The Association of University Presses

Directory 2018

The Association of University Presses
1412 Broadway, Suite 2135
New York, NY 10018

1775 Massachusetts Avenue, NW
Washington, DC 20036

Phone: 212.989.1010
Website: www.aupresses.org
Email: info@aupresses.org
Twitter: @aupresses

Published by the Association of University Presses
1412 Broadway, Suite 2135
New York NY 10018
© 2017 by the Association of University Presses, Inc.
All rights reserved.
Printed in the United States of America

International Standard Book Number 978-0-945103-04-2
Library of Congress Catalog Number 54-43046

Distributed to the Trade by:
The University of Chicago Press
11030 South Langley Avenue
Chicago, Illinois 60628
USA

Publication of this *Directory* was assisted by a generous grant from Thomson-Shore.

Contents

PREFACE 1
GENERAL INFORMATION FOR AUTHORS 2
On Submitting Manuscripts..4
SUBJECT AREA GRID 9
PRESSES PUBLISHING JOURNALS 20
DIRECTORY OF MEMBERS...22
Abilene Christian University Press...23
The University of Akron Press 24
The University of Alabama Press 25
University of Alaska Press..27
The University of Alberta Press 28
American Historical Association...29
American Psychiatric Association Publishing 30
The American School of Classical Studies at Athens...........................31
The American University in Cairo Press 32
Amherst College Press 33
Amsterdam University Press 34
The University of Arizona Press..36
The University of Arkansas Press 37
Army University Press 38
Athabasca University Press...39
Baylor University Press 40
Beacon Press...41
University of British Columbia Press 42
Brookings Institution Press...44
Bucknell University Press...45
University of Calgary Press 47
University of California Press 48
Cambridge University Press..50
Carnegie Mellon University Press 52
The Catholic University of America Press...53
Central European University Press..54
The University of Chicago Press 55
The Chinese University Press 59
University of Cincinnati Press 60
University Press of Colorado/Utah State University Press 61
Columbia University Press..62
Concordia University Press...64

Cork University Press	65
Cornell University Press	66
The University of Delaware Press	68
Duke University Press	69
University Press of Florida	72
Fordham University Press	74
Gallaudet University Press	75
George Mason University Press	76
Georgetown University Press	77
University of Georgia Press	79
Getty Publications	81
Harvard University Press	82
University of Hawai'i Press	84
University of Illinois Press	86
IMF Publications (International Monetary Fund)	88
Indiana University Press	90
INSTAP Academic Press	92
University of Iowa Press	93
Johns Hopkins University Press	94
University Press of Kansas	97
The Kent State University Press	98
The University Press of Kentucky	99
Leuven University Press/Universitaire Pers Leuven	101
Liverpool University Press	102
Louisiana State University Press	103
Manchester University Press	104
The University of Manitoba Press	106
Marine Corps University Press	107
Marquette University Press	108
University of Massachusetts Press	109
The MIT Press	110
McGill-Queen's University Press	113
Medieval Institute Publications	115
Mercer University Press	116
University of Michigan Press	117
Michigan State University Press	119
Minnesota Historical Society Press	121
University of Minnesota Press	122
University Press of Mississippi	124
University of Missouri Press	125

Modern Language Association of America	126
The Museum of Modern Art	127
The National Academies Press	128
National Gallery of Art	129
Naval Institute Press	130
University of Nebraska Press	132
University of Nevada Press	135
University Press of New England	136
University of New Mexico Press	138
UNSW Press Ltd	140
New York University Press	141
The University of North Carolina Press	143
University of North Texas Press	145
Northern Illinois University Press	146
Northwestern University Press	147
University of Notre Dame Press	148
Ohio University Press	150
Ohio State University Press	151
University of Oklahoma Press	152
Oregon State University Press	154
Otago University Press	155
University of Ottawa Press | Les Presses de l'Université d'Ottawa	156
Oxford University Press, Inc.	158
University of Pennsylvania Press	162
Pennsylvania State University Press	164
University of Pittsburgh Press	166
Princeton University Press	167
University of Puerto Rico Press	169
Purdue University Press	170
RAND Corporation	172
University of Regina Press	173
RIT Press	174
The University of Rochester Press	175
The Rockefeller University Press	176
Russell Sage Foundation	177
Rutgers University Press	178
Saint Joseph's University Press	179
SBL Press	180
The University of South Carolina Press	182
South Dakota Historical Society Press	183

Southern Illinois University Press 184
Stanford University Press 185
State University of New York Press 187
Syracuse University Press 189
Teachers College Press 190
Temple University Press..192
University of Tennessee Press 193
University of Texas Press...194
Texas A&M University Press 196
TCU Press...198
Texas Review Press 199
Texas Tech University Press...200
University of Tokyo Press 201
University of Toronto Press..202
Truman State University Press 205
United States Institute of Peace Press..206
W. E. Upjohn Institute for Employment Research...........................207
University of Utah Press 208
Vanderbilt University Press..209
The University of Virginia Press 210
University of Washington Press 212
Washington State University Press...214
Wayne State University Press 215
Wesleyan University Press..216
The University of the West Indies Press 217
West Virginia University Press 218
Wilfrid Laurier University Press..219
The University of Wisconsin Press...220
Wits University Press...221
The Woodrow Wilson Center Press...222
Yale University Press..223
ASSOCIATION PARTNERS..226
Baker & Taylor 226
Baker & Taylor Publisher Services 227
Books International..228
Brian Murphy Group 229
Firebrand Technologies 230
ITHAKA..231
ProQuest 232
Publishr.cloud 233

Thomson-Shore 234
Ubiquity Press..235
Virtusales Publishing Solutions..236
Westchester Publishing Services...237
International Sales Agents and Distributors...238
THE ASSOCIATION 241
Association of University Presses Central Office 242
2017-2018 Association Board of Directors..242
2017-2018 Association Committees and Task Forces 243
By-Laws (As revised August 29, 2017)..246
Guidelines on Admission to Membership
 and Maintenance of Membership..256
PERSONNEL INDEX 261

PREFACE

This *Directory* serves as a guide to the publishing programs and personnel of the 143 distinguished scholarly presses that have met the membership standards of the Association of University Presses. Updated annually, the *Directory* provides the most comprehensive information on these publishers available from any source. It belongs on the reference shelf of anyone connected to scholarly publishing: scholars preparing materials for publication, booksellers, librarians, scholarly presses interested in joining the Association, and, of course, the Association's own members.

The *Directory* is organized particularly for the convenience of authors, librarians, and booksellers who require detailed information about Association members and their wide-ranging publishing programs. The "Subject Area Grid," for example, provides a quick overview of the many disciplines published by the presses, indicating those most likely to publish a work in a given area. "On Submitting Manuscripts" gives advice to potential authors on preparing and submitting a scholarly manuscript for publication.

For further detail, individual press listings provide information on their editorial programs, journals published, and key staff members. Addresses, ordering information, and information on international sales representatives are also included. Detailed information on Association Partners is also listed.

The last section of the *Directory* focuses on the association and its purposes, and includes its by-laws, guidelines for admission to membership, and the names of the Association's Board of Directors, committees and task forces, and staff.

GENERAL INFORMATION FOR AUTHORS

What University Presses Do

University Presses perform services that are of inestimable value to the scholarly establishment, and also to the broader world of readers, and ultimately to society. If you are considering publishing with a university or other non-profit scholarly press, the following list should give you a good understanding of the scholarly publishing community.

• University Presses make available to the broader public the full range and value of research generated by university faculty.

• University Press books and journals present the basic research and analysis that is drawn upon by policymakers, opinion leaders, and authors of works for the general public.

• University Presses contribute to the variety and diversity of cultural expression at a time of global mergers and consolidation in the media industry.

• University Presses make common cause with libraries and other cultural institutions to promote engagement with ideas and sustain a literate culture.

• University Presses help to preserve the distinctiveness of local cultures through publication of works on the states and regions where they are based.

• University Presses give voice to minority cultures and perspectives through pioneering publication programs in ethnic, racial, and sexual studies.

• University Presses bring the work of overseas scholars and writers to English-language audiences by commissioning and publishing works in translation.

• University Presses rediscover and maintain the availability of works important to scholarship and culture through reprint programs.

• University Presses encourage cultural expression by publishing works of fiction, poetry, and creative nonfiction and books on contemporary art and photography.

• University Presses sponsor work in specialized and emerging areas of scholarship that do not have the broad levels of readership needed to attract commercial publishers.

• University Presses, through the peer review process, test the validity and soundness of scholarship and thus maintain high standards for academic publication.

• University Presses add value to scholarly work through rigorous editorial development; professional copyediting and design; and worldwide dissemination.

• University Presses are based at a wide array of educational institutions and thus promote a diversity of scholarly perspectives.

- University Presses encourage and refine the work of younger scholars through publication of the first books that establish credentials and develop authorial experience.

- University Presses make the works of English-language scholars available worldwide by licensing translations to publishers in other languages.

- University Presses commit resources to long-term scholarly editions and multivolume research projects, assuring publication for works with completion dates far in the future.

- University Presses add to the richness of undergraduate and graduate education by publishing most of the non-textbook and supplementary material used by instructors.

- University Presses collaborate with learned societies, scholarly associations, and librarians to explore how new technologies can benefit and advance scholarship.

- University Presses extend the reach and influence of their parent institutions, making evident their commitment to knowledge and ideas.

- University Presses demonstrate their parent institutions' support of research in areas such as the humanities and social sciences that rarely receive substantial Federal or corporate funding.

- University Presses help connect the university to the surrounding community by publishing books of local interest and hosting events for local authors.

- University Presses generate favorable publicity for their parent institutions through news coverage and book reviews, awards won, and exhibits at scholarly conferences.

- University Press staff act as local experts for faculty and administrators, providing guidance on intellectual property, scholarly communication, and the publishing process.

- University Presses provide advice and opportunities for students interested in pursuing careers in publishing.

On Submitting Manuscripts

JOURNAL ARTICLES

University presses have always been associated with publishing books of merit and distinction. This remains as true today as in the past, but less well appreciated is the extent to which university presses are active in publishing scholarly journals.

Journals form a major part of the publishing program of many presses, and more than half of the Association's members produce at least one periodical. (See page 2 for a list of presses publishing journals.)

Authors submitting papers to a journal should check a current issue for information on where to submit manuscripts and for guidelines on length and format. Editors of journals often have very precise requirements for manuscript preparation and may return articles that do not meet their specifications.

BOOK MANUSCRIPTS

Selecting a Publisher

If you are looking for a publisher for a book-length manuscript, do some research on which press may be best for your book. You should consider the reputation in your field of various presses and their editors, the design and production quality of their books, and the range and strength of their marketing efforts. To take advantage of group promotions and past experience, presses tend to specialize in certain subjects. Occasionally a press may take on a title in an unfamiliar area, but you are more likely to be successful in your submission if you choose one that knows the field. Use the "Subject Area Grid," which begins on page 9, to find out which presses publish titles in your field. You can then find more specific information about their interests under the listings of individual presses or by consulting their catalogs. If your book has a strong regional interest, consider the lists of the university presses active in your state to determine what types of regional books they publish.

You can also learn more about the list of each publisher by studying brochures received in the mail, reading book advertisements in journals, and by visiting press exhibits at academic meetings. At these exhibits you can meet acquisitions editors from the presses most active in the discipline and talk with them about your manuscript. Such talks can be very helpful to you and the editor in deciding if your manuscript would be suitable for a particular press. If you have already decided which press you would prefer for your book, call the appropriate editor before the meeting to make an appointment.

Preparing a Manuscript Prospectus

If you have selected a publisher but do not know an editor, you can use this directory to find the appropriate editor at that press. If you are not sure which editor to approach, write to the director of the press or to its editor-in-chief. Many Association member presses describe their submission guidelines on their Websites. It is best not to send the complete manuscript until you have been invited to do so. Presses vary in the amount of material they want to receive on a first submission, but some or all of the following materials are usually provided:

- a short, informative cover letter including a clear and concise description of your book and its notable features, your opinion of the audience for the book, information on the current status of the manuscript and expected completion date, and some details on the physical characteristics of the manuscript, such as length, number of illustrations, tables, appendices, etc.

- a table of contents

- a preface, introduction, or other brief sample of your manuscript

- a curriculum vitae or biographical notes

If the press is interested, the editor will invite you to submit the complete manuscript or inform you that he or she can proceed to review the materials you sent.

Preparing Your Manuscript for Review

Presses vary in their requirements for manuscript preparation. In general, the manuscript you submit for review should be as accurate and complete as possible. If a manuscript is carelessly prepared, reviewers may take offense at typographical errors or careless citations and spend precious review space discussing these problems instead of attending to the substance of your manuscript. If, for good reasons, your manuscript is incomplete, you should indicate what material is missing and provide your schedule for completion.

Although some presses will accept a single-spaced manuscript for review, it is best to double-space your text. A double-spaced manuscript is easier to read and may be required when your manuscript reaches the copyediting stage. For book publication, every element of the text should be double-spaced (including quotations, notes, bibliographies, appendices, figure legends, and glossaries). Once your manuscript is accepted for publication, your editor will advise you on any special requirements imposed by that press's house style.

The Review Process

Some university presses may give advance (i.e., conditional) contracts to experienced authors on the basis of incomplete or unreviewed manuscripts. Most, however, must obtain one or more reviews of a completed manuscript before presenting a project for the approval of the press's editorial board. As review procedures differ from press to press, check with the editor when you first submit the manuscript to find out what will be involved. He or she should be able to give you a tentative schedule for the review process. It is difficult to predict exactly how long it will take to reach a decision, since often readers' reports encourage authors to make further revisions to the manuscript and the manuscript is usually reviewed again after the author makes the revisions. If your manuscript is also under review at another publisher, be sure to let the editor know. Some editors will not review manuscripts that are under simultaneous consideration elsewhere; others will not object.

Preparing Your Manuscript for Publication

Most publishers will want an electronic version of your manuscript. Your manuscript should be keyboarded as simply as possible. There is no need to change fonts, type styles, and formats to differentiate between sections; in fact, this is counterproductive. The press's copyediting or production department will insert the proper typesetting codes for formatting extracts, different levels of headings, and so on. And keep in mind that your book will be designed by a professional. Many presses will send you their own guidelines for submitting manuscripts.

FURTHER READING

Abel, Richard, Lyman W. Newlin, Katina Strauch, and Bruce Strauch, eds. *Scholarly Publishing: Books, Journals, Publishers, and Libraries in the Twentieth Century*. Indianapolis: Wiley, 2001.

American Psychological Association. *Publication Manual of the American Psychological Association*. 6th ed. Washington, DC: APA Books, 2010.

Appelbaum, Judith. *How to Get Happily Published: A Complete and Candid Guide*. 5th ed. New York: Collins Reference, 1998.

Becker, Howard S. *Writing for Social Scientists: How to Start and Finish Your Thesis, Book, or Article*. 2nd ed. Chicago: University of Chicago Press, 2007.

Belcher, Wendy Laura. *Writing Your Journal Article in Twelve Weeks: A Guide to Academic Publishing Success*. Thousands Oaks, CA: SAGE Publications, 2009

Day, Robert A. and Barbara Gastel *How to Write and Publish a Scientific Paper*. 8th ed. Westport, CT: Greenwood Publishing Group, Inc., 2016.

Derricourt, Robin. *An Author's Guide to Scholarly Publishing*. Princeton: Princeton University Press, 1996.

Germano, William. *From Dissertation to Book*. 2nd ed. Chicago: University of Chicago Press, 2013.

Germano, William. *Getting it Published: A Guide for Scholars and Anyone Else Serious about Serious Books*. 3rd ed. Chicago: University of Chicago Press, 2016.

Hacker, Diana and Nancy Sommers. *A Writer's Reference with 2016 MLA Update*. 8th ed. Boston & New York: Bedford/St. Martin's, 2016.

Harman, Eleanor, Ian Montagnes, Siobhan McMenemy, and Chris Bucci eds. *The Thesis and the Book: A Guide for First-Time Academic Authors*. 2nd ed. Toronto: University of Toronto Press, 2003.

Huff, Anne Sigismund. *Writing for Scholarly Publication*. Thousand Oaks, CA: SAGE Publications, 1998.

Jensen, Joli. *Write No Matter What: Advice for Academics*. Chicago: University of Chicago Press, 2017.

Kasdorf, William E. *The Columbia Guide to Digital Publishing*. New York: Columbia University Press, 2003.

Katz, Michael J. *Elements of the Scientific Paper: A Step-by-Step Guide for Students and Professionals*. New Haven: Yale University Press, 1986.

Kaufman, Roy S. *Publishing Forms and Contracts*. New York: Oxford University Press, 2008.

Luey, Beth. *Handbook for Academic Authors*. 5th ed. New York: Cambridge University Press, 2009.

Luey, Beth, ed. *Revising Your Dissertation: Advice from Leading Editors*. 2nd ed. Berkeley: University of California Press, 2007.

Modern Language Association. *MLA Handbook*. 8th ed. New York: Modern Language Association of America, 2016.

Moxley, Joseph M. and Todd Taylor. *Writing and Publishing for Academic Authors*. 2nd ed. Lanham, MD: Rowman and Littlefield, 1996.

Mulvany, Nancy C. *Indexing Books*. 2nd ed. Chicago: University of Chicago Press, 2005.

Parsons, Paul. *Getting Published: The Acquisition Process at University Presses*. Knoxville: University of Tennessee Press, 1989.

Powell, Walter W. *Getting into Print: The Decision-Making Process in Scholarly Publishing*. Chicago: University of Chicago Press, 1985.

Strong, William S. *The Copyright Book: A Practical Guide*. 6th ed. Cambridge, MA: MIT Press, 2014.

Strunk, William J. and E. B. White. *The Elements of Style*. 4th ed. New York: Pearson Higher Education, 1999.

Swain, Dwight V. *Techniques of the Selling Writer*. Norman: University of Oklahoma Press, 1982.

Thompson, John. *Books in the Digital Age: The Transformation of Academic and Higher Education Publishing in Britain and the United States* Cambridge: Polity Press, 2005.

University of Chicago Press. *The Chicago Manual of Style*. 17h ed. Chicago: University of Chicago Press, 2017.

University of Chicago Press. *The Chicago Manual of Style Online*. 17th ed. Chicago: University of Chicago Press, 2017, http://www.chicagomanualofstyle.org/home.html

Wiser, James. *Open Book: A Librarian's Guide to Academic Publishing*. Santa Barbara, CA: Mission Bell Media, 2016.

Zerubavel, Eviator. *The Clockwork Muse: A Practical Guide to Writing Theses, Dissertations, and Books*. Cambridge, MA: Harvard University Press, 1999.

SUBJECT AREA GRID

This ten-page grid indicates the subject areas in which each press has a particularly strong interest.

Some presses are prepared to consider manuscripts of outstanding quality in areas other than those listed. For more detailed descriptions of press editorial programs, consult the individual listings in the "Directory of Members" section and contact the presses that interest you.

Subject	Abilene Christian	Akron	Alabama	Alaska	Alberta	A. Historical	A. Psychiatric	A. School Classical	Amherst	Amsterdam	Arizona	Arkansas	Army	Athabasca	Baylor	Beacon	British Columbia	Brookings	Bucknell	Cairo (American)	Calgary	California	Cambridge	Carnegie Mellon	Catholic	Central European	Chicago	Chinese
African Studies					●																	●	●				●	
African American Studies		●	●						●			●			●			●				●	●				●	
American Studies		●	●						●						●			●				●	●				●	
Anthropology			●	●	●				●	●	●			●		●	●		●		●	●	●				●	●
Archeology			●	●				●		●	●			●							●	○	●			●		●
Arts			●																		●	●				●		
Architecture			●	●		●	●	●		●											●	○	●			●		
Art Criticism			●						●					●		○			○		●		●			●		
Comics			●						●												●	○				●		
Dance	●		●						●													●				●		
Fashion and Textiles			●																				○				●	
Folk Art			●						●					●								●	○				●	
Film		●	●						●	●				●							●	●	●				●	
Fine Arts and Art History		●	●				●	●	●	●		●		●					●		●	●	○		●	●		
Music & Music Theory			●						●	●				●								●	●				●	●
Photography		●	●	●																	●	○	●			●		
Popular Culture			●						●	●			●	○								●	●			●		●
Television			●	○					●				●								○	●	●			●		
Theater			●						●				●					●				●	○			●	●	
Asian Studies			●						●	●				●	●							●	●				●	●
Biography and Memoir		●	●	●	●				●	●				●	●	●	○	●	●	●	●		●	○		●	●	●
Business and Management			●							●					○			●		○			●				●	●
Caribbean Studies		●							●						●			●				●	●				●	
Child Development			●												●								●					●
Classics						●	●	●						○					●			●	●		●	●	●	
Criminology			●											○			●					●	●				●	
Demography			●						●								●					●	●					●
Disability Studies			●						●				●		●	●	●	●				●	●			●		
European Studies			●						●	●				●			●		●			○	●			●		
Economics	●		●						●					●			●	●		●		○	●			●	●	
Education	●		●						●					●		●	●	●				●					●	●
Folklore			●						●							○						●					●	
Food & Agriculture		●	●	●										●		●	●					●						
Agriculture			●	●	●												●						●					
Cooking		●																				●	○					
Food & Culture		●		●	●							●	●		●		●	●				●	○			●		
History of Food			●												●		○					●	○			●	●	
Geography			●						●					●			○		●			●	●				●	
Gender and Sexuality Studies		●	●						●	●				●		○	●		●			●				●	●	●
LGBTQIA Studies		●	●	●					●	●				●	●				●	●	●					●		
Women's Studies			●	●					●	●				●	●		●	●	●			●					●	●
Health & Medicine			●				●		●					●			●	●				●						●
Addiction Studies			●											●			●	●					○					
Aging			●						●					●			●					●				●		
History of Medicine		●	●	●						●				○							●		●			●		
Public Health			●	●						●				●			●	●			●	●	●					●
History			●		●				●					●	○	●	●					●						●
African				●					●					●					●			●	●		●			
American	●	●	●	●					●		●	●	●	●		●						●	●	●	●		●	
Ancient			●			●	●	●	●					●					●			●	●				●	
Asian			●						●					●			●						●				●	●
Australasian									●					●									●					
British									●					●			●		●			●	●			●		
Canadian			●	●					●					●			●					●						
Caribbean									●					●		●			●		●	●				●		
Central American									●	●				●								●	●			●		
Eastern European				●					●														●		●			
European									●	●		●					●				○	●		●	●	●		
Latin American		●							●	●		●		●			●				●	●	●			●		
Medieval									●					●					●			●	●		●	●	●	
Middle Eastern									●					●		●			●			●	●				●	
South American			●						●		●			●								●	●	●			●	

● press acquires in this area
○ press is NOT actively acquiring in but may have a significant backlist in this area

Subject	Abilene Christian	Akron	Alabama	Alaska	Alberta	Amherst	A. Historical	A. Psychiatric	A. School Classical	Amsterdam	Arizona	Arkansas	Army	Athabasca	Baylor	Beacon	British Columbia	Brookings	Bucknell	Cairo (American)	Calgary	California	Cambridge	Carnegie Mellon	Catholic	Central European	Chicago	Chinese
Immigration			●		●						●			●	●	●						●	●			●	●	
Indigenous Studies		●	●	●	●						●			●		●	●				●	○	●				●	
Information and Communications		●	●		●					●				●			●					●						●
Information Science		●	●		●									●								●						
Internet Studies		●	●											●								●						
Journalism and Media Studies		●	●	●						●				●						●		●					●	●
Labor			●											●	●	●					●							
Language		●	●							●				○								●						●
Dictionaries and Lexicals		●	●	●													○					○			●			
Linguistic Theory		●	●							●												●					●	●
Language Texts		●															○		●		○		●		●			
Writing and Style Guides		●																				●	●		●			
Latin American Studies		●			●					●		○		●			●		●	●	●		●			○	●	
Law and Legal Studies	○	●	●		●					●				●		●					●	●			○	●	●	
Literature (Creative)		●								●												○						
Creative Nonfiction	●	●	●	●						●		●		●	●		●		●		●	○	●		●			
Fiction		●	●	●						●		○					●		●	●		○						
Poetry	●		●	●						●	●	●		●		●			●		●	○	○	●			●	●
Drama		●								●												○	○					
Children's		●								●				○					●			●	○	○				
Translations		●								●												○	○				●	●
Literature (Scholarly)		●		●		●				●				●	○		●					●			●			●
Literary Criticism		●	●	●	●	●				●				●			●		●	○	●	●		●	●			
History		●		●						●				●	●		●		●			●	●		●			
Theater Studies		●		●						●				●			●					●						
Medieval Studies			●		●						●			○					●		●	●		●	●			●
Military Studies		●	●								●		●	○		●						●						
Pacific Studies		●								●				○			○				●	●						
Philosophy		●								●				○					●			○	●		●	○	●	●
Political Science/Public Policy		●		●	●	●				●				●	○	●	●	●		●	●	○	●		○	●	●	
Psychology		●	●				●			●				○	●							●	●					●
Race and Class Studies	●		●	●	●					●	●			●	●	●						●	●			●	●	
Reference and Guidebooks		●												○			○		●			●			●			
Religion/Religious Studies	●		●	●		●				●				○	●	●	●					●	●		●		●	
Buddhism			●		●										●							●	●		●			
Christianity	●		●		●									●	●		●					●			●	●	●	
Hinduism			●		●										●							●	●		●			
Indigenous Religions		●	●		●									●	●							●			●			
Islam			●	●	●									●	●				●			●			●		●	
Judaism			●		●									●	●							●			●		●	
Renaissance Studies			●		●						○			○					●			●			●		●	
Science & Mathematics		●									○											●						
Astronomy		●								●												●						
Biological Science		●	●		●														○		●				●			
Botany		●	●		●						●											●				●		
Chemistry		●																				●						
Computer Science		●								●												●						
Ecology and Conservation		●	●								●	●			●						●	●				●		
Earth and Environmental	○	●	●	●							●	●			●						●	●				●		
Engineering		●																				●						
General		●													●							●	○				●	
History of Science	○	●	●							●					●							●					●	
Mathematics		●																				●						
Neuroscience		●				●									●							●						
Physics		●																				●						
Statistics		●																				●						
Zoology		●	●	●										●								●					●	
Slavic Studies			●	●							○				●		●					●			●			
Sociology		●	●	●						●				●	●	●			●		●	●			●	●	●	
Social Justice	●		●	●	●						●			●	●	●			●	○		●	●			●	●	
Sports		●	●	●	●							●		●		●					●	○						
Travel and Tourism		●		●	●									○		○			●		○							
Urban Studies		●	●	●			●				●			●		●			●	●		●				●	●	

● press acquires in this area
○ press is NOT actively acquiring in but may have a significant backlist in this area

Subject	Cincinnati	Colorado	Columbia	Concordia	Cork	Cornell	Delaware	Duke	Florida	Fordham	Gallaudet	George Mason	Georgetown	Georgia	Getty	Harvard	Hawaii	Illinois	IMF	Indiana	INSTAP	Iowa	Johns Hopkins	Kansas	Kent State	Kentucky	Leuven	Liverpool	Louisiana
African Studies	●								●							●		○	●										
African American Studies	●					●		●	●	●				●		●		○					●	●		●			●
American Studies	●					●	●	●	●	●		●		●		●		○					●	●	●	●			●
Anthropology	●	●				●		●	●	●						●	●	○	●						○	●			
Archeology		●			●	●			●					●	●		●	○			●					●			
Arts			●			●			●					●	●	●	●	○								●			
Architecture			●				●		●	●				●	●	●	●						●	●	○		●	●	
Art Criticism			●				●	●	●					●													●	●	
Comics			●											●												●			
Dance			●			●		●								●	●									●			
Fashion and Textiles			●											●	●										●				
Folk Art			●					●						●				●											
Film		●	●		●	●		●	●		●			●			●	●		●			○			●	●	●	
Fine Arts and Art History			●	○	●	●								●	●					●		●			○		●		
Music & Music Theory			●	○	●	●								●	●	●	●									○	●		
Photography			●	●			●	●	●					●	●												●		
Popular Culture			●	●		●	●							●		●	●	●		●		●	●	●	●		●	●	
Television			●			●																				●			
Theater			●			●	●	●	○					●				●				●				●			
Asian Studies	●	●	●			●	●	●						●		●	●	○								●	●	●	
Biography and Memoir		●			●			●	●	●	●	●	○	●		●	●	●	○				●	●	●	●			
Business and Management			●			●				●		●	●			●		●					●						
Caribbean Studies					●	●	●							●		●			○									●	●
Child Development	●									●				●					○										
Classics					●				●					●	●			○		○	●			●			●		
Criminology	●				●									●				○							●				
Demography																		○											
Disability Studies	●			●			●			●	●					●				●									
European Studies				●		●		●						●			●	○					○			●	●		
Economics		●						●			●			●			●			●			●			●			
Education	●				●	●	●			●	●	●		●				○								●			
Folklore		●		●	●	●									●	●	○	●						○				●
Food & Agriculture									●					●				●					●						
Agriculture					●									●						●		●		●					
Cooking									●					●						●									
Food & Culture		●	●					●	●					●		●	●					●		●		●	●	●	●
History of Food		●	●											●		●	●	●				●		●		●	●	●	●
Geography					●	●	●		●	●				●				●	○				●			●			●
Gender and Sexuality Studies	●		●			●	●	●		●				●		●	●	●	○				●	●			●		
LGBTQIA Studies		●	●				●	●						●			●	●					●						
Women's Studies		●	●	●	●	●	●		●	●				●		●	●	●		●			●						
Health & Medicine							●										●		○				●						
Addiction Studies																							●						
Aging	●		●	●										●									●						
History of Medicine							●			●				●									●	●		●			
Public Health		●		●	●	●		●					●				●						●		●				
History		●					●			●	●					●		○						●	●	●			
African									●							●				●								●	●
American		●			●	●	●	●		●		●		●		●		●				●	●	●		●		●	●
Ancient		●			●	●									●	●				●			●						
Asian						●		●						●	●		●									●			
Australasian						●				●						●													
British						●	●			●				●										●				●	
Canadian				●																									
Caribbean						●	●						●	●									●					●	
Central American		●				●	●						●	●														●	
Eastern European				●										●						●			●			●			
European				●	●	●	●		●			●		●	●			●		●			●			●			●
Latin American		●				●	●						●							○						●		●	
Medieval					●	●								●	●					○			○				●	●	
Middle Eastern	●	●							●	○				●				●								●			
South American		●				●	●						●	●															

● press acquires in this area
○ press is NOT actively acquiring in but may have a significant backlist in this area

Subject	Cincinnati	Colorado	Columbia	Concordia	Cork	Cornell	Delaware	Duke	Florida	Fordham	Gallaudet	George Mason	Georgetown	Georgia	Getty	Harvard	Hawaii	Illinois	IMF	Indiana	INSTAP	Iowa	Johns Hopkins	Kansas	Kent State	Kentucky	Leuven	Liverpool	Louisiana
Immigration	●	●		●		●		●	●							●	●	●	○				●				●	●	
Indigenous Studies	●	●		●		●		●								●	●	○					●	●					
Information and Communications				●					●		●					●		●		●			●						
Information Science				●												●				●			●						
Internet Studies						●										●							●						
Journalism and Media Studies				●				●	●				●			●		●					●				●		
Labor	●			●		●			●	○					●								●					●	
Language								●	●							●	●		○										
Dictionaries and Lexicals								●		●							●												
Linguistic Theory								●		●						●	●												
Language Texts										●							●												
Writing and Style Guides		●														●						●							
Latin American Studies	●	●						●	●							●		○										●	
Law and Legal Studies				●			●		●	●			○			●	●	●					●		●				
Literature (Creative)									●	●						●		○											
Creative Nonfiction		○					●			●													●						
Fiction									●					●			●						●	○		●			●
Poetry		○				●		○	●	●				●			●						●	○		●	●		●
Drama																	●												
Children's																													
Translations		●				●		●	●			●					●												
Literature (Scholarly)						●				●						●	●		○										
Literary Criticism			●	●	●	●	●	●	●	●			●			●	●			○			●	●		●	○	●	●
History			●	●	●	●	●	●	●	●			●			●	●						●	●		●		●	●
Theater Studies			●	●		●	●		●								●						●	○		●			
Medieval Studies						●	●	●		●	●				●		●		○				○			●		●	●
Military Studies						●			●		●		●		●		●	●	●	●			●	●		●			
Pacific Studies								●									●	●	○										
Philosophy		●					●	●	●	○			●				●	●	○				○				○	●	
Political Science/Public Policy	●	○	●	●		●	●	●	●		●	●	○	●		●	●	●					●	●	●	●	●		○
Psychology				●								●				●	●		○				●				○		
Race and Class Studies	●		●	●		●		●	●	●				●		●	●	●	●				●					●	●
Reference and Guidebooks	●								○			●		●		●	●	●					●			●			
Religion/Religious Studies		●				●		●		●			●	○		●	●	●	○				●			○	●		
Buddhism		●		●						●						●	●												
Christianity				●				●		●						●											●		
Hinduism														●		●													
Indigenous Religions																●													
Islam				●				○		●			●			●				●							●		
Judaism								○	●				●			●				●									
Renaissance Studies				●					●					●	●			○					○				●		
Science & Mathematics																●	●	○					●						
Astronomy		●														●							●						
Biological Science		●	●			●										●							●						
Botany		●				●																							
Chemistry																●													
Computer Science																													
Ecology and Conservation		●	●			●	●		●					●		●	●						●		●	●			
Earth and Environmental		●	●			●	●		●	●						●	●						●		●	●			●
Engineering																													
General			●													●	●						●						
History of Science							●									●	●						●			●			
Mathematics																●							●						
Neuroscience			●													●							●						
Physics																●							●						
Statistics																													
Zoology						●										●							●						
Slavic Studies						●										●		○		●									
Sociology	●	○	●	●	●	●		●		●				●		●	●	●	○										
Social Justice	●		●	●	●		●						●	●		●	●	●	●	○			●	●			●	●	●
Sports					●				●	●				●			●			○				●		●	●		
Travel and Tourism		●						●	●					●						○								●	
Urban Studies	●			●	●			●		●				●		●	●	●	○				●					●	●

● press acquires in this area
○ press is NOT actively acquiring in but may have a significant backlist in this area

Subject	McGill-Queen's	Manchester	Manitoba	Marquette	Marine Corps	Massachusetts	MIT	Medieval Institute	Mercer	Michigan	Michigan State	Minnesota	Minnesota Hist.	Mississippi	Missouri	MLA	MOMA	National Acad.	National Gallery	Naval	Nebraska	Nevada	New England	New Mexico	New South Wales	New York	North Carolina	North Texas
African Studies		●						○		●	●	●						●			●					●		
African American Studies		●				●	○		●	●	●	●	●	●	●						●			●		●	●	●
American Studies		●				●	○			●	●	●	●	●	●						●	●	●	●		●	●	●
Anthropology	●	●					●			○	●	●											●	○	●	●		
Archeology	●	●					●	●		●	○							●			●	●	●	○	○	●		
Arts	●				●	●	●				●	●	●								●	●		●			●	
Architecture	●	●			●	●	●			○	●	●	○	●	●		●		●						●	●	●	
Art Criticism	●						●				○	●					●		●		●			●		●		
Comics							○			●				●														
Dance	●	●					○			●	○	○					●				●			●				
Fashion and Textiles		●					●			○	●										●							
Folk Art	●						○			○				●					●				●			●		
Film	●	●					●			●		●		●	●		●				●			●	●			
Fine Arts and Art History	●	●	●				●	●		○	○	●					●		●		●	●		●		●	●	
Music & Music Theory	●				●	●		●	●	○	●	●	●							○							●	●
Photography	●	●	●				●			○	●	●	●				●		●		●	●		●		●		
Popular Culture	●	●			●	●	●		●	●	●	●	●								●	●		●		●	●	
Television	●						●			○		●									●			●		●		
Theater	●	●					●			●	○	○	●		●						●			●				
Asian Studies	●	●					●			○	●	●		●							●				●	●		
Biography and Memoir	●	●		○		●	●		●	○	●	●	●	●				●	●	●	●			●		●	●	●
Business and Management	●	●					●			●			○															
Caribbean Studies	●	●				○	○			○				●		●										●		
Child Development							●			○																		
Classics	●					○	○		●	●	○								●								○	
Criminology	●						○				●								●		●		●			●		●
Demography	●						●			○						●												
Disability Studies	●					●	○			●	●	●		●							●					●	●	
European Studies	●	●					○	○		○	●	●			●	●					●					●		
Economics	●	●					●			○	●			●				●										
Education	●				●	●				●	●				●		●						●		●			
Folklore	●						○			○	●			●	●	●							●				●	○
Food & Agriculture	●						●			●			●			●		●			●	●	●				●	
Agriculture							●			●		○		●		●			●						○			
Cooking	●						○			●	●	●										●	●				●	●
Food & Culture	●		●				●			●	●	●	●								●	●	●	●		●	●	
History of Food	●					●	●		●	●			●								●	●	●	●	●		●	
Geography	●		●			○	●				○	●						●			●	●	●	○				
Gender and Sexuality Studies	●	●				●	●			●	●			●	●	●					●			●		●	●	
LGBTQIA Studies	●	●				●	○			●	●	●		●		●					●			●		●	●	
Women's Studies	●	●				●	○			●	●	●	●	●	●						●		●	●		●	●	
Health & Medicine	●						●			○		●						●					●				●	●
Addiction Studies	●						○			○											●							
Aging	●						○			○								●						●				
History of Medicine	●	●	●		●		○			○	●	●					●				●	●		●		●		
Public Health	●	●					●			●	○	●			○			●				●	●	●	●	●		
History	●	●		○	●	●	○							●	●	●					●	●				●	●	●
African	●	●					○			●	●																	
American	●	●			●	●	●		●	●	●	●		●	●					●	●		●			●	●	●
Ancient	●					○	○		●	●	○								●		●		●				●	
Asian	●	●					○			●	○	●									●	●			●			
Australasian	●						○			○															●			
British	●	●					○			●	●			●				●			●							
Canadian	●	●	●				○			●											●	●		●				
Caribbean	●						○			●			●		●									●			●	
Central American	●						○			○												●		●				
Eastern European	●						○			○								●										
European	●	●			○	○				●	●		●					●		●	●							
Latin American	●	●					○			○			●								●		●		●			
Medieval	●					○	●		●	○																		
Middle Eastern							○			○								●									●	
South American	●						○			○											●		●				●	

● press acquires in this area
○ press is NOT actively acquired but may have a significant backlist in this area

Subject	McGill-Queen's	Manchester	Manitoba	Marquette	Marine Corps	Massachusetts	MIT	Medieval Institute	Mercer	Michigan	Michigan State	Minnesota	Minnesota Hist.	Mississippi	Missouri	MLA	MOMA	National Acad.	National Gallery	Naval	Nebraska	Nevada	New England	New Mexico	New South Wales	New York	North Carolina	North Texas
Immigration	●	●				●	●			○	●	●	●											●		●	●	●
Indigenous Studies	●		●					○		○	●		●	●	●	●					●			●	●	●		
Information and Communications	●	●				●	●				●							●			●							
Information Science							●			○								●										
Internet Studies	●						●			●	○	●						●									●	
Journalism and Media Studies	●	●				●	●			●	●	●		●	●						●						●	●
Labor	●						●			●	●	●	○		●												●	
Language	●						●			●	●										●							
Dictionaries and Lexicals	●							○			○	○																
Linguistic Theory	●						●				○																	
Language Texts							●			●	●	●									●				●	●	●	
Writing and Style Guides								○		●	○				●		●	●										
Latin American Studies	●	●						○		○	○	○	●		●	●					●			●			●	
Law and Legal Studies	●	●				●	●			○	○	●									●	●	●			●	○	●
Literature (Creative)	●							○													●	●	●			●		
Creative Nonfiction	●							○		●	○	●		○	●	●					●	●	●	●		●	●	●
Fiction						●	●		●	○	●	○	●	●							●	●	●			●		●
Poetry	●	●				●	●		●	○	●	○	●								●	●		●		●		●
Drama								○				○	○	○														
Children's								○				○							●					●				
Translations	●	●						○			○	●	●								●			●		●		
Literature (Scholarly)	●	●				●	●							●	●	●					●	●		●			●	●
Literary Criticism	●	●	●			●	●		●	○	●	●		●	●	●					●	●		●	●		●	●
History	●	●				●	●	●	●		●			●	●	●					●	●		●	●		●	
Theater Studies	●					●	●		●		●	○	○		●		●				●				●			
Medieval Studies	●	●		○			●	●		●	○	○																
Military Studies	●				●	●	●					○		●						●	●		●	●	●	●	●	●
Pacific Studies	●							○			○	●							●									
Philosophy	●	●		●		○	●		●		●	●			●						○							
Political Science/Public Policy	●	●			●	●	●			●	●	●	●		●						●	●		●		●	●	
Psychology	●						●				○							●			●					●		
Race and Class Studies	●					●	○			●	●	●	●	●							●					●	●	
Reference and Guidebooks		●					●				○		○							●					○		●	●
Religion/Religious Studies	●			●			○		●		○										●			●			●	●
Buddhism	●						○			●		○																
Christianity	●						○	●	●	○		○															●	●
Hinduism	●						○			●		○												●			●	
Indigenous Religions	●						○					○									●						●	●
Islam	●						○			●		○												●		●	●	●
Judaism	●						○	●	●	○	○			●							●		●				●	●
Renaissance Studies	●		○		●	●	○			○	○	○				●					●			●				
Science & Mathematics	●						●				●																	
Astronomy							●				○							●						●				
Biological Science	●						●				●							●						●				
Botany							●			●	●							●						●				
Chemistry							●				○							●										
Computer Science	●						●											●										
Ecology and Conservation	●					●	●			●	●	●	●	●				●					●	●		●	●	○
Earth and Environmental	●					●	●			●		●	●	●	●			●					●	●		●	●	○
Engineering							●				○							●										
General	●						●				○												●			●		
History of Science	●	●				●	●				●	●			●			●						●				
Mathematics							●				○							●										
Neuroscience	●						●				○							●						●				
Physics							●				○							●			●							
Statistics							●			○	●							●										
Zoology	●						●				●										●							
Slavic Studies	●					○					●								●									
Sociology	●	●				●	●			○	●	●						●						●			●	●
Social Justice	●			○		●	○			●	●	●													●		●	●
Sports	●	●				●	○		●		○	○	●	●	●						●			●		●	●	
Travel and Tourism						●	○			●	○	●													●			
Urban Studies	●	●		○		●	●			●	●	●		●				●			●	●				●		

● press acquires in this area
○ press is NOT actively acquiring in but may have a significant backlist in this area

	Northern Illinois	Northwestern	Notre Dame	Ohio	Ohio State	Oklahoma	Oregon State	Otago	Ottawa	Oxford	Pennsylvania	Penn State	Pittsburgh	Princeton	Puerto Rico	Purdue	RAND	Regina	RIT	Rochester	Rockefeller	Russell Sage	Rutgers	St. Josephs	SBL	South Carolina	South Dakota Hist.	Southern Illinois	Stanford	SUNY
African Studies			●							●		●		●				●		●			○					●		
African American Studies		●	●	●	●	●	●			●		●	●	●				●		●			●	●		●		●		●
American Studies	○	●		●	●		●			●	●	●		●				●		●			●						●	●
Anthropology	○		●		●	●		●	●	●		●	●	●		●	○			●	●								●	
Archeology			●		●	●		●	●	●	●	●		●										●			○			
Arts	○				●	●				●		●	●																	
Architecture	○		●		●		●			●	●	●	●	●				●		●								●		
Art Criticism		●	●		●		●			●	●	●																	●	
Comics			●	●								●								●			●							
Dance										●																				
Fashion and Textiles			●																											
Folk Art				○		●				○																				
Film		●	●	●	●					●			●	○		●		●		●	●		●					○		●
Fine Arts and Art History	●		●	●	○		●		●	●	○	●	●	●		●		●	○	●	●		○	●			○		●	
Music & Music Theory					●					●		●		●	○					●										
Photography					●		●		●	●		●		●	○			○		●									○	
Popular Culture		●	●	●	●	●				●		●								●			●							●
Television			●	●						●													●							
Theater	○	●		○			●		●	●													○						●	
Asian Studies	●		●					●		●	●			●				●					○						●	●
Biography and Memoir	●	○	●	●	●	●	●	●	●	●				●	●		●	●	●	●			●				●	●	●	●
Business and Management			●	●	○					●			●			●	●	●		●									●	
Caribbean Studies			●	○	●					●		●		●				●					●							●
Child Development				○					○	●				●		●	●					●								
Classics		●	●	●						●	●	●		●									○		●	○				
Criminology				○				●	●	●				●				●		●	●		●					●		
Demography										●					○	●		●												
Disability Studies										●	●		●			●		○					○							
European Studies	○	●	●		○					●	●		●	●		●		●		●										
Economics										●		●		●	●	●		●	●		●		●						●	
Education				○					●	●		●		●		●		●	●	●			●		●			○	●	
Folklore			○		●		●			●								●								●				
Food & Agriculture						●				●								●					●					●		
Agriculture	○		●	○						●				●	●	●												●		
Cooking			●							●																				
Food & Culture		●		●		●				●		●								●			●					●		
History of Food			●		●					●										●			●					●		
Geography					●					●		●		●		●				●			●							
Gender and Sexuality Studies		●		●			●		●	●		●				●	●			●			●						●	●
LGBTQIA Studies			○	●	●	●	●			●		●				●	●			●			●							●
Women's Studies	○	●		●	●	●	●	●		●				●		●	●	●		●			●		●	●	●	●	●	●
Health & Medicine										●		●								●			●							
Addiction Studies				●						●										●			●							
Aging										●										●		●	●							
History of Medicine			●	○					○	●	●	●	●					●		●	●		●				○			
Public Health			●	○						●		●		●	●	●		●		●		●		●						
History	●		●							●		●		●				●					●					●		
African			●							●		●								●										
American	●	●	●	●	○	●	●			●	●	●		●		●		●		●			●			●		●	●	●
Ancient				●						●	●	●		●										●					●	●
Asian	●		●							●		●		●															●	●
Australasian								●		●		●																		
British	○		●	○	○					●		●	●							●									●	●
Canadian									●									●												
Caribbean										●		●	●										●						●	
Central American			○	●						●		●	●										●						●	
Eastern European	●	●	●	○						●		●		●				●					●						●	
European	●	●	●	○						●	●	●	●	●				●					●						●	
Latin American		●	●	●		●				●		●	●	●	●					●			●						●	●
Medieval	●									●	●	●																		
Middle Eastern										●		●	●												●				●	●
South American			●							●		●											●						●	

● press acquires in this area
○ press is NOT actively acquiring in but may have a significant backlist in this area

	Northern Illinois	Northwestern	Notre Dame	Ohio	Ohio State	Oklahoma	Oregon State	Otago	Ottawa	Oxford	Pennsylvania	Penn State	Pittsburgh	Princeton	Puerto Rico	Purdue	RAND	Regina	RIT	Rochester	Rockefeller	Russell Sage	Rutgers	St. Josephs	SBL	South Carolina	South Dakota Hist.	Southern Illinois	Stanford	SUNY
Immigration					●	●			●	●													●	●				●		
Indigenous Studies	○	●		●	●	●	●	●	●	●								●								●				●
Information and Communications					●				●		●		●	●		●														
Information Science									●				●		●															
Internet Studies							●	●			●																			
Journalism and Media Studies	○		●	●		●			●		●		●	●	●	●				●			○						○	●
Labor						●			●	●												●	○					●	○	
Language						●						●	●																	
Dictionaries and Lexicals				○		○			●			●																		
Linguistic Theory				○	○				●		●		●	●															○	
Language Texts	○			○		●			●			●																		
Writing and Style Guides				○					●			●																●		
Latin American Studies		●	●	●	●	●				●			●	●	●		●			●			●			●			●	●
Law and Legal Studies	○			●	○	●			●	●	●			●	●		●					●							●	●
Literature (Creative)	○			●						●													●			●			●	●
Creative Nonfiction		●	●	●	●		●	●								●							●			●			●	●
Fiction	○	●	●	●	●	●	●	●	●					●									○			○			●	●
Poetry	○	●	●	●	●	○		●				●	●	●		●							○			○		●		
Drama		●		○																										
Children's																										●	●			
Translations	●	●		○					●		●			●									●					●		
Literature (Scholarly)	●		●						●	●			●	●									●					●		
Literary Criticism	●	●	●	○	●	○			●	●	●	●	●	●	●	●				●			●			●	○		●	●
History	●	●	●	○	○				●	●	●		●	●									●					●		
Theater Studies	○	●		○	○					●	●	●		●														●		
Medieval Studies			●		●				○		●			●																
Military Studies			●		●		●			●						○			●				●			●	●	●		●
Pacific Studies						●	●	●		●														●						
Philosophy	○	●	●	●					●	●		●	●	●		●		●	●							●			○	●	●
Political Science/Public Policy	●		●	●		●	●		●	●	●	●	●	●		●			●	●		●	●			●		●	●	●
Psychology								○			●	●	●									●								●
Race and Class Studies		●		●	●	●			●	●	●	●		●				●		●		●	●			●		●	●	●
Reference and Guidebooks		●	●				●		●	●			●	●		●												●	●	
Religion/Religious Studies	●	●						●		●		●		●		●				●				●	●			●		●
Buddhism								●	●			●													●					●
Christianity	●		●					●	●	●	●			●						●				●	●			●		●
Hinduism								●				●													●					●
Indigenous Religions					●	●		●				●						●							●			●		●
Islam		●						●	●	●		●								●					●			●		●
Judaism								●	●	●	●	●						●		●			●		●			●		●
Renaissance Studies		○			●				○	●	●	●		●						●			●							
Science & Mathematics											●			●	●	●														
Astronomy											●			●	●															
Biological Science							●				●			●	●					●										
Botany							●				●			●	●														○	
Chemistry											●			○																
Computer Science											●			●		●	●													
Ecology and Conservation		●			●		●				●			●	●	●	●													●
Earth and Environmental		●				●	●				●			●	●	●	●													●
Engineering			●								●												●							
General											●			●																
History of Science	○		●	●			●			●		●		●					●				●	●						
Mathematics											●			●	●															
Neuroscience											●			●																
Physics											●			●																
Statistics											●											●								
Zoology											●																			
Slavic Studies	●	●		●					●	●		●		●		●			●										●	
Sociology				●	○				●	●		●	●	●						●	●									
Social Justice		●						●	●	●						●		●		●	●				●			●	●
Sports	○		●	●								●							●			●						○		
Travel and Tourism				●		●																●						●		
Urban Studies	○			●	○	●	●		●	●	●		●							●	●							●	●	

● press acquires in this area
○ press is NOT actively acquiring in but may have a significant backlist in this area

	Syracuse	Teachers	Temple	Tennessee	Texas	Texas A&M	TCU	Texas Review	Texas Tech	Tokyo	Toronto	Truman State	U.S. Inst. Peace	Upjohn	Utah	Vanderbilt	Virginia	Washington	Wash. State	Wayne State	Wesleyan	West Indies	West Virginia	Wilfrid Laurier	Wisconsin	Wits	Woodrow Wilson	Yale
African Studies												•				•	•						•	•	•	•	•	•
African American Studies	•	•	•	•	•	•		•								•	•	•		•	○		•		•			•
American Studies	•		•	•	•		•	•	•							•	•	•	•	•	○			○				•
Anthropology	•		•	•	•	•				•	•				•	•		•	•	•			•	○	•	•		•
Archeology				•	•	•				•	•				•	•		•							•			•
Arts				•	•	•			•											•								•
Architecture			•	•	•	•				•	•					•	•	•		•			○					•
Art Criticism								•			•																	•
Comics				•							•																	
Dance																					•				•			•
Fashion and Textiles																												•
Folk Art																												
Film				•						•	•					•				•	○		•		•		•	•
Fine Arts and Art History	•				•	•				•	•							•	○				•		•			•
Music & Music Theory			•	•	•				•							•				•			•		•			•
Photography				•	•				•	•	•					•												•
Popular Culture	•			•	•					•						•				•					○		•	•
Television	•			•							•									•								•
Theater										•	•																•	•
Asian Studies		•								•	•	•				•							•			•		•
Biography and Memoir	○		•	•	•	•	•	•	•		•		○			•	•	•	•	•	•		•		•		•	•
Business and Management											•								•				•		•			•
Caribbean Studies			○	•							•					•	•		○	•		•	•					•
Child Development		•								•	•																	
Classics				•						•	•							○					•					•
Criminology		•						•																				
Demography										•	•																	
Disability Studies	•	•								•	•					•			•									
European Studies	•									•	•					•	•						•			•	•	•
Economics										•	•	•	•						•								•	•
Education	•	•	•		•			•		•	•		•			•			•		•		•	•	○			•
Folklore	•			•	•			•	•	•	•			•					•				•					
Food & Agriculture					•	•					•												•					
Agriculture					•						•												•					•
Cooking				•							•							•	○				•					•
Food & Culture				•	•		•				•						•	•		•		•	•					•
History of Food				•							•						•						•					•
Geography	•		•	•	•						•					•	•					•	•		•		•	•
Gender and Sexuality Studies		•	•							•	•					•	•	•		•		•	•		•			•
LGBTQIA Studies		•	•							•						•		•		•			•		•			•
Women's Studies	•	•		•	•	•		•	•	•						•		•	•	•			•	○	•		•	•
Health & Medicine				•						•																○		
Addiction Studies										•						•												
Aging				•						•	•					•												•
History of Medicine				•						•						•	•						•					•
Public Health				•						•	•							•	•				•					•
History	•			•	•	•				•	•					•		•								•	•	•
African											•					•	•						•		•	•	•	•
American	•		•	•	•	•	•	•	•		•		○			•	•	•	•	•	○		•		•	•	•	•
Ancient				•						•	•												•					•
Asian										•	•	•						•					•			•		•
Australasian																												•
British										•	•		•				•							○		•	•	•
Canadian											•							•			•		•		○		•	•
Caribbean			○	•							•					•	•				•			○				•
Central American				•							•					•								○				•
Eastern European											•	•							•						•			•
European	•	•								•	•	•				•	•		•						•		•	•
Latin American				•		•					•		•				•							○		•	•	•
Medieval											•							•										•
Middle Eastern	•			•							•		•		•		•											•
South American				•							•				•									○				•

● press acquires in this area
○ press is NOT actively acquiring in but may have a significant backlist in this area

Subject	Syracuse	Teachers	Temple	Tennessee	Texas	Texas A&M	TCU	Texas Review	Texas Tech	Tokyo	Toronto	Truman State	U.S. Inst. Peace	Upjohn	Utah	Vanderbilt	Virginia	Washington	Wash. State	Wayne State	Wesleyan	West Indies	West Virginia	Wilfrid Laurier	Wisconsin	Wits	Woodrow Wilson	Yale
Immigration		●		●						●	●			●		●	●	●								●		
Indigenous Studies	●	●		●	●	●	●			●	●	●				●	●	●	●				●	○	●		●	●
Information and Communications					●	○													●				●			●		
Information Science					●					●																		
Internet Studies										●																		●
Journalism and Media Studies	○		●						●												●		●		○	●	●	●
Labor			●	●	●					●					●	●		●							●		●	●
Language					●					●																		
Dictionaries and Lexicals										●	●	●		●		●									●			
Linguistic Theory										●															●			
Language Texts										●	●													○				
Writing and Style Guides										●	●																	
Latin American Studies			●	○	●		●			●		●				●								○		●	●	●
Law and Legal Studies										●	●	●				●	●						●		●	○		●
Literature (Creative)	●			●																					●			
Creative Nonfiction			●			●	●	●				●			●		●			●	●	●	●	●	●			
Fiction	○					●	●	●												●	●	●	●	●	●	●		●
Poetry	○						●	●			●				●					●	●	●	●	●	●			●
Drama	○															○									●			●
Children's																	●											
Translations	●				●												●			●	●		●	●				●
Literature (Scholarly)	●		●	●		●										○							●	●				●
Literary Criticism	●		●			●	●	●	●	●						●	●	○	●	●			●	●	●	●	●	●
History	●		●			●	●	●	●	●	●					●	●			●			●	●	●	●		●
Theater Studies										●															●			●
Medieval Studies										●	●						●							○				●
Military Studies				●		●				●		●				●			○				●			●		●
Pacific Studies										●		●				●										●		●
Philosophy	●		●							●	●					○	●									●	●	○
Political Science/Public Policy	●		●	○	●	●				●	●	●	●	●		●	●		●		●		●		●	●	●	●
Psychology	○									●	●					●			●						●			●
Race and Class Studies			●	●	●	●	●		●		●	●				●	●	●		●		●	●		●			●
Reference and Guidebooks										●				●		●	●	●		●			●				○	
Religion/Religious Studies	●		●	●	●					●	●	●				●	●			●						●		●
Buddhism										●						●	●											●
Christianity	●									●						●				○								●
Hinduism																	●											●
Indigenous Religions				●						●	●					●												●
Islam	●		●							●			●			●				●								●
Judaism	●		●							●						●			●									●
Renaissance Studies										●										○								●
Science & Mathematics						●																						
Astronomy											●														○			●
Biological Science					●						●	●																●
Botany	○				●						●	●																●
Chemistry											●																	
Computer Science											●																	
Ecology and Conservation	○					●	●			●	●	●								●			●		●			●
Earth and Environmental	○					●	●			●	●				●		●	●	●				●		●			●
Engineering											●																	
General																												●
History of Science										●	●						●											●
Mathematics											●																	●
Neuroscience											●																	●
Physics											●																	●
Statistics											●																	
Zoology					●						●														○			●
Slavic Studies										●	●									●					●	●		●
Sociology	●		●	●						●	●	●				●	●		●	●		●	●	○	●			●
Social Justice	●		●	●	●			●		●	●					●		●		●		●			●			●
Sports	●		●	●	●			●		●						●									●			●
Travel and Tourism					●	●														●					●			
Urban Studies				●	●	●				●	●			●		●	●			●					●	●	●	

● press acquires in this area
○ press is NOT actively acquiring in but may have a significant backlist in this area

PRESSES PUBLISHING JOURNALS

University presses have always been associated with publishing books of merit and distinction. This remains as true today as in the past, but less well appreciated is the extent to which university presses are active in publishing scholarly journals.

Journals form a major part of the publishing program of many presses, and more than half of the association's members produce at least one periodical. University presses publish several hundred scholarly periodicals, including many of the most distinguished in their respective fields.

Each individual press listing also gives the number of journals, if any, that a press publishes and usually lists the titles of journals under the press's editorial program. Many journals are available in both print and electronic versions. For information concerning a specific periodical, readers are advised to consult a copy of the publication before communicating with the press concerned.

The following Association member presses publish journals.

University of Akron Press
The University of Alabama Press
American Historical Association
American Psychiatric Association Publishing
The American School of Classical Studies at Athens
The American University in Cairo Press
Amsterdam University Press
The University of Arkansas Press
Army Press
Athabasca University Press
Brookings Institution Press
University of California Press
Cambridge University Press
The Catholic University of America Press
The University of Chicago Press
The Chinese University Press
University of Cincinnati Press
Cork University Press
Duke University Press
University Press of Florida
Fordham University Press
Gallaudet University Press
George Mason University Press
Georgetown University Press
Getty Publications
University of Hawai'i Press
University of Illinois Press
IMF Publications

Indiana University Press
The Johns Hopkins University Press
The Kent State University Press
Leuven University Press
Liverpool University Press
Manchester University Press
Marine Corps University Press
Marquette University Press
The MIT Press
Medieval Institute Publications
Michigan State University Press
Minnesota Historical Society Press
University of Minnesota Press
Modern Language Association of America
Naval Institute Press
University of Nebraska Press
The University of North Carolina Press
University of North Texas Press
Ohio State University Press
Otago University Press
University of Ottawa Press
Oxford University Press
University of Pennsylvania Press
Pennsylvania State University Press
University of Puerto Rico Press
Purdue University Press
RAND Corporation
RIT Press
The Rockefeller University Press
Russell Sage Foundation
SBL Press
South Dakota Historical Society Press
State University of New York Press
Temple University Press
University of Texas Press
Texas Review Press
Texas Tech University Press
University of Toronto Press, Inc.
Truman State University Press
Washington State University Press
Wayne State University Press
Wesleyan University Press
The University of the West Indies Press
West Virginia University Press
Wilfrid Laurier University Press
The University of Wisconsin Press

DIRECTORY OF MEMBERS

This section includes a wealth of information on the Association's member presses, including current street and mailing addresses, phone and fax numbers, email addresses, websites, and social media participation. Most presses also list their sales representatives/distributors for Canada, the UK, and Europe. (Addresses for these representatives are included on page 238)

Each entry contains important information describing that press's editorial program. This includes a list of disciplines published, special series, joint imprints, copublishing programs, and the names of journals published, if any.

Press staff are listed, wherever possible, by the following departments/order: director and administrative staff, acquisitions editorial, electronic publishing, manuscript editorial, design and production, marketing, journals, business, and information systems. In most cases the first person listed within a department is its head. Readers should note, however, that this method of organization is intended to promote ease of use, and is not always indicative of the lines of authority within an individual press.

Information on each press's membership status follows the staff listing. This includes date of press founding, type of membership (regular, affiliate, or introductory), year admitted to the Association, title output for 2016 and 2017, the number of journals published, and the total number of titles currently in print.

Abilene Christian University Press

ACU Box 29138
Abilene, TX 79699

Phone: 325.674.2720
Fax: 325.674.6471

Orders:
Phone: 325.674.2720 or 877.816.4455
Email: orders@acupressbooks.com

Websites and Social Media:
Website: www.acupressbooks.com;
www.leafwoodpublishers.com; www.acupressbookclub.com
Facebook: Facebook.com/ACUPress
Twitter: @ACUPress
YouTube: www.youtube.com/user/leafwoodpublishers

Staff
Director ACU Press & Leafwood Publishers: Jason Fikes (325.674.2720;
  email: jason.fikes@acu.edu)
Director of Sales & Operations: Duane Anderson (325.674.2720;
  email: duane.anderson@acu.edu)
Managing Editor: Managing Editor: Rebecka Scott (325.674.2761; email: rrs12c@acu.edu)
Office Manager: Lettie Morrow (325.674.2720; email: lettie.morrow@acu.edu)

Regular Member
Established: 1984

Admitted to the Association: 2008
(intro. member)
Admitted to the Association: 2012
(full member)

Title output 2016: 27
Titles currently in print: 582

Title output 2017: 33

Editorial Program
Religion in American culture; biblical studies and Christian spirituality theology; Texas regional studies; history and theory of higher education (with an emphasis on faith-based education); international and multicultural studies; literary works.
Special series: Christianity and Literature; Faith-Based Higher Education; History and Theology of the Stone-Campbell Movement; Texas History and Culture

The University of Akron Press

120 E. Mill Street, Suite 415
Akron, OH 44308

Phone: 330.972.5342
Fax: 330.972.8364

Cust. Service/Order Fulfillment:
Toll-free: 800.247.6553
Fax: 419.281.6883
Email: orders@btpubservices.com

Website and Social Media:
Website: www.uakron.edu/uapress
Facebook: www.facebook.com/UAkronPress
Twitter: @uakronpress
Instagram: @uakronpress

Canadian Representative:
Magenta Entertainment

UK Representative:
Roundhouse Group

Staff
Director: Jon Miller (330.972.6202; email: mjon@uakron.edu)
Editorial & Design: Amy Freels (330.972.5342;
 email: afreels@uakron.edu)
Production & Manufacturing: Thea Ledendecker (330.972.2795;
 email: thea@uakron.edu)
Marketing Manager: Julie Gammon (330.972.6962;
 email: jgammon@uakron.edu)

Regular Member
Established: 1988
Title output 2016: 6
Titles currently in print: 195

Admitted to the Association: 1997
Title output 2017: 10
Journals published: 1

Editorial Program
Regional trade books, scholarly books, and poetry, with special interests in applied politics, contemporary poetics, psychology, and regional culture and history. The Press distributes the publications of Principia Press. Submissions of poetry are only accepted during the annual poetry prize.
Journal: *The International Journal of Ethical Leadership*
Special series: Akron Series in Contemporary Poetics; Akron Series in Poetry; Bliss Institute Series; Center for the History of Psychology Series; Critical Editions in Early American Literature; & Law: Legal Issues Across Disciplines; and Ohio History and Culture

The University of Alabama Press

Street Address:
200 Hackberry Lane
Tuscaloosa, AL 35401

Phone: 205.348.5180
Fax: 205.348.9201
Email: (user I.D.)@uapress.ua.edu

Website and Social Media:
Website: www.uapress.ua.edu
Facebook: www.facebook.com/
   UniversityALPress
Twitter: @univofalpress

UK/European Distributor:
Eurospan

Mailing Address:
Box 870380
Tuscaloosa, AL 35487-0380

Order Fulfillment:
The University of Alabama Press
Chicago Distribution Center
11030 South Langley Avenue
Chicago, IL 60628
Phone: 773.568.1550
Fax: 773.660.2235

Canadian Representative:
Codasat Canada

Staff

Director: Linda Manning (205.348.1560; email: lmanning)
   Assistant to the Director: Kristen Hop (205.348.5180; email: khop)
   Rights and Permissions Coordinator: Claire Lewis Evans (205.348.1561; email: cevans)
Acquisitions Editorial: Dan Waterman, Editor-in-Chief and Acquisitions Editor, Humanities (literature and criticism, rhetoric and communication, African American studies, public administration, theater, law and legal studies) (205.348.5538; email: waterman)
   Senior Acquisitions Editors: Wendi Schnaufer (archaeology, anthropology, ethnohistory, Native American studies, food studies) (205.348.1568; email: wschnaufer); Elizabeth Motherwell (natural history and the environment, history of science, technology, agriculture, and medicine) (205.348.7108; email: emother)
   Acquisitions Editor: Donna Cox Baker (history) (205.348.7471; email: donna.baker@ua.edu)
Electronic Publishing: Claire Lewis Evans, Associate Editor for Digital and Electronic Publishing (205.348.1561; email: cevans)
Manuscript Editorial: Jon Berry, Managing Editor (205.348.9708; email: jberry)
   Assistant Managing Editor: Joanna Jacobs (205.348.1563; email: jjacobs)
   Project Editor: TBA (205.348.1565)
   Editorial Assistant: Carol Connell (205.348.5183; email: cconnell)
Design and Production: Rick Cook, Production Manager (205.348.1571; email: rcook)
   Art Director and Designer: Michele Quinn (205.348.1570; email: mquinn)
Marketing: Clint Kimberling, Director of Sales and Marketing (205.348.1566; email: ckimberling)
Sales Manager: Kristi Henson (205.348.9534; email: khenson)
   Marketing Coordinator: Blanche Sarratt (205.348.5180; email: bsarratt)
Business: Rosalyn Carr, Business Manager (205.348.1567; email: rcarr)
   Accounting Specialist: Allie Harper (205.348.1564; email: aharper)

University of Alabama Press continued

Regular Member
Established: 1945
Title output 2016: 80
Titles currently in print: 1,558

Admitted to the Association: 1964
Title output 2017: 71
Journals published: 3

Editorial Program
African American studies; American history; American literature and criticism; American religious history; American social and cultural history; anthropology; archaeology, American, Caribbean, southern and historical; creative non-fiction; ethnohistory; Judaic studies; Latin-American studies; linguistics, esp. dialectology; maritime history; military history; Native American studies; natural history and environmental studies; public administration; regional studies; rhetoric and communication; southern history and culture; sports history; theatre. Submissions are not invited in poetry, fiction, or drama.
Journals: *Journal of Community Engagement and Scholarship*; *Theatre History Studies*; *Theatre Symposium*
Special series: Alabama: The Forge of History; American Writers Remembered; Archaeology of the American South: New Directions and Perspectives; Atlantic Crossings; Caribbean Archaeology and Ethnohistory; Classics in Southeastern Archaeology; Contemporary American Indian Studies; Gosse Nature Guides; Historical Archaeology in South America; Jews and Judaism: History and Culture; Library of Alabama Classics; Modern and Contemporary Poetics; The Modern South; NEXUS: New Histories of Science, Technology, the Environment, Agriculture, and Medicine; NGOgraphies: Ethnographic Reflections on NGOs; Public Administration: Criticism and Creativity; Religion and American Culture; Rhetoric, Culture, and Social Critique; Rhetoric, Law, and the Humanities; Studies in American Literary Realism and Naturalism; War, Memory, and Culture
Imprints: Fiction Collective 2

University of Alaska Press

Mailing Address:
PO Box 756240
Fairbanks, AK 99775-6240

Phone: 888.252.6657; 907.474.5831
Fax: 907.474.5502

Website and Social Media:
Website: www.uapress.alaska.edu
Facebook: www.facebook.com/pages/
   University-of-Alaska-Press/44832289241
Twitter: @ualaskapress

Street Address:
1760 Westwood Way
Fairbanks, AK 99709

Orders:
Chicago Distribution Center
11030 South Langley Avenue
Chicago, IL 60628-3892
Phone: 800.621.2736
Fax: 800.621.8476

Staff
Director/Acquisitions Editor: Nate Bauer (907.474.2776; email: nate.bauer@alaska.edu)
Production Editor: Krista West (907.474.6413; email: krista.west@alaska.edu)
Publicity Coordinator: Dawn Montano (907.474.6544; email: dawn.montano@alaska.edu)
Sales and Marketing Coordinator: Laura Walker (907.474.5831;
   email: laura.walker@alaska.edu)
Editorial Assistant: Elizabeth Laska (907.474.6389; email: eplaska@alaska.edu)

Regular Member
Established: 1967
Title output 2016: 14
Titles currently in print: 255

Admitted to the Association: 1992
Title output 2017: 17

Editorial Program
The University of Alaska Press is recognized as the premier scholarly publisher of books relating to Alaska, the Pacific Rim, and circumpolar North. The Press publishes on topics that include history, politics, and literature; anthropology; Native American studies and art; science and natural history; energy and conservation; environmental studies; geography; biography and memoir; humanities and health; poetry and international poetry; photography; field guides; and children's literature. Submissions are invited in poetry, fiction, and literary nonfiction and should have a strong connection to Alaska or the circumpolar North.

The Press distributes publications for the following University of Alaska entities: UA Foundation; UA Museum of the North; Alaska Sea Grant College Program; Alaska Native Knowledge Network; and Alaska Native Language Center. The Press also serves as a distributor for various independent publishers.

Special series: Alaska Literary Series, Alaska Writer Laureate; Classic Reprint; Oral Biography; and Rasmuson Library Historical Translation
Special imprints: Snowy Owl (trade books)

The University of Alberta Press

Ring House 2
Edmonton AB T6G 2E1
Canada

Phone: 780.492.3662
Fax: 780.492.0719
Email: (user I.D.)@ualberta.ca

Website and Social Media:
Website: www.uap.ualberta.ca
Blog: holeinthebucket.wordpress.com
Facebook: www.facebook.com/pages/
   University-of-Alberta-Press-UAP/
   18764314500
Twitter: @UAlbertaPress

UK/European Distributor:
Gazelle Academic

Canadian Distributor:
University of Toronto Press
5201 Dufferin Street
Toronto ON M3H 5T8 Canada

Phone: 800.565.9523
Fax: 800.221.9985
Email: utpbooks@utpress.utoronto.ca

US Distributor:
Wayne State University Press
The Leonard N. Simons Building
4809 Woodward Avenue
Detroit MI 48201-1309
Phone: 800.978.7323
313.577.6120
Fax: 313.577.6131
Email: bookorders@wayne.edu

Staff
Director: Douglas Hildebrand (780.492.0717; email: dhildebr)
Business Administrator: Basia Kowal (780.492.3662; email: bkowal)
Scholar-in-Residence: Colleen Skidmore (780.492.1231; email: colleen.skidmore)
Senior Editor (Acquisitions): Peter Midgley (780.492.7714; email: pmidgley)
Editor (Production): Mary Lou Roy (780.492.9488; email: marylou.roy)
Digital Coordinator: Duncan Turner (780.492.4945; email: duncan.turner)
Design/Production: Alan Brownoff (780.492.8285; email: alan.brownoff)
Associate Director/Manager Planning & Operations: Cathie Crooks (780.492.5820; email: ccrooks)
Sales/Marketing Assistant: Monika Igali (780.492.7493; email: monika.igali)

Regular Member
Established: 1969
Title output 2016: 20
Titles currently in print: 893

Admitted to the Association: 1983
Title output 2017: 18

Editorial Program
UAlberta Press publishes in the areas of Indigenous studies, Canadian history, arctic and circumpolar studies, literature, anthropology, urban studies, African studies, Islamic studies, race and gender studies, biography, natural history and environmental studies, regional interest, travel narratives, and reference books.
Imprints: Pica Pica Press (textbooks); Gutteridge Books (trade books); Polynya Press (books on the circumpolar north).
Special series: Mountain Cairns—a series on the history and culture of the Canadian Rockies; Patterns of Northern Traditional Healing; Petrocultures; Robert Kroetsch: Canadian creative writing, short stories and poetry

American Historical Association

400 A Street, S.E.
Washington, DC 20003-3889

Phone: 202.544.2422
Fax: 202.544.8307
Email: aha@historians.org

Orders:
Oxford University Press
Phone: 800.445.9714
Email: orders.us@oup.com

Website and Social Media:
Website: www.historians.org
Blog: blog.historians.org
Facebook: www.facebook.com/AHAhistorians
Twitter: @AHAhistorians
YouTube: www.youtube.com/user/historiansorg

Staff
Executive Director: James R. Grossman (202.544.2422; email: jgrossman@historians.org)
Controller: Randy Norell (202.544.2422; email: rnorell@historians.org)
Editor, *American Historical Review*: Alex Lichtenstein (812.855.0027; email: ahredit@indiana.edu)
Director of Scholarly Communications and Digital Initiatives: Seth Denbo (202.544.1118 email: sdenbo@historians.org)
Editor, *Perspectives on History*: Allison Miller (202.450.5617; email: amiller@historians.org)
Associate Editor, Publications: Kritika Agarwal (202.544.2422 ext. 133; email: kagarwal@historians.org)
Associate Editor, Web Content and Social Media: Stephanie Kingsley (202.544.2422 ext. 117; skingsley@historians.org)
Editorial Assistant: Zoe Jackson (202.544.2422 ext. 119; email: zjackson@historians.org)

Regular Member
Established: 1884
Title output 2016: 2
Titles currently in print: 62

Admitted to the Association: 2005
Title output 2017: 2
Journals published: 1

Editorial Program
The AHA publishes a wide variety of periodical, annual, and other publications of service and interest to the historical profession and the general public. Primary publications are the journals, the *American Historical Review* (published by Oxford University Press) and the monthly news magazine *Perspectives on History*. The Association's other major publication is the annual *Directory of History Departments, Historical Organizations, and Historians*. Beyond that, the AHA publishes a wide range of topical booklets on the practice of history and historical topics. Both the booklets and the annual Directory are distributed by Oxford University Press. On the Web, the Association publishes articles, directories, and documentary materials. The AHA also maintains a daily blog for those interested in the study of the past and the practice of history, and a wiki on archives for history researchers.

American Psychiatric Association Publishing

800 Maine Avenue, SW
Washington, DC 20024

Phone: 703.907.7322
Fax: 703.907.1092
Email: appi@psych.org
Indiv: (user I.D.)@psych.org

Orders:
Phone: 800.368.5777; 703.907.7322
Fax: 703.907.1091

Website and Social Media:
Website: www.appi.org
Facebook: www.facebook.com/AmericanPsychiatricPublishing
Twitter: @APP_Publishing

European Distributor:
NBN International

Canadian Representative:
Login Brothers Canada

Staff
Interim Publisher: John J. McDuffie (703.907.7871; email: jmcduffie)
Executive Assistant: Erika Parker (703.907.7892; email: eparker)
Editor-in-Chief: Laura Roberts, M.D.,M.A. (703.907.7892)
Book Acquisitions Coordinator: Erika Parker (703.907.7892; email: eparker)
Director, Digital Publishing and Product Development: Tim Marney (703.907.8541; email: tmarney)
Managing Editor, Books: Greg Kuny (703.907.7872; email: gkuny)
Director of Production: Andrew Wilson (703.907.7882; email: awilson)
Director of Marketing and Sales: Patrick Hansard (703.907.7893; email: phansard)
Associate Director of Marketing: Christie Couture (703.907.7877; email: ccouture)
Editorial Director, Journals: Michael Roy (703.907.7894; email: mroy)
Director of Publishing and Business Operations: Debra Eubanks (703.907.8546; email: deubanks)

Regular Member
Established: 1981
Title output 2016: 23
Titles currently in print: 729

Admitted to the Association: 1993
Title output 2017: 32
Journals published: 5

Editorial Program
Clinical books and monographs in psychiatry and related fields; research monographs; medical textbooks; study guides; nonfiction trade books in mental health; annual review; and journals. *Diagnostic and Statistical Manual of Mental Disorders, 5th Edition*
Journals: *American Journal of Psychiatry; FOCUS; Journal of Neuropsychiatry; Psychiatric News; Psychiatric Services*
Special series: Clinical Manuals
Special imprints: American Psychiatric Association

The American School of Classical Studies at Athens

Publications Office:
6–8 Charlton Street
Princeton, NJ 08540-5232
Phone: 609.683.0800
Fax: 609.924.0578

Orders:
Casemate Academic
Phone: 610.853.9131
Fax: 610.853.9146
Email: info@casemateacademic.com

Website and Social Media:
Website: www.ascsa.edu.gr/publications
Twitter: @ascsapubs

UK Representative:
Oxbow Books

Canadian Representative:
Casemate Academic

Staff
Director of Publications: Carol A. Stein (ext. 16; email: castein@ascsa.org)
Editor of *Hesperia*: Jennifer Sacher (ext. 22; email: jsacher@ascsa.org)
Senior Project Editor: Colin Whiting (ext. 17; email: cwhiting@ascsa.org)
Project Editor: Destini Price (ext. 21; email dprice@ascsa.org)
Production Manager: Sarah George Figueira (ext. 18; email: sgf@ascsa.org)
Editorial Assistant: Megan R. M. Mendonça (ext. 26; email: mmendonca@ascsa.org)

Regular Member
Established: 1881

Admitted to the Association: 2008
(Introductory. Member)
Admitted to the Association: 2012
(Assoc. Member)

Title output 2016: 3
Titles currently in print: 147

Title output 2017: 7
Journals published: 2

Editorial Program
All fields of Greek archaeology, art, epigraphy, history, materials science, ethnography, and literature, from earliest prehistoric times onward. A particular focus is on publishing the work of the American School of Classical Studies at Athens, a research and teaching institutions founded in 1881 and based in Athens, Greece.
Journals: *Hesperia, The New Griffon*
Special series: Agora Picture Books; Ancient Art and Architecture in Context; The Argive Heraion; The Athenian Agora; Corinth; Gennadeion Monographs; Hesperia Supplements; Isthmia; Lerna; Nemea Valley Archaeological Project; Samothrace

The American University in Cairo Press

113 Kasr el Aini Street
PO Box 2511
Cairo, Egypt 11511

US Office:
420 Fifth Avenue
New York, NY 10018-2729

Phone: 202.2797.6926
Fax: 202.2794.1440
Email: aucpress@aucegypt.edu
Indiv: (user I.D.)@aucegypt.edu

Phone: 212.730.8800
Fax: 212.730.1600

Website and Social Media:
Websites: www.aucpress.com, www.hoopoefiction.com
Facebook: www.facebook.com/aucpress
Twitter: @aucpress
YouTube: www.youtube.com/user/aucpress

North American Distributor:
Oxford University Press
2001 Evans Road
Cary, NC 27513
Phone: 800.445.9714
Email: custserv.us@oup.com

UK and European Distributor:
I.B.Tauris
6 Salem Road
London W2 4BU
Phone: +44.20.7243.1225
Email: pdavighi@ibtauris.com

Staff
Director: Nigel Fletcher-Jones (202.2797.6888; email: nigel)
Executive Assistant to the Director: Sylvia Habib (email: sylvia)
Associate Director for Editorial Programs and Production: Miriam Fahmy (email: miriam)
Senior Commissioning Editor: Nadia Naqib (email: nnaqib)
Managing Editor: Nadine El-Hadi (email: nadine.elhadi)
Senior Online Editor: Ingrid Wassmann (email: wassmann)
Associate Director, Sales and Marketing: Trevor Naylor (email: trevornaylor)
Marketing and International Rights Manager: Basma El Manialawi (email: basma.manialawi)
North America Marketing Manager (NY City): Tarek El-Elaimy (202.730.8800, ext. 4546; email: telaimy)
North America Senior Acquisition Editor (NY City): Anne Routon (email: anne.routon)

Regular Member
Established: 1960
Title output 2016: 70
Titles currently in print: 800

Admitted to the Association: 1986
Title output 2017: 60
Journals published: 2

Editorial Program
The Press is recognized as the leading English-language publisher in the Middle East, and publishes a wide range of scholarly monographs, texts and reference works, and general interest books on ancient and modern Egypt and the Middle East, as well as Arabic literature in English translation (under the Hoopoe imprint), most notably the works of Egyptian Nobel laureate Naguib Mahfouz.
Journals: *Alif: Journal of Comparative Poetics; Cairo Papers in Social Science*

Copublishing programs: Numerous copublishing programs with US, UK, and European universities and trade publishers

Amherst College Press

Robert Frost Library, Amherst College
61 Quadrangle Drive
Amherst, MA 01002
Phone: 413.542.5709
Fax: 413.542.2662

<u>Website and Social Media:</u>
Website: acpress.amherst.edu
Blog: acpress.amherst.edu/blog/
Twitter: @amcollpress

Staff
Director: Mark Edington (413.542.5709; email: medington@amherst.edu)
Senior Acquisition Editor: Beth Bouloukos (413.542.5519;
   email: bbouloukos@amherst.edu)
Editor-in-Chief, New Books Network: Marshall Poe (email: mpoe@amherst.edu)

Introductory Member
Established: 2014
Title output 2016: 3

Admitted to the Association: 2014
Title output 2017: 3

Editorial Program
The Amherst College Press produces pathbreaking, peer-reviewed studies by scholars and makes it available to readers everywhere as digital, open-access work. Digital forms of all of our work—new studies, interviews with authors, and reviews of digital scholarly resources—is provided for use without cost through Creative Commons (4.0) licenses.
Special series: Laws | Literatures | Cultures; Public Works: Insights from the Humanities on Issues in the Public Square; Studies in Ethnomusicology

Amsterdam University Press

Nieuwe Prinsengracht 89
1018 VR Amsterdam
Netherlands

Phone: +31.20.4200050
Fax: +31.20.4203214
Email: info@aup.nl
Indiv: (user I.D.)@aup.nl

Website and Social Media:
Website: www.aup.nl
Facebook: www.facebook.com/
　AmsterdamUPress
Twitter: @AmsterdamUPress

US and Canadian Sales Representative:
University of Chicago Press
Phone: 773.702.7700

China and Hong Kong Representative:
China Publishers Service
Phone: +86 852 24911 436

Japan Representative:
Tim Burland
Phone: +81(0)3-3424 8977

India Representative:
MAYA Publishers PVT Ltd.
Phone: + 91 9811 555 197

Staff
Director: Jan-Peter Wissink (email: wissink)
Finance and Administration: Judith van Jaarsveld (email: jvanJaarsveld@holding.uva.nl);
　Daniela Pinnone (email: d.pinnone)
　Acquisition Editors: Saskia Gieling (Asian studies and social sciences) (email: s.gieling);
　Jeroen Sondervan (film & media) (email: j.sondervan); Inge van der Bijl (email: i.vd.bijl);
　Ebisse Rouw (email: e.rouw); Simon Forde (email: s.forde) Louise Visser (email: l.visser);
　Vanessa de Bueger (email: v.de.bueger)
Editorial Assistant: Atie Vogelenzang (email: a.vogelenzangdejong)
Manuscript Editorial: Chantal Nicolaes (Chief Editor) (email: c.nicolaes); Jaap Wagenaar
　(email: j.wagenaar)
Head of Production: Rob Wadman (email: r.wadman)
International Sales and Marketing: Vanessa de Bueger (email: v.d.bueger)
Orders: Michiel van der Drift (email: m.vander.drift)
Marketing & PR: Michiel van der Drift (head of marketing for the Netherlands and Belgium) (email: m.vander.drift)
International Marketing & PR: Vanessa de Bueger (Head of international marketing) (email:
　v.de.bueger); Anouk Brouwer (email: a.brouwer); Henriette Arndt (email: h.arndt)
Office Manager: Marina Jongkind (email: M.Jongkind)

Regular Member
Established: 1992
Title output 2016: NR
Titles currently in print: 1,100

Admitted to the Association: 2000
Title output 2017: NR
Journals published:　13

Editorial Program
Scholarly and trade titles (English and Dutch language) in Asian Studies, Media and Communication Studies, Social and Political Sciences, European History, and Linguistics. Textbooks for universities and higher education.

Journals: *Mens & Maatschappij* (People and Society); *Internationale Neerlandistiek* (International Dutch Studies); *Tijdschrift voor Genderstudies* (Journal for Gender Studies); *Tijdschrift voor Geschiedenis* (Journal of History); *Tijdschrift voor Sociale en Economische Geschiedenis* (Journal of Social and Economic History); *Taal & Tongval* (Language and Dialects); *NECSUS, European Journal for Media Studies*; *Algemeen Nederlands Tijdschrift voor Wijsbegeerte* (ANTW); *Nederlandse Taalkunde* (Dutch Linguistics); *Nederlandse Letterkunde* (Dutch Literature); *Tijdschrift voor Taalbeheersing* (Journal of Communications); *Sociologie* (Sociology); *Pedagogiek* (Pedagogy)

English series: Asian Borderlands; Asian Cities; Asian Heritages; Asian History; Asian Visual Cultures; China's Environment and Welfare; Consumption and Sustainability in Asia; Emerging Asia; Global Asia; Muslim Eurasia; New Mobilities in Asia; North East Asian Anthropologies; Religion and Society in Asia; Social Histories of Work in Asia; Amsterdam Archaeological Studies; Amsterdam Studies in the Dutch Golden Age; Central European Medieval Studies; Computer Applications and Quantitative Methods in Archaeology; Crossing Boundaries: Turku Medieval and Early Modern Studies; Early Christianity in the Roman World; Environmental Humanities in Pre-modern Cultures; Golden Age Lectures; Heritage and Memory Studies; Knowledge Communities; Landscape and Heritage Studies; Late Antique and Early Medieval Iberia; NIOD Studies on War; Holocaust, and Genocide; Premodern Crime and Punishment; Premodern Health, Disease, and Disability; Renaissance History, Art and Culture; Sources of Anglo-Saxon Literary Culture; The Early Medieval North Atlantic; Cities and Cultures; Eastern European Screen Cultures; Film Culture in Transition; Film Theory in Media History; Filmjaarboek; Framing Film; MediaMatters; Recursions; Televisual Culture; The Key Debates: Mutations and Appropriations in European Film Studies; Transmedia; Care & Welfare; Changing Welfare States; History of Science and Scholarship in the Netherlands; Protest and Social Movements; Work around the Globe: Historical Comparisons; Comprehensive Grammar Resources; Languages and Culture in History; Tekst in Context

German series: Justiz und NS-Verbrechen

Copublications: Princeton University Press (USA); University of California Press (USA); MIT Press (USA); Thames & Hudson (UK); Brandeis University Press (USA); Actes Sud (France); Lannoo Uitgeverij (Belgium); Uitgeverij Davidsfonds (Belgium); Mercatorfonds (Belgium); Arc Medieval Press (USA)

The University of Arizona Press

1510 E. University, 5th Floor
P.O. Box 210055
Tucson, AZ 85721-0055

Orders:
Chicago Distribution Center
Phone: 800.621.2736
Email: orders@press.uchicago.edu

Phone: 520.621.1441
Fax: 520.621.8899
Email: uapress@uapress.arizona.edu
Indiv: (user I.D.)@uapress.arizona.edu

Canadian Representative:
University of British Columbia Press

European Representative:
Eurospan

Website and Social Media:
Website: www.uapress.arizona.edu
Facebook: www.facebook.com/AZpress
Twitter: @AZpress

Staff

Director: Kathryn M. Conrad (520.621.1441; email: kconrad)
Assistant to the Director/Permissions: Julia Balestracci (520.621.3911; email: jbalestracci)
Editor-in-Chief: Kristen Buckles (Native American and Indigenous studies, Latin American studies, Border studies, Latina/o studies, history, regional) (520.621.7921; email: kbuckles)
Senior Editor: Allyson Carter (anthropology, archaeology, ecology, natural history, Native American and Indigenous studies, Latin American studies, environmental science, astronomy and space sciences, regional) (520.621.3186; email: acarter)
Assistant Editor: Scott DeHerrera (literature) (520.621.5919; email: sdeherrera)
Editing, Design, and Production Manager/Production Editor: Amanda Krause (520.621.5915; email: akrause)
Production Coordinator: Sara Thaxton (520.621.7916; email: sthaxton)
Art Director and Book Designer: Leigh McDonald (520.621.5824; email: lmcdonald)
Marketing and Sales Manager: Abby Mogollón (520.621.8656; email: amogollon)
Publicity Manager: Rosemary Brandt (520.621.3920; email: rbrandt)
Exhibits Manager/Marketing Assistant: Nora Evans-Reitz (520.621.4913; email: nevansreitz@email.arizona.edu)
Accounts Payable: Susan Fasciani (520.626.3041; email: sfasciani)

Regular Member

Established: 1959
Title output 2016: 47
Titles currently in print: 1,544

Admitted to the Association: 1962
Title output 2017: 103

Editorial Program

Specialties strongly identified with the universities in the state and other significant nonfiction of regional and national interest. Especially strong fields include anthropology and archaeology; environmental science; history; Latin American studies; Latina/o studies and literature; Native American and Indigenous studies and literature; and space sciences.

The Press also distributes titles from Ironwood Press; the Arizona State Museum; Statistical Research, Inc.; SWCA, Inc.; Center for Desert Archaeology; Center for Sustainable Envi-

ronments; Crow Canyon Archaeological Center; and The Gila River Indian Community.
Special series: Amerind Studies in Anthropology; Anthropological Papers of the University of Arizona; Archaeology of Indigenous-Colonial Interactions in the Americas; Arizona-Sonora Desert Museum Studies In Natural History; Biodiversity in Small Spaces; Camino del Sol; Critical Green Engagements; Critical Issues in Indigenous Studies; The Feminist Wire Books; La Frontera: People and Their Environments in the U.S.-Mexico Borderlands; Global Change / Global Health; Latin American Landscapes; Latinx Pop Culture; The Mexican American Experience; Modern American West; Native Peoples of the Americas; Southwest Center Series; Space Science Series; Sun Tracks; Women's Western Voices

The University of Arkansas Press

McIlroy House
105 North McIlroy Avenue
Fayetteville, AR 72701-1201

Phone: 800.626.0090
Email: info@uapress.com
Indiv: (user I.D.)@uark.edu

Website and Social Media:
Website: www.uapress.com
Facebook: www.facebook.com/UARKPRESS
Twitter: @uarkpress

Customer Service/Orders:
University of Arkansas Press
c/o Chicago Distribution Center
11030 South Langley Avenue
Chicago, IL 60628
Phone: 800.621.2736
Fax: 773.702.7212
Email: orders@press.uchicago.edu

Canadian Representative:
Scholarly Book Services

UK/European Representative:
Eurospan

Staff
Director: Mike W. Bieker (479.575.3859; email: mbieker)
Editor-in-Chief: David Scott Cunningham (479.575.5767; email: dscunnin)
Production Manager: Liz Lester (479.575.6780; email: lizl)
Manuscript Editor: Molly Rector (479.575.4724; email: mbrector)
Marketing: Melissa King, Director of Marketing and Sales (479.575.7715; email: mak001)
Marketing/Advertising Designer: Charlie Shields (479.575.7258; email: cmoss)
Business Manager: Sam Ridge (479.575.3858; email: sridge)
UAP Distribution Services:
Distribution Services Manager: Sam Ridge (479.575.3858; email: sridge)

Regular Member
Established: 1980
Title output 2016: 20
Titles currently in print: 648

Admitted to the Association: 1984
Title output 2017: 25
Journals published: 1

Editorial Program
African American history, art, civil rights studies, food studies, Middle East studies, Ozarks studies, poetry, political science, regional studies, Southern history, sports studies, Civil War studies, women's studies
Journal: *Philosophical Topics*
Special series: The Arkansas Character; CantoMundo Poetry Series; The Civil War in the West; Etel Adnan Poetry Series; Fay Jones Collaborative Series; Food and Foodways; Miller

-37-

University of Arkansas Press continued

Williams Poetry Series; Ozarks Studies; Portraits of Conflict; The Simms Series; Sport, Culture, and Society

Army University Press

290 Stimson, Unit 1
Fort Leavenworth, KS 66027

Phone: 913.684.9327/2127
Email: usarmy.leavenworth.tradoc.mbx.csi-rp
　@mail.mil

Book Orders:
Mr. Ken Gott (913.684.2138/email: kendall.d.gott.civ@mail.mil)

Journal Orders:
Linda Darnell (913.684.9327/email: linda.j.darnell.civ@mail.mil)

Websites and Social Media:
Website: www.armyupress.army.mil/
Twitter: @ArmyUPress
YouTube: www.youtube.com/channel/UCX9G3c6jkROVZ0tXr4gvUKQ/featured?disable_polymer=1 s

Staff
Director/Editor-in-Chief: COL Kate Guttormsen (913.684.9331; email:
　erica.l.cameron.mil@mail.mil)
Deputy Director: Dr. Donald P. Wright (913.684.2088; email:
　donald.p.wright.civ@mail.mil)
Administrative Officer: Amy Castillo (913.684.2127: email: amy.k.castillo.civ@mail.mil)

Introductory Member
Established: 2015 (merger of Combat Studies Institute Press and Military Review)
Admitted to the Association: 2015
Title output 2016: 10
Titles currently in print: 11

Title output: 2017: 8
Journals published: 2

Editorial Program
Established to publish on topics for military professionals. Areas of emphasis include history, strategy, leadership, doctrine, training, military education and general policy issues.
Journals: *Military Review* (3 Versions; English, Portuguese, and Spanish); *Journal of Military Learning*
Special series: Art of War Papers; Leavenworth Papers; Occasional Papers on Global War on Terror

Athabasca University Press

Peace Hills Trust Tower
1200, 10011–109 Street
Edmonton, AB T5J 3S8 Canada

Phone: 780.497.3412
Fax: 780.421.3298
Email: aupress@athabascau.ca

Website and Social Media:
Website: www.aupress.ca
Facebook: www.facebook.com/AUPress1
Twitter: @au_press
YouTube: www.youtube.com/user/aupresst

UK, Europe, Middle East, & Africa Orders:
Combined Academic Publishers
Windsor House
Email: enquiries@combinedacademic.co.uk

Canadian Orders:
University of British Columbia Press
c/o UTP Distribution

Phone: 800.565.9523/416.667.7791
Fax: 800.221.9985/416.667.7832
Email: utpbooks@utpress.utoronto.ca

US Orders:
University of Washington Press
c/o Hopkins Fulfillment Service
Phone: 800.537.5487/410.516.6965
Fax: 410.516.6998
Email: hfscustserv@press.jhu.edu

Asia and Pacific:
East West Export Books

China, Hong Kong, Taiwan, and Korea:
Asia Publishers Services Ltd.

Staff
Acting Director: Megan Hall (780.428.2067; email: mhall@athabascau.ca)
Marketing and Editorial Assistant: Karyn Wisselink (780.497.3408; email: kwisselink@athabascau.ca)
Senior Editor: Pamela Holway (780.428.7278; email: pholway@athabascau.ca)
Associate Editor: Connor Houlihan (780.392.1204; email: connorh@athabascau.ca)
Journals and Digital Coordinator: Kathy Killoh (780.421.2528; email: kathyk@athabascau.ca)
Marketing & Production Coordinator: Megan Hall (780.428.2067; email: mhall@athabascau.ca)
Digital Design Technician: Sergiy Kozakov (780.421.5846; email: sergiyk@athabascau.ca)
IT Systems Administrator/Coordinator: Shubhash Wasti (780.421.2526; email: shubhash@athabascau.ca)
Fulfillment Administrator: Linda Kadis (780.421.5062; email: lkadis@athabascau.ca)

Regular Member
Established: 2007

Title output 2016: 15
Titles currently in print: 123

Admitted to the Association:
2008 (intro. member)
Admitted to the Association:
2011 (full member)
Title output 2017: 15
Journals published: 7

Editorial Program
Our geographical focus is on Canada, the North American West, and the Circumpolar North. One of our mandates is to publish innovative and experimental works (in both fiction

Athabasca University Press continued

and non-fiction) that challenge established canons, subjects, and formats. As we are dedicated to making AU Press publications accessible to a broad readership through open access technologies, we cultivate the areas of open, distance, and e-learning. We promote forms such as diary, memoir, and oral history. AU Press also publishes websites (under its imprint) with content that has scholarly parameters and standards, especially grey literature on distance learning and primary sources in labour studies, Métis and Aboriginal Studies, gender studies, and the environment.

Journals: *Alternate Routes; The Canadian Journal of Learning and Technology (CJLT); Canadian Folk Music/Musique folklorique canadienne; International Review of Research in Open and Distance Learning (IRRODL); The Journal of Distance Education; Journal of Research Practice (JRP); Labour/Le Travail; Oral History Forum d'histoire orale; The Trumpeter*

Web-based publications: *Aurora; Canadian Theatre Encyclopedia*

Special series: Canadian Plays; Cultural Dialectics; Fabriks: Studies in the Working Class; Global Peace Studies; Issues in Distance Education; Mingling Voices; OPEL: Open Paths to Enriched Learning; Our Lives: Diary, Memoir, and Letters; Recovering the Past: Studies in Archaeology; The West Unbound: Social and Cultural Studies; Working Canadians: Books from the CCLH

Baylor University Press

Street Address:
1920 South 4th Street
Waco, TX 76706-2529

Phone: 254.710.3164
Fax: 254.710.3440
Email: (user I.D.)@baylor.edu

Website and Social Media:
Website: www.baylorpress.com
Facebook: www.facebook.com/BaylorPress
Twitter: @Baylor_Press

Mailing Address:
One Bear Place # 97363
Waco, TX 76798-7363

Orders:
Baylor University Press
c/o Hopkins Fulfillment Service
P.O. Box 50370
Baltimore, MD 21211-4370
Phone: 800.537.5487 or 410.516.6956
Fax: 410.516.6998

UK Representative:
Gazelle

Staff
Director: Carey Newman (254.710.3522; email: carey_newman)
Business: Madeline Wieters, Finance and Operations Manager (254.710.1285; email: madeline_wieters)
Design and Production: Diane E. Smith, Associate Director/Director of Production and Design (254.710.2563; email: diane_smith)
Ebooks: Jenny Hunt Associate Director/Director of Digital Publishing (254.710.3236; email: jenny_hunt)
Sales and Publicity Manager: David Aycock (254.710.1465; email: david_aycock)

Regular Member
Established: 1897
Title output 2016: 39
Titles currently in print: 477

Admitted to the Association: 2007
Title output 2017: 43

Editorial Program
Established in 1897, Baylor University Press publishes forty new titles each year in the following academic areas: religion & public life; rhetoric & religion; religious studies & theology; religion & literature; religion & philosophy; religion & higher education. In accordance with Baylor University's mission, the Press strives to serve the academic community by producing works of excellent quality that integrate faith and understanding.

Special series: Baylor Handbook on the Greek New Testament; Baylor Handbook on the Hebrew Bible; Charles Edmondson Historical Lectures; Documents of Anglophone Christianity Series; The Making of the Christian Imagination; New Perspectives on Latina/o Religion; Provost's Series; Studies in Christianity and Literature; Studies in Religion and Higher Education; Studies in Rhetoric and Religion; World Christianity

Beacon Press

24 Farnsworth Street
Boston, MA 02210

UK Representative:
Publishers Group UK

Phone: 617.742.2110
Fax: 617.723.3097
Marketing/Publicity/Subsidiary
Rights Fax: 617.742.2290
Email: permissions@beacon.org
Indiv: (user I.D.)@beacon.org

Canadian Representative:
Penguin Random House Canada

Website and Social Media:
Website: www.beacon.org
Blog: www.beaconbroadside.com
Facebook: www.facebook.com/beaconpress
Twitter: @BeaconPressBks
YouTube: www.youtube.com/user/BeaconBroadside

Staff
Director: Helene Atwan (email: hatwan)
  Assistant to the Director: Maya Fernandez (email: mfernandez)
Editorial: Gayatri Patnaik, Editorial Director (email: gpatnaik)
  Executive Editor: Amy Caldwell (email: acaldwell)
  Senior Editors: Rakia Clark (email: rclark); Joanna Green (email: jgreen)
  Contracts Director and Director of Beacon Press Audio: Melissa Nasson (email: mnasson)
  Editors: Will Myers (email: wmyers); Rachael Marks (email: rmarks)
Production: Marcy Barnes, Production Director & Digital Publishing Director
  (email: mbarnes)
Managing Editor: Susan Lumenello (email: slumenello)
Creative Director: Bob Kosturko (email: bkosturko)
Marketing: Tom Hallock, Associate Publisher (email: thallock)

Beacon Press continued

Director of Sales and Marketing: Sanj Kharbanda (email: skharbanda)
Director of Communications: Pamela MacColl (email: pmaccoll)
Publicity Manager: Caitlin Meyer (email: cmeyer)
Associate Marketing Manager: Emily Powers (email: epowers)
Assistant to the Associate Publisher: Kennia Joseph (email: kjoseph)
Business: Cliff Manko, Chief Financial Officer (email: cmanko)
Director of Business Operations: Greg Kanter (email: gkanter)
Accounts Payable/Receivable: Jill Dougan (email: jdougan)

Regular Member
Established: 1854
Title output 2016: 60
Titles currently in print: 1,026

Admitted to the Association: 1988
Title output 2017: 57

Editorial Program
Beacon Press, the non-profit publisher affiliated with the Unitarian Universalist Association, publishes works for the general reader, specializing in African American, Native American, and Asian American studies; anthropology; current affairs; education; environmental studies; gay and lesbian studies; public health; religion; and women's studies.
Special series and joint publishing programs: The Beacon Press/Simmons College Series on Race, Education, and Democracy; The King Legacy; Queer Action/Queer Ideas, Revisioning American History

University of British Columbia Press

2029 West Mall
University of British Columbia
Vancouver, BC V6T 1Z2 Canada

Phone: 604.822.5959
Toll-free (in Canada): 877.377.9378
Fax: 604.822.6083
Toll-free fax (in Canada): 800.668.0821
Email: (user I.D.)@ubcpress.ca

Website and Social Media:
Website: www.ubcpress.ca
Facebook: UBC Press
Twitter: @UBCPress
YouTube: UBCPressChannel
Instagram: instagram.com/ubcpress

Canadian Orders and Returns:
University of Toronto Press
5201 Dufferin Place
Toronto, ON M3H 5T8 Canada
Phone: 416.667.7791
Fax: 416.667.7832
Email: utpbooks@utpress.utoronto.ca

US Orders and Returns:
University of Washington Press
C/O Hopkins Fulfillment Service
PO Box 50370
Baltimore, MD 21211-4370 USA
Phone: 800.537.5487; 410.516.6956
Email: hfscustserv@press.jhu.edu

Distributors
The University of Washington Press (US); Combined Academic Publishers (UK, Europe, Middle East, and Africa); East West Export Books (Asia and Pacific); Special Book Services Ltd. (South America)

Staff
Director: Melissa Pitts (604.822.6376; email: pitts)
Assistant to the Publisher and Permissions Manager: Valerie Nair (604.822.4161; email: nair)
Acquisitions Editorial: Darcy Cullen, Associate Director—Acquisitions (Vancouver) (BC studies, Canadian history, gender & sexuality studies, Indigenous studies, transnational and multicultural Studies) (604.822.5744; email: cullen); Randy Schmidt, Senior Editor (Kelowna) (Asian studies, diplomatic history, law and socio-legal studies, military history, political history, political science) (250.764.4761; email: schmidt); James MacNevin, Senior Editor (Toronto) (communications & media studies, environmental history, environmental and resource studies, health and food studies, sociology, urban studies and planning); Nadine Pedersen, Editorial Coordinator (604.827.1795; email: pedersen)
Production Editorial: Holly Keller, Assistant Director—Production and Editorial Services (604.822.4545; email: keller)
Editors: Ann Macklem (604.822.0093; email: macklem); Lesley Erickson (604.822.4548; email: lerickson); Megan Brand (604.822.5885; email: brand); Katrina Petrik (604.822.6436; email: petrik)
Marketing and Sales: Laraine Coates, Marketing Manager (604.822.6486; email: coates)
Academic Marketing Manager: Harmony Johnson (604.822.1978; email: johnson)
Digital Publishing Coordinator: Krista Bergstrom (604.822.5790; email: bergstrom)Publicist and Events Manager: Kerry Kilmartin (604.822.8244; email: kilmartin) Catalogues and Advertising Manager: Alexa Love (604.822.4546; email: love)
Agency and Digital Marketing Coordinator: Megan Malashewsky (604.822.8226; email: malashewsky)
Inventory and Distribution Coordinator: Liz Hudson (604.822.1221; email: hudson); Marketing Assistant and Front Desk: David Ly (604.822.5959; email: ly)
Finance: Steve Young, Asst. Director—Finance & Operations (604.822.8938; email: young)
Finance Assistant: Derick Chan (604.822.5370; email: chan)

Regular Member
Established: 1971　　　　　　　　　　　Admitted to the Association: 1972
Title output 2016: 59　　　　　　　　　Title output 2017: 62
Titles currently in print: 1,035

Editorial Program
Scholarly books and serious nonfiction, with special interest in First Nations culture politics and linguistics, Canadian history, environmental history and policy, resources, Canadian politics, globalization, multiculturalism, urban planning, Asian studies, and sexuality and gender studies.
Special series: Asia Pacific Legal Culture and Globalization; Asian Religions and Society; Brenda and David McLean Canadian Studies; C.D. Howe Series in Canadian Political History; Canada and International Relations; Canadian Democratic Audit; Communication, Strategy, and Politics; Contemporary Chinese Studies; Disability, Culture, and Politics; Equality|Security|Community; Ethnicity and Democratic Governance; First Nations Languages; Globalization and Autonomy; Histories of Substance; Law and Society; Legal Dimensions; Nature|History|Society; Pacific Rim Archaeology; Purich's Aboriginal Issues; RBCM Handbooks; Pioneers of British Columbia; Sexuality Studies; Shared: Oral and Public History; Studies in Canadian Military History; Sustainability and the Environment; Urbanization in Asia; Women and Indigenous Studies; Women's Suffrage and the Struggle for Democracy

University of British Columbia Press continued

Imprints: UBC Press; On Point Press; Purich Books; On Campus; and Pacific Educational Press

Brookings Institution Press

1775 Massachusetts Avenue, N.W.
Washington, DC 20036-2103

Phone: : 202.797.6429
Email: books@brookings.edu
Indiv: firstinitiallastname@brookings.edu

Customer Service/Orders:
Perseus Distribution
210 American Drive
Jackson, TN 38301
Phone: 1.800.343.4499
Fax: 1.800.351.5073

Website and Social Media:
Website: www.brookings.edu/press
Twitter: @BrookingsPress

UK Representative:
Eurospan Group

Canadian Representative:
Perseus Distribution

Staff
Director: William Finan (202.536.3637)
Financial Manager: Ben Cahen (202.797.6163)
Digital and Marketing Manager: Steven Roman (202.536.3609)
Rights Manager and Editorial Associate: Kristen Harrison (202.536.3604)
Managing Editor: Janet Walker (202.536.3613)
Production Coordinator: Elliott Beard (202.536.3618)
Assistant Director: Yelba Quinn (202.536.3619)
Media Relations Manager: Carrie Engel (202.797.4364)
Marketing Coordinator: Adam Juskewitch (202.540.7773)
Distribution Manager: Laura Baida (202.741.6557)
Bookstore Manager: Frederick King (202.797.6429)

Regular Member
Established: 1916
Title output 2016: 40
Titles currently in print: 1,665

Admitted to the Association: 1958
Title output 2017: 40
Journals published: 3

Editorial Program
Economics, government, and international affairs, with emphasis on the implications for public policy of current and emerging issues confronting American society. The Press publishes books written by the Institution's resident and associated staff members, as well as manuscripts acquired from outside authors.

The Institution also publishes three journals: *Brookings Papers on Economic Activity*, *Economia* (copublished with the Latin American and Caribbean Economic Association), and *Behavioral Science and Policy*, the Journal of the Behavioral Science and Policy Association.

The Press distributes publications for organizations such as the Asian Development Bank Institute, the American Chamber of Commerce to the European Union, the Bertelsmann

Foundation, the Carnegie Endowment for International Peace, the Centre for Economic Policy Research, the Century Foundation Press, Economica, the Center for Global Development, the Institute for the Study of the Americas, the International Labor Organization, the Japan Center for International Exchange, the OECD, the Royal Institute for International Affairs, the Trilateral Commission, the United Nations University Press, and the World Trade Organization.

Bucknell University Press

Street Address Until March 15, 2018:
6 Taylor Hall
Bucknell University
Lewisburg, PA 17837

After March 15, 2018
Hildreth-Mirza Hall
Bucknell University
Lewisburg, PA 17837

Phone: 570.577.3674
Email: universitypress@bucknell.edu
Indiv.: (User I.D.)@bucknell.edu

Website and Social Media:
Website: www.bucknell.edu/universitypress
Blog: upress.blogs.bucknell.edu
Facebook: www.facebook.com/BucknellUP
Twitter: @BucknellUPress

UK:
Rowman & Littlefield

Australia, New Zealand and Papua New Guinea:
Co Info Pty Ltd

UK/European/Asian Representative:
Eurospan

Mailing Address:
1 Dent Drive
Lewisburg, PA 17837

Orders (USA and Canada):
Until July 1, 2018
Rowman & Littlefield
Blue Ridge Summit, PA 17214
Phone: 800.462.6420
Fax: 800.338.4550
Website: www.rowman.com
Email: orders@rowman.com

Orders
After July 1, 2018
In conjuction with Rutgers UP
c/o Chicago Distribution Center
11030 S Langley Ave, Chicago, IL 60628
Phone: 773.702.7010
Fax: 800.621.8476

Europe:
Durnell Marketing Ltd.

Canadian Representative:
Scholarly Book Services

Staff
Director: Greg Clingham (570.577.1552; email: clingham)
Managing Editor: Pamelia Dailey (570.577.3674; email: pad024)
Acquisitions Editorial: Greg Clingham (Transits, Apercus, 17th-19th century studies, Hispanic studies) (email: clingham); Logan J. Connors (French and Francophone theater) (email: logan.connors@miami.edu); Kevin L. Cope (humanities & public policy); Carmen Gillespie (Griot) (email: gillespie); Anibal Gonzalez (Latin American studies) (email: anibal.gonzalez@yale.edu); John S. Rickard (Irish writers) (email: rickard); Richard B. Sher

Bucknell University Press continued

(18th-century Scotland) (email: rbsher6@gmail.com); Karin Schutjer (Studies in the Age of Goethe) (email: kschutjer@ou.edu); Alfred Siewers (Susquehanna River) (email: asiewers)
Editorial Assistant: Tong Tong (email: tt015)
Design: Adrienne Beaver (email: abeaver)

Introductory Member
Established: 1968   Admitted to the Association: 2016
Title output 2016: 29   Title output 2017: 26
Titles currently in print: 227

Editorial Program
Comparative eighteenth-century studies; English and American literary criticism, especially early modern to mid nineteenth century; cultural studies; Luso-Hispanic studies; Latin American literature and theory; contemporary Irish writers; French and Francophone theatre; Africana studies; environmental studies; literary memoirs; poetry (occasionally).

Special series: Aperçus: Histories Texts Cultures; Bucknell Studies in Latin American Literature and Theory; Contemporary Irish Writers; Griot Project Book (in association with the Griot Institute for Africana Studies at Bucknell); New Studies in the Age of Goethe (in association with the Goethe Society of North America); Scènes francophones: Studies in French and Francophone Theater; Stories of the Susquehanna Valley (in association with the Center for Sustainability and the Environmental at Bucknell); Studies in Eighteenth-Century Scotland (in association with the Eighteenth-Century Scottish Studies Society); Transits: Literature, Thought & Culture 1650-1850.

University of Calgary Press

2500 University Drive N.W.
Calgary, AB T2N 1N4 Canada

Phone: 403.220.7578
Fax: 403.282.0085
Email: ucpress@ucalgary.ca

Canadian Distribution & Orders:
uniPRESSES
c/o Georgetown Terminal Warehouses
34 Armstrong Avenue
Georgetown, ON L7G 4R9 Canada
Phone (toll-free): 877.864.8477
Fax (toll-free): 877.864.4272
Email: orders@gtwcanada.com

Website and Social Media:
Website: www.press.ucalgary.ca
Facebook: www.facebook.com/UCalgaryPress
Twitter: @UCalgaryPress
YouTube: www.youtube.com/channel/UCmpSYUJVXlHG6p8mn-Ps4hw

US Distribution & Orders:
Longleaf Services, Inc.
Orders@longleafservices.org
116 S. Boundary St, Chapel Hill, NC
27514-3808 USA
Phone: 800.272.6817
Email inquiries: customerservice
  @longleafservices.org

UK/Africa/Middle East/European
Distributor:
Gazelle Book Services, Ltd.
White Cross Mills, High Town, Lancashire
LA1 4XS UK
Phone: 011 44 (0)1524 63232
Email: sales@gazellebooks.co.uk

Staff
Director: Brian Scrivener (403.220.3511; email: brian.scrivener@ucalgary.ca)
Operations Manager: Michelle Lipp (403.220.8221; email: mlipp@ucalgary.ca)
Editorial (Acquisitions) & Marketing Coordinator: Helen Hajnoczky (403.220.4208; email: helen.hajnoczky@ucalgary.ca)
Graphic Design & Print Management: Melina Cusano (403.220.8719; email: macusano@ucalgary.ca)
Marketing Specialist: Alison Cobra (403.220.3979; email: alison.cobra@ucalgary.ca)
Digital Services & Fulfilment Coordinator/Accounts: Ethel Cuesta (403.220.7736; email: ucpmail@ucalgary.ca)

Regular Member
Established: 1981

Admitted to the Association: 2002
(Affiliate member: 1992-95)

Title output 2016: 10
Titles currently in print: 372

Title output 2017: 17

Editorial Program
At the University of Calgary Press we publish peer-reviewed scholarly books that connect local experience to the global community, helping to create a deeper understanding of human dynamics in a changing world. Through Open Access publishing, we make our authors' research accessible to the widest possible audience.

   Publishing interests include: Arctic and northern studies; foreign affairs and public policy; energy, environment & ecology; environmental history; Indigenous and Métis studies; Cana-

University of Calgary Press continued

dian literature; contemporary Canadian art & architecture; African studies; Latin American & Caribbean studies; Western Canada; media & communications; gender studies; urban studies.
Special series: Africa: Missing Voices; Art in Profile; Arts in Action; Beyond Boundaries (Canadian Defense and Strategic Studies); Brave & Brilliant (poetry & fiction); Canadian History and Environment; Cinemas Off Centre; Energy, Ecology, and Environment; Global Indigenous Issues; Latin American and Caribbean Studies; Northern Lights (arctic & circumpolar studies); Small Cities Studies in Community & Cultural Engagement; The West (western history)
Co-publishing programs: The Arctic Institute of North America; Latin American Research Centre; Centre for Military, Security & Strategic Studies; Mount Royal University, Faculty of Arts

University of California Press

155 Grand Avenue, Suite 400
Oakland, CA 94612-3758

Phone: 510.883.8232
Fax: 510.836.8910
Email: askucp@ucpress.edu
Indiv: firstname.lastname@ucpress.edu

Website and Social Media:
Website: www.ucpress.edu
Journals website: www.ucpress.edu/journals
Blog: www.ucpress.edu/blog
Facebook: www.facebook.com/ucpress
Twitter: @ucpress
YouTube: UCPressVideo

Order Fulfillment:
Ingram Publisher Services
210 American Drive
Jackson, TN 38301
Phone: 800.343.4499
Fax: 800.351.5073
Email: pd_orderentry@ingramcontent.com

UK/European Office:
John Wiley & Sons Ltd
European Distribution Centre
New Era Estate,
Oldlands Way Bognor Regis
West Sussex PO22 9NQ UK
Phone: +44 (0) 1243 843291
Fax: +44 (0) 1243 843302
Email: customer@wiley.com

Staff
Interim Director: Erich van Rijn (510.883.8240)
  Assistant to the Director: Susan Owen (510.883.8319)
Director of Finance and Operations: Denise Feinsod (510.883.8323)
Director Publishing Operations: Erich van Rijn (510.883.8264)
Digital Science Publisher: Dan Morgan (510.883.8330)
Journals Publisher: David Famiano (510.883.8270)
Editorial Director: Kim Robinson (regional studies, Mark Twain) (510.883.8283)Sponsoring
  Editors: Raina Polivka (music, cinema, media studies) (812.322.6722); Niels Hooper (US History, American studies, Pacific world, western history, world history, Middle East studies) (510.883.8300); Nadine Little (art history, museum copublications) (510.883.8284); Kate Marshall (anthropology, food studies, Latin American studies, environmental studies)

(510.883.8285); Reed Malcolm (anthropology, Asian studies, global studies, Luminos/ Open Access) (510.883.8313); Maura Roessner (criminology, law and society, criminal justice) (510.883.8298); Eric Schmidt (classical studies, medieval studies, pre-modern history, the ancient world to late antiquity) (510.883.8263); Naomi Schneider (sociology, public anthropology, contemporary social issues, global health) (510.883.8302); Lyn Uhl (communications) (617.905.3681); Chris Johnson (psychology) (973.896.3184)
Director of Editing, Design, and Production: Scott Norton (510.883.8320)
Managing Editor: Kate Warne (510.883.8289)
Lead Production Coordinator: Angela Chen (510.883.8233)
Art Director: Lia Tjandra (510.883.8292)
Journals Production & Publishing Technology Manager: Gabe Alvaro (510.883.8266)
Director of Marketing and Sales: Elena McAnespie (510.883.8262)
Director of PR & Communications: Peter Perez (510.883.8318)
Human Resources: Denise Feinsod (510.883.8323)

Regular Member
Established: 1893
Title output 2016: 198
Titles currently in print: 4,729
Admitted to the Association: 1937
Title output 2017: 185
Journals published: 32

Editorial Program
Anthropology, art history, Asian studies, communication, Latin American studies, Middle Eastern studies, classical studies, environmental studies, film, food studies, history; late antiquity, law & society, media studies, medieval studies, music, natural history, global health, criminology, criminal justice, psychology, regional studies, religion, sociology. Submissions are not invited in original poetry or fiction.

Journals: *The American Biology Teacher; Asian Survey; California History; Classical Antiquity; Collabra: Psychology; Elementa; Federal Sentencing Reporter; Feminist Media Histories, Film Quarterly; Gastronomica: Historical Studies in the Natural Sciences; Huntington Library Quarterly; International Review of Qualitative Research; The Journal of Musicology; Journal of Palestine Studies; Journal of the American Musicological Society; Journal of the Society of Architectural Historians; Journal of Vietnamese Studies; Mexican Studies/Estudios Mexicanos; Music Perception; New Criminal Law Review; Nineteenth-Century Literature; 19th-Century Music; Nova Religio; Pacific Historical Review; The Public Historian; Qualitative Communication Research; Religion and American Culture; Representations; Rhetorica; Sociology of Development; Southern California Quarterly; Studies in Late Antiquity*

Special series: American Crossroads; Ancient Philosophies; The Anthropology of Christianity; Asia Pacific Modern; Asia: Local Studies/Global Themes; Berkeley Series in British Studies; California Natural History Guides; California/Milbank Books on Health and the Public; California Series in Law, Politics, and Society; California Series in Public Anthropology; California Studies in 19th-Century Music; California Studies in 20th-Century Music; California Studies in Food and Culture; California World History Library; The Clark Kerr Lectures on the Role of Higher Education in Society; The Collected Writings of Robert Duncan; Defining Moments in American Photography; Documents of Twentieth Century Art; Ernest Bloch Lectures; Franklin D. Murphy Lectures; Ethnographic Studies in Subjectivity; Freshwater Ecology Series; From Indochina to Vietnam: Revolution and War in a Global Perspective; Gender and Justice; Hellenistic Culture and Society; The Marcus Garvey and Universal Negro Improvement Association Papers; Mark Twain Papers; The Middle Awash Series; Music of the African Diaspora; New Perspectives on Chinese Culture and Society;

University of California Press continued

The Norman and Charlotte Strouse Edition of the Writings of Thomas Carlyle; Origins of Human Behavior and Culture; The Phillips Books Prize Series; Reproductive Justice: A New Vision for the 21st Century; Sather Classical Lectures; Sociology in the 21st Century; South Asia Across the Disciplines; Sport in World History; The Works of Mark Twain; The World's Finest Wines; Transformation of the Classical Heritage; Weimar and Now: German Cultural Criticism; Western Histories; Wildavsky Forum Series

Cambridge University Press

North American Office:
One Liberty Plaza
New York, NY 10017

Head (UK) Office:
University Printing House
Cambridge CB2 8BS UK

Phone: 212.337.5000
Fax: 212.691.3239
Email: firstinitiallastname@cambridge.org

Customer Service:
Email: customer_service@cambridge.org
Phone: 1.800.872.7423

Website and Social Media:
Website: www.cambridge.org
Blog: www.cambridgeblog.org
Facebook: www.facebook.com/CambridgeUniversityPress
Twitter: @CambridgeUP
YouTube: www.youtube.com/user/CambridgeUP
Google +: plus.google.com/112563436639321822653/posts
LinkedIn: www.linkedin.com/company/cambridge-university-press

Staff
Chief Executive: Peter Phillips (UK)
Managing Director, Academic Publishing: Amanda Hill (UK)
NY Office:
Managing Director, Americas and ELT: Michael Peluse (212.337.6551)
Senior Vice President for Academic, Americas & Director of Scholarly Communications Research and Development: Brigitte Shull (212.337.5965)
Academic Publishing:
Book Editors: Matthew Bennett (Director of Higher Education Publishing); Sara Doskow (political science); David Repetto (Executive Publisher, psychology); John Berger (law); Lauren Cowles (math, computer science); Robert Dreesen (politics, sociology); Steve Elliott (engineering); Matt Gallaway (law); Deborah Gershenowitz (American and Latin American history and politics); Diana Gillooly (math and statistics); Kaitlyn Leach (mathematical sciences); Matt Lloyd (Executive Publisher, earth sciences); Karen Maloney (Executive Publisher, economics and finance); Beatrice Rehl (Publisher, classics, religion, archaeology); Ray Ryan (literature), Stephen Acerra (psychology and economics)
Journals:
STM Publisher, Aaron Johnson & Ann Avouris
   STM Journal Editors: Jessica Bradley; Marissa Murray-Harrison

HSS Publisher: Mark Zadrozny & Ann Avouris
HSS Journal Editors: Chris Robinson, Amy Laurent, Lisa Arrington, and Hal Moore
Sales and Marketing:
Vice President of Business Development: Al Cascio
   Institutional Sales Managers: Stephanie Kaelin; Kellie O'Rourke
   Retail Sales Manager: Thomas Willshire
   Rights and Permissions: Adam Hirschberg
   Business Development Representatives: Christina Ko and Valeria Guagnini
   Senior Marketing Manager, End User Marketing: Michael Duncan
   College Sales Manager: Pam Cooper
   Associate Marketing Director, Library Marketing: Larry Grodsky
   Marketing Manager, Library Marketing: Susan Soule
Production:
Production Director, Journals: Edward Carey
ELT Publishing:
Editorial Director: Jeff Krum
   Adaptations & Versioning Unit Manager: Danielle Power
   US/Canada Sales Director: Michelle Velissariou
   Associate Business Unit Director: John Ade
   Senior National Sales Manager, ELT/Classics: Mike Woods
   Senior Business Performance Manager: Aniko Banfi
   Publishing Manager, ELT: Wendalyn Nichols
   Associate Director of Market Research: Jose Antonio Mendez
Operations:
HR: Giuseppe Rotella and Brendan Burke
Associate Director Customer Services: Marianne Headrick
Global Warehousing Manager: Edward Galante

Regular Member
Established: 1534
American Branch: 1949
Title output 2016: 1,782
Titles currently in print: 55,000
Admitted to the Association: 1950
Title output 2017: 1,378
Journals published: 360

Editorial Program
A broad range of academic books, journals, digital and online products in the humanities, social sciences, science, engineering, technology, engineering, medical and health sciences; including pre-eminent lists in social and political sciences; biological, physical and earth sciences; mathematics; psychology, psychiatry and neuroscience; law, history and religious studies. Cambridge also publishes for the global education market and is one of the world's leading English language teaching/ESL publishers.

Carnegie Mellon University Press

5032 Forbes Avenue
Pittsburgh, PA 15289-1021

Phone: 412.268.2861
Fax: 412.268.8706
Email:
cmupress@andrew.cmu.edu.com

Website and Social Media:
Website: www.cmu.edu/universitypress
Facebook: www.facebook.com/CarnegieMellonUniversityPress

Order Fulfillment/Customer Service:
Carnegie Mellon University Press
c/o University Press of New England
1 Court Street
Lebanon, NH 03766
Phone: 800.421.1561
Fax: 603.448.9429
Website: www.upne.com/distributed/dist_cmu.html

Staff
Director: Gerald Costanzo (poetry editor) (email: gc3d@andrew.cmu.edu)
Senior Editor: Cynthia Lamb (nonfiction acquisitions) (email: cynthial@andrew.cmu.edu)
Production Coordinator: Connie Amoroso (email: camoroso@andrew.cmu.edu)
Accounts Administrator: Anna Houck (email: am2x@andrew.cmu.edu)

Regular Member
Established: 1972
Title output 2016: 11
Titles currently in print: 308

Admitted to the Association: 1991
Title output 2017: 12

Editorial Program
Carnegie Mellon University Press' particular strength lies in literary publishing: Carnegie Mellon Poetry Series, Carnegie Mellon Classic Contemporaries Series (the reissuing of significant early poetry and fiction collections by important contemporary writers), Carnegie Mellon Series in Short Fiction, Poets in Prose Series (memoir in the form of poets writing about their writing lives, poetry criticism, guidebooks and handbooks about the writing of poetry, and Carnegie Mellon Series in Translation. Additionally, the Press publishes in regional social history (titles that explore the rich history of Pittsburgh and Western Pennsylvania), art history, the performing arts (original plays and adaptations), literary analysis, education, and Carnegie Mellon University history.

The Catholic University of America Press

240 Leahy Hall
620 Michigan Avenue, N.E.
Washington, DC 20064

Phone: 202.319.5052
Fax: 202.319.4985
Email: (user I.D.)@cua.edu

Customer Service:
HFS
PO Box 50370
Baltimore, MD 21211
Phone: 800.537.5487
Fax: 410.516.6998

Website and Social Media:
Website: cuapress.org
Facebook: www.facebook.com/pages/
  The-Catholic-University-of-America-Press/232124655084
Twitter: @CUAPress

Warehouse (Returns only):
HFS
RETURNS
c/o Maple Press Co.
Lebanon Dist. Center
704 Legionaire Drive
Fredericksburg, PA 17026

UK Representative:
Eurospan

Canadian Representative:
Brunswick Books

Staff
Director: Trevor Lipscombe (email: lipscombe)
  Assistant to the Director: Libby Newkumet (email: newkumet)
Acquisitions Editors: John Martino (philosophy, theology) (email: martinoj); Trevor Lipscombe (all other fields)
Managing Editor: Theresa Walker (email: walkert)
  Editorial Assistant: Tanjam Jacobson (email: jacobsot)
Design and Production: Anne Kachergis (Kachergis Book Design, 14 Small Street North, Pittsboro, NC 27312)
Marketing Manager: Brian Roach (email: roach)
  Marketing Assistant: Catherine Szczybor (email: szczyborc)
Journals Coordinator: Cait Duggan (email: dugganc)

Regular Member
Established: 1939
Title output 2016: 40
Titles currently in print: 1,010

Admitted to the Association: 1985
Title output 2017: 40
Journals published: 10

Editorial Program
American and European history (both ecclesiastical and secular); American and European literature; philosophy; political theory; theology. Periods covered range from late antiquity to modern times, with special interest in late antiquity, early Christianity, and the medieval period.
Journals: *Newman Studies Journal; The Thomist: A Speculative Quarterly Review; Antiphon: A Journal for Liturgical Renewal; Nova et Vetera; The Catholic Historical Review; Pierre d'Angle;*

Catholic University of America Press continued

The Jurist: Studies in Church Law and Ministry; U.S. Catholic Historian; The Bulletin of Medieval Canon Law; and Quaestiones Disputatae
Special series: *Sacra Doctrina*; Catholic Moral Thought; The Fathers of the Church: A New Translation; Library of Early Christianity; Medieval Texts in Translation; Publications of the American Maritain Association (distributed); Studies in Philosophy and the History of Philosophy; Thomas Aquinas in Translation; IPS Monograph Series of the Institute for the Psychological Sciences (distributed); Sapientia Press (distributed); Franciscan University Press (distributed); Association of American Franciscan History (distributed); Humanum Academic Press (distributed).

Central European University Press

Street Address:
H-1051 Budapest
Oktober 6 utca 14.
Hungary

Phone: +36 1 327 3138
Fax: +36 1 327 3183
Email: ceupress@press.ceu.edu
Indiv.: (user ID)@ceu.hu

Website and Social Media:
Website: www.ceupress.com
Blog: ceupress.blogspot.hu
Facebook: www.facebook.com/ceupress
Twitter: @CEUPress

Mailing Address:
H-1051 Budapest,
Nador utca 11
Hungary

US and Canadian Orders:
Books International
Phone: 703.661.1500
Email: todd@booksintl.com

European Orders:
NBN International

UK Representative:
Oxford Publicity Partnership

Asia and the Pacific:
East West Export Books
Phone: 808.956.8830

Staff
Director: Krisztina Kos (36.1.327.3844; email: kosk)
Deputy Director: Peter Inkei (36.1.327.3181; email: inkeip)
Editors: Jozsef Litkey (36.1.327.3000/2096; email: litkeij); Nora Voros (36.327.3136; email: vorosn); Linda Kunos (36.327.3136; email: kunosl)
Financial Manager: Noemi Szabo (36.1.327.3141; email: szabon)
US Sales Manager: Abel Meszaros (732.763.8816; email: meszarosa)
Marketing Manager: Agnes Barla-Szabo (36.1.327.3138; email: barla-szaboa)

Regular Member
Established: 1993
Title output 2016: 20
Titles currently in print: 345

Admitted to the Association: 2014
Title output 2017: 27

Editorial Program
Reflecting the intellectual strengths and values of its parent institution, the press publishes books on the political philosophy and practices of open society, history, legal studies, nationalism, human rights, conflict resolution, Jewish studies, economics, medieval studies, literature, and international relations.

The publishing program of CEU Press focuses on issues of Central and Eastern Europe; it is also committed to the past and present history, society, culture and economy of the countries of the former Soviet Union and its neighbors. In the last couple of years, the Press has been expanding its list to include books in the field of higher education policy, gender studies, media studies and art history.

Special series: Central European Medieval Texts; CEU Medievalia; CEU Press Classics; CEU Studies in the History of Medicine; Discourses of Collective Identity in Central and Southeast Europe 1770–1945: Texts and Commentaries; Historical Studies in Eastern Europe and Eurasia; Natalie Zemon Davies Annual Lecture Series; The National Security Archive Cold War Readers

The University of Chicago Press

1427 E. 60th Street
Chicago, IL 60637-2954

Phone: 773.702.7700
Fax: 773.702.2705 (Books Acquisitions)
     773.702.9756 (Books Marketing)
     773.834.3480 (Journals Marketing)
     773.753.4247 (Journals Production)
Email: (user I.D.)@uchicago.edu

Website and Social Media—Books:
Website www.press.uchicago.edu
Chicago Blog: pressblog.uchicago.edu
Twitter: @UChicagoPress
Facebook: facebook.com/UniversityofChicagoPress
Tumblr: uchicagopress.tumblr.com
Instagram: UChicagoPress
Goodreads: goodreads.com/UChicagoPress
LibraryThing: www.librarything.com/profile/UChicagoPress

Website and Social Media—Journals:
Website: www.journals.uchicago.edu
Facebook: www.facebook.com/UChicagoJournals
Twitter: @ChicagoJournals

Chicago Distribution Center
11030 South Langley Avenue
Chicago, IL 60628
Phone: 773.702.7000
Fax: 773.702.7212

UK Representative:
Yale Representation Ltd.

Canadian Representative:
The University Press Group

University of Chicago Press continued

Staff
Director: Garrett P. Kiely (773.702.8878; email: gkiely)
Deputy Director: Christopher Heiser (773.702.2998; email: cheiser)
Assistant to the Director and Deputy Director: Ellen M. Zalewski (773.702.8879; email: emz1)
Executive Director of Information Technology: Patti O'Shea (773.702.8521; email: poshea)
IT Operations Manager Information Technology Support: Derek Simmons (773.702.0510; email: dcsimmons)
Human Resources Manager: Alice Lloyd (773.702.7303; email: alloyd)
Digital Publishing Manager: Krista Coulson (773.702.5862; email: kcoulson)

Books Division
Acquisitions Editorial:
Editorial Director: Alan Thomas (773.702.7644; email: athomas2)
  Editors: Susan Bielstein (art, architecture, ancient archeology, classics, film studies) (773.702.7633; email: smb1); Timothy Mennel (American history, regional publishing) (773.702.0158; email: tmennel);Elizabeth Branch Dyson (ethnomusicology, education, philosophy) (773.702.7637; email: edyson); Marta Tonegutti (music) (773.702.0427; email: mtonegutti); Douglas Mitchell (history, sociology, sexuality studies, rhetoric) (773.702.7639; email: dmitchel); Randolph Petilos (medieval studies, poetry in translation) (773.702.7647; email: rpetilos); Karen Darling (history, philosophy, and social studies of science) (773.702.7641; email: darling); Jane Macdonald (economics, business, finance) (773.702.7638; email: janem); Chuck Myers (political science, law and society) (773.702.7648; email: myersc); Miranda Martin (linguistics) (773.702.5270; email: mirandam); Priya Nelson (anthropology, history) (773.702.4759; email: pnelson); Kyle Wagner (religious studies) (773.702.1006; email: kwagner); Mary Laur (reference, geography and cartography) (773.702.7326; email: mlaur)
  Paperback Editor: Margaret Hivnor (773.702.7649; email: mhivnor1)
Director of Intellectual Property: Laura Leichum (773.702.6096; email: lleichum)
International Rights Manager: Beatrice Bourgogne (773.702.7741; email: bbourgogne)
Manuscript Editorial: Jenni Fry, Managing Editor (773.702.5328 email: jennifry)
Design and Production: Jill Shimabukuro, Design and Production Director (773.702.7653; email: jshimabu)
Marketing; Carol Kasper, Marketing Director (773.702.7733; email: ckasper)
  Associate Marketing Director and Promotions Director: Levi Stahl (773.702.0289; email: levi)
  Senior Promotions Managers: Melinda Kennedy (773.702.2945; email: mkennedy1); Nick Lilly (773.702.7740; email: nlilly); Kristen Raddatz (773.702.1964; email: kraddatz)
  Promotions Managers: Ben Balskus (773.834.8708; email: balskus); Tristan Bates (773.702.0279; email thbates); Brian Carroll (773.702.7678; email: carrollb2); Tyler McGaughey (773.702.4216; email: tmcaughey)
  Promotion Assistant: Mollie McFee (773.702.7740; email: mmcfee)
  Marketing and Sales Specialist-Ref. Library: James Lilly (773.702.7957; email: jlilly)
  Advertising Manager: Anne Osterman (773.702.7897; email: abwolver)
  Senior Exhibits Manager: Eric DeTratto (773.834.7201; email: edetratto)
  Marketing Design Manager: Mary Shanahan (773.702.7697; email: meshanah)
  Graphic Artist: Brian Beerman (773.702.7849; email: bbeerman)

Sales: John Kessler, Associate Marketing Director/Sales Director (773.702.7248; email: jck1)
  Sales and Distribution Associate: Robert Hoffman (773.702.0340; email: rmh)
  Special Sales and Inventory Manager: Joseph Peterson (773.702.7723; email: jpeterson)
  Sales Representatives: Bailey Walsh (Midwest) (email: bgw); Blake Delodder (East Coast) (email: bdelodder); Gary Hart (West Coast) (email: ghart)
  International Sales Manager: Micah Fehrenbacher (773.702.7898; email: micahf)
  E-commerce/Direct-to-Consumer Sales: Dean Blobaum, Electronic Marketing Manager (773.702.7706; email: dblobaum)
  Marketing Systems Coordinator: Tom McGraw (773.702.6674; email: tmcgraw)
  Direct Mail Associate: Teresa Fagan (773.702.7887; email: tfagan)
  Reference Marketing: Jenny Ringblom, Reference Marketing Manager (773.702.3233; email: ringblom)
  Reference Special Sales and Senior Promotions Manager: Lauren Salas (773.702.0890; email: lsalas)
  Marketing Specialist *CMOS*: Carol Saller (773.702.7493; email: s333)
  Marketing Client Distribution: Carol Kasper, Director (773.702.7733; email: ckasper)
  Marketing Distribution Client Manager.: Steven Pazik (773.834.1916; email: spazik)

Journals Division
Director, Journals Division: Michael Magoulias (773.753.2669; email: mmagoulias)
  Publisher, Journals Acquisitions: Kari Roane (773.702.7362; email: kroane)
  Publishers: Gordon Rudy (773.702.2448; email: grudy); Valerie Bajorat (773.702.7521; email: vbajorat); Andrew Seagram (773.702.4673; email: aseagram)
  Director of Strategic Partnerships and Analytics: Kate Duff (773.702.7688; email: kduff)
  Publishing Operations Manager: Ashley Towne (773.753.4241; email: atowne)
  Manager of Electronic Publishing Technology: Michael Boudreau (773.753.3298; email: mboudrea)
  Manager of Subscription Fulfillment: Rich Connelly (773.753.3601; email: rec1)
  Manager of Editorial Processes: Mary E. Leas (773.702.7961; email: lea8)
  Chief Manuscript Editor, Science Journals: Mary Nell Hoover (773.702.7679; email: mnh2)
  Assistant Chief Manuscript Editor, General Journals: Brendan Carrick (773.702.7676 email: bjc)
  Marketing Manager, Team Leader: Tiffany Adams (773.834.0432; email: tiffanyadams)
  Marketing Managers: Rose Rittenhouse (773.834.4075: email: rittenhouse)
  Marsha Ross (773.702.8185; email: mar)
  Licensing Manager: Chaz Oreshkov (773.834.1793; email: oreshkov);
  Marketing Analyst: Edward Rhyne (773.702.0157; email: erhyne)
  Exhibits and Advertising Coordinator: Andrea Parker (773.702.0224; email: adparker)

Chicago Distribution Center Services
Director, Chicago Distribution Services: Joseph D'Onofrio (773.702.7020; email: jdonofrio)
  Senior Operations Manager: Mark Stewart (773.702.7024; email: stewart44)
  Senior Client Liaison Manager: Saleem Dhamee (773.702.7014; email: sdhamee)
  Customer Service Manager: Karen Hyzy (773.702.7109; email: khyzy)
  Asst. Manager, Customer Service/Instructor Trainer Title Management: Latrice Allen (773.702.7112; email: lallen)
  Credit and Collections, A/R Manager: Cynthia Bastion (773.702.7167; email: cab9)
  Director of Accounting: Bob Peterson (773.702.7036; email: xrwp)
  Manager, Chicago Digital Distribution Center: Kewon Bell (773.702.7238; email: kewon-bell)

University of Chicago Press continued

M.I.S. Manager: Christopher Jones (773.702.7229; email: cdjones)
Royalty/Rights Manager: Cassandra Wisniewski (773.702.7062; email: cwisniew)
Warehouse Office Manager: Gail Candreva-Szwet (773.702.7080; email: gcandrev)
Production Manager: Tammy Paul (773.702.7081; email: tpaul)
Journals Warehouse Manager: Don P. Collins (773.702.7245; email: dpcollins)
Returns Manager: Jenn Stone (773.834.3687; email: jstone1)
Inventory Control Manager: Dennis Kraus (773.834.3499; email: kraus)
BiblioVault
BiblioVault Manager: Kate Davey (773.834.4417; email: kdavey)

Regular Member
Established: 1891
Title output 2016: 311
Titles currently in print: 5,000

Admitted to the Association: 1937
Title output 2017: 329
Journals published: 73

Editorial Program
Scholarly, course, and general-interest works in: Anthropology; Art and Architecture; Asian Studies; Business; Cartography and Geography; Classics; Economics and Finance; Education; Film and Media Studies, History; Law; Life Sciences; Linguistics; Literary Criticism; Musicology; Philosophy; Political Science; Reference; Religious Studies; Science Studies; Sociology; Writing and Publishing. Closed to submissions in fiction and poetry.

Journals: *Afterall; American Art; American Journal of Education; American Journal of Sociology; The American Naturalist; American Political Thought; Archives of American Art Journal; Art Documentation; The Biological Bulletin; The China Journal; Classical Philology; Comparative Education Review; Critical Historical Studies; Critical Inquiry; Current Anthropology; Economic Development and Cultural Change; The Elementary School Journal; English Literary Renaissance; Ethics; Freshwater Science; Gesta; Getty Research Journal; HAU: Journal of Ethnographic Theory; History of Humanities; History of Religions; HOPOS; International Journal of American Linguistics; International Journal of Plant Sciences; Isis; The Journal of African American History; Journal of Anthropological Research; Journal of the Association for Consumer Research; The Journal of the Association of Environmental and Resource Economists; The Journal of Geology; Journal of Human Capital; Journal of Labor Economics; Journal of Law and Courts; The Journal of Law and Economics; The Journal of Legal Studies; The Journal of Modern History; Journal of Near Eastern Studies; Journal of Political Economy; The Journal of Politics; The Journal of Religion; Journal of the Society for Social Work and Research; Know: A Journal on the Formation of Knowledge; Library Quarterly; Marine Resource Economics; Metropolitan Museum Journal; Modern Philology; The Papers of the Bibliographical Society of America; Philosophy of Science; Physiological and Biochemical Zoology; Polity; The Quarterly Review of Biology; Renaissance Drama; Renaissance Quarterly; Res: Anthropology and Aesthetics; Schools; Signs; Signs and Society; Social Service Review; Source: Notes in the History of Art; Speculum; I Tatti Studies in the Italian Renaissance; West 86th; Winterthur Portfolio*
Annuals: *Crime and Justice; Innovation Policy and the Economy; NBER Macroeconomics Annual; Tax Policy and the Economy; Osiris; Spenser Studies; Supreme Court Economic Review; The Supreme Court Review*

The Chinese University Press

The Chinese University of Hong Kong
Sha Tin
New Territories, Hong Kong

North American Distributor:
Columbia University Press
c/o Perseus Distribution
Phone: 800.944.8648/731.988.4440
Email: cup_book@columbia.edu

Phone: +852.3943.9800
Fax: +852.2603.7355
Email: cup@cuhk.edu.hk
Indiv: (user I.D.)@cuhk.edu.hk

UK and European Distributor:
Eurospan Group
c/o Turpin Distribution
Phone: +44 (0) 1767 604972
Email: eurospan@turpin-distribution.com

Website and Social Media:
Website: www.chineseupress.com
Facebook: www.facebook.com/
　TheChineseUniversityPress
Weibo: weibo.com/cupress
Twitter: @CUHKPress

Other Areas:
(Customer Service and Orders)
The Chinese University Press
Phone: +852 39439800
Fax: +852 26037355
Email: cup-bus@cuhk.edu.hk

Australian Distributor:
Footprint Books

Staff
Director: Qi GAN (+852.3943.9818; email: ganqi)
Secretary to the Director: Tina Chan (+852.3943.9810; email: tinachan)
Editorial: Ying LIN, Managing Editor (+852.3943.9811; email: linying)
Acquisitions Editor: Minlei YE (+852.3943.9812; email: minleiye)
Production: Kingsley Ma, Manager (+852.3943.9808; email: kwaihungma)
Business/Marketing: Angelina Wong, Manager (+852.3943.9822; email: laifunwong)

Regular Member
Established: 1977
Title output 2016: NR
Titles currently in print: 946

Admitted to the Association: 1981
Title output 2017: NR
Journals published: 8

Editorial Program
Bilingual publication of academic and general trade titles. Areas of interest include Chinese studies in literature, history, philosophy, languages, and the arts. The Press also publishes books on business, government, medicine, as well as dictionaries and general books in both the English and Chinese languages.

Journals: *Asian Journal of English Language Teaching*; *The China Review*; *Communication & Society*; *Daoism: Religion, History and Society*; *Journal of Chinese Studies*; *Journal of Translation Studies*, *International Journal for the Study of Humanistic Buddhism*

Special series: Bibliography and Index Series; Bilingual Series on Modern Chinese Literature; Ch'ien Mu Lectures in History and Culture; Educational Studies Series; Hong Kong Taxation; Institute of Chinese Studies Monograph Series; International Poetry Nights in Hong Kong Series (IPNHK); Jintian Series of Contemporary Chinese Writing; Young Scholars Dissertation Awards, Translation Series

University of Cincinnati Press

Street Address:
Rieveschl 503C
Cincinnati OH 45221-0033
Phone: 513.556.1515
Email: ucincinnatipress@ucmail.uc.edu

Mailing Address:
Langsam Library
2911 Woodside Dr
ML 0033
Cincinnati OH 45221-0033

Website and Social Media:
Website: ucincinnatipress.uc.edu/
Twitter: @ucincipress

Staff
Director: Elizabeth Scarpelli (513.556.1494; email: Elizabeth.Scarpelli@uc.edu)
   Staff Executive Asst: Kathi Miniard (513.556.1515; email: miniarkn@ucmail.uc.edu)
Acquisitions Editor: Michael Duckworth (513.556.1424, 206.495.2501;
   email: michael.duckworth@uc.edu)
Scholarly Communications Library Publishing Coordinator (CLiPS): Mark Konecny
   (513.556.2511; email: mark.konecny@uc.edu)
Business Affairs Director: Deborah Myree, Business Affairs Director (Library and Press)
   (513.556.1551; email: debora.myree@uc.edu)
IT Developer: Sean Crowe (Library and Press) (513.556.1899; email: sean.crowe@uc.edu)

Introductory Member
Established: 2016
Title output 2016: 0
Titles currently in print: 2

Admitted to the Association: 2017
Title output 2017: 1
Journals published: 3

Editorial Program
Serious works of non-fiction in social justice across HSS, STEM and business, transdisciplinary works in community engagement and collective impact. The press publishes scholarly monographs and serious works for a wide audience of scholars and practitioners which move beyond discipline-specific approaches to create new rigorous perspectives across HSS, STEM and Business. Our books focus on issues, solutions and strategies which highlight and improve underserved and underrepresented populations and disparities in access, equity, and privilege throughout the world. Additionally, the Press publishes in all areas and all subjects related to Regional Studies in the Greater Cincinnati area. The press invites open and subscription model journals related to areas of publication to submit proposals.

Joint imprints and co-publishing programs: University of Cincinnati Library Publishing Services (CLiPS)

University Press of Colorado/Utah State University Press

Colorado Address:
245 Century Circle
Suite 202
Louisville, CO 80027

Phone: 720.406.8849
Fax: 720.406.8849
Email: (user I.D.)@upcolorado.com

Utah Address:
3078 Old Main Hill
Merrill-Cazier Library
Logan, UT 84322-3078
Phone: 720.406.8849
Fax: 720.406.8849

Distributor:
Chicago Distribution Center
11030 South Langley Ave.
Chicago, IL 60628

Phone: 800.621.2736
Fax: 800.621.8476

European and International Representative:
National Book Network International

Websites and Social Media:
Websites: www.upcolorado.com; www.usupress.com
Facebook: www.facebook.com/pages/The-University-Press-of-Colorado/347439013387; www.facebook.com/pages/Utah-State-University-Press/164439110276267
Twitter: @UPColorado

Staff
Director: Darrin Pratt (email: darrin)
Assistant Director/Managing Editor: Laura Furney (email: laura)
Acquisitions Editor (USUP Imprint): Rachael Levay (email: rachael@usupress.com)
Acquisitions Editor (Colorado Imprint): Jessica d'Arbonne (email: jessica)
Production Manager: Dan Pratt (email: dan)
Marketing & Sales Manager: Beth Svinarich (email: beth)

Regular Member
Established: 1965
Title output 2016: 54
Titles currently in print: 809

Admitted to the Association: 1982
Title output 2017: 48

Editorial Program
Physical sciences; natural history; ecology; American history; Western history; anthropology; archaeology; composition studies; folklore studies; Native American studies; Western women's history; Mormon history; and regional (Mountain West) titles.

The Press also copublishes with and distributes titles for the Denver Museum of Natural History, the Colorado Historical Society Colorado State University's Cooperative Extension, the Center for Literary Publishing, History Colorado, the Institute for Mesoamerican Studies, the WAC Clearinghouse, and Western Press Books.

Special series: Atomic History & Culture; The George and Sakaye Aratani Nikkei in the Americas Series; Leonard J. Arrington Lecture Series; Life Writings of Frontier Women; May Swenson Poetry Award Series; Mesoamerican Worlds; Mining the American West; Timberline Books

Columbia University Press

61 West 62nd Street, Fl. 3
New York, NY 10023-7015

Phone: 212.459.0600
Fax: 212.459.3677
Email: (user I.D.)@columbia.edu

Distributed by Ingram Academic Services:
210 American Drive
Jackson, TN 38301
Orders and Customer Service
Phone: 800.343.4499
Email: IPSJacksonOrders@ingramcontent.com

Website and Social Media:
Website: cup.columbia.edu
Blog: cupblog.org
Facebook: www.facebook.com/ColumbiaUniversityPress
Twitter: @ColumbiaUP
Pinterest: ColumbiaUP

UK Office:
University Press Group
LEC 1 – New Era Estate
1 Oldlands Way, Bognor Regis
West Sussex PO22 9SA
Phone: +44 1243 842165
Fax: +44 1243 842167

Staff
Administration
Associate Provost and Director: Jennifer Crewe (ext. 7145; email: jc373)
Executive Assistant to the Director: Sheniqua Larkin (ext. 7142; email: sl2805)
Associate Director and Director of Operations and Sales: Brad Hebel (ext. 7130; email: bh2106)
Financial Manager: Robert Abrams (ext. 7119; email: ra2555)
Director of Human Resources: James Pakiela (ext. 7109; email: jp2483)
Director of Rights and Contracts: Justine Evans (ext. 7128; email: je2217)
Director, Editing, Design, and Production: Marielle Poss (ext. 7155; email: mtp2147)
IT Director: Greg Lara (ext. 7132; email: gl2298)
Development and Grants Manager: Suela Thomas (ext. 7131; email: st3031)
Acquisitions
Editorial Director: Eric I. Schwartz (sociology, behavioral science) (ext. 7118; email: es3387)
　Associate Provost and Director: Jennifer Crewe (food studies) (ext. 7145; email: jc373)
　Publisher for the Life Sciences: Patrick Fitzgerald (ext. 7136; email: pf2134)
　Publisher, Columbia Business School Publishing: Myles Thompson (ext. 7161; email: mt2312)
　Publisher for Philosophy and Religion: Wendy Lochner (ext. 7121; email: wl2003)
　Editors: Philip Leventhal (literary studies, film studies, journalism) (ext. 7159; email: pl2162); Bridget Flannery-McCoy (American history, economics) (ext. 7136; email: bmf7136); Christine Dunbar (Asian humanities, Asian and Russian literature in translation) (ext. 7141; email: cd2654); Caelyn Cobb (politics IR, comparative; security studies; history—global, Asia, Middle East) (ext. 7107; email: cc4141); Stephen Wesley (American politics and foreign relations; social work) (ext 7203, email: sw2729)
EDP (Editing, Design, and Production)
Assistant Managing Editor: Leslie Kriesel (ext. 7110; email: lrk11)
　Senior Manuscript Editor: Susan Pensak (ext. 7139; email: srp4)
　Director of Design and Production: Jennifer Jerome (ext. 7177; email: jj352)
　Associate Production Manager: Jessica Schwarz (ext. 7114; email: js2447)

Art Director: Julia Kushnirsky (ext. 7102; email: jk3151)
Senior Designers: Lisa Hamm (ext. 7105; email: lh400); Milenda Lee (ext. 7103; email: ml2657); Chang Jae Lee (ext. 7140; email: chl32)
Designer: Noah Arlow (ext. 7178; email: na2407)
Publishing Systems Manager: Michael Haskell (ext. 7162; email: mh2100)
Managing Editor for Reference and Electronic Publishing: Stephen Sterns (ext. 7148; email: ss724)

Marketing and Sales
Promotions Director: Meredith Howard (ext. 7126; email: mh2306)
Assistant Marketing Director/Direct Marketing Manager: Todd Lazarus (ext. 7152; email: tdl10)
Advertising Manager: Elena Iaffa (ext. 7124; email: ei2131)
Sales Consortium Manager/Southeast Sales Representative: Catherine Hobbs (email: catherinehobbs@earthlink.net)
Mid-West Sales Representative: Kevin Kurtz (email: kkurtz5@earthlink.net)
West Coast Sales Representative: William Gawronski (email: wgawronski@earthlink.net)
Northeast Sales Representative: Connor Broughan (email: cb2476)
Digital Products Representative: Herbert Plummer (ext. 7112; email: hp2356)
Metadata and Social Media Manager: Maritza Herrera-Diaz (ext. 7115; email: mh3850)

Finance and Operations
Accounts Receivable & Royalty Manager: Louis Gabriele (ext. 7108; email: lmg2210)

Regular Member
Established: 1893   Admitted to the Association: 1937
Title output 2016: 182   Title output 2017: 185
Titles currently in print: 4,191

Editorial Program
Scholarly, general interest, and professional books, and upper-level textbooks in the humanities; social sciences; earth and life sciences; business and economics; and social work. Subjects include animal studies; Asian studies; behavioral science; botany; conservation and environmental science; criminology; ecology; evolutionary studies; film; finance and business economics; gender studies; history; international relations; journalism; literary and cultural studies; media studies; Middle East studies; philosophy; political philosophy; political science; religion; social work; and sociology. General reference works in print and electronic formats. The Press publishes poetry, fiction, and drama in translation only. It is the publisher of Wallflower Press titles worldwide.

Columbia University Press is the distributor in the United States, Canada, and Latin America for American Institute of Buddhist Studies; Agenda Publishing; Auteur Publishing; Barbara Budrich Publishers; Chinese University Press; Columbia Books on Architecture and the City; East European Monographs/Maria Curie-Skłodowska University Press; Harrington Park Press; Hong Kong University Press; ibidem Press; Jagiellonian University Press; Peterson Institute for International Economics; Social Science Research Council; Transcript Verlag; Tulika Books; and University of Tokyo Press.

Special series, joint imprints, and/or co-publishing programs: American Academy of Religion Lectures on the History of Religions; Arts and Traditions of the Table; Asia Perspectives; Biology and Resource Management; Columbia Business School Publishing; Columbia Classics in Philosophy; Columbia Classics in Religion; Columbia History of Urban Life; Columbia Journalism Review Books; Columbia Readings of Buddhist Literature; Columbia

Columbia University Press continued

Series in Race, Inequity, and Health; Columbia Series in Science and Religion; Columbia Studies in the History of U.S. Capitalism; Columbia Studies in International History; Columbia Studies in Terrorism and Irregular Warfare; Columbia Themes in Philosophy, Social Criticism and the Arts; Complexity in Ecological Systems; Contemporary Asia In the World; Critical Moments in Earth History; Critical Perspectives on Animals; Cultures of History; Empowering the Powerless; End of Life Care; Energy Markets and Geopolitics; European Perspectives; Film and Culture; Foundations of Social Work Knowledge; Gender and Culture; Gender, Theory and Religion; Global Chinese Culture; History and Society of the Modern Middle East; Initiative for Policy Dialogue at Columbia; Introduction to Asian Civilizations; Insurrections: Critical Studies in Religion, Politics, and Culture; Kenneth J. Arrow Lecture Series; Leonard Hastings Schoff Lectures; Literature Now; The Middle Range; Modern Asian Literature; Modern Chinese Literature from Taiwan; New Directions in Critical Theory; Political Thought/Political History; Read Russia; Records of Western Civilization; Religion, Culture, and Public Life; Russian Library; Social Science Research Council Books; Society and the Environment, Translations from the Asian Classics; Weatherhead Books on Asia; Wellek Library Lectures; Woodrow Wilson Center Press.

Concordia University Press

1400 de Maisonneuve Blvd. West, LB 509.04
Montreal, Quebec H3G 1M8

Phone: 514.848.2424 ext. 7748
Fax: 514.848.2882
Email: press@concordia.ca

Website and Social Media:
Website: www.concordia.ca/press
Twitter: @ConcordiaPress

Staff
Editor-in-Chief: Geoffrey Little (email: geoffrey.little@concordia.ca)
Editorial and Production Coordinator: Meredith Carruthers (email: meredith.carruthers@concordia.ca)

Introductory Member
Established: 2016   Admitted to the Association: 2015

Editorial Program
Concordia University Press publishes books and pamphlets in the arts, humanities, and social sciences that engage with the themes of life, knowledge, and creation.

Life, including lifespan and aging; gender and sexuality; migration and diaspora; indigeneity; disability; the natural environment and sustainability; sense, emotion and affect; human and non-human rights; risk studies; cities and urban centers; and industrial and post-industrial communities. Knowledge, including memory, the past, and the future; digital and post-digital environments; the creation, formation, and curation of knowledge publics; oral history and storytelling; media; and translation and translation studies. Creation, including making and maker cultures; sculpture; painting; photography; fibre arts; literature; poetics; theatre; performance; cinema; video arts; and games and gaming studies.

Cork University Press

Youngline Industrial Estate, Pouladuff Road
Cork, Ireland

Phone: +353 21 490 2980
Fax: + 353 21 431 5329
Email: corkuniversitypress@ucc.ie

Website and Social Media:
Website: www.corkuniversitypress.com
Blog: corkuniversitypress.org
Facebook: www.facebook.com/CorkUP
Twitter: @CorkUP

UK Representative:
Marston Book Services

US Representative:
Longleaf Services
116 South Boundary Street
Chapel Hill, NC 27514-3808
Phone: 800.848.6224
Fax: 800.272.6817
Email: customerservice@longleafservices.org

Irish Representative:
Gill & MacMillan

Staff
Director: Mike Collins (email: mike.collins@ucc.ie)
Editorial and Production: Maria O'Donovan (email: maria.odonovan@ucc.ie)

Regular Member
Established: 1925
Title output 2016: 10
Titles currently in print: 200

Admitted to the Association: 2002
Title output 2017: 7
Journals published: 1

Editorial Program
While the Press specializes in the broad field of Irish Culture, its subject range extends across the fields of music, art history, literary criticism and poetry. However, the focus of our list is in the areas of Irish cultural history, archaeology and landscape studies.
Journal: *Irish Review*
Special series: Síreacht

Cornell University Press

Sage House
512 East State Street
Ithaca, NY 14850

Phone: 607.882.2219
Fax: 607.277.2374
Email: (user I.D.)@cornell.edu

Website and Social Media:
Website: cornellpress.cornell.edu; threehillsbooks.com
Twitter: @CornellPress
Blog: sagehouse.blog
Facebook: CornellPress
Instagram: cornelluniversitypress
YouTube: CornellPressNews

Order Fulfillment:
Longleaf Services, Inc.
116 South Boundary Street
Chapel Hill, NC 27514-3808

Phone: 800.848.6224
Fax: 800.272.6817
Email: customerservice@longleafservices.org

Global Distributor (except Australia/New Zealand):
Combined Academic Publishers

Canada Distributor:
Codasat Canada Ltd.

Australia Distributor:
Footprint Books

Staff
Director: Dean J. Smith (607.882.2226; email: djs486)
Subsidiary Rights Manager: Tonya Cook (email: tcc6)
Acquisitions Editorial: Mahinder S. Kingra, Editor-in-Chief (humanities, medieval studies, literary studies, classics) (607.882.2239; email: msk55)
  Editorial Director, ILR Press: Frances Benson (workplace issues, labor, class studies, health care, sociology, anthropology of work, higher education) (607.882.2218; email: fgb2)
  Executive Editor: Roger Haydon (international relations, comparative politics, East and Central Asian studies, Slavic/Eurasian studies, Middle East studies) (607.882.2236; email: rmh11)
  Senior Editors: Emily Andrew (military history, modern European history, Asian history, contemporary US politics & society) (416.429.0322; email: ea424); James Lance (anthropology, geography, global urban studies) (413.727.2265; email: jml554); Michael J. McGandy (US history, New York region, urban history, US urban development & policy) (607.882.2250; email: mjm475)
  Editor, Comstock Publishing Associates: Katherine H. Liu (natural history & nature writing, ornithology, herpetology & ichthyology, mammalogy, entomology, botany & plant sciences, environmental studies) (607.882.2247; email: khl8)
  Editor, Southeast Asia Program Publications: Sarah E. M. Grossman (Southeast Asian studies, anthropology, political science, history, cultural studies) (607.255.4359; email: sg265)
  Assistant Editor: Bethany Wasik (archaeology) (607.882.2218; email: bethany.wasik)
  Acquisitions Assistants: Meagan Dermody (607.882.2255; email: mbd89); Ellen F. Murphy (607.882.2249; email: efm66)
Manuscript Editorial: Ange Romeo-Hall, Managing Editor (607.882.2257; email: asr8)

Digital Publishing Editor and Senior Production Editor: Karen Laun (607.882.2240; email: kml35)
Senior Production Editors: Karen T. Hwa (607.882.2237; email: kth9); Susan Specter (607.882.2259; email: sps19)
Production Editors: Sara Ferguson (607.882.2261; email: srf3); Jennifer Savran Kelly (607.882.2261; email: jds75)
Design and Production: Karen Kerr, Manager (607.882.2238; email: kg99)
  Senior Designer: Scott Levine (607.882.2241; email: sel37)
  Designer: Richanna Patrick (607.882.2253; email: rp12)
  Senior Production Coordinator: Diana Silva (607.882.2258; email: drs68)
  Production Coordinator: William L. Oates (607.882.2260; email: wlo6)
Marketing: Martyn Beeny, Marketing Director (607.882.2197; email: mb2545)
  Special Sales Rep & Metadata Specialist: Nathan Gemignani (607.882.2234; email: ndg5)
  Digital Marketing Manager: Jonathan Hall (607.882.2235; email: jlh98)
  Marketing Designer: Elizabeth L. Kim (607.882.2231; email: elk5)
  Exhibits/Awards/Advertising Coordinator: David Mitchell (607.882.2251; email: dwm23)
  Publicity Manager: TBA
Business: Lynn Benedetto, Business Operations Manager (607.882.2210; email: lad23)
  Accounting: William O'Dell Wehling (607.882.2211; email: wvo3)
  Administration, Royalties, Copyright: Michael Morris (607.882.2256; email: mam278)
IT Administrator: Patrick Garrison (607.882.2233; email: plg6)
Permissions & Rights Coordinator: Stephanie Munson (607.882.2252; email: sm120)

Regular Member
Established: 1869   Admitted to the Association: 1937
Re-established in present form: 1930
Title output 2016: 116   Title output 2017: 126
Titles currently in print: 2,919

Editorial Program
Nonfiction, with particular strengths in anthropology, archaeology, Asian studies, classics, geography, higher education, history (U.S., European, Asian, and military), law, literary and cultural studies, medieval studies, New York City and State, politics and international relations, religion, Slavic studies, sociology, and urban studies. Under the ILR Press imprint, books in labor relations, class and workplace issues, and health care policy. Books in the life sciences, environmental studies, and natural history are published under Comstock Publishing Associates imprint, and books on Southeast Asian history, culture, and society, as well as the journal Indonesia, are published under the Southeast Asia Program (SEAP) Publications imprint. Books about New York State for a trade audience are published under the Three Hills imprint. Submissions are not invited in poetry or fiction.

Cornell University Press is the distributor in North America for Leuven University Press. Special imprints: Comstock Publishing Associates; ILR Press; Southeast Asia Program Publications; Three Hills

Special series, joint imprints and/or copublishing programs: Agora Editions; American Institutions and Society; Brown Democracy Medal; Cornell Global Perspectives; Cornell Series in Environmental Education; Cornell Series on Land: New Perspectives in Territory, Development, and Environment; Cornell Studies in Classical Philology; Cornell Studies in Money; Cornell Studies in Political Economy; Cornell Studies in Security Affairs; Corpus Juris: The Humanities in Politics and Law; The Culture and Politics of Health Care Work;

Cornell University Press continued

Expertise: Cultures and Technologies of Knowledge; Islandica; Myth and Poetics II; Persian Gulf Studies; Police/Worlds: Studies in Security, Crime, and Governance; Religion and American Public Life; Signale: Modern German Letters, Cultures, and Thought; Studies of the Weatherhead East Asian Institute; The United States in the World

The University of Delaware Press

Street/Mailing Address:
200A Morris Library
181 South College Avenue
Newark, DE 19717-5267

Phone: 302.831.1149
Fax: 302.831.6549
Email: joestrei@udel.edu
Website: library.udel.edu/udpress/

Orders:
Rowman & Littlefield
4501 Forbes Blvd., Suite 200
Lanham, MD 20706
Phone: 800.462.6420
Email: custserv@rowman.com
Online orders: www.rowman.com

Staff
Director: Julia Oestreich (302.831.1149; email: joestrei@udel.edu)

Introductory Member
Established: 1922
Title output 2016: 15
Titles currently in print: 700

Admitted to the Association: 2014
Title output 2017: 15

Editorial Program
The University of Delaware Press publishes mainly in the fields of literary studies, especially Early Modern, eighteenth- and nineteenth-century literature; Eighteenth-Century Studies; art history; French studies; and historical/cultural studies of Delaware and the Eastern Shore. Our publishing program in literary studies and art history has expanded, and submissions that deal with the Late Medieval period through the contemporary era are welcome, as are those that address literature, art, or culture in the United Kingdom, Continental Europe, Asia, the United States, Latin America, or the Caribbean. Our series focus on works that are interdisciplinary, transnational, and/or trans-temporal in nature.
Special series: Cultural Studies of Delaware and the Eastern Shore; Studies in Seventeenth- and Eighteenth-Century Art and Culture; Early Modern Exchange; Swift and His Contemporaries; Performing Celebrity; Early Modern Feminisms
Co-publishing partners: John Cabot University Press; University Museums (of the University of Delaware)

Duke University Press

Street Address:
905 West Main Street
Suite 18-B
Durham, NC 27701

Mailing Address:
Box 90660
Durham, NC 27708- 0660

Phone: 919.687.3600
Faxes: 919.688.4574 (general)
Email: info@dukepress.edu
Indiv:
firstinitiallastname@dukeupress.edu or
firstname.lastname@dukeupress.edu
(unless otherwise indicated)

Orders and Customer Service:
Phone: 888.651.0122; 919.688.5134
Fax: 888.651.0124; 919.688.2615

Warehouse:
Duke University Press
Distribution Center
120 Golden Drive
Durham, NC 27705
Phone: 919.384.0733

Website and Social Media:
Website: www.dukeupress.edu
Blog: dukeupress.wordpress.com/
Facebook: www.facebook.com/DukeUniversityPress
Twitter: @DUKEpress

UK/European Representative:
Combined Academic Publishers

Canadian Representative:
Lexa Publishers' Representatives

Staff
Director: Stephen A. Cohn (919.687.3606)
Office of the Director
  Administrative Assistant to the Director/Development Coordinator: Bonnie Perkel (919.687.3685)
Executive Support Group
  Associate Director for Digital Publishing: Allison Belan (919.687.3683)
  Assistant Director for Contracts and Licensing: Cathy Rimer-Surles (919.687.8005)
  Manager, Rights and Permissions: Diane Grosse (919.687.8020)
Administration
  Director of Administration: Robyn L. Miller, Manager (919.687.3633)
  Accounting Manager: Cynthia Durham (919.687.3661)
  Budget and Logistics Manager: Bonnie Conner (919.687.3693)
  HR Manager: Thomas Devine (919.687.8018)
  IT Manager: Nicholas Sullivan (919.687.3641)
  Warehouse Manager: Don Griffin (919.384.1244)
Books
  Editorial Director: Ken Wissoker (anthropology, cultural studies, Asian Studies, post-colonial theory, lesbian and gay studies, construction of race, gender and national identity, new media, literary theory and criticism, film and television, popular music, social studies of science, visual studies) (212.817.7248; email: kwiss@duke.edu)
  Senior Editor and Editorial Department Manager: Courtney Berger (social and political theory, transnational American studies, Native American and indigenous studies, gender and sexuality studies, African American studies, Asian American studies, critical ethnic

Duke University Press continued

studies, science and technology studies, media studies, literary studies, and geography) (919.687.3652)
Editor: Gisela Fosado (anthropology, sociology, American and Atlantic World history, gender and sexuality studies, race and ethnicity, African American and Africana studies, environmental studies, and Latin American and Latinx Studies) (919.687.3632)
Editor: Elizabeth Ault (African Studies, Urban Studies, Middle East Studies, Geography, Theory from the South, Black and Latinx studies, disability studies, trans studies, and critical prison studies) (919.687.8022)
Associate Editor: Miriam Angress (religion, world history, women's studies, creative nonfiction, World Readers, Latin American Readers) (919.687.3601)

Journals Publishing & Partnerships
Journals Director: Rob Dilworth (919.687.3624)
Senior Editor: Erich Staib (919.687.3664)
Director of Publishing Services, Project Euclid: Leslie Eager (919.687.3630)

Editing, Design, and Production
Director of Editing Design and Production: Nancy Hoagland (919.687.3629)
Editorial Production Manager: Jessica Ryan (919.687.3666)

Editing (Books)
Senior Project Editor: Liz Smith (919.687.8006)
Project Editors: Susan Albury (919.687.3669); Sara Leone (919.687.3681); Christi Stanforth (919.687.8016); Chris Catanese (919.687.8003)

Editing (Journals)
Senior Managing Editor: Ray Lambert (919.687.3625)
Senior Project Editor: Charles Brower (919.687.3688)
Assistant Managing Editors: Roy Pattishall; Keller Kaufman-Fox; Elizabeth Jones; Joel Luber; Chris Mazzarra

Design (Books)
Design Manager: Amy Buchanan (919.687.3651)
Book Designers: Heather Hensley (919.687.3658); Matt Tauch (919.687.3676)

Design (Journals)
Designer: Sue Hall (919.687.3620)

Production (Books)
Production Manager: TBA
Production Specialists: Kelsea Smith (919.687.8019); Venus Bradley (919.687.3643)

Productions (Journals)
Production Manager: TBA
Senior Production Coordinator: Cynthia Gurganus (919.687.3691)
Production Coordinators: Nancy Sampson; Nathan Moore; Amy Walter; Lisa Savage; Erica Tucker Woods
Production Assistant: Taylor Brock

Marketing and Sales
Director of Marketing and Sales: Cason Lynley (919.687.3631)

Customer Relations
Customer Relations Manager: Amanda Kolman (919.687.3602)
Digital Access and Journals Coordinator: Amber Carey (919.687.3612)

Digital Access and Books Coordinator: Patrick Coleff (919.687.3617)
<u>Library Relations and Sales</u>
  Library Relations and Sales Manager: Kim Steinle (919.687.3655)
  Digital Collections Sales Manager: Katja Moos (919.687.8014)
  Library Sales Coordinator: Kristen Twardowski (919.687.3627)
  Sales and Marketing Research Coordinator: TBA
  Data Analyst: George Black (919.687.3614)
<u>Marketing (Books)</u>
  Books Marketing & Sales Senior Manager: Michael McCullough (919.687.3604)
  Publicity and Advertising Manager: Laura Sell (919.687.3639)
  Books Sales Manager: Jennifer Schaper (919.687.3680)
  Marketing Designer and Awards Coordinator: Emily Lawrence (919.687.3650)
  Publicity and Advertising Assistant: Jessica Castro-Rappl (919.687.3637)
  Direct Marketing Manager and Sales Associate: Julie Thomson (919.687.3603)
  Exhibits Manager: Helena Knox (919.687.3647)
  Metadata and Digital Systems Manager: H. Lee Willoughby-Harris (919.687.3646
  Copywriter: Christopher Robinson (919.687.3663)
  Senior Marketing Assistant: Chad Royal (919.687.3649)
<u>Marketing (Journals)</u>
  Journals Marketing Manager: Jocelyn Dawson (919.687.3653)
  Library Marketing Outreach Manager: Mandy Brannon (919.687.8027)
  Publicist and Exhibits Coordinator: Katie Smart (919.687.8029)
  Digital Marketing Coordinator: Kasia Repeta (919.687.8019)
  Library Marketing and Exhibits Coordinator: Leslie Eager (919.687.8027)
  Marketing Designer and Advertising Coordinator: Dan Ruccia (919.687.8013)

Regular Member
Established: 1921 (as Trinity College Press)   Admitted to the Association: 1937
Title output 2016: 120   Title output 2017: 130
Titles currently in print: 2,807   Journals published: 56

Editorial Program
Scholarly books in the humanities and social sciences, with lists in art criticism and history; visual studies; cultural studies; gay and lesbian studies; gender studies; American studies; American history; African American studies; Asian American studies; Native American & indigenous studies; cultural anthropology; minority politics and post-colonial issues; Latin American studies; Asian studies; South Asian studies; African studies; Middle East studies; European studies; music; film, TV and media studies; literary theory and history; environmental studies; political science and political theory; legal studies; religion; sociology and social theory; and science studies

Journals: *American Literary Scholarship; American Literature; American Speech; Annals of Functional Analysis; Archives of Asian Art; Banach Journal of Mathematical Analysis; boundary 2; Camera Obscura; Collected Letters of Thomas and Jane Welsh Carlyle; Common Knowledge; Comparative Literature; Comparative Studies of South Asia, Africa and the Middle East; Cultural Politics; differences; Duke Mathematical Journal; East Asian Science, Technology and Society; Eighteenth-Century Life; English Language Notes; Environmental Humanities; Ethnohistory; French Historical Studies; Genre; GLQ: A Journal of Lesbian and Gay Studies; Hispanic American Historical Review; History of Political Economy; Journal of Chinese Literature and Culture;*

Duke University Press continued

*Journal of Health Politics, Policy and Law; Journal of Korean Studies; Journal of Medieval and Early Modern Studies; Journal of Middle East Women's Studies; Journal of Music Theory; Kyoto Journal of Mathematics; Labor; Mediterranean Quarterly; Meridians; minnesota review; Modern Language Quarterly; New German Critique; Nka; Notre Dame Journal of Formal Logic; Novel; Pedagogy; Philosophical Review; Poetics Today; positions; Public Culture; Qui Parle; Radical History Review; Small Axe; Social Text; South Atlantic Quarterly; Theater; Tikkun; TSQ: Transgender Studies Quarterly; Twentieth-Century Literature; World Policy Journa*l
Special series, joint imprints and/or copublishing programs: ANIMA; American Encounters: Global Interactions; Asia-Pacific: Culture, Politics and Society; Collected Letters of Thomas and Jane Welsh Carlyle; C. L. R. James Archives; Console-ing Passions; Body/Commodity/Text; Critical Global Health: Evidence, Efficacy, Ethnography; Design Principles for Teaching History; Ecologies for the Twenty-First Century; Experimental Futures; Global Insecurities; Improvisation, Community, and Social Practice; Latin America in Translation; Latin America Otherwise: Languages, Empires, Nations; Latin America Readers; The Morgan Lectures; Narrating Native Histories; New Americanists; Next Wave: New Directions in Women's Studies; Objects/Histories: Perverse Modernities; Post-Contemporary Interventions; Public Planet; Radical Perspectives: A Radical History Review Book Series; Refiguring American Music; SIC; Sign, Storage, Transmission; Social Text Books; Theory Q; World Readers

University Press of Florida

15 N.W. 15th Street
Gainesville, FL 32603

Phone: 352.392.1351
Fax: 352.392.0590
Email: (user I.D.)@upress.ufl.edu

Orders:
Phone: 800.226.3822
Fax: 352.392.7302
Toll free fax: 800.680.1955

Website and Social Media:
Website: upress.ufl.edu
Blog: Floridabookshelf.wordpress.com
Facebook: www.facebook.com/Floridapress
Twitter: @floridapress
YouTube: floridapress
Instagram: floridapress

UK Representative:
Eurospan

Canadian Representative:
Scholarly Book Services

Staff
Director: Meredith Morris Babb (ext. 206; email: mb)
Editor-in-Chief/Deputy Director: Linda Bathgate (ext. 236; email: lbathgate)
  Senior Acquisitions Editor: Sian Hunter (919.428.8813; email: sian)
  Assistant Acquisitions Editor: Stephanye Hunter (ext. 201; email: sah)

Acquisitions Assistants: Ali Sundook (ext. 211; email: ans); Jane Pollack (ext. 219; email: jane); Daniel Dufy (ext. 203; email daniel)
Editorial, Design & Production: Michele Fiyak-Burkley, Associate Director & EDP Manager (ext. 222; email: mf)
   Assistant Director, Managing Editor: Marthe Walters (ext. 212; email: marthe)
   Project Editor: Eleanor Deumens (ext. 217; email: eleanor)
   Editorial Assistant: Valerie Melina (ext. 213; email: valerie)
   Design Director: Larry Leshan (ext. 221; email: ll)
   Senior Designer: Robyn Taylor (ext. 218; email: rt)
   Production Coordinators: Anja Jimenez (ext. 220; email: anja); Marisol Amador (ext. 216; email: marisol)
Associate Director of Sales and Marketing: Romi Gutierrez (ext. 232; email: romi)
   Advertising/Direct Mail Manager: Rachel Doll (ext. 235; email: rd)
   Metadata Manager: Ale Gasso (ext. 243; email: ale)
   Publicist and Rights Manager: Samantha Zaboski (ext. 233; email: sz)
   Exhibits and Awards Coordinator: Olivia Isaacs (ext. 238; email: olivia)
Journals Manager: Lauren Phillips (ext. 227; email: lauren)
Business: Peter Van Woerden, Associate Director for Finance (ext. 209; email: peter)
   Accountant/AP: Sandra Dyson (ext. 210; email: sd)
   AP/Credit/Collections Manager: Jackie Panetta (ext. 207; email: jackie)
   Order Entry: Chris Warner (352.392.6867; email: orders)
   Warehouse and Shipping Manager: Charles Hall (352.392.6867; email: charles)
IT Manager: Bryan Lutz (ext. 215; email: bryan)

Regular Member

Established: 1945
Title output 2016: 74
Titles currently in print: 3,500
Admitted to the Association: 1950
Title output 2017: 82
Journals published: 6

Editorial Program

Floridiana; New World archaeology; conservation biology; Latin American studies; Caribbean studies; African American studies; American history and culture; Native American studies; medieval and modernist literature and literary criticism; dance; natural history; humanities. Submissions are not invited in prose fiction, poetry, or memoirs.

Journals: *Bioarchaeology International, Journal of Global South Studies, Forensic Anthropology, Florida Tax Review, Rhetoric of Health and Medicine, Subtropics*

Fordham University Press

Joseph A. Martino Hall
45 Columbus Avenue, 3rd Floor
New York, NY 10023

Phone: 718.817.4795
Fax: 347-842-3083
Email: (user I.D.)@fordham.edu

Orders:
Ingram Publisher Services / Jackson
210 American Drive
Jackson, TN 38301
Phone: 800.343.4499
ipsjacksonorders@ingramcontent.com

Website and Social Media:
Website: www.fordhampress.com
Blog: www.fordhamimpressions.com
Facebook: www.facebook.com/FordhamUP
Twitter: @fordhampress
Pinterest: www.pinterest.com/fordhampress
Empire State Editions: www.empirestateeditions.com
Empire State Editions Twitter: @E_S_Editions
Empire State Editions Facebook: www.facebook.com/EmpireStateEditions
YouTube: www.youtube.com/fordhampress1
Instagram: Fordham_press

European Representative:
Combined Academic Publishers Ltd.

Canadian Representative:
Canadian Manda Group

Staff
Director: Fredric W. Nachbaur (646.868.4201; email: fnachbaur)
Editorial Associate and Assistant to the Director: Will Cerbone (646.868.4203; email: wcerbone)
Editorial Director: Richard W. Morrison (646.868.4208; email: rmorrison7)
Acquisitions Editor: Thomas Lay (646.868.4209; email: tlay)
Managing Editor: Eric Newman (646.868.4210; email: ernewman)
Design and Production Manager: Ann-Christine Racette (646.868.4202; email: aracette)
Marketing Director: Kate O'Brien-Nicholson (646.868.4204; email: bkaobrien)
Assistant Marketing Manager: Kathleen A. Sweeney (646.868.4205; email: kasweeney)
Business Manager: Margaret M. Noonan (646.868.4206; email: mnoonan)
Assistant Business Manager: Marie Hall (646.868.4207; email: mhall21)

Regular Member
Established: 1907
Title output 2016: 103
Titles currently in print: 1,068

Admitted to the Association: 1938
Title output 2017: 91
Journals published: 1

Editorial Program
Fordham University Press publishes primarily in the humanities and social sciences, with emphasis on the fields of African American studies, American studies, anthropology, communication and media studies, gender studies, history, literature, philosophy, religion, theology,

and urban studies. Additionally, the Press publishes books focusing on the New York region and books of interest to the general public.

The Press distributes the publications of Creighton University Press; University of San Francisco Press; St. Joseph's University Press; Rockhurst University Press; The Institution for Advanced Study in the Theater Arts (IASTA); Center for Migration Studies; and St. Bede's Publications.

Journal: *Joyce Studies Annual*

Imprints: Empire State Editions: Dedicated to publishing books about the New York region.

Special series: American Philosophy; Bordering Religions: Concepts, Conflicts, and Conversations; Berkeley Forum in the Humanities; Catholic Practice in North America; Commonalities; Critical Studies in Italian America; Comparative Theology: Thinking Across Traditions; Dante's World: Historicizing Literary Cultures of the Due and Trecento; Donald McGannon Research Center's Everett C. Parker Book Series; Fordham Series in Medieval Studies; Forms of Living; The Future of the Religious Past; Groundworks: Ecological Issues in Philosophy and Theology; International Humanitarian Affairs; Just Ideas; Meaning Systems; Lit Z; Medieval Philosophy: Texts and Studies; The North's Civil War; Orthodox Christianity and Contemporary Thought; People and the Environment; Perspectives in Continental Philosophy; POLIS: Fordham Series in Urban Studies; Psychoanalytic Interventions; Poets Out Loud; Reconstructing America; Thinking Out Loud; Transdisciplinary Theological Colloquia; Verbal Arts: Studies in Poetics; and World War II: The Global, Human, and Ethical Dimension

Gallaudet University Press

800 Florida Avenue, N.E.
Washington, DC 20002-3695

Phone: 202.651.5488
Fax: 202.651.5489
Email: (user I.D.)@gallaudet.edu

Website and Social Media:
Website: gupress.gallaudet.edu
Facebook: GallaudetUniversityPress
Twitter: @GallaudetPress
YouTube: www.youtube.com/channel/ c/GallaudetUniversityPress

Orders:
Gallaudet University Press
Chicago Distribution Center
11030 South Langley Avenue
Chicago, IL 60628
Phone: 800.621.2736
TTY: 888.630.9347
Fax: 800.621.8476

European Distributor:
University Chicago Press/John Wiley

Pacific-Asian Area Representative:
East-West Export Books, Inc.

Staff
Director and Acquistions: Ivey Pittle Wallace (202.651.5662; email: ivey.wallace)
Managing Editor: Deirdre Mullervy (202.651.5967; email: deirdre.mullervy)
Production Coordinator: Donna Thomas (202.651.5144; email: donna.thomas)
Marketing and Fulfillment Manager: Angela Leppig (202.651.5661; email: angela.leppig)
   Marketing Assistant: Valencia Simmons (202.651.5488; email: valencia.simmons)
Business: Donna Thomas (202.651.5444; email: donna.thomas)

Gallaudet University Press continued

Regular Member
Established: 1980
Title output 2016: 12
Titles currently in print: 418

Admitted to the Association 1983
Title output 2017: 14
Journals published: 2

Editorial Program
Scholarly books and serious nonfiction from all disciplines as they relate to the interests and culture of people who are deaf, hard of hearing, or experiencing hearing loss. Particular areas of emphasis include signed languages, sign language dictionaries, linguistics, interpretation, deaf culture, deaf education, deaf history, disability studies, biography and autobiography, parenting, and special education, as well as instructional works and children's literature with sign language or deafness themes.
 The Press distributes select titles from Signum Verlag (Hamburg, Germany).
Journals: *American Annals of the Deaf; Sign Language Studies*
Special imprints: Kendall Green Publications; Clerc Books
Special series: Deaf Education; Deaf Lives; Gallaudet Classics in Deaf Studies; Interpreter Education; Sociolinguistics in Deaf Communities; Studies in Interpretation

George Mason University Press

4400 University Drive MS 2FL
Fairfax, VA 22030-4444

Phone: 703.993.3636
Email: gmupress@gmu.edu
Indiv. email: (user I.D.)@gmu.edu

Orders:
University of Virginia Press
Phone: 1.800.831.3406
Website: www.upress.virginia.edu/order
Email: vapress@virginia.edu

Website and Social Media:
Website: publishing.gmu.edu/
Blog: publishing.gmu.edu/news/
Twitter: @MasonPublish
GitHub: github.com/masonpublishing/

UK Representative:
Eurospan

Canadian Representative:
Scholarly Book Services

Staff
Head, Mason Publishing: John W. Warren (703.993.3636; email: jwarre13)
Scholarly Communications and Copyright Officer: Claudia Holland (703.993.2544; email: chollan3)
Coordinator, University Dissertation & Thesis Services: Sally Evans (703.993.2222; email: sevans13)
Associate University Librarian for Digital Programs and Services: Wally Grotophorst (703.993.9905; email: wallyg)
Dean of Libraries and University Librarian: John Zenelis (703.993.2491; email: jzenelis)

Introductory Member
Established: 2007
Title output 2016: 0
Titles currently in print: 7

Admitted to the Association: 2014
Title output 2017: 3
Journals published: 6

Editorial Program
Mason Publishing Group provides support and resources to the George Mason University community for creating, curating, and disseminating scholarly, creative, and educational works. Mason Publishing Group consolidates robust digital publishing programs and services within the University Libraries, which has been developing expertise and increased capacity in scholarly publishing for several years. The George Mason University Press supports the academic mission of George Mason University by publishing peer-reviewed, scholarly works for a diverse, worldwide readership. Subject areas include regional titles including history of Northern Virginia and Washington DC; education, online learning, research methods and technology; political science, public policy, and global affairs; environmental studies and conservation.
Journals: *Journal of Mason Graduate Research*; *Narrative and Conflict*; *New Voices in Public Policy*; *Philosophy and Public Policy*; and *The Writing Campus*
Conference Proceedings: *Open Scholarship Initiative Proceedings; Innovations in Teaching and Learning*

Georgetown University Press

3520 Prospect Street, NW, Suite 140
Washington, DC 20007

Phone: 202.687.5889
Fax: 202.687.6340
Email: gupress@georgetown.edu
Indiv: (user I.D.)@georgetown.edu
Indiv: (First name.last name)@georgetown.edu

Orders:
US: c/o Hopkins Fulfillment Service
PO Box 50370
Baltimore, MD 21211
Phone: 800.537.5487
Fax: 410.516.6998
Email: hfscustserv@press.jhu.edu

Website and Social Media:
Website: www.press.georgetown.edu
Blog: georgetownuniversitypress.tumblr.com
Facebook: www.facebook.com/georgetownup
News blog: georgetownup.wordpress.com
Pinterest: pinterest.com/georgetownup
Twitter:@gupress
YouTube: www.youtube.com/user/GeorgetownUP
Tumblr: georgetownuniversitypress.tumblr.com

UK/European Distributor:
NBN International

Canadian Representative:
Brunswick Books

Staff
Interim Director: Hope LeGro (202.687.4704; email: hjs6)
Director, Georgetown Languages, and Assistant Director of the Press: Hope LeGro
  (202.687.4704; email: hjs6)

Georgetown University Press continued

Digital Editor, Georgetown Languages: TBA
Acquisitions Editor, Languages: Clara Totten (202.687.2988; email: cls86)
  Senior Acquisitions Editor, Political Science and International Affairs: Donald Jacobs (202.687.5218; email: dpj5)
Editorial, Design, and Production Manager: Glenn Saltzman (202.687.6251; email: gls43
  Editorial and Production Coordinator: Kathryn Owens (202.687.0159; email: kao51)
Marketing and Sales Director: Virginia Bryant (202.687.9856; email: vvb6
  Marketing Coordinator: Cherylann Pasha (202.687.3671; email: cmp259)
  Publicity Manager: Jacqueline Beilhart (202.687.9298; email: jb594)
  Digital Publishing and Rights Manager: TBA (202.687.7687)
  Contracts, Permissions, and Journals Coordinator: TBA (202.687.4462)
Business Manager and Assistant Director of the Press: Ioan Suciu (202.687.5641; email: suciui)
  Accountant: Sulah Kim (202.687.8151; email: slk33)

Regular Member

Established: 1964	Admitted to the Association: 1986
Title output 2016: 50	Title output 2017: 42
Titles currently in print: 886	Journals published: 3

Editorial Program
Disciplines: international affairs; languages and linguistics; religion and ethics; and regional.
Journals: *Al-cArabiyya: Journal of the American Association of Teachers of Arabic; Georgetown Journal of International Affairs; Journal of the Society of Christian Ethic*s
Special series: Advancing Human Rights; American Governance and Public Policy; Georgetown Classics in Arabic Language and Linguistics; Georgetown Shorts; Georgetown Studies in Spanish Linguistics; Georgetown University Round Table on Languages and Linguistics; Moral Traditions; Public Management and Change; Religion and Politics; South Asia in World Affairs

University of Georgia Press

Main Library, Third Floor
320 S. Jackson Street
Athens, GA 30602

Phone: 706.542.1007
Fax: 706.542.2558
Indiv: (user I.D.)@uga.edu

Website and Social Media:
Website: www.ugapress.org
Blog: ugapress.wordpress.com
Facebook: www.facebook.com/UGAPress
Goodreads: www.goodreads.com/UGAPress
Instagram: instagram.com/ugapress
Twitter: @UGAPress
YouTube: UGAPress

World Distributor:
Eurospan

Fulfillment:
University of Georgia Press
c/o Longleaf Services, Inc.
116 Boundary St.
Chapel Hill, NC 27514-3808

Returns:
Longleaf Services – Returns
c/o Ingram Publisher Services
1250 Ingram Drive
Chambersburg, PA 17202

Orders and Customer Service:
Phone: 800.848.6224 or 919.966.7449
Fax: 800.272.6817 or 919.962.2704
Orders email: orders@longleafservices.org
Email: customerservice@longleafservices.org

Staff

Director: Lisa Bayer (706.542.0027; email: lbayer)
  Assistant to the Director: Katherine La Mantia (706.542.1007; email: katglm)
Intellectual Property Manager (Contracts & Rights): Jordan Stepp (706.542.7175; email: jstepp)
Director of Development: Chantel Dunham (706.542.0628; email: cdunham)
Acquisitions Editorial: Mick Gusinde-Duffy, Executive Editor for Scholarly and Digital Publishing (history; human geography/urban studies; American studies) (706.542.9907; email: mickgd)
  Executive Editor: Walter Biggins (American literary & cultural studies, history of the Americas, African American studies, narrative/creative nonfiction) (706.542.4728; email: wbiggins)
  Acquisitions Editor: Patrick Allen (popular/public history, regional interest, landscape architecture; environmental studies) (706.542.6004; email: pallen)
  Assistant Acquisitions Editor: Beth Snead (animal studies) (706.542.7613; email: bsnead)
  Editorial Assistant: Katherine La Mantia (706.542.1007; email: katglm)
Editorial Design and Production: Jon Davies, Assistant Director for Editorial, Design, and Production (706.542.2101; email: jdavies)
  Assistant Editorial, Design, and Production Manager: Melissa Bugbee Buchanan (706.542.4488; email: melissa.buchanan)
  Production Editor and Reprints Coordinator: Rebecca Norton (706.542.4643; email: ranorton)
  Senior Designer and Art Director: Erin Kirk New (706.769.0879; email: ekirknew)
  Senior Designer and Production Manager: Kaelin Broaddus (706.542.3889; email: kaelinb)
  Production Editor: Thomas Roche (706.542.2491; email: thomas.roche)

University of Georgia Press continued

Marketing and Sales: David Des Jardines, Director of Marketing and Digital Initiatives (706.542.9758; email: ddesjard)
Publicist and Social Media Manager: Jason Bennett (706.542.9263; email: jason.bennett)
Marketing Content and Exhibits Manager: Christina Cotter (706.542.0134; email: ccotter)
Business: Phyllis Wells, Assistant Director and Business Manager (706.542.7250; email: pwells)
Senior Accountant: Marena Smith (706.542.0753; email: marena)
Accounts Payable and Permissions Coordinator: Stacey Hayes (706.542.2606; email: sbhayes)
Distributor Liaison: Jeri Headrick (706.542.9921 email: headrick)
The New Georgia Encyclopedia Project (www.georgiaencyclopedia.org)
Managing Editor: Ed Hatfield (404.523.6220, ext. 121; email: edward.hatfield)

Regular Member
Established: 1938
Title output 2016: 60
Titles currently in print: 1,800

Admitted to the Association: 1940
Title output 2017: 65

Editorial Program
Humanities and social sciences with particular interests in Atlantic world, American, and southern history; civil rights history; legal history; environmental history; African American studies; geography; urban studies; creative nonfiction; international relations; natural history; environmental studies; American and southern literature; American studies; cinema and media studies; food studies; popular culture; and regional trade titles.
Special series and imprints: Animal Voices/Animal Worlds; Children, Youth, and War; Critical Studies in the History of Landscape Design; Crux: The Georgia Series in Literary Nonfiction; Early American Places; Environmental History and the American South; Geographies of Justice and Social Transformation; Georgia Review Books; Georgia River Network Guidebooks; Masters of Modern Landscape Design; The Morehouse College King Collection Series on Civil and Human Rights; Music of the American South; New Perspectives on the Civil War Era; The New Southern Studies; Politics and Culture in the Twentieth-Century South; Print Culture and the South; Race in the Atlantic World, 1700-1900; Since 1970: Histories of Contemporary America; Sociology of Race and Ethnicity Series; The South on Screen; Southern Foodways Alliance Studies in Culture, People, and Place; Studies in Security and International Affairs; Southern Legal Studies; UnCivil Wars; The United States and the Americas; A Wormsloe Foundation Nature Book; A Wormsloe Foundation Publication
Literary competitions: Flannery O'Connor Award for Short Fiction; Georgia Poetry Prize; The Association of Writers and Writing Programs Award for Creative Nonfiction; Cave Canem Poetry Prize; National Poetry Series
Lecture series: Mercer University Lamar Memorial Lectures; George H. Shriver Lecture Series in Religion in American History

Getty Publications

1200 Getty Center Drive
Suite 500
Los Angeles, CA 90049-1682

Phone: 310.440.7365
Fax: 310.440.7758
Email: pubsinfo@getty.edu
Indiv: (user I.D.)@getty.edu

Orders:
Chicago Distribution Center
11030 South Langley Avenue
Chicago, IL 60628
Phone: 800.621.2736
Fax: 800.621.8476
Email: custserv@press.uchicago.edu

Website and Social Media:
Website: www.getty.edu/publications
Facebook: www.facebook.com/GettyPublications
Tumblr: gettypubs.tumblr.com
Twitter: @GettyPubs

UK/European Distributors:
Yale University Press UK

UK/Sales Representative:
Yale University Press UK

Canada Sales Representative:
Lexa Publishers Representatives

Staff
Publisher: Kara Kirk (310.440.6066; email: kkirk)
Getty Research Institute: Michele Ciaccio (310.440.7453; email: mciaccio)
Getty Conservation Institute: Cynthia Godlewski (310.440.6805; email: cgodlewski)
Editor-in-Chief: Karen Levine (310.440.6525; email: klevine)
Rights & Permissions: Leslie Rollins (310.440.7102; email: lrollins)
Design and Production: Karen Schmidt (310.440.6504; email: kschmidt)
Associate Publisher: Maureen Winter (310.440.6117; email: mwinter)
Digital Publications Manager: Greg Albers (310.440.6067; email: galbers)

Regular Member
Established: 1982
Title output 2016: 25
Titles currently in print: 610

Admitted to the Association: 1989
Title output 2017: 35
Journals published: 1

Editorial Program
Scholarly and general interest publications on the visual arts; conservation and the history of art and the humanities; and areas related to the work of the Getty Research Institute, the Getty Conservation Institute, the Getty Foundation, and the collections of the J. Paul Getty Museum: antiquities, decorative arts, drawings, manuscripts, paintings, photographs, and sculpture.
Journal: *Getty Research Journal*
Imprints: Getty Research Institute; Getty Conservation Institute; J. Paul Getty Museum; and Getty Publications

Harvard University Press

79 Garden Street
Cambridge, MA 02138-1499

Phone: 617.495.2600
Faxes: 617.495.5898 (General)
617.495.2611 (Editorial)
617.495.2606 (Sales/Marketing)
Email:
firstname_lastname@harvard.edu

Customer Service/Orders:
Harvard University Press
c/o TriLiteral-LLC
100 Maple Ridge Drive
Cumberland, RI 02864-1769
Phone: 800.405.1619 (US & Canada)
401.531.2800 (all others)
Faxes: 800.406.9145 (US & Canada)
401.531.2801 (all others)

Website and Social Media:
Website: www.hup.harvard.edu
Blog: harvardpress.typepad.com
Facebook: www.facebook.com/HarvardPress
Twitter: @Harvard_Press
YouTube: www.youtube.com/user/harvardupress

European Office:
Harvard University Press
Vernon House
23 Sicilian Avenue
London WC1A 2QS United Kingdom
Email: info@harvardup.co.uk
Phone: 011.44.20.3463.2350

Staff
Director: George Andreou (617.495.2601)
CFO/COO: Dan Wackrow (617.495.2613)
Director of Intellectual Property: Stephanie Vyce (617.495.2603)
Assistant Director and Editor-in-Chief: Susan Wallace Boehmer (617.495.2624)
   Executive Editor for Life Sciences: Janice Audet (617.495.2674)
   Executive Editor for Physical Sciences and Technology: Jeff Dean (617.495.1226)
   General Editor: Andrew Kinney (617.495.9015)
   Executive Editor-at-Large: Thomas LeBien (617.496.2681)
   Senior Executive Editor-at-Large (Europe) and Senior Executive Editor for Economics (Global): Ian Malcolm (011.44.7843.301.029)
   Executive Editor for History: Kathleen McDermott (617.495.4703)
   Senior Executive Editor for History and Contemporary Affairs: Joyce Seltzer (212.337.0280)
   Executive Editor-at-Large: Sharmila Sen (617.495.8122)
   Executive Editor for the Humanities: Lindsay Waters (617.495.2835)
   Editorial Manager: David Foss (617.496.8170)
   Managing Editor for Manuscript Development and Preparation: Christine Thorsteinsson (617.495.5951)
   Managing Editor for Digital Projects and Metadata: Emily Arkin (617.496.4690)

Director of Design and Production: Tim Jones (617.495.2669)
  Assistant Production Director: Abigail Mumford (617.496.9421)
  Design Manager: Lisa Roberts (617.495.5129)
Assistant Director/Sales and Marketing Director: Susan Donnelly (617.495.2606)
  Sales Manager/Digital Content Manager: Vanessa Vinarub (617.495.2650)
  Assistant Marketing Manager: Gregory Kornbluh (617.496.3281)
  Promotion Manager: Sheila Barrett (617.495.2618)
  Special Sales: Briana Ross (617.384.7515)
  Exhibits Manager/Business Analyst: Val Hunt (617.495.2607)
  Sales and Marketing Manager (Europe): Richard Howells (011.44.20.3463.2350)
  Publicity Manager (Europe): Rebekah White (011.44.20.3463.2350)

Regular Member

Established: 1913	Admitted to the Association: 1937
Title output 2016: 275	Title output 2017: 274
Titles currently in print: 8,500	

Editorial Program
Scholarly books and serious works of general interest in the humanities, the social and behavioral sciences, the natural sciences, medicine, and technology. The Press does not normally publish poetry, fiction, festschriften, memoirs, symposia, or unrevised doctoral dissertations.

The Press distributes publications for a number of Harvard University departments and affiliates: Archaeological Exploration of Sardis, Center for Hellenic Studies, Center for the Study of World Religions, David Rockefeller Center for Latin American Studies, Department of Celtic Languages and Literatures, Department of the Classics, Department of Comparative Literature, Department of English, Department of Music, Department of Near Eastern Languages and Civilizations, Department of South Asian Studies, Derek Bok Center, Dumbarton Oaks Research Library and Collection, FXB Center for Health and Human Rights, Harvard Center for Middle Eastern Studies, Harvard College Library, Harvard Divinity School, Harvard Global Equity Initiative, Harvard University Asia Center, Harvard University Center for Jewish Studies, Harvard University Graduate School of Design, Houghton Library of the Harvard College Library, Ilex Foundation, Islamic Legal Studies Program, Harvard Law School, Peabody Museum Press, Harvard School of Public Health, the Ukrainian Research Institute of Harvard University, and Villa I Tatti.
Special imprints: The Belknap Press
Special series, joint imprints, and/or copublishing programs: The Adams Papers; Bernard Berenson Lectures; Carl Newell Jackson Lectures; Charles Eliot Norton Lectures; Dumbarton Oaks Medieval Library; Edwin L. Godkin Lectures; Edwin O. Reischauer Lectures; Harvard Historical Studies and Monographs; Harvard Studies in Business History; I Tatti Renaissance Library; I Tatti Renaissance Monographs; John Harvard Library; Loeb Classical Library (print and digital); Loeb Classical Monographs; Mary Flexner Lectures; Murty Classical Library of India; Nathan I. Huggins Lectures; Oliver Wendell Holmes Lectures; Revealing Antiquity; Tanner Lectures; W.E.B. Du Bois Lectures; William E. Massey Sr. Lectures

University of Hawai'i Press

2840 Kolowalu Street
Honolulu, HI 96822-1888

Phone: 808.956.8257
Fax: 808.988.6052
Email: (user I.D.)@hawaii.edu

Orders:
Phone: 888.UHPRESS; 808.956.8255
Fax: 800.650.7811; 808.988.5203

Website and Social Media:
Website: www.uhpress.hawaii.edu
Blog: uhpress.wordpress.com
Facebook: www.facebook.com/pages/University-of-Hawaii-Press/200519105362
Twitter: @UHPRESSNEWS
Instagram: @uhpress

European Distributor:
Eurospan

Canadian Distributor:
Scholarly Book Services

Staff
Interim Director: Joel Cosseboom (808.956.6292; email: cosseboo)
   Administrative Assistant, Rights and Permissions: Alison Kleczewski (808.956.8257; email: alison38)
Acquisitions Editorial: Pamela Kelley, Executive Editor (808.956.6207; email: pkelley)
   Editors: Masako Ikeda (808.956.8696; email: masakoi); Stephanie Chun (808.956.6426; email: chuns)
   Editorial Associates: Debra Tang (808.956.8694; email: dtang); Emma Ching (808.956.6426; email: emma6)
Digital Publishing Manager: Trond Knutsen (808.956.6227; email: tknutsen)
Managing Editors: Cheryl Loe (808.956.8276; email: cheryl.loe); Grace Wen (808.956.8834; email: gracewen)
Design and Production: Santos Barbasa, Manager (808.956.8877; email: barbasa)
   Production Editors: Lucille Aono (808.956.6328; email: lucille); Mardee Melton (808.956.2858; email: mmelton)
   Fiscal Support Specialist: Terri Miyasato (808.956.8275; email: terrimiy)
Marketing: Royden Muranaka, Interim Marketing Manager (808.956.6214; email: royden)
   Product Manager: Steven Hirashima (808.956.8698; email: stevehir)
   Promotion Manager: Carol Abe (808.956.8697; email: abec)
   E-Marketing Specialist: Blaine Tolentino (808.956.4262; email: blainemt)
Journals: Pamela Wilson, Manager (808.956.6790; email: pwilson6)
   Managing Editor: Alicia Upano (808.956.8398; email: aupano)
   Production Editor: Emily Benton (808.956.4492; email: bentone)
   Administrative Assistant: Norman Kaneshiro (808.956.8833; email: uhpjourn)
East-West Export Books: Royden Muranaka, International Sales Manager (808.956.6214; email: royden)
   Assistant: Kiera Nishimoto (808.956.8830; email: eweb)
Business: Ku'ulei Arakaki, Administrative Officer (808.956.6218; email: shunya)
   Fiscal Officer: Kyle Watanabe (808.956.6228; email: kshiga21)

Order Processing: Cindy Yen (808.956.8256; email: cyen); Danny Li (808.956.6279; email: wingon)
Warehouse: Kyle Nakata, Clifford Newalu (808.956.3357; email: uhpwhse)
IT: Collin Wong (808.956.6209; email: cwong808)

Regular Member

Established: 1947   Admitted to the Association: 1951
Title output 2016: 86   Title output 2017: 90
Titles currently in print: 2,034   Journals published: 24

Editorial Program
Asian, Pacific, and Asian American studies in history; art; anthropology; architecture; economics; sociology; philosophy and religion; languages and linguistics; law; literature; performing arts; political science; physical and natural sciences; regional studies.

Journals: *Asian Perspectives; Asian Theatre Journal; Azalea; Biography; Buddhist-Christian Studies; China Review International; The Contemporary Pacific; Cross-Currents; Hawaiian Journal of History; Journal of Daoist Studies; Journal of Korean Religions; Journal of the Southeast Asian Linguistics Society; Journal of World History; Korean Studies; Language Documentation and Conservation; Manoa; Oceanic Linguistics; Pacific Science; Palapala; Philosophy East and West; Review of Japanese Culture and Society; Trans-Humanities; U.S.-Japan Women's Journal; Yearbook of the Association of Pacific Coast Geographers*

Special series, joint imprints, and/or copublishing programs: ABC Chinese Dictionary; ASAA (Asian Studies Association of Australia) Southeast Asia Publications; Asia Pacific Flows; Asia Pop!; Biography Monographs; Confucian Cultures; Contemporary Buddhism; Critical Interventions; Dimensions of Asian Spirituality; Food in Asia and the Pacific; Hawaiʻinuiakea; Hawaiʻi Studies on Korea; Indigenous Pacifics; Intersections: Asian and Pacific American Transcultural Studies; KLEAR Textbooks in Korean Language (Korean Language Education and Research Center/Korea Foundation); Korean Classics Library: Historical Materials; Korean Classics Library: Philosophy and Religion; Kuroda Institute Classics in East Asian Buddhism; Kuroda Institute Studies in East Asian Buddhism; Modern Korean Fiction; Music and Performing Arts of Asia and the Pacific; Nanzan Library of Asian Religion and Culture; The New Oceania Literary Series; Oceanic Linguistics Special Publications; Pacific Islands Archaeology; Pacific Islands Monographs; PALI Language Texts; Perspectives on the Global Past; Pure Land Buddhist Studies; Society for Asian and Comparative Philosophy; Southeast Asia: Politics, Meaning, and Memory; Spatial Habitus: Making and Meaning in Asia's Architecture; Studies of the Weatherhead East Asian Institute (Columbia University); Topics in the Contemporary Pacific

University of Illinois Press

1325 S. Oak Street
Champaign, IL 61820-6903

Phone: 217.333.0950
Fax: 217.244.8082
Email: uipress@uillinois.edu
Journals: journals@uillinois.edu
Indiv: (user I.D.)@uillinois.edu

Website and Social Media:
Website: www.press.uillinois.edu
Blog: www.press.uillinois.edu/wordpress
Journals Blog: www.press.uillinois.edu/journals/blog
Facebook: www.facebook.com/UniversityofIllinoisPress
Twitter: @IllinoisPress
Instagram: @illinoispress

Warehouse Address and Orders:
University of Illinois Press
c/o Chicago Distribution Center
11030 South Langley Avenue
Chicago, IL 60628

Orders:
Books: 800.621.2736
Email: orders@press.uchicago.edu
Journals: 866.244.0626

UK/European Representative:
Combined Academic Publishers

Canadian Representative:
Scholarly Book Services

Asia Representative:
B.K. Norton

Australia & New Zealand:
Footprint Books Pty Ltd.

Staff

Director: Laurie Matheson (217.244.4685; email: lmatheso)
  Assistant to the Director: Kathy O'Neill (217.244.4691; email: oneill2)
  Outreach & Development and Acquisitions Assistant: Julie R. Laut (217.300.4126; email: jlaut2)
Acquisitions Editorial: Laurie Matheson, Director (music) (217.244.4685; email: lmatheso)
  Senior Acquisitions Editors: Dawn Durante (African American studies; women's, gender, and sexuality studies; American studies; religion) (217.265.8491; email: durante9); Daniel Nasset (communication and information studies, film and media, military history, Chicago politics and urban studies, sports history) (217.244.5182; email: dnasset)
  Acquisitions Editor: James Engelhardt (Appalachian studies, folklore, labor studies, Lincoln studies, regional trade) (217.244.1040; email: jengel04)
  Associate Acquisitions Editor: Marika Christofides (anthropology, food studies, science fiction studies) (217.300.7842; email: mchristo)
  Assistant Acquisitions Editor: Alison K. Syring Bassford (217.300.5933; email: asyring2)
Editorial, Design, and Production
  Assistant Director and EDP Manager: Jennifer Comeau (217.244.3279; email: jlcomeau)
  Assistant Managing Editor: Jennifer Clark (217.244.8041; email: jsclark1)
  Senior Editor: Tad Ringo (217.265.0238; email: tringo)
  Production Manager: Kristine Ding (217.244.4701; email: kding)
  Production Coordinator: Tamara Shidlauski (217.265.0940; email: shidlaus)
  Desktop Publishers: Lisa Connery (217.244.1311; email: lconnery); Kirsten Dennison (217.244.9892; email: kdennisn); Jim Proefrock (email: proefroc)

Art Director: Dustin Hubbart (217.333.9227; email: dhubbart)
Designer: Jennie Fisher (217.244.7156; email: jholz)
Marketing
  Marketing and Sales Manager: Michael Roux (217.244.4683; email: mroux)
  Sales and Course Adoption Coordinator: Ami Reitmeier (217.244.4703; email: reitmeir)
  Publicity Manager: Heather Gernenz (217.300.2687; email: gernenz2)
  Exhibits Manager: Margo Chaney (217.244.6491; email: mechaney)
  Rights & Permissions and Awards Manager: Angela Burton (217.300.2883; email: alburton)
  Direct Marketing & Advertising Manager: Denise Peeler (217.244.4690; email: dpeeler)
  Catalog & Copywriting Coordinator: Kevin Cunningham (email: rkcunnin)
  Sales and Marketing Assistant: Roberta Sparenberg (217.333.6494; email: sparnbrg)
Journals
  Journals Manager: Clydette Wantland (217.244.6496; email: cwantlan)
  Associate Journals Manager: Jeff McArdle (217.244.0381; email: jmcardle)
  Senior Production Editor: Heather Munson (217.244.6488; email: hmunson)
  Journals Production Editors: Kate Kemball (217.244.7411; email: kemball2); Kristen Dean-Grossmann (217.265.9186; email: kdeangro)
  Journals Circulation Manager: Cheryl Jestis (866.244.0626; email: jestis)
  Journals Marketing Manager: Alexa Colella (217.244.5610; email: acolella)
Information Systems
  Electronic Publisher: Paul Arroyo (217.244.7147; email: parroyo)
  Manager of Information Technology: Louis W. Mesker (217.244.8025; email: lmesker)
  Database Administrator: Leslie DeLucia (217.244.6498; email: ldelucia)
  Web Programmer: Bob Repta (217.244.0854; email: repta)
Business
  Chief Financial Officer: Alice Ennis (217.244.0091; email: atennis)
  Accounts Receivable: Sandy Sullivan (217.244.0628; email: ssulliva)
  Accounts Payable: Jennifer Barbee (217.244.7958; email: jjbarbee)

Regular Member

Established: 1918   Admitted to the Association: 1937
Title output 2016: 100   Title output 2017: 113
Titles currently in print: 2,400   Journals published: 38

Editorial Program

Scholarly books and serious nonfiction, with special interests in African American studies, American history, American music, anthropology, Appalachian studies, Asian American studies, critical theory, cultural studies, communications, cinema studies, ethnic studies, folklore, food studies, Latino/a studies, Lincoln studies, military history, religious studies, sport history, women's studies, labor and working-class history

Journals: *American Journal of Psychology; American Journal of Theology & Philosophy; American Literary Realism; American Music; American Philosophical Quarterly; Black Music Research Journal; Bulletin of the Council for Research in Music Education; Connecticut History Review; Ethnomusicology; Feminist Teacher; History of Philosophy Quarterly; History of the Present; Illinois Classical Studies; Illinois Heritage; Jazz & Culture; Journal of the Abraham Lincoln Association; Journal of Aesthetic Education; Journal of American Ethnic History; Journal of American Folklore; Journal of Animal Ethics; Journal for the Anthropological Study of Human Movement; Journal of Appalachian Studies; Journal of Civil and Human Rights; Journal of Edu-*

University of Illinois Press continued

cation Finance; Journal of English and Germanic Philology; Journal of Film & Video; Journal of the Illinois State Historical Society; Journal of Mormon History; Journal of Sport History; Music and Moving Image; The Pluralist; Polish American Studies; The Polish Review; Process Studies, Public Affairs Quarterly; Scandinavian Studies; Utah Historical Quarterly, Visual Arts Research; Women, Gender and Families of Color; World History Connected

Special series, joint imprints, and/or copublishing programs: African American Music in Global Perspective; American Composers; The Asian American Experience; Bach Perspectives; The Beauvoir Series; Beethoven Sketchbook Series; Common Threads; Contemporary Film Directors; Disability Histories; Dissident Feminisms; Feminist Media Studies; Folklore Studies in a Multicultural World; The Geopolitics of Information; Global Studies of the United States; Heartland Foodways; The History of Communication; The History of Emotions; History of Military Occupations; Interpretations of Culture in the New Millennium; The Knox College Lincoln Studies Center; Latinos in Chicago and the Midwest; Lemann Institute for Brazilian Studies Series; Modern Masters of Science Fiction; Music in American Life; The New Black Studies Series; New Perspectives on Gender in Music; NWSA/University of Illinois First Book Prize; Sport and Society; Studies in Sensory History; Studies in Sports Media; Studies of World Migrations; Topics in the Digital Humanities; Transformations: Womanist, Feminist, and Indigenous Studies; The Urban Agenda; Working Class in American History; Women Composers; Women and Film History International; Women, Gender, and Sexuality in American History; Women in Print

IMF Publications (International Monetary Fund)

Street Address:
700 19th Street, NW
Washington, DC 20431

Mailing Address:
Publications Services
P.O. Box 92780
Washington, DC 20090

Phone: 202.623.7430
Fax: 202.623.7201
Email: publications@imf.org

Orders:
202.623.7430
202.623.7201
Website: www.bookstore.imf.org

Website and Social Media:
Websites: www.bookstore.imf.org; www.elibrary.imf.org; www.imf.org
Blog: blogs.imf.org
Twitter: @IMFNews
YouTube: www.youtube.com/user/imf
Facebook: www.facebook.com/imf

Canadian Representative:
Renouf Publishing Co. Ltd.

UK/European Representative:
Eurospan Group

Staff
Publisher: Jeffrey Hayden (202.623.8354; email: jhayden@imf.org)
Associate Publisher: Linda Griffin Kean (202.623.4124; email: lkean@imf.org)

Rights Manager/Acquisitions Editor/Conference Manager: Patricia Loo (202.623.8296; email: ploo@imf.org)
Editorial Assistants: Madje G. Amega (202.623.7010; email: mamega@imf.org); Josh Hyoun Woo Park (202.623.4248; email: hpark@imf.org)
Electronic Publishing Officer: Jim Beardow (202.623.7899; email: jbeardow@imf.org)
Digital Publishing Officer: Akshay Modi (202.623.8964; email: amodi@imf.org)
Editors: Joseph Procopio (202.623.9258; email: jprocopio@imf.org); Gemma Diaz (202.623.7114; email: gdiaz@imf.org); Linda Long (email: 202.623.6591; email: llong@imf.org)
Production Associate: Houda Berrada (202.623.7035; email: hberrada@imf.org)
Marketing Associate: Sandra Carrollo (202.623.9554; email: scarrollo@imf.org)
Licensing and Contracts Agent: Alexa Smith (952.944.5729; email: asmith2@imf.org)
Finance Administrator: Cristina Pagan (202.623.4824; email: cpagan@imf.org)
Process Management Consultant: John Brenneman (202.623.7092; email: jbrenneman@imf.org)

Regular Member

Established: 1948
Title output 2016: 57
Titles currently in print: 833

Admitted to the Association: 2011
Title output 2017: 66
Journals published: 2

Editorial Program

The International Monetary Fund publishes a wide variety of books, periodicals, and electronic products covering economics, international finance, monetary issues, statistics, and exchange rates.

Journals: *Finance & Development; IMF Economic Review*

Special series: Departmental Papers; Occasional Papers; Staff Discussion Notes; Technical Notes and Manuals; World Economic and Financial Surveys (includes World Economic Outlook, Fiscal Monitor, Global Financial Stability Report, and Regional Economic Outlooks); Working Papers

Joint imprints and copublishing programs: Select titles copublished with John Wiley & Sons, MIT Press, Oxford University Press, Palgrave Macmillan, Routledge, and Yale University Press.

Indiana University Press

Office of Scholarly Publishing
Herman B Wells Library 350
1320 E. 10th Street
Bloomington, IN 47405

Phone: 812.855.8817
Phone: 800.842.6796
Email: iupress@indiana.edu
Indiv: (user I.D.)@indiana.edu

Fulfillment Center:
C/O Ingram Publisher Services
1280 Ingram Drive
Chambersburg, PA 17202

Orders: 800.648.3013
Fax: 812.855.8507
Email (vendors): pubsupport@ingramcontent.com
Email (individuals): iuporder@indiana.edu

Canadian Representative:
Lexa Publishers' Representative

UK/European Representative:
Combined Academic Publishers

Website and Social Media:
Web: iupress.indiana.edu
Blog: iupress.typepad.com/blog
Twitter: @iupress
Facebook: www.facebook.com/iupress
Google+: plus.google.com/115444288032700584669
YouTube: www.youtube.com/iupress
Pinterest: www. pinterest.com/iupforeign/

Staff

Director, Indiana University Press and Digital Publishing: Gary Dunham (email: dunhamg)
Acquisitions Editorial: Dee Mortensen, Editorial Director (African studies, Judaism and Judaica, philosophy, and religious studies) (email: mortense)
  Acquisition Editors: Jennika Baines (global and international studies) (email: bainesj); Janice Frisch (music, film and media, folklore) (email: frischj); Ashley Runyon (trade and regional) (email: asrunyon); Peggy Solic (Well House Books) (email: pegsolic)
  Acquisition Assistants: Paige Rasmussen (email: parasmus); Kate Schramm (email: katschra)
Operations: Michael Regoli, Director of Publishing Operations (email: regoli)
  Lead Project Manager/Editor: David Miller (email: Dm60)
  Project Managers: Nancy Lightfoot (email: nlightfo); Darja Malcolm-Clarke (email: dmalcolm); Rachel Rosolina (email: rrosolin)
  Senior Artists and Book Designers: Pam Rude (email: psrude); Jennifer Witzke (email: jwitzke)
  Online Publishing Manager: Dan Pyle (email: dapyle)
  Journals Production Manager: Sherondra Thedford (email: sherthed)
  Production Manager: Laura Hohman (email: lhohman)
  Publishing Services Coordinator: Tony Brewer (email: tbrewer)
  Production Assistant: Rachel Kindler (email: rkindler)
Marketing and Sales: Dave Hulsey, Associate Director and Marketing and Sales Director (email: hulseyd)
  Trade Marketing and Publicity Manager: Michelle Sybert (email: msybert)

Scholarly Marketing and Publicity Manager: Julie Davis (email: julmsmit)
Electronic Marketing Manager: Jon Meerdink (email: jmeerdin)
Publicity Coordinator: Theresa Halter (email: thalter)
Sales and Marketing Assistant: Rhonda Van Der Dussen (email: rdussen)
Rights and Permissions Manager: Stephen Williams (email: smw9)
Business and Operations: Michael Noth, Fiscal Officer (email: mnoth)
  Human Resources Officer: Jennifer Chaffin (email: jlchaffi)
  Staff Accountant: Brent Starr (email: brstarr)
  Assistant Business Manager for Network Systems and Order Processing: Janie Pearson (email: cjfender)
  Assistant Business Manager for Accounts Receivable & Customer Service: Kim Bower (email: kchilder)

Regular Member

Established: 1950   Admitted to the Association: 1952
Title output 2016: 160   Title output 2017: 180
Titles currently in print: 3,450   Journals published: 32

Editorial Program

African studies; anthropology; ethnomusicology; film and media studies; folklore; international studies; Irish studies; Jewish and Holocaust studies; Middle East studies; military history; music; paleontology; philosophy; public health; railroad history; religion; Russian and East European studies; science; women's and gender studies.

Journals: *Africa Today; ACPR: African Conflict and Peacebuilding Review; Aleph: Historical Studies in Science & Judaism; Antisemitism Studies; Black Camera; Chiricu; e-Service Journal; Ethics & the Environment; Film History; The Global South; History & Memory; Indiana Journal of Global Legal Studies; Israel Studies; Jewish Social Studies; Journal of Feminist Studies in Religion; JFR: Journal of Folklore Research; Journal of Islam and Muslim Studies; Journal of Modern Literature; Journal of the Ottoman and Turkish Studies Association; Journal of World Philosophies; Meridians: feminism, race, transnationalism; Nashim: A Journal of Jewish Women's & Gender Issues; Pakistan Journal of Historical Studies; Philanthropy and Education; PMER: Philosophy of Music Education Review; Prooftexts: A Journal of Jewish Literary History; Recreation, Parks, and Tourism in Public Health; Research in African Literatures; Spectrum: The Journal of Black Men; Teaching and Learning Inquiry; Transactions of the Charles S. Peirce Society: A Quarterly Journal in American Philosophy; Transition; Victorian Studies*

Special series: African Expressive Cultures; African Systems of Thought; American Philosophy; Counterpoints: Music and Education; Digital Game Studies; Excavations at Ancient Halieis; Excavations at Franchthi Cave, Greece; Global African Voices; Global Research Studies; The Helen and Martin Schwartz Lectures in Jewish Studies; Indiana Repertoire Guides; Indiana Series in Middle East Studies; Indiana Series in the Philosophy of Religion; Indiana Series in Sephardi and Mizrahi Studies; Indiana Studies in Biblical Literature; Indiana-Michigan Series in Russian and East European Studies; Jewish Literature and Culture; Life of the Past; Material Vernaculars; The Modern Jewish Experience; Music and the Early Modern Imagination; Music, Nature, Place; Musical Meaning and Interpretation; New Anthropologies of Europe; New Directions in National Cinema; Philanthropic and Nonprofit Studies; Polis Center Series on Religion and Urban Culture; Profiles in Popular Music; Public Cultures of the Middle East and North Africa; Publications of the Early Music Institute; Railroads Past and Present; Readings in African Studies; Religion in North America; Russian Music Studies; Scholarship of Teaching and Learning; Selections from the Writings of

Indiana University Press continued

Charles S. Peirce; Spatial Humanities; Special Publications of the Folklore Institute, Indiana University; Studies in Antisemitism; Studies in Continental Thought; Tracking Globalization; Twentieth-Century Battles; The Variorum Edition of the Poetry of John Donne; World Philosophies; Writings of Charles S. Peirce: A Chronological Edition; The Year's Work: Studies in Fan Culture and Cultural Theory

INSTAP Academic Press

2133 Arch St.
Suite 301
Philadelphia, PA 19146

Phone: 215.568.8041
Email: instappress@hotmail.com
Website: www.instappress.com

Orders:
Casemate Academic
Phone: 610.853.9131
www.oxbowbooks.com/dbbc/

UK Representative:
Oxbow Books
Tel. +44 (0)1865 241249
Website: www.oxbowbooks.com/oxbow/

Staff
Director: Susan Ferrence (215.568.8041; email: sferrence@instappress.com)

Introductory Member
Established: 2001
Title output 2016: 4
Titles currently in print: 65

Admitted to the Association: 2015
Title output 2017: 5

Editorial Program
The Institute for Aegean Prehistory (INSTAP) was founded in 1982 to support projects relevant to the history of the Aegean world from the Paleolithic to the 8th century B.C. In 2001, INSTAP Academic Press was started to help publish projects dealing with the subject of Aegean Prehistory. The Press is a scholarly publisher specializing in the publication of primary source material from archaeological excavations as well as individual studies dealing with material from the prehistoric periods. All publications are in English.
Special series: Prehistory Monographs, INSTAP Archaeological Excavation Manuals

University of Iowa Press

Editorial Office:
119 West Park Road
100 Kuhl House
Iowa City, IA 52242-1000

Phone: 319.335.2000
Fax: 319.335.2055
Email: (user I.D.)@uiowa.edu

Website and Social Media:
Website: www.uiowapress.org
Blog: buroakblog.blogspot.com/
Facebook: www.facebook.com/UIowaPress
Twitter: @UIowaPress

Order Fulfillment:
University of Iowa Press
c/o Chicago Distribution Center
11030 South Langley Avenue
Chicago, IL 60628
Phone: 800.621.2736
Fax: 800.621.8476

UK/European Representative:
Eurospan

Staff
Director: Jim McCoy (319.335.2013; email: james-mccoy)
   Assistant to the Director: Gemma de Choisy (319.335. 3424, email: gemma-dechoisy)
Rights and Permissions: Michelle Moode (319.384.2008; email: UIPress-Permissions)
Editorial:
Acquisitions Editors: Ranjit Arab (natural history, regional history, anthropology/archaeology, fan studies, food studies, performance studies) (319.384.1910; email:ranjit-arab@uiowa.edu); Jim McCoy (poetry, short fiction, general trade, literary nonfiction, literary criticism)
   Editorial Assistant: Meredith Stabel (319.335.2022; email: meredith-stabel)
Managing Editor: Susan Hill Newton (319.335.2011; email: susan-hillnewton)
Design and Production: Karen Copp, Associate Director and Design and Production Manager (319.335.2014; email: karen-copp)
Marketing: Allison Thomas Means, Marketing Manager (319.335.3440; email: allison-means)

Regular Member
Established: 1969
Title output 2016: 40
Titles currently in print: 760

Admitted to the Association: 1982
Title output 2017: 36

Editorial Program
American literary criticism and history, women's studies, contemporary American literature; memoirs; short fiction (award winners only); poetry (award winners and invited submissions only); creative nonfiction; regional studies; regional natural history; theatre history and criticism; American studies; food studies; fan studies; public humanities; veteran's affairs.
Special series: Bur Oak Books and Bur Oak Guides; Contemporary North American Poetry; Iowa Poetry Prize; Iowa Prize in Literary Nonfiction; Iowa Short Fiction Award and John Simmons Short Fiction Award; Iowa and the Midwest Experience; Iowa Whitman Series; Kuhl House Poets; Muse Books; New American Canon; Sightline Books: The Iowa Series in Literary Nonfiction; Studies in Theatre History and Culture; Writers in Their Own Time

Johns Hopkins University Press

2715 N. Charles Street
Baltimore, MD 21218-4363

Phone: 410.516.6900
Fax: 410.516.6998/6968
Email: (user I.D.)@press.jhu.edu

Website and Social Media:
Website: www.press.jhu.edu
Blog: jhupressblog.com
Facebook: www.facebook.com/
   JohnsHopkinsUniversityPress
Twitter: @JHUPress
YouTube: JHUPress
Pinterest: www.pinterest.com/jhupress/
SoundCloud: www.soundcloud.com/jhupress

Distribution Center:
C/O Maple Logistics Solutions
Lebanon Distribution Center
704 Legionaire Drive
Fredericksburg, PA 17026

Orders and Customer Service:
Phone: 800.537.5487 (HFS)
Phone: 800.548.1784 (Journals)
Phone: 410.516.6989 (MUSE)

UK Representative:
Oxford Publicity Partnership Ltd

UK Distribution
John Wiley & Sons Limited

Staff

Director: Barbara Kline Pope (410.516.6971; email: bkp)
Assistant to the Director: TBA (410.516.6971)
Rights and Permissions Manager: Kelly Rogers (410.516.6063; email: klr)
Office and Facilities Coordinator: Nora Reedy (410.516.7035; email: ncr)
Director, Finance and Administration: Erik Smist (410.516.6941; email: eas)
Chief Information Officer: Timothy D. Fuller (410.516.3844; email: tdf)
Acquisitions Editorial: Gregory M. Britton, Editorial Director (higher education) (410.516.6919; email: gb)
   Senior Editors: TBA (American history/American studies) (410.516.6917); Tiffany Gasbarrini (life sciences) (410.516.6999; email: tg); Matthew McAdam (history of STEM, humanities, and ancient studies) (410.516.6903; email: mxm)
   Editors: Robin Coleman (public health and health policy) (410.516.6997; email: rwg); Joe Rusko (health and wellness) (410.516.6904); email: jr)
   Assistant Editor: Catherine Goldstead (Literary studies) (410.516.7353; email: cg)
Project MUSE: Wendy J. Queen, Director (410.516.3845; email: wjq)
   Associate Director, Finance & Operations, Project MUSE: Nicole Kendzejeski (410.516.6969; email: nak)
   Director, Marketing and Sales: Melanie B. Schaffner (410.516.3846; email: mbs)
   Manager, International Sales: Ann Snoeyenbos (410.516.6992; email: aps)
   Sales Manager: Douglas Storm (217.823.0286; email: das)
   Customer Service Coordinator: Lora Czarnowsky (410.516.2890; email: llc)
   Business Solutions Analyst: Elizabeth R. Windsor (410.516.6510; email: brw)
Manuscript Editorial: Juliana M. McCarthy, Managing Editor (410.516.6912; email: jmm)
   Senior Production Editors: Andre M. Barnett (410.516.6995; email: amb); Deborah L. Bors (410.516.6914; email: dlb); Kimberly F. Johnson (410.516.6915; email: kfj); Mary

Lou Kenney (410.516.6897; email: mk)
  Associate Production Editor: Hilary S. Jacqmin (410.516.6901; email: hsj)
  Assistant Manuscript Editor: Kyle Howard Kretzer (410.516.6901; email: khk)
Design and Production: John Cronin, Design & Production Manager (410.516.6922; email: jgc)
  Art Director: Martha Sewall (410.516.6921; email: mds)
  Senior Book Designer: Glen Burris (410.516.6924; email: gmb)
  Production Controller, Prepress and Printing: Patty Weber (410.516.3855; email: pw)
  Production Controller, Electronic Media: Carol Eckhart (410.516.3862; email: cle)
  Production Coordinator, Digital Archive: Jennifer Paulson (410.516.7872; email: jcp)
Marketing: Kerry Cahill, Sales Director (410.516.6936; email: kpc)
  Sales Associate: Devon Renwick (410.516.6951; email: dbr)
  Marketing & Sales Coordinator: Catherine Bergeron (410.516.6934; email cab)
  Associate Marketing Director: Claire McCabe Tamberino (410.516.6935; email: cmt)
  Publicity Manager: Gene Taft (410.516.4162; email: gat)
  Publicity & Community Relations Officer: Jack Holmes (410.516.6928; email: jmh)
  Publicist: Emma All (410.516.6902; email: ea)
  Digital Promotions Coordinator: Robin Rennison (410.516.6972; email: rr)
Journals: William Breichner, Publisher (410.516.6985; email: wmb)
  Journals Fulfillment Systems Project Manager: Matt Brook (410.516.6899; email: mb)
  Director, Sales and Marketing: Lisa Klose (410.516.6689; email: llk)
  Journals Production Manager: Carol Hamblen (410.516.6986; email: crh)
  Journals Operations Manager: Shannon Fortner, (410.516.6038, email: stf)
  Journals Subscription Manager: Robert White Goodman (410.516.6964; email: rwg)
  Journals Assistant Subscription Manager: Kathleen Young (410.516.6944; email: kmy)
  Manager, Public Relations & Advertising: Brian Shea (410.516.7096; email: bjs)
Business: Tony Jacobson, Accounting Manager (410.516.6974; email: tlj)
Fulfillment: Davida G. Breier, Manager, Fulfillment Operations (410.516.6961; email: dgb)
  Customer Service Supervisor, Fulfillment Operations Terrence J. Melvin (410.516.4449; email: tjm)
  Customer Service Coordinator: Alicia C. Catlos (410.516.4441; email: acc)
  Credit & Collections: Christopher Walsh, Accounts Receivable Coordinator (410.516.3854; email: cdw)

Regular Member

Established: 1878
Title output 2016: 142
Titles currently in print: 3,634

Admitted to the Association: 1937
Title output 2017: 135
Journals published: 88

Editorial Program

History (American, ancient, history of science, technology, and medicine); humanities (literary and cultural studies, ancient studies); medicine and health (consumer health, public health); science (biology, physics, and natural history); mathematics; higher education; reference books; and regional books.

  The Press through Hopkins Fulfillment Service (HFS, *hfs.jhu.edu* and HFSBooks.com) handles book order processing and distribution for: Baylor University Press, Catholic University of America Press, Center for Talented Youth, Georgetown University Press, Johns Hopkins University Press, University Press of Kentucky, Maryland Historical Society, Univer-

Johns Hopkins University Press continued

sity of Massachusetts Press, University of New Orleans Press, University of Washington Press, and University of New Orleans Press.
The Press, in cooperation with participating publishers, manages Project MUSE© (*muse.jhu.edu*). Project MUSE provides electronic subscription access to full-text content from 670 periodicals and 50,000 books published by more than 260 not-for-profit scholarly publishers in the humanities and the social sciences.

Other digital publishing initiatives include electronic versions of *The Complete Prose of T. S. Eliot: The Critical Edition*; *The Early Republic*; *The Johns Hopkins Guide to Literary Theory and Criticism*; *The Papers of Dwight David Eisenhower*; the *Encyclopedia of American Studies*; and the *World Shakespeare Bibliography*

Journals: *African American Review; American Imago; American Jewish History; American Journal of Mathematics; American Journal of Philology; American Quarterly; Arethusa; Arizona Quarterly Book History; ariel, Bookbird; The Bulletin of the Center for Children's Books; The Bulletin of Historical Society; Bulletin of the History of Medicine; Callaloo; The CEA Critic; Children's Literature; Children's Literature Association Quarterly; Classical World; College Literature: Configurations; Dante Studies; diacritics; Dickens Quarterly; Eighteenth-Century Studies; Encyclopedia of American Studies; The Emily Dickinson Journal; ELH: English Literary History; Feminist Formations; German Studies Review; The Henry James Review; The Hopkins Review; Hispania; Human Rights Quarterly; Journal of Asian American Studies; Journal of College Student Development; Journal of Colonialism and Colonial History; Journal of Democracy; Journal of Early Christian Studies; Journal of Health Care for the Poor and Underserved; Journal of Late Antiquity Journal of Modern Greek Studies; Journal of the History of Childhood and Youth; Journal of the History of Philosophy; Journal of Women's History; Kennedy Institute of Ethics Journal; Late Imperial China; L'Esprit Créateur; Leviathan; Library Trends; The Lion and the Unicorn; Literature and Medicine; MLN; Modern Fiction Studies; Modernism/Modernity; Narrative Inquiry in Bioethics and Digital Philology; New Literary History; Partial Answers: Journal of Literature and the History of Ideas; Perspectives in Biology & Medicine; Philosophy and Literature; Philosophy, Psychiatry, and Psychology; Poe Studies; portal: Libraries and the Academy; Postmodern Culture; Reviews in American History; Progress In Community Health Partnerships: Research, Education, and Action; Reviews in Higher Education; SAIS Review; SEL: Studies in English Literature; Sewanee Review; Shakespeare Bulletin; Shakespeare Quarterly; South Central Review; Spiritus: A Journal of Christian Spirituality; Social Research; Studies in American Fiction; Studies in the Novel , Technology & Culture; Substance; Theatre Journal; Theatre Topics; Theory and Event; The Wallace Stevens Journal; Transactions of the American Philological Association; Twentieth-Century China; Victorian Periodical Review; Victorian Review; World Shakespeare Bibliography Online*

The Press also handles subscription fulfillment for Imagine, a publication of the Center for Talented Youth of The Johns Hopkins University, Penn State University Press, The Ohio State University Press, The University Press of Florida, Catholic University of America Press, and Georgetown University Press.

Special series, joint imprints, and/or copublishing programs: The Complete Poetry of Percy Bysshe Shelley; Documentary History of the First Federal Congress; Johns Hopkins: Poetry and Fiction; The Johns Hopkins Studies in the History of Technology; The Papers of Frederick Law Olmsted; The Papers of Thomas A. Edison; New Series in NASA History; Critical University Studies; Tech.EDU

University Press of Kansas

2502 Westbrooke Circle
Lawrence, KS 66045-4444

Phone: 785.864.4154
Fax: 785.864.4586
Email: upress@ku.edu
Indiv: (user I.D.)@ku.edu

Website and Social Media:
Website: www.kansaspress.ku.edu
Facebook: www.facebook.com/kansaspress
Blog: www.universitypressblog.dept.ku.edu/
Twitter: @Kansas_Press
You Tube: www.youtube.com/channel/UCaQrdXflKJRGp0Dr7S6E_cg
Instagram: www.instagram.com/kansas_press/

Warehouse Address:
2445 Westbrooke Circle
Lawrence, KS 66045-4440
Phone: 785.864.4156

Orders:
Phone: 785.864.4155
Email: upkorders@ku.edu

UK/European Representative:
Eurospan

Canadian Representative:
Scholarly Book Services

Staff
Interim Director: Conrad Roberts (785.864.9158; email: cerobert)
Administrative Assistant/Permissions Coordinator: Andrea Laws (785.864.9125; email: alaws09)
Editorial: Joyce Harrison, Editor-in-Chief (military history and intelligence studies (785.864.9162; email: joyce)
  Acquisitions Editors: David Congdon (political science, law, presidential studies, US political history, American political thought) (785-864-6059; email: dcongdon); Kim Hogeland (American Studies, environmental history, western history, Native American studies, regional studies) (785.864.9161; email: khogeland)
  Editorial Assistant (785.864.9185; email: upkacqasst@ku.edu)
Manuscript Editorial, Design and Production:
  Managing Editor: Kelly Chrisman Jacques (785.864.9186; email: kjchrism)
  Production Editor: Larisa Martin (785.864.9169; email: lmartin)
  Production Assistant: Colin Tripp (785.864.9123; email: ctripp)
Marketing: Michael Kehoe, Marketing and Sales Director (785.864.9165; email: mkehoe)
  Publicity Manager: Derek Helms (785.864.9170; email: dhelms)
  Direct Mail & Exhibits Manager: Debra Diehl (785.864.9166; email: ddiehl)
  Art Director & Webmaster: Karl Janssen (785.864.9164; email: kjanssen)
  Marketing Assistant: Suzanne Galle (785.864.9167; email: sgalle)
Business: Conrad Roberts, Interim Director and Business Manager (785.864.9158; email: ceroberts)
  Customer Service Coordinator: Katy Willson (785.864.9159; email: kwillson)

University Press of Kansas continued

Regular Member
Established: 1946
Title output 2016: 63
Titles currently in print: 1,731

Admitted to the Association: 1946
Title output 2017: 70

Editorial Program
American history; military and intelligence studies; western history; Native American studies; American government and public policy; presidential studies; constitutional and legal studies; environmental studies; American studies and popular culture; Kansas, the Great Plains, and the Midwest. The Press does not consider fiction, poetry, or festschriften for publication.
Special series, joint imprints, and/or copublishing programs: American Political Thought; American Presidential Elections; American Presidency; Constitutional Thinking; CultureAmerica; Environment and Society; Kansas Nature Guides; Landmark Law Cases and American Society; Modern First Ladies; Modern War Studies; Studies in Government and Public Policy; US Army War College Guides to Civil War Battles

The Kent State University Press

Street Address:
1118 University Library
1125 Risman Drive
Kent, OH 44242-0001

Mailing Address:
1118 University Library
PO Box 5190
Kent, OH 44242-0001

Phone: 330.672.7913
Fax: 330.672.3104
Email: (user I.D.)@kent.edu

Orders:
Phone: 419.281.1802
Fax: 419.281.6883

Website and Social Media:
Website: www.kentstateuniversitypress.com
Facebook: www.facebook.com/kentstateuniversitypress
Twitter: @KentStateUPress

UK/European Representative:
Eurospan

Canadian Representative:
Scholarly Book Services

Staff
Director: Susan Wadsworth-Booth (330.672.8009; email: swadswor2)
Acquisitions: Will Underwood, Acquiring Editor (330.672.8094; email: wunderwo)
Editorial: Mary D. Young, Managing Editor (330.672.8101; email: mdyoung)
Design and Production: Christine A. Brooks, Manager (330.672.8092; email: cbrooks)
Assistant Design and Production Manager: Darryl M. Crosby (330.672.8091; email: dcrosby)
Marketing: Susan L. Cash, Manager (330.672.8097; email: scash)

Regular Member

Established: 1965　　　　　　　　　　Admitted to the Association: 1970
Title output 2016: 33　　　　　　　　Title output 2017: 25
Titles currently in print: 740　　　　　Journals published: 2

Editorial Program
History: American Civil War era; true crime; sports; Ohio/Midwestern studies; fashion/costume; material culture. Literature: US (to ca. 1970); regional/Midwestern; British (Inklings). Regional literary nonfiction; poetry only through Wick Poetry Center; no fiction other than in Literature and Medicine series.
Journals: *Civil War History*; *Ohio History*
Special series: American Abolitionism and Antislavery; The Civil War Era in the South; Civil War in the North; Civil War Soldiers and Strategies; Classic Sports; Costume Society of America; Interpreting American History; Literature and Medicine; New Studies in US Foreign Relations; Reading Hemingway; Teaching Hemingway; Translation Studies; True Crime History; Wick Poetry Prize

The University Press of Kentucky

663 South Limestone Street
Lexington, KY 40508-4008

Phone: 859.257.8400
Fax: 859.257.7975
Email: (user I.D.)@uky.edu

Website and Social Media:
Website: www.kentuckypress.com
Blog: kentuckypress.wordpress.com
Facebook: www.facebook.com/
　KentuckyPress
Twitter: @KentuckyPress
YouTube: YouTube.com/univpressofky

Warehouse Address:
Maple Press Lebanon Distribution Center
704 Legionaire Drive
Fredericksburg, PA 17026

Orders:
c/o Hopkins Fulfillment Services
PO Box 50370
Baltimore, MD 21211
Phone: 800.537.5487 or 410.516.6956
Fax: 410.516.6998
Email: hfscustserv@ press.jhu.edu

UK/European Representative:
Eurospan

Canadian Representative:
Brunswick Books

Staff
Director: Leila W. Salisbury (859.257.8432; email: lsalisbury)
　Assistant to the Director: Tasha Ramsey (859.257.7919; email: tasha.ramsey)
Acquisitions Editors: Anne Dean Dotson (African American studies, American and southern history, American studies, Appalachian studies, film studies, general interest and scholarly books about Kentucky and the region, popular culture) (859.257.8434; email: adwatk0); Melissa Hammer (American history, Asian studies, foreign policy and diplomatic history, international studies, military history, political science, political theory, public policy) (859.257.8150; email: melissa.hammer); Patrick O'Dowd (agrarian studies, ecology and conservation, fiction and poetry, general interest and scholarly books about Kentucky and the region, nature and environmental history) (859.257.9492; email: patrick.odowd)
Managing Editor: David Cobb (859.257.4252; email: dlcobb2)

University Press of Kentucky continued

Senior Supervising Editor: Ila McEntire (859.257.8433; email: ila.mcentire)
   Project Editor: Sarah Olson (859.257.8435; email: saol222)
   Production and Fulfillment Manager: Teresa W. Collins (859.257.8404; email: teresa.collins)
   Production Manager: Pat Gonzales (859.257.4669; email: pagonz0)
Director of Marketing and Sales: Stephanie Williams (email: TBA)
   Publicity and Rights Manager: Mack McCormick (859.257.5200; email: permissions)
   Direct Promotions and Exhibits Manager: Katie Cross Gibson (859.257.2817; email: krcr222)
   Marketing Assistant: Jackie Wilson (859.257.6855; email: jacqueline.wilson)
Business Manager: TBA
Information Technology Manager: Tim Elam (859.257.8761; email: taelam2)
   Administrative Assistant: Robert Brandon (859.257.8400; email: rbrandon)

Regular Member
Established: 1943
Admitted to the Association: 1947
Title output 2016: 68
Title output 2017: 69
Titles currently in print: 1,886

Editorial Program
Scholarly books in the fields of American history; military history; film studies; international studies; folklore and material culture; popular culture; African American studies; Asian studies, serious nonfiction of general interest. Regionally, the Press maintains an interest in Kentucky and the Ohio Valley, Appalachia, and the upper South. Submissions of fiction and poetry are only accepted during an annual review period.
Special series: American Warriors; Asia in the New Millennium; Aviation & Air Power; Battles and Campaigns; Civil Rights and the Struggle for Black Equality in the Twentieth Century; Culture of the Land: A Series in the New Agrarianism; Essential Readers in Contemporary Media; Foreign Military Studies: Kentucky Remembered: An Oral History Series; Material Worlds; New Books for New Readers; New Directions in Southern History; The Ohio River Valley; Place Matters: New Directions in Appalachian and Regional Studies; Religion in the South; Screen Classics; Studies in Conflict, Diplomacy, and Peace; Thomas D. Clark Studies in Education, Public Policy, and Social Change; Topics in Kentucky History; University Press of Kentucky New Poetry & Prose Series; Understanding and Improving Health for Minority and Disadvantaged Populations; Virginia at War.

Leuven University Press/Universitaire Pers Leuven

Minderbroedersstraat 4 - bus 5602
B-3000 Leuven
Belgium

Phone: +32 16 32 53 45
Fax: +32 16 32 53 52
Email: info@lup.be
Indiv. (user I.D.)@lup.be

Website and Social Media:
Website: www.lup.be
Facebook: www.facebook.com/pages/
   Leuven-University-Press/130250583714129
Twitter: @LeuvenUP
LinkedIn: leuven-university-press

UK and European Orders:
NBN International

US Representative:
Cornell University Press
Sage House
512 East State Street
Ithaca, NY 14850
Phone: 607.277.2338
Email: cupressinfo@cornell.edu

US Orders:
Longleaf Services
customerservice@longleafservices.org

Staff
Director and Acquisitions Editorial: Veerle De Laet (+32.16.32.81.26; email: veerle.delaet)
Acquisitions Editorial: Mirjam Truwant (+32.16.32.31.27; email: mirjam.truwant)
Manuscript Editorial: Beatrice Van Eeghem (+32.16.32.53.40; email: beatrice.vaneeghem)
Production: Patricia di Costanzo (+32.16.32.53.53; email: patricia.dicostanzo)
Marketing: Annemie Vandezande (+32.16.32.53.51; email: annemie.vandezande)
Customer Service and Order Processing: Margreet Meijer (+32.16.32.53.50; email: margreet.meijer)

Regular Member
Established: 1971
Title output 2016: 43
Titles currently in print: 900

Admitted to the Association: 2005
Title output 2017: 41
Journals published: 6

Editorial Program
Scholarly publications with emphasis on music, art & theory, text & literature, history & archaeology, philosophy & religion, and society, law & economics

Journals: *DiGeSt. Journal of Diversity and Gender Studies*; *Humanistica Lovaniensia: Journal of Neo-Latin Studies*; *HEROM, Journal on Hellenistic and Roman Material Culture*; *Music Theory and Analysis*; *Nieuwe Tijdingen. Over vroegmoderne geschiedenis*; *Transdisicplinary Insights*

Special series: Ancient and Medieval Philosophy - Series 1: Ancient and Medieval Philosophy - Series 2: Henrici de Gandavo Opera Omnia; Ancient and Medieval Philosophy - Series 3: Francisci de Marchia Opera Philosophica et Theologica; Avisos de Flandes; CeMIS Migration and Intercultural Studies; Current Issues in Islam; Orpheus Institute Series; Dynamics of Religious Reform; Egyptian Prehistory Monographs; Historisch Denken; Figures de l'Inconscient; Figures of the Unconscious; ICAG Studies; Jean François Lyotard Writings on Contemporary Art and Artists; Kadoc-Artes; Kadoc-Studies on Religion, Culture and Society; Lieven Gevaert Series; Mediaevalia Lovaniensia-Series 1/Studia; Plutarchea Hypomne-

Leuven University Press continued

mata; Sagalassos; Society, Crime & Criminal Justice; Studia Paedagogica; Studies in Archaeological Sciences; Studies in European Comics and Graphic Novels; Studies in Musical Form; Supplementa Humanistica Lovaniensia

Liverpool University Press

4 Cambridge Street
Liverpool L69 7ZU, UK

US Orders:
Oxford University Press
Phone: 800.445.9714

Phone: +44 151.7942233
Email: lup@liv.ac.uk
Indiv: (user I.D.)@liv.ac.uk

UK Representative:
Turpin Distribution

Website and Social Media:
Website: www.liverpooluniversitypress.co.uk
Twitter: @LivUniPress

Staff
Managing Director: Anthony Cond (+44.151.7942237; email: a.cond)
Editorial Director: Alison Welsby (+44.151.7942231; email: a.welsby)
Head of Production: Patrick Brereton, (+44.151.7943133; email: p.brereton)
Head of Journals : Clare Hooper (+44.151.7943135; email: c.hooper)
Finance Director: Justine Greig (+44.151.7942232; email: j.greig)
Head of Sales: Jennie Collinson, (email: j.collinson)
Books Marketing Manager: Heather Gallagher (email: h.c.gallagher)

Regular Member
Established: 1899
Title output 2016: 85
Titles currently in print: 500

Admitted to the Association: 2013
Title output 2017: 100
Journals published: 28

Editorial Program
Scholarly books in ancient, medieval, Irish, slavery and labour history. The modern languages, notably French and Francophone and Hispanic and Lusophone Studies. Science Fiction criticism, contemporary poetry criticism and sculpture. Occasional Liverpool trade titles, building on the city's significance in global migration and popular culture.
Journals: *Australian Journal of French Studies; British Journal of Canadian Studies; Bulletin of Hispanic Studies; Byron Journal; Catalan Review; Comma, Contemporary French Civilization; Essays in Romanticism; European Journal of Language Policy; Extrapolation; Francosphères; Historical Studies in Industrial Relations; Hunter Gatherer Research International Development Planning Review; Journal of Literary and Cultural Disability Studies; Labour History Review; Modern Believing; Music, Sound, and the Moving Image; Québec Studies; Romani Studies; Science Fiction Film and Television; Sculpture Journal; Town Planning Review*
Special series: Contemporary French and Francophone Cultures; Contemporary Hispanic and Lusophone Cultures; Exeter Medieval Texts and Studies; Liverpool Science Fiction Texts

and Studies; Reappraisals in Irish History; Liverpool English Texts and Studies; Liverpool Studies in International Slavery; Migrations and Identities; Public Sculpture of Britain; Poetry &....; Postcolonialism Across the Disciplines; Studies in Labour History; Translated Texts for Historians

Louisiana State University Press

338 Johnston Hall
Louisiana State University
Baton Rouge, LA 70803

Phone: 225.578.6294
Email: (user I.D.)@lsu.edu

Website and Social Media:
Website: www.lsupress.org
Blog: blog.lsupress.org
Facebook: www.facebook.com/LSUPRESS
Twitter: @lsupress

Canadian Distributor:
Scholarly Book Services

Warehouse, Orders and Cust. Service:
Longleaf Services
116 S. Boundary St
Chapel Hill, NC 27514-3808

Phone: 800.848.6224
Fax: 800.272.6817
Email: customerservice@longleafservices.org

Staff
Director: MaryKatherine Callaway (225.578.6144; email: mkc)
Assistant to the Director, Subrights and Permissions: Erica Bossier (email: ebossie)
Acquisitions Editorial: Rand Dotson, Editor-in-Chief (southern history, southern roots music and Atlantic World history) (225.578.6412; email: pdotso1); Margaret Lovecraft (Louisiana and regional general interest, environmental studies, landscape architecture) (225.578.6319; email: lovecraft); James Long (literary studies, media studies, fiction, foodways) (225.578.6433; email: jlong12); Jennifer Keegan (fan studies, Caribbean history, contemporary social justice/civil rights issues in the South) (225.578.6453; email: jennifer-keegan)
Manuscript Editorial: Lee Sioles, Managing Editor (225.578.6467; email: lsioles)
   Senior Editor: Catherine Kadair (email: clkadair)
Design and Production: Laura Gleason, Associate Director and Production Manager (225.578.6469; email: lgleasn)
   Assistant Production Manager: Amanda Scallan (email: amandas)
Marketing: Erin Rolfs, Assistant Director and Marketing Manager (225.578.8282; email: erolfs)
   Publicist: M'Bilia Meekers (email: mmeekers)
   Digital Initiatives and Database Manager: Robert Keane (email: rkeane)
   Assistant Marketing Manager/Exhibits and Advertising Coordinator: Kate Barton (email: kbart04)
Financial Operations Manager: Rebekah Brown (225.578.6415; email: rbrown1)
Subsidiary Rights: McIntosh & Otis, Inc., 353 Lexington Ave., New York, NY 10016 (212.687.7400)
The Southern Review

Louisiana State University Press continued

Fiction and Nonfiction Editor: Emily Nemens (225.578.5159; email: enemens)
Prose Editor: Jessica Faust (225.578.0896; email: jfaust1)

Regular Member
Established: 1935
Title output 2016: 71
Titles currently in print: 2,128

Admitted to the Association: unknown
Title output 2017: 64

Editorial Program
Humanities and social sciences, with special emphasis on Southern history and literature; regional studies; environmental studies; poetry; Louisiana roots music, and foodways.
Special series, joint imprints and/or copublishing programs: Antislavery, Abolition, and the Atlantic World; Conflicting Worlds; Making the Modern South; Southern Biography; Southern Literary Studies; Southern Messenger Poets; Barataria Poetry; Yellow Shoe Fiction; Natural World of the Gulf South; Reading the American Landscape; The Southern Table; distribute books for Pleiades Press.

Manchester University Press

Oxford Road
Manchester, M13 9NR
United Kingdom
Telephone: +44 (0)161 275 2310
Email: mup@manchester.ac.uk

Website and Social Media:
Website: www.manchesteruniversitypress.co.uk
Blog: www.manchesteruniversitypress.co.uk/articles
Twitter: @ManchesterUP, @MUPJournals, @GothicMUP, @MedievalSources
Facebook: www.facebook.com/ManchesterUniversityPress
Instagram: www.instagram.com/manchester_university_press

Distribution
Worldwide (excluding The Americas)
NBN International

The Americas
Oxford University Press
Phone: 919.677.0977

UK Representative
Yale University Press

US Representative
Oxford University Press

European Representative
Andrew Durnell

Ireland
Robert Towers

Australia and New Zealand
Footprint Books Pty Ltd

Asian Representative
Publisher's International Marketing Ltd

The Middle East
Ward International (Book Export) Ltd

India
The White Partnership

Staff
Chief Executive: Simon Ross (email: sross@manchester.ac.uk)
Editorial Director and Senior Commissioning Editor: Emma Brennan (history, art history and design) (email: emma.brennan@manchester.ac.uk)
　Senior Commissioning Editor: Matthew Frost (literature, theatre and film) (email: matthew.j.frost@manchester.ac.uk)
　Senior Commissioning Editor: Tony Mason (politics and economics) (email: anthony.r.mason@manchester.ac.uk)
　Senior Commissioning Editor: Tom Dark (social sciences) (email: thomas.dark@manchester.ac.uk)
　Journals Manager/Senior Commissioning Editor: Meredith Carroll (archeology) (email: meredith.carroll@manchester.ac.uk)
　Contracts Coordinator: Deborah Smith (email: deborah.m.smith@manchester.ac.uk)
　Assistant Editors: Paul Clarke (email: paul.m.clarke@manchester.ac.uk); Robert Byron (email: robert.byron@manchester.ac.uk); Alun Richards (email: alun.richards@manchester.ac.uk)
Head of Sales: Shelly Turner (email: shelly.turner@manchester.ac.uk)
Head of Marketing: Chris Hart (email: chris.hart@manchester.ac.uk)
　Rights and Distribution Coordinator: Marilyn Cresswell (email: m.cresswell@manchester.ac.uk)
　Sales and Marketing Coordinator: Bethan Hirst (email: bethan.hirst@manchester.ac.uk)
　Sales and Marketing Executive: Rebecca Mortimer (email: rebecca.mortimer@manchester.ac.uk)
　Sales Assistant/Export Sales: Melanie Richards (email: melanie.richards@manchester.ac.uk)
Production and Operations Director: John Normansell (email: john.normansell@manchester.ac.uk)
　Production Editors: Danielle Shepherd (email: danielle.shepherd@manchester.ac.uk); Elizabeth Beck (email: elizabeth.beck@manchester.ac.uk)
　Production Manager: David Appleyard (email: david.appleyard@manchester.ac.uk)
　Managing Production Editor: Lianne Slavin (email: lianne.slavin@manchester.ac.uk)
Head of Finance: Sarah Roper (email: sarah.roper@manchester.ac.uk)
　Accounts Controller: Claudette Johnson (email: claudette.johnson@manchester.ac.uk)
　Publishing Support Assistant: Olivia Rye (email: olivia.rye@manchester.ac.uk)

Regular Member

Established: 1904	Admitted to the Association: 2013
Title output 2016: 170	Title output 2017: 179
Titles currently in print: 2,194	Journals published: 7

Editorial Program
History; art history; critical theory, cultural studies; literature and theatre; film and media; architecture; medieval studies; social science; international relations; philosophy, sociology; politics; economics
Journals: *Bulletin of the John Rylands Library; Film Studies; Gothic Studies; Human Remains and Violence: An Interdisciplinary Journal; James Baldwin Review; Journal of Humanitarian Affairs; Redescriptions*

The University of Manitoba Press

Street Address:
301 St. John's College
University of Manitoba
Winnipeg Manitoba R3T 2M5
Canada

Phone: 204.474.9495
Fax: 204.474.7556
Email: uofmpress@umanitoba.ca

Website and Social Media:
Website: uofmpress.ca
Blog: uofmpress.ca/blog
Facebook: www.facebook.com/UofMPress
Twitter: @umanitobapress

Canadian Orders:
University of Toronto Press
Phone: 800.565.9523
Email: utpbooks@utpress.utoronto.ca

US Orders:
Michigan State University Press
c/o Chicago Distribution Center
Phone: 800.621.2736

UK and European Orders:
Eurospan Group
Email: eurospan@turpin-distribution.com

Canadian Representative:
Ampersand and Company

Staff
Director and Editor: David Carr (204.474.9242; email: carr@cc.umanitoba.ca)
Managing Editor: Glenn Bergen (204.474.7338; email: D.Bergen@umanitoba.ca)
Acquisitions Editor: Jill McConkey (204.474.8840; email: jill.mcconkey@umanitoba.ca)
Marketing: David Larsen, Sales and Marketing Supervisor (204.474.9998; email: david.larsen@cc.umanitoba.ca)
Promotions and Publicity Coordinator: Ariel Gordon (204.474.8048; email: gordojd@cc.umanitoba.ca)

Regular Member
Established: 1967
Title output 2016: 14
Titles currently in print: 178

Admitted to the Association: 2011
Title output 2017: 14

Editorial Program
Native studies; Native history; Canadian history; the Arctic and the North; ethnic and immigration studies; Aboriginal languages; Canadian literary studies, especially Aboriginal literature; political studies; environmental studies; regional trade titles.
Special series: Contemporary Studies on the North; Critical Studies in Aboriginal History (formerly Manitoba Studies in Native History); First Voices, First Texts (Aboriginal literary reprints); Studies in Immigration and Culture: Human Rights and Social Justice; Publications of the Algonquian Text Society

Marine Corps University Press

111 South Street
Quantico, VA 22134

Phone: 703.432.4880
Email: MCU_Press@usmcu.edu

Orders:
MCU Press
Phone: 703.432.4880
Email: MCU_Press@usmcu.edu

Website and Social Media:
Website: www.usmcu.edu/mcupress
Facebook: MC UPress
Twitter: @MC_UPress

Staff
Senior Editor/E & D Branch Chief: Angela Anderson (703.432.4880; email: angela.anderson@usmcu.edu)
Managing Editors: Jason Gosnell (email: Jason.gosnell@usmcu.edu)
Editors: Stephani Miller (email: stephani.miller@usmcu.edu)
Acquisitions: Dr. Alexandra Kindell (email: alexandra.kindell@usmcu.edu)
Designers: Rob Kocher (email: robert.kocher@usmcu.edu); Young-hee Krouse (email: younghee.krouse@usmcu.edu)
Circulation Assistant: Jeff Moravetz (email: Jeffrey.moravetz@usmcu.edu)

Introductory Member
Established: 2008
Title output 2016: 5
Titles currently in print: 31

Admitted to the Association: 2015
Title output 2017: 6
Journals published: 1

Editorial Program
Marine Corps University Press (MCUP) recognizes the importance of an open dialogue between scholars, policy makers, analysts, and military leaders and of crossing civilian-military boundaries to advance knowledge and solve problems. To that end, MCUP launched the Marine Corps University Journal (*MCU Journal*) in 2010 to provide a forum for interdisciplinary discussion of national security and international relations issues and how they impact the Department of Defense, the Department of the Navy, and the U.S. Marine Corps directly and indirectly. Though the press focuses on military topics, it does not accept biographies or historical fiction.

Journal: *MCU Journal*

Marquette University Press

1415 West Wisconsin Avenue
Box 3141
Milwaukee, WI 53201-3141

Phone: 414.288.1564
Fax: 414.288.7813
Email: (user I.D.)@marquette.edu

Website and Social Media:
Website: marquette.edu/mupress
Facebook: www.facebook.com/MarquetteUPress
Twitter: @MarquetteUPress

UK/European Distributor:
Eurospan

Warehouse Address:
30 Amberwood Parkway
Ashland, OH 44805

Orders and Customer Service:
Phone: 800.247.6553; 419.281.1802
Fax: 419.281.6883

Canadian Representative:
Scholarly Book Services

Staff
Director: James South (414.288.1564; email: james.south)
Business, Marketing, Production: Maureen Kondrick (414.288.1564; email: maureen.kondrick)
Journals: James South
Journals Marketing: Pamela K. Swope (800.444.2419; email: pkswope@pdcnet.org)

Regular Member
Established: 1916
Title output 2016: 12
Titles currently in print: 455

Admitted to the Association 1998
Title output 2017: 7
Journals published: 1

Editorial Program
Philosophy; theology; history; urban studies; journalism; education; regional studies; and mediæval history.
Journal: *Philosophy & Theology*
Special series: Aquinas Lecture; Marquette Studies in Philosophy; Mediæval Philosophical Texts in Translation; Marquette Studies in Theology; Père Marquette Lecture; Reformation Texts with Translation: Biblical Studies, Women in the Reformation, Late Reformation; Klement Lecture (Civil War); Urban Studies Series; Diederich Studies in Media and Communication.

University of Massachusetts Press

East Experiment Station
671 North Pleasant Street
Amherst, MA 01003

Phone: 413.545.2217
Fax: 413.545.1226
Email: (user I.D.)@umpress.umass.edu
(unless otherwise indicated)

Website and Social Media:
Website: www.umass.edu/umpress
Facebook: www.facebook.com/umasspress
Twitter: @umasspress
Blog: umasspress.wordpress.com

Canadian Representative:
Scholarly Book Services

Boston Office:
Brian Halley
UMass Boston
100 Morrissey Boulevard
Boston, MA 02125

Orders:
c/o Hopkins Fulfillment Services
PO Box 50370
Baltimore, MD 21211
Phone: 800.537.5487
Fax: 410.516.6998
Email: hfscustserv@press.jhu.edu

UK/European Distributor:
Eurospan

Staff
Director: Mary Dougherty (413.545.4990; email: mvd)
Acquisitions Editorial: Matt Becker, Executive Editor (413.545.4989; email: mbecker)
Boston Editor: Brian Halley, Senior Editor (617.287.5610; email: brian.halley@umb.edu)
Editorial, Design, and Production: Sally Nichols, Manager (413.545.4997; email: snichols
Production Editor: Rachael DeShano (413.545.4998; email: rdeshano@umass.edu)
Business: Yvonne Crevier, Business Manager (413.545.4994; email: ycrevier)
Marketing: Courtney Andree, Marketing Manager (413.545.4987; email: cjandree)

Regular Member
Established: 1963
Title output 2016: 34
Titles currently in print: 1,000

Admitted to the Association: 1966
Title output 2017: 40

Editorial Program
Scholarly books and serious nonfiction, with special interests in African American studies; American history; American studies; biography; childhood and youth studies; disability studies; educational studies; environmental studies; gender and sexuality studies; history of the book; history of New England; journalism and media studies; literary and cultural studies; Native American studies; public history; science and technology studies; transnational studies; and urban studies.
Imprints: Bright Leaf: Books that Illuminate
Special series, joint imprints and/or copublishing programs: African American Intellectual History; American Popular Music; The Amherst Series in Law, Jurisprudence, and Social Thought; AWP Award Series in Short Fiction (Grace Paley Prize); Childhoods: Interdisciplinary Perspectives on Children and Youth; Culture and Politics in the Cold War and Beyond; Environmental History of the Northeast; Juniper Prizes (poetry and fiction); Library of American Landscape History (Designing the American Park); Massachusetts Studies in

University of Massachusetts Press continued

Early Modern Culture; Native Americans of the Northeast; Public History in Historical Perspective; Science/Technology/Culture; Studies in Print Culture and the History of the Book; Veterans

The MIT Press

1 Rogers Street
Cambridge, MA 02142-1315
Phone: 617.253.5646 (main)
Fax: 617.258.6779
Email: (user I.D.)@mit.edu

Journals:
Phone: 800.207.8354 (US/Can)
Phone: 617.253.2864 (main)
Fax: 617.258.6779
Email: journals-cs@mit.edu

Website and Social Media:
Website: mitpress.mit.edu
Blog: mitpress.mit.edu/blog
Facebook: www.facebook.com/mitpress
Twitter: @mitpress
YouTube: mitpress
Instagram: mitpress
Tumblr: mitpress

Book Orders/Customer Service:
Phone: 800.405.1619 (US/Can);
401.531.2800 (International)
Fax: 800.406.9145 (US/Can);
401.531.2801 (International)
Email: mitpress-orders@mit.edu

London Office:
The MIT Press, Ltd.
Suite 2, 1 Duchess Street
London, W1W 6AN, UK
United Kingdom
Phone: +44 (20) 7306 0603
Fax: +44 (20) 7306 0604
Email: info@mitpress.org.uk

Staff
Director: Amy Brand (617.253.4078; email: amybrand)
Assistant to the Director: Gayle Sherman (617.253.5255; email: gsherman)
Director of Finance and Operations: Brent Oberlin (617.253.5250; email: brento)
Director for Strategic Initiatives: Terry Ehling (617.258.0583; email: ehling)
Director of Technology: Bill Trippe (617.452.3747; email: trippe)
Director of Business Development: Bill Smith (617.253.0629; email: smithwmj)
Editorial Director: Gita Manaktala (information science, communications) (617.253.3172; email: manak)
 Editors: Matthew Browne (life sciences, neuropsychiatry, global health) (email: brownem); Susan Buckley (education) (617.253.0763; email: susanb); Beth Clevenger (environmental studies) (617.253.4113; email: eclev); Roger Conover (art, architecture, visual culture) (617.253.1677; email: conover); Victoria Hindley (art, architecture) (617.253.3842; email: vhindley); Katie Helke (science, technology & society) (617.253.0974; email: helkekat); Philip Laughlin (cognitive science, philosophy, bioethics, Bradford Books) (617.252.1636; email: laughlin); Marie Lee (computer science) (617.253.1588; email: marielee); Marc Lowenthal (linguistics, Boston Review, Semiotext(e), Zone Books) (617.258.0579; email:

lowentha); Jermey Matthews (physical sciences, mathematics, engineering) (617.715.2048; email: jnamatt); Robert Prior (life sciences, neuroscience, engineering) (617.253.1584; email: prior); Doug Sery (new media, game studies, design) (617.253.5187; email: dsery); Emily Taber (economics, business, finance) (617.253.1585; email: etaber)
Managing Editor: Michael Sims (617.253.2080; email: msims)
Design Manager: Yasuyo Iguchi (617.253.8034; email: iguchi)
Production Manager: Janet Rossi (617.253.2882; email: janett)
Marketing and Promotions: Katie Hope, Director of Marketing and Author Relations (617.258.0603; email: khope)
   Advertising and Digital Marketing Manager: Amanda Markell (617.253.3516; email: amarkell)
   Exhibits Manager: Kate Hensley (617.258.5764; email: khensley)
   Institutional Marketing Manager: Amy Harris (617.258.0595; email: aeharris)
   Publicity Manager: Colleen Lanick (617.253.2874; email: colleenl)
   Subsidiary Rights Manager: Pamela Quick (617.253.0080; email: quik)
   Textbook Manager: Michelle Pullano (617.253.3620; email: mpullano)
   Sales Manager: David Goldberg (617.253.8838; email: davidgol)
   International Sales and Marketing Manager: Jessica Lawrence-Hurt (617.258.0582; email: jclh)
Journals Director: Nick Lindsay (617.258.0594; email: nlindsay)
   Journals and Digital Products Customer Service Manager: Abbie Hiscox (617.452.3765; email: hiscox)
   Journals Editorial & Production Manager: Rachel Besen (617.258.0585; email: rbesen)
   Journals Subsidiary Rights Manager: Pamela Quick (617.253.0080; email: quik)
Warehouse: Robert O'Handley, Director of Operations (email: bob.ohandley@triliteral.org)
   Customer Service Manager: Cathy Morrone (800.405.1619; email: cathy.morrone@triliteral.org)

Regular Member

Established: 1961	Admitted to the Association: 1961
Title output 2016: 262	Title output 2017: 374
Titles currently in print: 5,342	Journals published: 36

Editorial Program

Architecture; artificial intelligence; bioethics; biology; business; cognitive sciences; communication; computer science; contemporary art; design; earth sciences; economics; education; engineering; environmental and urban studies; finance; game studies; information sciences; life sciences; linguistics; management; mathematics; natural history; new media studies; neuroscience; philosophy; physical sciences; performing arts; photography; political science; psychology; regional/MIT titles; science, technology, and society (STS); visual and cultural studies.

Co-publishing and distribution programs: Afterall Books; Alphabet City; Boston Review Books; Goldsmiths Press; MITxPress; Perspecta; SA+P Press; Semiotext(e); Strange Attractor Press; Whitechapel Documents of Contemporary Art; Zone Books

Journals: *African Arts; American Journal of Health Economics; Artificial Life; ARTMargins; Asian Development Review; Asian Economic Papers; Computational Linguistics; Computational Psychiatry; Computer Music Journal; Daedalus; Design Issues; Education Finance and Policy; Evolutionary Computation; Global Environmental Politics; Grey Room; Innovations; Interna-*

MIT Press continued

tional Security; JoDS: Journal of Design and Science; Journal of Cognitive Neuroscience; Journal of Cold War Studies; The Journal of Interdisciplinary History; Leonardo; Leonardo Music Journal; Linguistic Inquiry; Nautilus; Network Neuroscience; Neural Computation; The New England Quarterly; October; Open Mind: Discoveries in Cognitive Science; PAJ: A Journal of Performance and Art; Perspectives on Science; Presence: The Review of Economics and Statistics; TDR: The Drama Review; Thresholds

Special series: Acting with Technology; Adaptive Computation and Machine Learning; Afterall: One Work; Alvin Hansen Symposium Series on Public Policy; American Academy Studies in Global Security; American and Comparative Environmental Policy; Annotating Art's Histories; Arne Ryde Memorial Lectures; Basic Bioethics; BCSIA Studies in International Security; Boston Review Books; Bradford Books; Cairoli Lectures; Cellular and Molecular Neuroscience; Centre for European Policy Studies (CEPS); CESifo Book; CESifo Seminar; Cognitive Neuroscience; Computational Molecular Biology; Computational Neuroscience; Cooperative Information Systems; Current Studies in Linguistics; Dahlem Workshop Reports; Design Thinking, Design Theory Developmental Cognitive Neuroscience; Dibner Institute Studies in the History of Science and Technology; Digital Communication; Digital Libraries & Electronic Publishing; Documentary Sources in Contemporary Art; Documents Books; Documents of Contemporary Art; Earth System Governance; Economic Learning and Social Evolution; Electronic Culture; Engineering Studies; Engineering Systems; Essential Knowledge; Food, Health, and the Environment; Gaston Eyskens Lectures; George Santayana: Definitive Works; Global Environmental Accord: Strategies for Sustainability and Institutional Innovation; History and Foundation of Information Science; History of Computing; Information Revolution and Global Politics; Information Policy; Infrastructures; Inside Technology; Intelligent Robotics and Autonomous Agents; International Security Readers; Issues in Clinical and Cognitive Neuropsychology; Issues in the Biology of Language & Cognition; Jean Nicod Series; John D. & Catherine T. MacArthur Foundation Series on Digital Media and Learning; Lemelson Center Studies in Invention and Innovation; Leonardo Books; Life and Mind; Linguistic Inquiry Monographs; Lionel Robbins Lectures; Munich Lectures; Neural Information Processing; October Books; October Files; Ohlin Lectures; Perspecta: The Yale Architecture Journal; Philosophical Psychopathology: Disorders in Mind; Platform Studies; Playful Thinking; Politics, Science, and the Environment; Representation and Mind; Scientific and Engineering Computation; Semiotext(e); Short Circuits; Simplicity: Design, Technology, Business, Life; Social Neuroscience; Software Studies; Special Issues of Physica D; Structural Mechanics; Strüngmann Forum Reports; Studies in Contemporary German Social Thought; Studies in Neuropsychology & Neurolinguistics; Sustainable Metropolitan Communities Books; Tax Policy and the Economy; Technologies of Lived Abstraction; Topics in Contemporary Philosophy; Transformations: Studies in the History of Science and Technology; Urban and Industrial Environments; Vienna Series in Theoretical Biology; Walras-Pareto Lectures; Wicksell Lectures; Work Books; Writing Architecture; Writing Art; Yrjo Jahnsson Lectures Series; Zeuthen Lecture Series
Idea Commons: ARTECA; MIT CogNet

McGill-Queen's University Press

Montreal Office:
1010 Sherbrooke Street West
Suite 1720
Montreal, QC H3A 2R7
Canada

Phone: 514.398.3750
Fax: 514.398.4333
Email: mqup@mcgill.ca
Indiv: (user I.D.)@mcgill.ca

Kingston Office:
Douglas Library Building
93 University Avenue
Kingston, ON K7L 5C4
Canada

Phone: 613.533.2155
Email: mqup@queensu.ca

Website and Social Media:
Website: www.mqup.ca/
Blog: www.mqup.ca/blog/
Facebook: www.facebook.com/McGillQueensUP
Twitter: @McGillQueensUP
YouTube: www.youtube.com/user/McGillQueens
Tumblr: mqup.tumblr.com/

Canadian Distributor:
Georgetown Terminal Warehouses
34 Armstrong Avenue
Georgetown, ON L7G 4R9
Canada
Phone: 877.864.8477
Fax: 877.864.4272
Email: orders@gtwcanada.com

US Distributor:
Chicago Distribution Center
11030 South Langley Avenue
Chicago, IL 60628
USA
Phone: 800.621.2736
Fax: 800.621.8476
Email: orders@press.uchicago.edu

UK/European Distributor:
Marston Book Services Ltd

Staff
Executive Director: Philip J. Cercone (Montreal, 514.398.3750; email: philip.cercone)
Finance and Business Manager: Regan Toews (514.398.5336; email: regan.toews)
Rights and Special Projects Manager: Natalie Blachere (514.398.2121; email: natalie.blachere)
Information Systems Administrator: Alex Stoica (514.398.4419; email: alex.stoica)
Publishing Administrator: Paloma Friedman (514.398.2911; email: paloma.friedman)
Accounts Payable: Carmie Vacca (514.398.5792; email: carmie.vacca)
   Accounting Clerk (Receivables): Tricia Henry (514.398.1825; email: tricia.henry)
Editor-in-Chief: Jonathan Crago (514.398.7480; email: jonathan.crago)
   Senior Editor: Kyla Madden (514.398.2056; email: kyla.madden)
   Editors: Mark Abley (514.398.6652; email: mark.abley); Jacqueline Mason (514.398.2250; email: jacqueline.mason); Khadija Coxon (613.533.2155; email: khadija.coxon@queensu.ca); Richard Ratzlaff (647.580.9333; email: richard.ratzlaff@queensu.ca); Richard Baggaley

McGill-Queen's University Press continued

(+44.1295.720025; richard.baggaley.mqup@mcgill.ca)
Editorial Assistants: Joanne Pisano (514.398.1823; email: joanne.pisano); Finn Purcell (514.398.3279; email: finn.purcell)
Managing Editor: Ryan Van Huijstee (514.398.3922; email: ryan.vanhuijstee)
Assistant Managing Editor: Kathleen Fraser (514.398.2068; email: kathleen.c.fraser)
Production Manager: Elena Goranescu (514.398.7395; email: elena.goranescu)
Assistant Production Manager: Rob Mackie (514.398.1342; email: robert.mackie)
Production Assistant: Andrew Pinchefsky (514.398.6996; email: andrew.pinchefsky)
Marketing Director and Associate Director: Susan McIntosh (514.398.6306; email: susan.mcintosh)
Sales Manager: Jack Hannan (514.398.5165; email: jack.hannan)
Educational Sales Administrator: Roy Ward (514.398.7177; email: roy.ward)
Direct Mail & Exhibits Coordinator: Filomena Falocco (514.398.2912; email: filomena.falocco)
Online Marketing and Data Manager: Shannon Wood (514.398.6166; email: shannon.wood)
Marketing Assistant: Jennifer Roberts (514.398.2914; email: marketing.mqup)
Publicist: Jacqueline Davis (514.398.2555; email: jacqueline.davis)

Regular Member
Established: 1969 as a joint press
Admitted to the Association: 1963 (as McGill University Press)
Title output 2016: 136   Title output 2017: 142
Titles currently in print: c. 3,180

Editorial Program
Scholarly books and well-researched studies of general interest in the humanities and social sciences, including anthropology, especially North American native peoples; architecture; Arctic and northern studies; art history; biography; Canadian studies; Canadian literature; classics; communication and media studies; cultural studies; demography; economics; education; environmental studies; ethnic studies; European studies; film studies; folklore and material culture; gender studies; geography; health and society; history; history of medicine; history of science; Irish and Gaelic studies; law; linguistics; literary criticism; medieval and renaissance studies; military studies; music history and theory; native studies; philosophy; poetry; photography; political economy; political science; public administration; public affairs; public health; Quebec studies; religious studies; Slavic and Eastern European studies; sociology; theatre; urban studies; and women's studies.
Special series: Advancing Studies in Religion; Art of the State; Arts Insights; Canada Among Nations; Canada: The State of the Federation; Canadian Association of Geographers Series in Canadian Geography; Canadian Public Administration; Carleton Library; Central Problems of Philosophy; Central Works of Philosophy; Centre for Editing Early Canadian Texts; CHORA: Intervals in the Philosophy of Architecture Comparative Charting of Social Change; Continental European Philosophy; Critical Perspectives on Public Affairs; Culture of Cities; Democracy, Diversity, and Citizen Engagement; Fields of Governance: Policy-Making in Canadian Municipalities; Fontanus Monograph; Footprints; Foreign Policy, Security, and Strategic Studies; Fundamentals of Philosophy; Global Dialogue on Federalism; Global

Dialogue on Federalism Booklet; Governance and Public Management; Harbinger Poetry; How Ottawa Spends; Hugh MacLennan Poetry; Human Dimensions in Foreign Policy, Military Studies, and Security Studies; Innovation, Science, Environment; International Social Survey Programme; Library of Political Leadership; McGill-Queen's French Atlantic Worlds Series; McGill-Queen's Native and Northern; McGill-Queen's Studies in Ethnic History; McGill-Queen's Studies in Gender, Sexuality, and Social Justice in the Global South; McGill-Queen's Studies in the History of Ideas; McGill-Queen's Studies in the History of Religion; McGill-Queen's/Associated Medical Services Studies in the History of Medicine, Health, and Society; McGill-Queen's/Beaverbrook Canadian Foundation Studies in Art History; McGill-Queen's Rural, Wildland, Resource Studies; McGill-Queen's Studies in Urban Governance; Migration and Diversity: Comparative Issues and International Comparisons; Nordic Voices; Philosophy Now; Philosophy and Science; Public Policy; Queen's Policy Studies; Rethinking Canada in the World; Rupert's Land Record Society; Social Union; Studies in Christianity and Judaism; Studies in Nationalism and Ethnic Conflict; Studies on the History of Quebec/Études d'histoire du Québec; Thematic Issues in Federalism; Understanding Movements in Modern Thought; War and European Society, Women's Experience.

Medieval Institute Publications

Street Address:
100 E Walwood Hall
Western Michigan University
Kalamazoo, MI 49008-5432, USA
Phone: 269.387.8754
Fax: 269.387.8750

Mailing Address:
Western Michigan University
1903 W. Michigan Ave.
Kalamazoo, MI 49008-5432, USA

Website and Social Media:
Website: arc-humanities.org/
WMU website: wmich.edu/
    medievalpublications
Blog: arc-humanities.org/blog/
Twitter: @ArcMedieval_MIP
YouTube: www.youtube.com/channel/UC93THfM-dMmZAi8ljvCuldw

North American Distributor:
ISD
70 Enterprise Drive, Suite 2
Bristol, CT 06010, USA

For Rest of the World:
NBN International
10 Thornbury Rd
Plymouth PL6 7PP, United Kingdom

Staff
Director and Editor-in-Chief: Simon Forde (email: simon.forde@arc-humanities.org)
Managing Editor: Theresa M. Whitaker (email: theresa.m.whitaker@wmich.edu)
Production Editor: Thomas P. Krol (email: thomas.p.krol@wmich.edu)
Finance and Assistant Managing Editor: Marjorie Harrington (email: mdvl_pub_office@wmich.edu)

Medieval Institute Publications continued

Regular Member
Established: 1978

Admitted to the Association: 2011
(Intro. Member)
Admitted to the Association: 2015
(Assoc. Member)

Title output 2016: 20
Titles currently in print: 230

Title output 2017: 27
Journals published: 3

Editorial Program
Publications in archeology, art history, dance, drama, history, literature, music, philosophy, and theology of the European Middle Ages and early modern period, with very occasional publications on the history of science and technology.
Special series: MIP imprint: Research in Medieval and Early Modern Culture; Studies in Medieval and Early Modern Culture; Early Drama, Art, and Music; Publications of the Richard Rawlinson Center; Studies in Iconography: Themes and Variations; Festschriften, Occasional Papers, and Lectures; TEAMS Publications; History and Cultures of Food, 1300-1800; Late Tudor and Stuart Drama; The Northern Medieval World; Ludic Cultures, 1100-1700
Arc imprint: The Medieval Globe; Black Sea World; CARMEN Studies and Monographs; Medieval Islamicate World; Monasticism and Spirituality, East and West; Beyond Medieval Europe; Collection Development, Cultural Heritage and Digital Humanities; Connected Histories in the Early Modern World; Cross-Cultural Engagements; Medieval Media Culture; Past Imperfect; Arc Impact; Reference Works
Journals: *Medieval Prosopography; Studies in Iconography; The Medieval Globe*
Joint Imprint: Arc Humanities Press

Mercer University Press

1501 Mercer University Drive
Macon, GA 31207

Orders:
Phone: 866.895.1472
Email: mupressorders@mercer.edu

Phone: 478.301.2880
Fax: 478.301.2585
Email: (user I.D.)@mercer.edu

Website and Social Media:
Website: www.mupress.org
Blog: merceruniversitypress.wordpress.com/
Facebook: www.facebook.com/MercerUniversityPress
Twitter: @mupress

Staff
Director and Acquisitions: Marc A. Jolley (email: jolley_ma)
Production: Marsha Luttrell, Publishing Assistant (email: luttrell_mm)
Marketing: Mary Beth Kosowski, Director of Marketing and Sales (email: kosowski_mb)
Business: Regenia (Jenny) Toole, Business Office (email: toole_rw)

Customer Service: Heather Comer (email: Comer_hm)

Regular Member
Established: 1979
Title output 2016: 33
Titles currently in print: 485+

Admitted to the Association: 2000
Title output 2017: 33

Editorial Program
Regional trade titles and serious works of nonfiction in history, particularly in the history of the United States (with an emphasis on the American South), the history of religion, and the history of literature; Southern regional studies; literature and literary criticism; Southern literary fiction; poetry; African American studies; political science; natural history.
Special series: Baptists; Civil War Georgia; the International Kierkegaard Commentary; Mercer Classics in Biblical Studies; the Mercer Commentary on the Bible; the Melungeons; Mercer Paul Tillich Series; Mercer Flannery O'Connor Series; Music and the American South; Sports and Religion; Voices of the African Diaspora.
Book Awards: The Ferrol Sams Award for Fiction; The Adrienne Bond Award for Poetry; The Will D. Campbell Award for Creative Nonfiction

University of Michigan Press

839 Greene Street
Ann Arbor, MI 48104-3209

Phone: 734.764.4388
Fax: 734.615.1540
Email: um.press@umich.edu
Indiv: (user I.D.)@umich.edu

Orders:
University of Michigan Press
c/o Chicago Distribution Center
11030 S. Langley Avenue
Chicago, IL 60628
Phone: 800.621.2736, 773.702.7000
Fax: 800.621.8476, 773.702.7212

Website and Social Media:
Website: www.press.umich.edu
Blog: blog.press.umich.edu
Facebook: www.facebook.com/pages/University-of-Michigan-Press/37383103953
Twitter: @UofMPress
YouTube: youtube.com/umichpress

UK and European Representative:
Eurospan

Staff
Director: Charles Watkinson (734.936.0452; email: watkinc)
Director of Strategic Initiatives and Partnerships: Rebecca Welzenbach (734.615.0038; email: rwelzenbach)
Senior Administrative Assistant: Chris Butchart-Bailey (734.763.7751; email: chrisbu)
Acquisitions Editorial:
Editorial Director: Mary Francis (music, media studies, digital scholarship,digitalculturebooks.org) (734.763.4134; email: mfranci)
  Editors: Ellen Bauerle (classical studies, medieval studies, African studies) (734.615.6479; email: bauerle); LeAnn Fields (theater and performance studies, American studies)

University of Michigan Press continued

(734.647.2463; email: lfields); Elizabeth Demers (political science, international studies) (734.763.6419; email: esdemers); Scott Ham (regional) (734.764.4387; email: scottom); Christopher Dreyer (Asian studies, German studies) (734.647.2463; email: mikage)
Editorial Associates: Susan Cronin (734.936.2841; email: sjcronin); Danielle Coty (734.763.4134; email: dcoty); Sarah Dougherty (734.763.1664; email: sarahdoe)
English as a Second Language: Kelly Sippell, ELT Manager and Executive Acquisitions Editor (734.764.4447; email: ksippell)
Assistant Marketing Manager: Jason Contrucci (734.936.0459; email: contrucc)

Publishing Production:
Director of Publishing Production: Jillian Downey (734.615.8114; email: jilliand)
  Managing Editor: Marcia LaBrenz (734.647.4480; email: mlabrenz)
  Production Editors: Mary Hashman (734.936.0461; email: mhashman); Kevin Rennells (734.763.1526; email: rennells)
  Senior Designer: Paula Newcomb (734.763.6417; email: newcombp)
  Designer: Heidi Dailey (734.764.4128; email: hdailey)
  Reprints Coordinator: Rosemary Lacy (734.763.0170; email: rabush)

Publishing Services:
Director of Publishing Services: Jason Colman (734.647.6017; email: taftman)
  Senior Digital Production Coordinator: Patrick Goussy (email: pgoussy)
  Production Coordinators: Jaclyn Sipovic (email: sipovicj); Lauren Stachew (email: lstachew); Amanda Karby (email: akarby)

Marketing and Sales:
Director of Sales, Marketing, and Outreach: Renee Tambeau (734.936.0388; email: rtambeau)
  Publication Sales Manager: Shaun Manning (734.763.0163; email: shaunman)
  Publicity and Promotions Coordinator: Sam Killian (734.763.0163; email: killians)
  Intellectual Property Coordinator: Bryan Birchmeier (734.764.4330; email: bryanbir)

Publishing Technology Group:
Publishing Technology Group Director: Jeremy Morse (734.615.5739; email: jgmorse)
  Project Manager: Melissa Baker-Young (734.764.6802; email: mbakeryo)
  Front End Developer & UI Designer: Jonathan McGlone (734.763.4260; email: jmcglone)
Systems Administrator: James Vanderwill (734.936.3636; email: jvanderw)
Business: Gabriela Beres, Business Manager (734.936.2227; email: gsberes)
  Accountant: Jeanne Wren (734.763.0146; email: jawren)
  Accounts Payable: Linda Rowley (734.647.9083; email: lrowley)

Regular Member

Established: 1930   Admitted to the Association: 1963
Title output 2016: 106   Title output 2017: 104
Titles currently in print: 5,512

Editorial Program

Scholarly and trade works in political science; performing arts (theater, performance studies, music, media studies); classics; American Studies (disability studies, gender studies, race and ethnicity, class studies); Michigan and Great Lakes; African studies; Asian studies; German studies; English language teaching textbooks.

The Press distributes works for Michigan's Center for Chinese Studies, Center for Japanese Studies, the Center for South and Southeast Asian Studies; the American Academy in Rome, and the American Society of Papyrologists.

Special series: African Perspectives; Analytical Perspectives on Politics; The CAWP Series in Gender and American Politics;; Class: Culture; Contemporary Political and Social Issues; Configurations: Critical Studies of World Politics; Corporealities: Discourses of Disability; Critical Performances; Digital Rhetoric Collaborative; Great Lakes Environment; International Series on the Research of Learning and Instruction of Writing; Jazz Perspectives; Kelsey Museum Studies; Landmark Video Games; Law and Society in the Ancient World; Law, Meaning, and Violence; Legislative Politics and Policy Making; The Memoirs of the American Academy in Rome; Michigan Classical Commentaries; Michigan Modern Dramatists; Michigan Papyri; Michigan Series in English for Academic and Professional Purposes; The Michigan Series on Teaching Multilingual Writers; Michigan Studies in International Political Economy; Michigan Studies in Political Analysis; New Comparative Politics; The New Media World; The Papers and Monographs of the American Academy in Rome; Perspectives on Contemporary Korea; Poets on Poetry; The Politics of Race and Ethnicity; Social History, Popular Culture, and Politics in Germany; Societas: Historical Studies in Classical Culture; Theater: Theory/Text/Performance; Thomas Spencer Jerome Lectures; Tracking Pop; Triangulations: Lesbian/Gay/Queer/Theater/Drama/Performance

Michigan State University Press

1405 South Harrison Road, Suite 25
East Lansing, MI 48823-5245

Phone: 517.355.9543
Director's Office Fax: 517.353.6766
Email: msupress@msu.edu
Indiv: (user I.D.)@msu.edu

Orders:
Chicago Distribution Center
11030 S. Langley Ave.
Chicago, IL 60628
Phone: 800.621.2736; (Int'l) 773.702.7000
Fax: 800.621.8476; (Int'l) 773.702.7212

Website and Social Media:
Website: msupress.org
Facebook: facebook.com/MSUPress
Twitter: @msupress

Staff

Director: Gabriel Dotto (European history; cultural history/humanities; urban studies, transportation history & architectural history) (517.884.6900; email: dotto)
Editor-in-Chief/Assistant Director: Julie L. Loehr (Great Lakes studies and regional history; environmental and natural sciences; agricultural sciences; ethnohistory) (517.884.6905; email: loehr)
Senior Acquisitions Editor: J. Alex Schwartz (US history; sociology; criminology; political science; African studies and African fiction) (517.884.6906; email: as)
Acquisitions Assistant: Terika Hernandez (517.884.6001; email: herna376)
Coordinating Editor, College of Arts & Letters projects: Kurt Milberger (517.884.7907; email: milberg2)
Managing Editor: Kristine Blakeslee (517.884.6912; email: blakes17)
Digital Production Specialist: Annette Tanner (517.884.6910; email: tanneran)

Michigan State University Press continued

Project Editor: Anastasia Wraight (517.884.6911; email: wraighta)
Marketing & Sales Manager: Julie Reaume (517.884.6920; email: reaumej)
  Promotions Editor: Elise Jajuga (517.884.6918; email: jajugael)
  Website Coordinator: Dawn Martin (517.884.6919; email: marti778)
Journals Production Editor: Natalie Eidenier (517.884.6915; email: eidenie1)
Finance/Business Officer: Julie Wrzesinski (517.884.6922; email: wrzesin2)
  Logistics: Brett Robinson (517.884.6909; email: whpress)
Information Systems: Jesse Howard (517.884.6908; email: howard10)

Regular Member
Established: 1947   Admitted to the Association: 1992
                                            (Previous membership, 1951-1972)
Title output 2016: 35   Title output 2017: 44
Titles currently in print: 714   Journals published: 10

Editorial Program
Scholarly books and general nonfiction with areas of special interest in African studies; African American studies; anthropology, Agricultural Science; American studies; American Indian studies; Armenian studies; environmental science and natural history; Great Lakes studies; history; immigration studies; Latino/a studies; politics and the global economy; mimetic theory; sociology; US history; urban studies; women's studies.

The Press distributes publications for Ecovision; University of Manitoba Press; the Michigan State University Museum; Ruth Mott Foundation.

Journals: *Contagion: Journal of Violence, Mimesis, and Culture; CR: The New Centennial Review; Fourth Genre: Explorations In Nonfiction; French Colonial History; Journal for the Study of Radicalism; Journal of West African History; Northeast African Studies; QED: A Journal in GLBTQ Worldmaking; Real Analysis Exchange; Rhetoric & Public Affairs*

Special series: African History and Culture Series; African Humanities and the Arts Series; Algonquian Series; American Food In History Series; American Indian Studies Series (related imprint: Makwa Enewed); The Animal Turn Series; Arab Literature and Language Series; Armenian Series; Breakthroughs in Mimetic Theory Series; Environmental Research Series; Discovering the Peoples of Michigan Series; International Race and Education Series; Latinos in the United States Series; Rhetoric and Public Affairs Series; Rhetorical History of the United States Series; Ruth Simms Hamilton African Diaspora Series; Studies in Violence, Mimesis, and Culture Series; Transformations in Higher Education: The Scholarship of Engagement Series

Minnesota Historical Society Press

345 Kellogg Blvd. West
Saint Paul, MN 55102

Phone: 651.259.3200
Fax: 651.297.1345
Email: (user I.D.)@mnhs.org

Orders:
Ingram Publisher Services
www.ingramcontent.com
One Ingram Boulevard
La Vergne, TN 37086
Phone: 615.793.5000

Website and Social Media:
Websites: www.mnhspress.org; www.mnopedia.org
www.mnhs.org/market/mhspress/minnesotahistory/
E-Marketing: edelweiss.abovethetreeline.com/HomePage.aspx?pubOrgID=MINN
Blog: discussions.mnhs.org/10000books/
Facebook: www.facebook.com/Minnesota-Historical-Society-Press-44328618980/
Twitter: @mnhspress, @mnopedia

UK/European Distributor:
Lightning Source International

Canadian Distributor:
Scholarly Book Service

Staff
Acting Director: Josh Leventhal (651.259.3218; email: josh.leventhal)
Acquisitions: Josh Leventhal, Ann Regan, Shannon Pennefeather
Editor-in-Chief, Rights and Permissions: Ann Regan (651.259.3206; email: ann.regan)
Managing Editor: Shannon Pennefeather (651.259.3212; email: shannon.pennefeather)
Design and Production: Dan Leary (651.259.3209; email: daniel.leary)
Digital Production: Robin Moir (651.259.3211; email: robin.moir)
Sales and Marketing Director: Mary Poggione (651.259.3204;
    email: mary.poggione)
    Publicity and Promotions: Alison Aten (651.259.3203;
    email: alison.aten)
Sales Manager: Serenity Shanklin (651.259.3202; email: serenity.shanklin)
Journals: Laura Weber (651.259.3207; email: laura.weber)
MNopedia (online Minnesota encyclopedia) Editor: Linda Cameron (651.259.3216; email:
    linda.cameron)

Affiliate Member
Established: 1851
Title output 2016: 16
Titles currently in print: 500+

Admitted to the Association: 2001
Title output 2017: 16
Journals published: 1

Editorial Program
The Minnesota Historical Society Press is a leading publisher of the history and culture of Minnesota and the Upper Midwest. The Press advances research, supports education, serves the local community, and expands the reputation of the Minnesota Historical Society through the publication of books and digital works, the Minnesota History journal, and the free, digital encyclopedia, *MNopedia*.

Minnesota Historical Society Press continued

Journal: *Minnesota History*
Digital: *MNopedia, an Encyclopedia of Minnesota; Minnesota History* app (iPad and Android tablets)
Special series: Minnesota Byways; Native Voices; People of Minnesota; the Northern Plate
Imprints: MNHS Press; Borealis Books

University of Minnesota Press

111 Third Avenue South
Suite 290
Minneapolis, MN 55401-2552

Phone: 612.301.1990
Fax: 612.301.1980
Email: (user I.D.)@umn.edu

Orders:
University of Minnesota Press
Chicago Distribution Center
11030 South Langley Avenue
Chicago, IL 60628
Phone: 800.621.2736; 773.568.1550
Fax: 800.621.8476; 773.660.2235

Website and Social Media:
Website: www.upress.umn.edu
Blog: www.uminnpressblog.com
Facebook: www.facebook.com/pages/Minneapolis-MN/University-of-Minnesota-Press/40070783448
Twitter: @UMinnPress
YouTube: www.youtube.com/user/UMinnPress
Tumblr: uminnpress.tumblr.com

UK Distributor:	UK Representative:
NBN Plymbridge	Combined Academic Publishers

Staff
Director: Douglas Armato (612.301.1989; email: armat001)
  Associate Director and Test Division Manager: Beverly Kaemmer (612.301.1956; email: kaemm002)
  Rights and Permissions: Jeff Moen (612.301.1995; email: moenx017)
  Outreach and Development: Molly Fuller (612.301.1991; email: fulle154)
Acquisitions Editorial: Jason Weidemann, Editorial Director (geography, sociology, anthropology) (612.301.1992; email: weide007)
  Senior Editors: Pieter Martin (architecture, art and visual studies, political science, urban studies) (612.301.1993; email: marti190); Danielle Kasprzak (literary and cultural studies, cinema, media) (612.301.0122; email: kasp0079); Erik Anderson (regional, Scandinavian studies) (612.301.1996; email: and00900)
Managing Editor: Laura Westlund (612.301.1985; email: westl003)
  Assistant Managing Editor: Michael Stoffel (612.301.1994; email: stoff004)
Design and Production: Daniel Ochsner, Manager (612.301.1981; email: ochsn013)
  Assistant Design and Production Manager: Rachel Moeller (612.301.1984; email: moel0067)

Manifold Digital Projects Editor: Terence Smyre (612.301.0073; email: smyre)
Marketing: Emily Hamilton, Assistant Director of the Book Division (612.301.1936; email: eph)
Sales Manager: Matt Smiley (612.301.1931; email: mwsmiley)
Publicist: Heather Skinner (612.301.1932; email: skinn077)
Direct Mail and Web Marketing Manager: Maggie Sattler (612.301.1934; email: sattl014)
Business: Susan Doerr, Assistant Director, Digital Publishing and Operations (612.301.1987; email: doer0012)
Journals: Susan Doerr, Business; Jason Weidemann, Acquisitions
IT Systems: John Henderson (612.301.1955; email: hende291)

Regular Member

Established: 1925
Title output 2016: 110
Titles currently in print: 3,438

Admitted to the Association: 1937
Title output 2017: 119
Journals published: 10

Editorial Program
Literary and cultural studies; social and political theory; cinema and media studies; art and visual studies; digital culture; feminist studies; gay and lesbian studies; anthropology; architecture; geography; international relations; Native American studies; personality assessment, clinical psychology and psychiatry; philosophy; and Upper Midwest studies.

Journals: *Buildings & Landscapes; Critical Ethnic Studies; Cultural Critique; Future Anterior; Journal of American Indian Education; Mechademia; The Moving Image; Native and Indigenous Studies Journal; Verge; Wicazo Sa Review*

Special series, joint imprints, and/or copublishing programs: Borderlines; Contradictions; Critical American Studies; Cultural Studies of the Americas; difference incorporated; Electronic Mediations; Fesler-Lampert Minnesota Heritage Book Series; First Peoples: New Directions in Indigenous Studies; Globalization and Community; Indigenous Americas; Minnesota Studies in the Philosophy of Science; MMPI-2 Monographs; MMPI-A Monographs; Posthumanities; Public Worlds; Quadrant; Social Movements, Protest, and Contention; Theory and History of Literature

University Press of Mississippi

3825 Ridgewood Road
Jackson, MS 39211-6492

Phone: 601.432.6205
Fax: 601.432.6217
Email: press@mississippi.edu
Indiv: (user I.D)@mississippi.edu

Website and Social Media:
Website: www.upress.state.ms.us
Blog: upmississippi.blogspot.com
Facebook: www.facebook.com/UPMiss
Twitter: @UPMiss
Instagram: instagram.com/upmississippi
Pinterest: www.pinterest.com/upm/
Tumblr: upm.tumblr.com

Warehouse Address:
Maple Logistics Solutions
Lebanon Distribution Center
704 Legionaire Drive
Fredericksburg, PA 17026

Orders:
Phone: 800.737.7788; 601.432.6205

Canadian Representative:
Scholarly Book Services

UK Representative:
Eurospan

Staff

Director: Craig W. Gill (601.432.6371; email: cgill) (film studies, music, ethnomusicology, regional trade)
  Rights and Permissions Manager/Administrative Assistant: Cynthia Foster (601.432.6205; email: cfoster)
  Assistant to the Director: Emily Bandy (601.432.6206; email: ebandy)
Acquisitions Editorial:
  Acquisitions Editors: Vijay Shah (601.432.6102; email: vshah) (history, Caribbean studies, American studies, African American studies, ethnic studies, comics studies); Katie Keene (601.432.6459; email: kkeene) (folklore, literature, children's literature studies, television studies)
  Editorial Assistants: Lisa McMurtray (601.432.6272; email: lmcmurtray); Mary Heath (601.432.6459; email: mheath)
Electronic Publishing: Steve Yates, Associate Director/Marketing Director (601.432.6695; email: syates)
Manuscript Editorial: Shane Gong Stewart, Project Manager (601.432.6249; email: sgong)
  Project Editor: Valerie Jones (601.432.6554; email: vjones)
  Associate Project Editor: Kristi Ezernack (601.432.6249; email: kezernack)
Design and Production: Todd Lape, Production and Design Manager (601.432.6558; email: tlape)
  Senior Book Designer: Pete Halverson (601.432.6559; email: phalverson)
  Book Designer: Jennifer Mixon (601.432.6557; email: jmixon)
Marketing and Sales: Steve Yates, Associate Director/Marketing Director (601.432.6695; email: syates)
  Data Services and Course Adoptions Manager: Kathy Burgess (601.432.6105; email: kburgess)

Publicity and Promotions Manager: Courtney McCreary (601.432.6424; email: cmccreary)
Electronic, Exhibits, and Direct-to-Consumer Sales Manager: Kristin Kirkpatrick (601.432.6795; email: kkirkpatrick)
Marketing Assistant: Jordan Nettles (601.432.6274; email: jnettles)
Business: Tonia Lonie, Business Manager (601.432.6551; email: tlonie)
Customer Service and Order Supervisor: Sandy Alexander (601.432.6704; email: salexander)

Regular Member
Established: 1970
Title output 2016: 133
Titles currently in print: 1,400

Admitted to the Association: 1976
Title output 2016: 137

Editorial Program
Scholarly and trade titles in African American studies; African Diaspora studies; American studies, literature, history, and culture; art and architecture; Caribbean studies; children's literature studies, comics studies; ethnic studies; folklore; film studies; media studies; memoir; music; ethnomusicology; natural sciences; photography; popular culture; regional studies; serious nonfiction of general interest; Southern studies; sports; women's studies; other liberal arts.
Special series: African Diaspora Material Culture; American Made Music; America's Third Coast; Caribbean Studies; Chancellor Porter L. Fortune Symposium in Southern History; Children's Literature Association; Civil Rights in Mississippi; Conversations with Comics Artists; Conversations with Filmmakers; Critical Approaches to Comics Artists; Faulkner and Yoknapatawpha; Folklore Studies in a Multicultural World; Great Comic Artists; Heritage of Mississippi; Hollywood Legends; Literary Conversations; Margaret Walker Alexander Series in African American Studies; Race, Rhetoric, and Media; Television Conversations; Willie Morris Books in Memoir and Biography

University of Missouri Press

113 Heinkel Bldg.
201 S. 7th Street
Columbia, MO 65211-1344

Phone: 573.882.7641
Fax: 573.884.4498
Email: upress@missouri.edu
Indiv: (user ID)@missouri.edu

Website and Social Media:
Website: upress.missouri.edu
Blog: umissouripress.blogspot.com/
Facebook: University of Missouri Press
Twitter: @umissouripress

Orders:
University of Missouri Press
c/o Chicago Distribution Center
11030 South Langley Avenue
Chicago, IL 60628-3830
Phone: 800.621.2736
Fax: 800.621.8476
Email: orders@press.uchicago.edu

Canadian Representative:
Scholarly Book Services

Europe, Middle East & Africa Representative:
Eurospan

Asia & the Pacific Representative:
East-West Export Books

University of Missouri Press continued

Staff
Director: David Rosenbaum (email: rosenbaumd)
Acquisitions: Andrew Davidson, Editor-in-Chief (573.882.9997; email: davidsonaj)
 Acquisitions Editor: Gary Kass (573.884.1277; email: kassg)
 Associate Acquisitions Editor: Mary Conley (573.882.8344; email: conleyms)
 Editorial, Production, and Design Coordinator: Drew Griffith (573.882.3044; email: griffithd)
Marketing: TBA, Marketing and Sales Manager (573.882.9672)
 Marketing Coordinator: Deanna Davis (573.882.3000; email: davisdea)
 Marketing Assistant: Ryan Eidson (573.882.8735; email: eidsonr)
Business: Tracy Tritschler, Business Manager (573.882.9459; email: tritschlert)

Regular Member
Established: 1958
Title output 2016: 41
Title currently in print: 1,226

Admitted to the Association: 1960
Title output 2017: 39

Editorial Program
American history and culture, including intellectual history, military history, and biography; African American studies; Native American studies; women's studies; American and British literary criticism; history and practice of journalism; political science; bioethics, and regional studies and the natural history of Missouri and the Midwest.
Special series: Advances in Organizational Psychodynamics; American Military Experience; Journalism in Perspective; Mark Twain and His Circle; Shades of Blue and Gray; Sports in American Culture; Studies in Constitutional Democracy

Modern Language Association of America

85 Broad Street, Suite 500
New York, NY 10004-2434

Phone: 646.576.5000
Fax: 646.458.0030
Email: info@mla.org
Indiv: firstinitiallastname@mla.org

Book Orders:
Phone: 646.576.5161
Fax: 646.576.5160
Email: bookorders@mla.org

Website and Social Media:
Website: www.mla.org
Blog: commons.mla.org
Twitter: @MLAnews, @MLAstyle
Facebook: www.facebook.com/modernlanguageassociation/
YouTube: www.youtube.com/channel/UCleB07C9Cj_KDToGMe7GEGQ

Staff
Executive Director: Paula M. Krebs (646.576.5102)
Director of Scholarly Communication: Angela Gibson (646.576.5016)
Senior Acquisitions Editor: James C. Hatch (646.576.5044)

Acquisitions Editor: Jaime Cleland
Coordinator of Permissions: Marcia E. Henry (646.576.5042)
Head of Book Publications: Erika Suffern (646.576.5134)
Head of Periodical Publications: Sara Pastel (646.576.5031)
Head of Digital Initiatives: Nicky Agate (646.576.5114)
Head of Print Production: Judith Altreuter (646.576.5010)
Head of Online Production: Tom Lewek (646.576.5033)
Head of Marketing and Sales: Kathleen Hansen (646.576.5018)

Regular Member
Established: 1883
Title output 2016: 6
Titles currently in print: 313
Admitted to the Association: 1992
Title output 2017: 8
Journals published: 6

Editorial Program
Scholarly, pedagogical, and professional books on language and literature.
Journals: *ADE and ADFL Bulletins; MLA International Bibliography; MLA Newsletter; PMLA; Profession*
Book series: Approaches to Teaching World Literature; New Variorum Edition of Shakespeare; Options for Teaching; Teaching Languages, Literatures, and Cultures; Texts and Translations; World Literatures Reimagined

The Museum of Modern Art

11 West 53rd Street
New York, NY 10019

Phone: 212.708.9512
Fax: 212.333.6575 or 212.708.9779
Email: moma_publications@moma.org
Indiv: firstname_lastname@moma.org

Orders:
Individuals: 800.447.6662
www.momastore.org
Trade: 212.627.9484/www.artbook.com

Website and Social Media:
Website: www.moma.org
Facebook: www.facebook.com/MuseumofModernArt
Twitter: @MuseumModernArt
Instagram: @TheMuseumofModernArt
YouTube: www.youtube.com/MoMAvideos
Tumblr: moma.tumblr.com

UK Representative:
Thames & Hudson

Canadian Representative:
ARTBOOK | D.A.P.

Staff
Publisher: Christopher Hudson (212.708.9445)
Department Coordinator: Cerise Fontaine (212.708.9512)
Editor: Emily Hall (212.708.9511)
Editor: Rebecca Roberts (212.708.9883)

Museum of Modern Art continued

Assistant Editor: Maria Marchenkova (212.708.9418)
Rights Coordinator: Adedoyin Samuel (212.708.9741)
Production Director: Marc Sapir (212.708.9745)
Production Manager: Matthew Pimm (212.708.9742)
Senior Designer: Amanda Washburn (212.708.6572)
Marketing and Production Senior Coordinator: Hannah Kim (212.708.9449)
Associate Business Manager: Bryan Stauss (212.708.9743)

Regular Member
Established: 1929
Title output 2016: 16
Titles currently in print: 350

Admitted to the Association: 2008
Title output 2017: 25

Editorial Program
Modern and contemporary art, including painting, sculpture, drawings, prints and illustrated books, photography, film, media and performance, architecture and design
Special series: MoMA Artist Series; MoMA Design Series; MoMA Primary Documents; Studies in Modern Art

The National Academies Press

500 Fifth Street, N.W.
Washington, DC 20001

Bookstore phone: 202.334.2612
Fax: 202.334.2793
Email: (user I.D.)@nas.edu

Orders (US and Canada):
Phone: 800.624.6242; 202.334.3313
Fax: 202.334.2451
Email: zjones@nas.edu

UK Distributor:
Marston Book Services

Website and Social Media:
Website: www.nap.edu
Facebook: www.facebook.com/NationalAcademies
Twitter: @theNASEM

Staff
Co-Executive Directors: Sandy Adams (202.334.3328; email: sadams); Alphonse MacDonald (202.334.3625; email amacdonald)
Managing Editor: Rachel Marcus (202.334.2275; email: rmarcus)
Production Manager: Dorothy Lewis (202.334.2409; email: dlewis)
Marketing & Sales Manager: Barbara Murphy (202.334.1902; email: bmurphy)
Business Manager: Rachel Levy (202.334.3329; email: rlevy)
Customer Service Manager: Zina Jones (202.334.3116; email: zjones)

Regular Member
Established: 1864
Title output 2016: 205
Titles currently in print: 6,993

Admitted to the Association: 1988
Title output 2017: 175

Editorial Program
Primarily scholarly, policy-oriented titles in agricultural sciences; behavioral and social sciences; biology; chemistry; computer sciences; earth sciences; economics; education; energy; engineering; environmental issues; industry; international issues; materials science; medicine; natural resources; nutrition; physical sciences; public policy issues; statistics; transportation; and urban and rural development.

National Gallery of Art

Street Address:
Sixth Street and Constitution Avenue NW
Washington, DC

Mailing Address:
2000B South Club Drive
Landover, MD 20785

Phone: 202.842.6200
Fax: 202.408.8530
Email: (firstinitial-lastname)@nga.gov

Online shop:
shop.nga.gov

Customer Service/Order Fulfillment:
800.697.9350

Website and Social Media:
Website: www.nga.gov
Facebook: www.facebook.com/NationalGalleryofArt
Twitter: @ngadc

Staff
Editor-in-Chief: Emiko K. Usui (202.842.6205; email: e-usui)
Deputy Publisher and Production Manager: Chris Vogel (202.842.6209; email: c-vogel)
Senior Editors: Tam Bryfogle (202.842.6498; email: t-bryfogle); Julie Warnement (202.842.6136; email: j-warnement)
Associate Senior Editor: John Strand (202.842.6613; email: j-strand)
Editor: Caroline Weaver (202.842.6032; email: c-weaver)
Assistant Editor: Lisa Wainwright (202.842.6669; email: l-wainwright)
Managing Editor of CASVA Publications: Cynthia Ware (202.842.6204; email: c-ware)
Design Manager: Wendy Schleicher (202.789.4601; email: w-schleicher)
Designers: Brad Ireland (202.789.3082; email: b-ireland); Rio DeNaro (202.842.6697; email: r-denaro)
Print and Digital Production Associate: John Long (202.842.6423; email: j-long)
Production Assistant: Mariah Shay (202.842.6758; email: m-shay)
Permissions Coordinator: Sara Sanders-Buell (202.842.6719; email: s-sanders-buell)
Rothko Research Associate: Laili Nasr (202.842.6779; email: l-nasr)
Associate Curator, Mark Rothko Catalogue Raisonné: Adam Greenhalgh (202.842.6323; email: a-greenhalgh)
Program Assistant: Katie Brennan (202.842.6200; email: k-brennan)

Regular Member
Established: 1941
Title output 2016: 11
Titles currently in print: 40 print
(125 backlist in PDF Library)

Admitted to the Association: 1992
Title output 2017: 10

National Gallery of Art continued

Editorial Program
The National Gallery publishes exhibition catalogues on all subjects and permanent collection catalogues (including Western art of the early Renaissance through the contemporary era); National Gallery of Art Online Editions; a symposium series; Studies in the History of Art, in conjunction with the Center for Advanced Study in the Visual Arts; educational online programs and catalogues; exhibition brochures and wall texts; online features for permanent collection and special exhibitions; scholarly and popular publications based on objects in the museum's collections; scholarly publications on conservation; educational materials and guides for use by the public and by teachers and schools; and the calendar of events, film and music programs, bulletins, and all Gallery ephemera. Unsolicited manuscripts are not invited.

Naval Institute Press

291 Wood Road
Annapolis MD 21402-5034

Orders:
Phone: 800.233.8764

Phone: 410.268.6110
Fax: 410.295.1084/5
Email: firstinitiallastname@usni.org

Website and Social Media:
Website: www.nip.org
Facebook: www.facebook.com/NavalInstitute
Twitter: @USNIBooks

UK/European Representatives:
Eurospan Group

Canadian Representatives:
Scholarly Book Service

Staff
Director: Richard A. Russell (410.295.1031)
Editorial Director: Paul Merzlak (410.295.1072)
   Gordon England Chair of Professional Naval Literature: Thomas J. Cutler (410.295.1038)
   Senior Acquisitions Editor/Subsidiary Rights Manager: Susan Todd Brook (410.295.1037)
   Senior Acquisitions Editor for Professional Development Content: Jim Dolbow (410.295.1034)
  Senior Acquisitions Editor: Laura Davulis (410.295.1025)
   Acquisitions Editor: Glenn Griffith (410.295.1067)
   Assistant Acquisitions Editor/Editorial Lead, Graphic Novels: Gary Thompson (410.295.1030)
   Assistant Editor and Digital Assets Coordinator: Taylor Skord (410.295.1096)
   Assistant Editor: David Bowman (410.295.1029)
  Managing Editor: Susan Corrado (410.295.1032)
   Senior Production Editor: Emily Bakely (410.295.1020)
   Production Editor: Marlena Montagna (410.295.1040)
   Managing Editor for Digital Content and Production: Kelly Oaks (410.295.1079)

Director of Sales and Marketing: Claire Noble (410.295.1039)
  Sales Manager: Robin Noonan (410.295.1046)
  Publicity Manager: Jacqline Barnes (410.295.1028)
  Marketing Manager: Meagan Szekley (410.295.1033)
Oral History Program, U.S. Naval Institute
  Director: Richard A. Russell (410.295.1031)
  Manager: Eric Mills (410.295.1063)
Journals, U.S. Naval Institute:
Proceedings, Editor-in-Chief: Fred Rainbow (410.295.1092)
Naval History, Editor-in-Chief: Richard Latture (410.295.1076)
Publisher, U.S. Naval Institute: William M. Miller III (410.295.1068)
Chief Financial Officer, U.S. Naval Institute: Chip Wallen (410.295.1707)

Regular Member
Established: 1898   Admitted to the Association: 1949
Title output 2016: 90   Title output 2017: 85
Titles currently in print: 1,500   Journals published: 2

Editorial Program
General military subjects; military biography; naval history and literature; naval and military reference; navigation; military law; naval science; sea power; shipbuilding; professional guides; nautical arts and lore; technical guides; veterans affairs; fiction.
Journals: *Naval History; Proceedings*
Special series: Bluejacket Books (paperback); Blue and Gold Professional Library; Leatherneck Classics; New Perspectives on Maritime History and Nautical Archaeology; Scarlet & Gold Professional Library; Studies in Naval History and Seapower

University of Nebraska Press

1111 Lincoln Mall
Lincoln, NE 68588-0630

Phone: 402.472.3581
Fax 402.472.6214
Email: pressmail@unl.edu
Email: (user I.D.)@unl.edu

Orders:
University of Nebraska Press
Longleaf Services
116 S. Boundary Street
Chapel Hill, NC 27514-3808
Phone: 800.848.6224
Fax: 800.272.6817
Email: customerservice@longleafservices.org

Website and Social Media:
Website: www.nebraskapress.unl.edu;
  bisonbooks.com;
  potomacbooksinc.com
Blog: unpblog.com
Facebook: www.facebook.com/NebraskaPress
www.facebook.com/JewishPublicationSociety
www.facebook.com/PotomacBooks
Twitter: @UnivNebPress @PotomacBooks @JewishPub
Pinterest: UnivNebPress
Instagram: instagram.com/univnebpress

UK Distributor:
Combined Academic Publishers
Potomac: Casemate UK Ltd

Canadian Distributor:
Codasat Canada Ltd.

Asia/Pacific Distributor:
Eurospan

Staff

Director: Donna A. Shear (402.472.2861; email: dshear2)
Assistant Director for Business/CFO: Tera Beermann (402.472.0011; email: tbeermann2)
Rights and Permissions: Leif Milliken (402.472.7702; email: lmilliken2)
Editor-in-Chief: Alisa Plant (European and world history, regional trade) (402.472.4311; email: aplant2)
  Senior Editors: Bridget Barry (U.S. and world history, geography, environmental studies) (402.472.0645; email: bbarry2); Matthew Bokovoy (Native American and Indigenous studies, borderlands history) (402.472.4452; email: mbokovoy2); Rob Taylor (sports, spaceflight) (402.472.0325; email: rtaylor6)
  Editors: Alicia Christensen (American studies, cultural criticism, creative works) (402.472.0317; email: achristensen6)
  Potomac Books Editor: Tom Swanson (402.472.5945; email: tswanson3)
  Associate Editors: Courtney Ochsner (402.472.4282; email: cochsner2); Heather Stauffer (402.472.5821; email: unp-hstauffer)
  Editorial Assistants: Natalie O'Neal (402.472.5937; email: noneal2); Emily Wendell (402.472.5940; email: ewendell2)
  JPS Acquisitions: Rabbi Barry L. Schwartz (bschwartz@jps.org); Joy Weinberg (jweinberg@jps.org)

Editorial, Design, and Production: Ann Baker, Manager, EDP (402.472.0095; email: abaker2)
Project Editors: Joeth Zucco (402.472.0199; email: jzucco2); Sara Springsteen (402.472.4008; email: sspringsteen1); Elizabeth Zaleski (402.472.3638; email: ezaleski2)
EDP Editorial Assistant: Margaret Mattern (402.472.3473; email: mmattern2)
Assistant Production Manager: Alison Rold (402.472.7706; email: arold1)
Book Production Associate: Terry Boldan (402.472.0890; email: tboldan2)
Designers: Andrea Shahan (402.472.7718; email: ashahan1); Roger Buchholz (402.472.7713; email: rbuchholz1); Nathan Putens (402.472.5943; email: nputens2)
Production Designer: Lindsey Auten (402.472.7716; email: lauten2)
Compositors: Mikala Kolander (402.472.1505; email: mkolandar2); Erin Cuddy (402.472.0318; email: ecuddy2)
Marketing and Sales: Manager: Mark Heineke (402.472.7946; email: mheineke2)
Sales Coordinator: Rob Buchanan (402.472.0160; email: rbuchanan1)
Publicity Manager: Rosemary Sekora (402.427.7710; email: rsekora)
Publicists: Tayler Lord (402.472.3632; email: tlord2); Anna Weir (402.472.5938; email: aweir)
Direct Mail Manager: Tish Fobben (402.472.4627; email: pfobben2)
Advertising and Exhibits Coordinator: Amy Lage (402.472.2759; email: alage2)
Electronic Marketing Coordinator: Erica Corwin (402.472.9313; email: ecorwin1)
Marketing Designer: John Klopping (402.472.5949; email: jklopping2)
Journals Management & Publishing Solutions: Manjit Kaur, Manager (402.472.7703; email: mkaur2)
Marketing and Fulfillment Manager: Joyce Gettman (402.472.8330; email: jgettman2)
Marketing Associate: Laurel Ybarra (402.472.5988; email: lybarra3)
Fulfillment Coordinator: Odessa Anderson (402.472.8536; email: oanderson2)
Project Supervisor: Joel Puchalla (402.472.3572; email: jpuchalla4)
Project Coordinator: Weston Poor (402.472.2292; email: wpoor2)
Desktop Compositor: Lacey Losh (402.472.5028; email: llosh2)
Business Services:
Senior Accountant and Analyst: Mark Francis (402.472.5804; email: mfrancis2)
Royalty Accountant & Accounts Receivable: Odessa Anderson (402.472.8536; email: oanderson2)
Accounts Payable: Claire Schwinck (402.472.7711; email: cschwinck2)
Business Assistant: Barbara Townsend (402.472.3581; email: btownsend2)
Digital Assets and IT: Jana Faust, Manager (402.472.0171; email: jfaust2)
Coordinator: Grey Castro (402.472.3663; email: gcastro3)

Regular Member

Established: 1941	Admitted to the Association: Unknown
Title output 2016: 142	Title output 2017: 142
Titles currently in print: 3,300	Journals published: 30

Editorial Program
Native American and Indigenous studies; American and European history; Western Americana; Latin America; sports; anthropology; geography; environmental studies; American studies; cultural criticism; creative works. JPS imprint: bible, bible commentary, Jewish history and culture. Potomac imprint: biography and memoir, Civil War history, military

University of Nebraska of Press continued

studies, world and national affairs.

The Press distributes for the American Foreign Service, the Buros Institute of Mental Measurement, Confederated Salish Tribes, Salish Kootenai College Press, the Society for American Baseball Research, and Whale & Star Press.

Journals: *American Indian Quarterly; Anthropological Linguistics; Collaborative Anthropologies; Frontiers: A Journal of Women's Studies; Great Plains Quarterly; Great Plains Research; Hotel Amerika; Journal of Austrian Studies; Journal of Black Sexuality and Relationships; Journal of Literature and Trauma Studies; Journal of Sports Media; Legacy: A Journal of American Women Writers; Middle West Review; Native South; NINE: A Journal of Baseball History & Culture; Nineteenth-Century French Studies; Nouvelles Etudes Francophones; Resilience: A Journal of the Environmental Humanities; Storyworlds: A Journal of Narrative Studies; Studies in American Indian Literatures; Studies in American Naturalism; symploke: A Journal for the Intermingling of Literary, Cultural, and Theoretical Scholarship; The Gettysburg Magazine; The Undecidable Unconscious: A Journal of Deconstruction and Psychoanalysis; Western American Literature; Women and Music: A Journal of Gender and Culture*; and *Women in German Yearbook: Feminist Studies in German Literature and Culture*

Imprints: Bison Books; JPS (The Jewish Publication Society); Potomac Books

Book series: African Poetry; American Indian Lives; American Lives; American Transnationalism; Anthropology of Contemporary North America; At Table; Bison Frontiers of Imagination; Boas Papers Documentary Edition; Borderlands and Transnational Studies; Cather Studies; Comprehensive History of the Holocaust; Complete Letters of Henry James; Critical Studies in the History of Anthropology; Cultural Geographies + Rewriting the Earth; Discover the Great Plains; Early American Places; Early Modern Cultural Studies; Ethnohistories of the Americas; Expanding Frontiers; Flyover Fiction; France Overseas; Frontiers of Narrative; Great Campaigns of the Civil War; Historical Archaeology of the American West; Histories of Anthropology Annual; History of the American West; Indians of the Southeast; Indigenous Education; Indigenous Films; Journals of the Lewis and Clark Expedition; Law in the American West; The Mexican Experience; Native Literatures of the Americas; Native Storiers; New Hispanisms; New Visions in Native American and Indigenous Studies; Our Sustainable Future; Outdoor Lives; Outward Odyssey; Papers of William F. "Buffalo Bill" Cody; Polar Studies; Politics and Governments of the American States; Postwestern Horizons; Prairie Schooner Book Prize in Fiction; Prairie Schooner Book Prize in Poetry; Provocations; Race and Ethnicity in the American West; Recovering Languages and Literacies of the Americas; Sports, Media, and Society; Studies in Antisemitism; Studies in the Anthropology of North American Indians; Studies in the Native Languages of the Americas; Studies in Pacific Worlds; Studies in War, Society, and the Military; Ted Kooser Contemporary Poetry; This Hallowed Ground: Guides to Civil War Battlefields; Willa Cather Scholarly Edition; Women and Gender in the Early Modern World; Women in the West

JPS series: Celebrating the Jewish Year; Folktales of the Jews; Jewish Choices, Jewish Voices; JPS Anthologies of Jewish Thought; JPS Bible Commentary; JPS Guides; JPS Scholar of Distinction; JPS Torah Commentary; The Rubin JPS Miqra-ot Gedolot: The Commentators' Bible

University of Nevada Press

Continuing Education Building,
Mail Stop 0166
Reno, NV 89557-0166

Phone: 775.682.7389
Email: (user I.D.)@unpress.nevada.edu

Order Fulfillment:
Chicago Distribution Center
11030 South Langley Ave.
Chicago, IL 60628
Phone: 800.621.2736
Fax: 800.621.8476

Website and Social Media:
Website: www.unpress.nevada.edu
Facebook: www.facebook.com/universitynevadapress

Canadian Representative:
Scholarly Book Services

UK Representative:
Eurospan

Staff
Director: Justin Race (775.682.7389; email: jrace)
Acquisitions Editor: Justin Race
Marketing & Sales Manager: Sara Hendricksen (775.682.7395; email: shendricksen)
Editorial, Design & Production Manager: Virginia Fontana (775.682.7391; email: vfontana)
Business Manager: JoAnne Banducci (775.682.7387; email: jbanducci)

Regular Member
Established: 1961
Title output 2016: 16
Titles currently in print: 415

Admitted to the Association: 1982
Title output 2017: 22

Editorial Program
Scholarly and general interest books about the history, literature, anthropology, archaeology, and natural history of the American West, Nevada, and the Great Basin. Additional interests include books dealing with the Basque peoples of Europe and the Americas; Native American Studies; mining; environmental studies; and gaming and gambling.
Special series: America's National Parks; Basque Studies; Cultural Ecologies of Food in the 21st Century; Gambling Studies; Migration, Demography, & Environmental Change: Global Challenges; Mining and Society; The Urban West; Waterscapes: History, Cultures, and Controversies; Wilbur S. Shepperson Series in Nevada History;

University Press of New England

1 Court Street, Suite 250
Lebanon, NH 03766-1358

Phone: 603.448.1533
Fax: 603.448.7006
Email: university.press@dartmouth.edu
Indiv: (user I.D.)@dartmouth.edu

Website and Social Media:
Website: www.upne.com
Blog: upne.blogspot.com
Facebook: www.facebook.com/
   UniversityPressOfNewEngland
Twitter: @UPNEpub

Canadian Representative:
Sales: Ampersand Inc.
Distribution: University of Toronto Press

Customer Service/Order Fulfillment:
Phone: 800.421.1561
Fax: 603.448.9429

Warehouse:
UPNE Fulfillment Center
c/o Maple Logistics Solutions
Lebanon Distribution Center
704 Legionaire Drive
Fredricksburg, PA 17026

European Representative:
Oxbow Books Ltd.

Staff

Director: Michael P. Burton (ext. 241; email: michael.p.burton)
   Assistant to the Director, Permissions Manager: Kara L. Caputo (ext. 201; email: kara.l.caputo)
Associate Director, Operations: Thomas M. Johnson (ext. 251; email: thomas.m.johnson)
Editor-in-Chief: TBA (603.448.1533, ext. 222)
   Acquisitions Editors: Stephen P. Hull (ext. 225; email: stephen.p.hull); Richard Pult (ext. 226; email: richard.pult)
Manuscript Editorial: Amanda A. Dupuis, Managing Editor (ext. 243; email: amanda.a.dupuis)
   Production Editor: Susan A. Abel (ext. 244; email: susan.a.abel)
Design and Production: Eric M. Brooks, Assistant Director, Design and Production (ext. 211; email: eric.m.brooks)
   Designer: Mindy B. Hill (email: mindy.b.hill)
   Production Coordinator: Douglas C. Tifft (ext. 245; email: douglas.c.tifft)
   Production Assistant: Kate L. Tarbell (ext. 217; email: kate.l.tarbell)
Marketing: TBA, Assistant Director, Marketing & Sales (ext. 234)
   Sales & Trade Exhibits Manager: Sherri L. Strickland (ext. 238; email: sherri.l.strickland)
   Publicity and Subsidiary Rights Manager: Barbara L. Briggs (ext. 233; email: barbara.l.briggs)
   New Media Marketing Coordinator: Catherine A. Grabill (ext. 237; email: catherine.a.grabill)
   Sales & Exhibit Coordinator: Susan Sylvia (ext. 236; email: susan.sylvia)
Business: Thomas M. Johnson, Associate Director, Operations (ext. 251; email: thomas.m.johnson)
   Accounting Supervisor: Donna Youngman (ext. 252; email: donna.youngman)

Accounting Associate: Timothy E. Semple (ext. 253; email: timothy.e.semple)
Order Fulfillment Supervisor: Barbara A. Benson (ext. 255; email: barbara.a.benson)
Senior Customer Service Clerk: Barbara F. McBeth (ext. 256; email: barbara.f.mcbeth)
IT: David R. Bellows, Systems Administrator/Webmaster (ext. 257; email: david.r.bellows)

Regular Member
Established: 1970   Admitted to the Association: 1975
Title output 2016: 54   Title output 2017: 56
Titles currently in print: 778
Publishes books under the consortium member imprints of Brandeis University Press, Dartmouth College Press, ForeEdge Books, and University Press of New England.

Editorial Program
General trade, scholarly, instructional, and reference works for scholars, teachers, students, and the public. The Press concentrates in Jewish studies, American studies, New England studies, cultural studies, ethnic studies, literary criticism, and history; art, architecture, photography, and material culture; music, dance, and popular culture; languages; natural sciences, nature and the environment; marine ecology and maritime culture; health and medicine; military history; current events, social issues, and true crime.

The Press, through UPNE Book Partners, handles book order processing and distribution for: Academia Press; Autumn House Press; Bauhan Publishing; Carnegie Mellon University Press; Cavankerry Press; Chipstone Foundation; Duquesne University Press; Four Way Books; Historic New England; International Polar Institute Press; University of New Hampshire Press; New Issues Poetry and Prose; Nightboat Books; Northeastern University Press; Oberlin College Press; Omnidawn Publishing; Saturnalia Books; Sheep Meadow Press; Tagus Press; Vermont Folklife Center; The Warring States Project; and Wesleyan University Press.
Special series: Becoming Modern: New Nineteenth-Century Studies; Brandeis Series in American Jewish History, Culture and Life; Collected Writings of Rousseau; Geisel Series in Global Health and Medicine; HBI Series on Gender, Culture, Religion, and Law; HBI Series on Jewish Women; Interfaces: Studies in Visual Culture; Mandel Lectures in the Humanities; Menahem Stern Jerusalem Lectures; New England and the World; Re-Mapping the Transnational: A Dartmouth Series in American Studies; Schusterman Series in Israel Studies; Seafaring America; Tauber Institute Series for the Study of European Jewry

University of New Mexico Press

Mailing Address:
MSC05 3185
1 University of New Mexico
Albuquerque NM 87131-0001

Phone: 505.277.3495
Fax: 505.277.3343
Email: unmpress@unm.edu
Indiv: (user I.D.)@unm.edu
(unless otherwise indicated)

Website and Social Media:
Website: www.unmpress.com
Facebook: www.facebook.com/pages
   /University-of-New-Mexico-Press/109620976711
Twitter: @UNMPress

Street Address:
1717 Roma NE
NE Albuquerque NM 87106-4509

Business and Order Fulfillment:
1312 Basehart Road SE
Albuquerque NM 87106-4363

Orders:
Phone: 800.249.7737; 505.272.7777
Fax: 505.272.7778
Email: custserv@unm.edu

UK/European Representative:
Eurospan

Canadian Representative:
Codasat Canada

Staff
Interim Director: Richard Schuetz (505.277.3284; email: rschuetz)
   Rights and Royalties Coordinator: Briony Jones (505.925.9512; email: briony)
Executive Editor: Clark Whitehorn (406.422.6771; email: clarkw) (anthropology, archaeology, Chicano/a studies, history, Latin American studies, Native studies, natural history)
   Senior Acquisitions Editor: Elise McHugh (505.277.3327; email: elisemc) (American literature and criticism, poetry, fiction, art, photography)
Managing Editor: James Ayers (505.277.3324; email: ayers)
   Production Editor: Morgan Podraza (505.277.3436, email: mpodraza)
   Assistant Acquisitions Editor/e-book Production Coordinator: Sonia Dickey (505.277.2153; email: soniad)
Art Director: Lisa Tremaine (505.277.3333; email: ltremaine)
   Book Designer: Felicia Cedillos (505.277.2293; email: fcedillo)
Sales and Marketing Manager: Katherine White (505.277.3294; email: kwhite03)
   Publicist: TBA
   Marketing Associate: Jennifer de Garmo (505.277.3289; email: jdegarmo)
   Sales Representative: Richard Fugini (505.272.7544; email: rfugini)
Associate Director for Business Operations: Richard Schuetz (505.277.3284; email: rschuetz)
   Fiscal Services: Lyudmila Markova (505.272.7774; email: milam)
   Accounts Receivable/Payable: Tiffany Rawls (505.272.7775; email: trawls)
   Customer Service and Credit Manager: Stewart Marshall (505.925.9506; email: stewartm)
   Customer Service Associates: Susan Hoffman (505.925.9508; email: soozjh)
   Warehouse Manager: Susan Coatney (505.272.7770; email: susanc)
IT Support Manager: Darrell Banward (505.277.0978; email: dbanward)

Regular Member
Established: 1929
Title output 2016: 64
Titles currently in print: 1,200

Admitted to the Association: 1937
Title output 2017: 64

Editorial Program
Scholarly books, fiction, poetry, and literary nonfiction, with special interests in social and cultural anthropology; archaeology of the Americas; art, architecture, and photography; Chicano/a studies; frontier history; legal studies, especially water issues; American literature; Latin American studies; Native studies; and books that deal with important aspects of Southwest or Rocky Mountain states, including natural history and land grant studies
Special series, joint imprints, and/or copublishing programs: Barbara Guth Worlds of Wonder Science Series for Young Readers; Diálogos Series; Latin America in the World – The World in Latin America; Histories of the American Frontier; Mary Burritt Christiansen Poetry Series; Pasó por Aquí Series on the Nuevomexicano Literary Heritage; Recencies Series on Twentieth-Century American Poetics; Archaeologies of Landscapes in the Americas Series; Cambio Series on Business, Economics, and Society in Latin America; Querencias Series on Transnational Culture of the U.S./Mexico Borderlands; Contextos Series on Latino/a Contemporary Issues; Religions of the Americas; School for Advanced Research Copublications; River Teeth Literary Nonfiction Prize; Southwest Adventure

UNSW Press Ltd

Street Address:
University of New South Wales
Cliffbrook Campus
45 Beach Street
Coogee, NSW 2034, Australia

Phone: +61 2 8936 0100
Fax: +61 2 8936 0040
Email: enquiries@newsouthpublishing.com

Website and Social Media:
Website: www.unswpress.com
www.newsouthbooks.com.au
Blog: www.newsouthpublishing.com
Facebook: www.facebook.com/NewSouth-Books-Australia-131239900263716/
Twitter: @newsouthbook
Instagram: instagram.com/newsouthbooks/

Mailing Address:
University of New South Wales
Sydney NSW 2052, Australia

Orders:
TL Distribution
15-23 Helles Ave
Moorebank NSW 2170
Australia
Phone: +61 2 8778 9999
Email: orders@tldistribution.com.au
www.bookshop.unsw.edu.au/

USA & Canada Representative:
Independent Publishers Group
814 North Franklin Street
Chicago, IL 60610
Email: frontdesk@ipgbook.com

UK Representative:
Eurospan

Staff

Director: Kathy Bail (+61 2 8936 0017; email: kathy.bail@unswpress.com.au)
Chief Operating Officer: David Moody (+61 2 8936 0012; email: david.moody@unswpress.com.au)
NewSouth Books (sales & marketing) Director: Nella Soeterboek (+61 2 8936 0027; email: nella.s@newsouthbooks.com.au)
  Executive Publisher: Phillipa McGuinness (+61 2 8936 0018; email: p.mcguinness@newsouthpublishing.com.au)
  Publisher: Elspeth Menzies (+61 2 8936 0019; email: e.menzies@newsouthpublishing.com.au)
  Editors: Deborah Nixon (+61 2 8936 0030; email: deborah.nixon@newsouthpublishing.com.au); Paul O'Beirne (+61 2 8936 0024; email: p.obeirne@newsouthpublishing.com.au); Emma Hutchinson (+61 2 8936 0031; email: e.hutchinson@newsouthpublishing.com.au)
  National Sales Manager: Jane Kembrey (+61 2 9385 9028; email: jane.kembrey@newsouthbooks.com.au)
  Digital & Production Manager: Rosie Marson (+61 2 8936 0028; email: r.marson@newsouthbooks.com.au)
Retail Director: Mark Halliday (+61 2 9385 6655; email: mark@bookshop.unsw.edu.au)
Information Systems: Brett Haydon (+61 2 8936 0038; email: brett.haydon@unswpress.com.au)

Regular Member
Established: 1962
Title output 2016: 50
Titles currently in print: 500

Admitted to the Association: 2015
Title output 2017: 46

Editorial Program
Literary and illustrated non-fiction across two imprints—NewSouth (trade) and UNSW Press (scholarly and specialist). We publish thought-provoking, well-written books in areas such as history, particularly the history of Australia (with an emphasis on Indigenous history and culture), military history, political science, natural history, environmental studies, popular science and medicine, art, architecture and biography. Select titles are published in partnership with organizations such as the Australian War Memorial, the State Library of NSW and the State Library of Victoria, as well as state galleries and museums. Our books prompt debate and tackle social, political, and scientific issues.

New York University Press

838 Broadway, 3rd Floor
New York, NY 10003-4812

Phone: 212.998.2575
Fax: 212.995.3833
Email: orders@nyupress.edu
Indiv: firstname.lastname@nyu.edu

Website and Social Media:
Website: www.nyupress.org
Blog: www.fromthesquare.org
Facebook: www.facebook.com/fromthesquare
Twitter: @NYUpress
YouTube: www.youtube.com/user/NYUPressOnline
Tumblr: nyupress.tumblr.com

Orders and Customer Service:
Phone: 855.802.8236

Distributor:
Ingram Publishing Services (IPS)
One Ingram Blvd.
La Vergne, TN 37086
Website: ipage.ingramcontent.com
Phone 855.8028236
Email: ips@ingramcontent.com

UK/European Representative:
Combined Academic Publishers

Staff
Director: Ellen Chodosh (212.998.2573)
  Assistant to the Director/Sales Assistant: Matthew Blon (212.992.9745)
Subsidiary Rights Administrator: Margie Guerra (212.998.2540)
Acquisitions Editorial: Eric Zinner, Associate Director and Editor-in-Chief (cultural and media studies, literary studies, American studies, twentieth-century American history) (212.998.2544)
  Executive Editor: Ilene Kalish (sociology, criminology, politics) (212.998.2556)
  Editor: Clara Platter (American history, military history, law) (212.998.2570)
  Senior Editor: Jennifer Hammer (religion, Jewish studies, psychology, anthropology) (212.998.2491)
  Editorial Director, Library of Arabic Literature: Chip Rossetti (212.998.2433)
  Assistant Editor, Library of Arabic Literature: Amanda Yee (212.998.2575)
  Associate Editor: Alicia Nadkarni (film and media studies) (212.998.2426)
  Assistant Editor: Maryam Arain (212.992.9013)
  Editorial Assistant: Amy Klopfenstein (212.998.4252)

New York University Press continued

Editorial Assistant: Dolma Ombadykow (212.998.6832)
Digital Scholarly Publishing Specialist: TBA
Production and Design Manager: Charles Hames (212.998.2628)
Managing Editor: Dorothea Halliday (212.998.2575)
  Assistant Production Manager: Adam Bohannan (212.998.2578)
  Production Editor: Alexia Traganas (212.992.9998)
  Editing and Production Specialist: Edith Alston (212.992.7303)
Marketing and Sales: Mary Beth Jarrad, Marketing and Sales Director (212.998.2588)
  Publicity Manager: Betsy Steve (212.992.9991)
  Marketing and Publicity Coordinator: Sydney Garcia (212.998.2571)
  Publicist and Subsidiary Rights Administrator: Margie Guerra (212.998.2540)
Business: Laura Bisberg, Business Director (212.998.2569)
  Accounts Payable and Royalties Coordinator: Susan Hamilton (212.998.2524)
  Senior Operations Supervisor: Kevin Cooper (212.998.2546)

Regular Member
Established: 1916
Admitted to the Association: 1937
Title output 2016: 140
Title output 2017: 140
Titles currently in print: 2,960

Editorial Program
American history; law; sociology; Asian American studies; African American studies; Latino/a studies, political science; criminology; psychology; gender studies; cultural and literary studies; media, film, and communications; urban studies; Jewish studies; anthropology; religion; environmental studies; New York regional interest.

    NYU Press is the exclusive North American distributor for Monthly Review Press, and the world-wide distributor for New Village Press.

Special series: Alternative Criminology; America and the Long Nineteenth Century; American History and Culture; Biopolitics; American Literatures Initiative; Children and Youth in America; Citizenship and Migration in the Americas; Clay Sanskrit Library; Critical Cultural Communications; Cultural Front; Culture, Labor, History; Early American Places; Families, Law, and Society; Gender and Political Violence; The History of Disability; Intersections: Transdisciplinary Perspectives on Genders and Sexualities; Library of Arabic Literature; Modern and Contemporary Catholicism; Nation of Newcomers; New and Alternative Religions; New Perspectives on Crime, Deviance, and Law; NOMOS; North American Religions; NYU Series in Social & Cultural Analysis; Postmillennial Pop; Psychology and Crime; Psychology of Law; Qualitative Studies in Psychology; Religion and Social Transformation; Religion, Race, and Ethnicity; Re-imagining North American Religions; Qualitative Studies in Psychology; Qualitative Studies in Religion; Sexual Cultures
Imprints: Washington Mews Books. Books of regional and cultural interest

The University of North Carolina Press

116 South Boundary Street
Chapel Hill, NC 27514-3808

Phone: 919.966.3561
Fax: 919.966.3829
Email: uncpress@unc.edu
Indiv: first name.last name@uncpress.org

Website and Social Media:
Website: www.uncpress.org
Blog: uncpressblog.com
Facebook: www.facebook.com/UNCPress
Twitter: @uncpressblog
YouTube: www.youtube.com/user/UNCPress

Longleaf Services:
Phone: 800.848.6224
Fax: 800.272.6817
Email: customerservice@longleafservices.org
Website: longleafservices.org

UK/European Representative:
Eurospan

Canadian Representative:
Scholarly Book Services

Staff
Director: John Sherer (919.962.3748)
  Executive Assistant: Laura Gribbin (919.962.0358)
Director of Development: Joanna Ruth Marsland (919.962.0924)
Director of Office of Scholarly Publishing Services: John McLeod (919.962.8419)
Acquisitions Editorial:
  Editorial Director: Mark Simpson-Vos (American studies, Native American and Indigenous studies, Civil War and military history, music, regional trade) (919.962.0535)
  Executive Editors: Charles Grench (history) (919.962.0481); Elaine Maisner (religious studies, Latin American and Caribbean studies, cooking and foodways, regional trade) (919.962.0810)
  Senior Editor: Brandon Proia (history, current affairs, African American studies, environmental history) (919.962.0482)
  Editor: Lucas Church (regional trade, Southern studies, literary studies, sociology, health and medicine) (919.962.0536)
  Associate Editor: Jessica Newman (gender and sexuality studies) (919.962.4200)Acquisitions Assistants: Jad Adkins (919.962.0538); Andrew Winters (919.962.0390), Cate Hodorowicz (919.962.9515)
Manuscript Editorial:
  Managing Editor: Mary Caviness (919.962.0545)
  Assistant Managing Editors: Jay Mazzocchi (919.962.0546); Stephanie Wenzel (919.962.0366)
  Editor: Ian Oakes (919.962.0549)
Design and Production:
  Director of Design and Production: Kim Bryant (919.962.0571)
  Senior Designer: Jamison Cockerham (919.843.8021)
  Senior Designer & Reprints Manager: Rebecca Evans (919.962.0575)

University of North Carolina Press continued

Production Manager: Michelle Wallen (919.962.0577)
Book Designer and Production Associate: Sally Scruggs (919.962.0569)
Digital Assets Coordinator: Marjorie Fowler (919.962.0471)
Marketing:
Assistant Director & Senior Director of Marketing & Digital Business Development: Dino Battista (919.962.0579)
Sales Manager: Susan Garrett (919.962.0475)
Director of Publicity: Gina Mahalek (919.962.0581)
Publicity Assistant: Michaela Dwyer (919.962.0585)
Digital Initiatives and Database Director: Ellen Bush (919.962.0582)
Exhibits Manager & Awards Coordinator: Ivis Bohlen (919.962.0594)
Marketing Designer: Joanne Thomas (919.962.0590)
Marketing Assistant: Anna Faison (919.843.7897)
Journals:
Journals Manager: Suzi Waters (919.962.4201)
Journals & OSPS Production Coordinator: Sam Dalzell (919.962.0572)
Business:
Associate Director & CFO: Robbie Dircks (919.962.1400)
Controller: Jami Clay (919.962.4203)
Accounts Payable Manager & Accounting Assistant: Deborah Strickland (919.962.4204)
Accounting Associate: Dylan Stroupe (919.962.0530)
Information Systems:
Information Technology Manager: Tom Franklin (919.962.4196)
Desktop Support Specialist & Systems Administrator: Josef Kalna (919.962.0486)
Longleaf Services:
Executive Director: Clay Farr (919.962.0540); email: clay.farr@longleafservices.org)
Operations Manager: BJ Smith (919.962.1230; email: BJ.smith@ longleafservices.org)
Editorial, Design, & Production Manager: Lisa Stallings (919.962.0544; email: lisa.stallings@longleafservices.org)
Client Sales and Marketing Manager: Jen Slajus (919.962.0369; email: jen.slajus@longleafservices.org)
EDP Associate: Ihsan Taylor (919.962.9569; email: ihsan.taylor@longleafservices.org)
Customer Service Manager: Andrew Routh (919.962.1231); email: andrew.routh@longleafservices.org)
Credit Manager: Terry Miles (919.962.1263); email: terry.miles@longleafservices.org)
Finance Associate: Amanda Doboszenski (919.445.8767; email: amanda.doboszenski@longleafservices.org)

Regular Member

Established: 1922
Title output 2016: 103
Titles currently in print: 4,200

Admitted to the Association: 1937
Title output 2017: 123
Journals published: 11

Editorial Program
African American studies; American and European history; American literature; American studies; ancient history and classics; business and entrepreneurship; cooking and foodways;

craft and craft history; diplomatic history; gender and sexuality; geography; Latin American studies; legal history; military history; Native American and Indigenous studies; nature and environmental studies; politics; popular culture; public policy; regional trade and North Caroliniana; religious studies; social medicine; sociology; southern studies; Women's studies. Submissions are not invited in fiction, poetry, or drama.
Journals: *Appalachian Heritage; The Comparatist; Early American Literature; The High School Journal; Journal of Best Practices in Health Professions Diversity; Journal of the Civil War Era; North Carolina Literary Review; south: a scholarly journal; Southeastern Geographer; Southern Cultures; Studies in Philology*
Special series: Civil War America; Critical Indigeneities; David J. Weber Series in the New Borderlands History; Documentary Arts and Culture; Envisioning Cuba; Ethnographies of Religion; Flows, Migrations, and Exchanges; Gender and American Culture; Islamic Civilization and Muslim Networks; The John Hope Franklin Series in African American History and Culture; Justice, Power, and Politics; Latin America in Translation/en Traducción/em Traducão; The New Cold War History; New Directions in Southern Studies; The Steven and Janice Brose Lectures in the Civil War Era; Studies in Social Medicine; Studies in the History of Greece and Rome; Studies in United States Culture
Joint imprints: Omohundro Institute of Early American History and Culture, sponsored by the College of William and Mary
Distributed publishers: Editorial A Contracorriente; North Carolina Office of Archives and History; North Carolina State Extension; Reacting Consortium Press; University of North Carolina Department of Romance Studies; UNC School of Government

University of North Texas Press

1155 Union Circle #311336
Denton, TX 76203

Phone: 940.565.2142
Fax: 940.565.4590
Email: firstname.lastname@unt.edu

Website and Social Media:
Website: untpress.unt.edu
Facebook: www.facebook.com/UniversityOfNorthTexasPress
Twitter: @untpress
Pinterest: NorthTexasPress

Orders:
Phone: 800.826.8911

UK Representative:
Eurospan

Canadian Representative:
Scholarly Book Services

Staff
Director: Ronald Chrisman
  Assistant to the Director: April Eubanks
  Assistant Director/Managing Editor: Karen DeVinney
Marketing Manager: Elizabeth Whitby

Regular Member
Established: 1988
Title output 2016: 24
Titles currently in print: 500

Admitted to the Association: 2003
Title output 2017: 24
Journals published: 3

University of North Texas Press continued

Editorial Program
Humanities and social sciences, with special emphasis on Texas history and culture, military history, western history, music, criminal justice, folklore, multicultural topics, nature writing, natural and environmental history, culinary history, and women's studies. Submissions in poetry and fiction are invited only through the Vassar Miller and Katherine Anne Porter Prize competition.
Journals: *Journal of Schenkerian Studies; Military History of the West; Theoria*
Special series: A. C. Greene; Al Filo: Mexican American Studies; American Military Studies; Frances B. Vick; Great American Cooking; Katherine Anne Porter Prize in Short Fiction; North Texas Crime and Criminal Justice; North Texas Lives of Musicians; North Texas Military Biography and Memoir; Philosophy and the Environment; Practical Guide; Publications of the Texas Folklore Society; Southwestern Nature Writing Series; Temple Big Thicket; Texas Local; Vassar Miller Prize in Poetry; War and the Southwest; Western Life

Northern Illinois University Press

2280 Bethany Road
DeKalb, IL 60115

Phone: 815.753.1075
Fax: 815.753.1845
Email: (user I.D.)@niu.edu

Website and Social Media:
Website: www.niupress.niu.edu
www.switchgrass.niu.edu
Facebook: www.facebook.com/NIUPress
www.facebook.com/SwitchgrassBooks
Twitter: @NIUPress

Orders:
Chicago Distribution Center
11030 S. Langley Ave.
Chicago, IL 60628
Phone: 800.621.2736
Fax: 800.621.8476
Email: orders@press.uchicago.edu

UK Distributor:
John Wiley Distribution Center

Staff
Interim co-Directors: Amy Farranto (email: afarranto); Nathan Holmes (815.753.9908; email: nholmes1)
  Assistant to the Director: Pat Yenerich (815.753.1075; email: pyenerich)
Acquisitions Editor: Amy Farranto (email: afarranto) (Russian studies, European history, religion, philosophy, political science, U.S. Civil War, midwestern regional studies, Southeast Asian studies, and fiction)
Managing Editor: Nathan Holmes (815.753.9908; email: nholmes1)
Production Manager: Yuni Dorr (815.753.9906; email: ydorr)
Marketing Manager: Lori Propheter (815.753.9905; email: lpropheter)

Regular Member
Established: 1965
Title output 2016: 20
Titles currently in print: 539

Admitted to the Association: 1972
Title output 2017: 20

Editorial Program
U.S. Civil War; European history; Russian studies; religion; philosophy; political science; Southeast Asian studies; regional studies on Chicago and the Midwest; Midwest literary fiction.
Special series: Early American Places; Orthodox Christian Studies; Russian Studies, Southeast Asian Studies
Imprint: Switchgrass Books

Northwestern University Press

629 Noyes Street
Evanston, IL 60208-4210

Phone: 847.491.2046
Fax: 847.491.8150
Email: nupress@northwestern.edu
Indiv: (user I.D.)@northwestern.edu

Orders:
Northwestern University Press
Chicago Distribution Center
11030 South Langley Avenue
Chicago, IL 60628
Phone: 800.621.2736; 773.568.1550
Fax: 800.621.8476; 773.660.2235

Website and Social Media:
Website: www.nupress.northwestern.edu
Facebook: www.facebook.com/pages/Northwestern-University-Press/116644703843
Instagram: instagram.com/nupress
Tumblr: northwesternup.tumblr.com
Twitter: @NorthwesternUP

UK Distributor:
Eurospan

Canadian Distributor:
Scholarly Book Service

Staff
Director: Jane Bunker (847.491.8111; email: j-bunker)
Editor-in-Chief: Gianna Mosser (847.467.1279; email: g-barbera)
  Acquisitions Editors: Trevor Perri (scholarly) (847.491.7384; email: trevor.perri); Jill Petty (email: j-petty) (trade) (847.467.5949)
  Acquisitions Coordinator: Maggie Grossman (847.491.8113; email: m-grossman)
Managing Editor and Manager of Design and Production: Anne Gendler (847.491.3844; email: a-gendler)
  Special Projects Editor: Nathan MacBrien (847.467.7362; email: nathan.macbrien)
  Creative Director: Marianne Jankowski (847.467.5368; email: ma-jankowski)
  Production Manager: Morris (Dino) Robinson (847.467.3392; email: morris-robinson)
Director of Marketing and Publicity: JD Wilson (847.467.0319; email: jdwilson)
  Sales/Subsidiary Rights Manager and Poetry Editor: Parneshia Jones (847.491.7420; email: p-jones3)
  Marketing Manager: Greta Bennion (847.491.5315; email g-bennion)

Northwestern University Press continued

Digital Content and Systems Coordinator: Emily Dalton (847.467.2434; email: emily.dalton)
Business Manager: Kirstie Felland (847.491.8310; email: kfelland)
Intellectual Property Specialist: Liz Hamilton (847.491.2458; email: emhamilton)

Regular Member
Established: 1959
Title output 2016: 62
Titles currently in print: 1,339
Admitted to the Association: 1988
Title output 2017: 70

Editorial Program
The Press publishes in African-American studies; Chicago regional; comparative literature; critical ethnic studies; critical theory; fiction; German studies; history; Jewish Studies; literary criticism; literature in translation; philosophy; poetry; Slavic studies; theater and performance studies; trade nonfiction; women's studies.
Distributed presses: Lake Forest College Press; Tia Chucha Press
Imprints: Curbstone; Marlboro; TriQuarterly; Hydra
Special series: Critical Insurgencies, Diaeresis; Flashpoints; Jewish Lives; Northwestern World Classics; the Northwestern-Newberry Edition of the Writings of Herman Melville; Performance Works; Rereading Ancient Philosophy; Rethinking the Early Modern; Second to None: Chicago Stories; Studies in Phenomenology and Existential Philosophy; Studies in Russian Literature and Theory
Literary Competitions: Cave Canem Northwestern University Press Poetry Prize; Drinking Gourd Chapbook Poetry Prize; Global Humanities Translation Prize

University of Notre Dame Press

310 Flanner Hall
Notre Dame, IN 46556

Phone: 574.631.6346
Fax: 574.631.8148
Email: undpress.1@nd.edu
Indiv: (user I.D.)@nd.edu

Orders:
University of Notre Dame Press
Chicago Distribution Center
11030 South Langley Avenue
Chicago, IL 60628
Phone: 800.621.2736
Fax: 800.621.8476

Website and Social Media:
Website: www.undpress.nd.edu
Facebook: www.facebook.com/UNDpress/
YouTube: www.youtube.com/user/UofNotreDamePress
Pinterest: pinterest.com/undpress

UK/European Representative:
Eurospan

Staff
Director: Steve Wrinn (574.631.3265; email: swrinn)
Senior Acquisitions Editor: Eli Bortz (574.631.4912; email ebortz)
 Acquisitions Editor: Stephen Little (574.631.4906; email: slittle2)
 Executive Assistant: Robyn Karkiewicz (574.631.4913; email: karkiewicz.2)
Manuscript Editorial: Matthew Dowd, Managing Editor (574.631.4914; email: mdowd1)
 Manuscript Editor: Elizabeth Sain (574.631.4911; email: sain.6)
Design and Production: Wendy McMillen, Manager (574.631.4907; email: mcmillen.3)
 Digital Asset Coordinator: Jennifer Bernal (574.631.3266; email: bernal.7)
Marketing: Kathryn Pitts, Manager (574.631.3267; email: pitts.5)
 Marketing and Promotions Assistant: Susan Berger (574.631.4905; email: susan.m.berger)
IT Program Manager: Paul Ashenfelter (574.631.7415; email: pashenfe)
 Coordinator of Office Services: Gina Bixler (574.631.6346; email: bixler.1)

Regular Member
Established: 1949   Admitted to the Association: 1959
Title output 2016: 43   Title output 2017: 55
Titles currently in print: 1,000

Editorial Program
Religion; theology; philosophy; ethics; political science; medieval and early modern studies; classics; Catholic studies; business ethics; American history; European history; European Studies, Latin American studies; religion and literature; Irish studies; history and philosophy of science; international relations; literary criticism; peace studies; patristics; political science, political theory. Submissions are not invited in the hard sciences, mathematics, psychology, or novel-length fiction.

Special series, joint imprints, and/or copublishing programs: Andrés Montoya Poetry Prize; The African American Intellectual Heritage; Catholic Ideas for a Secular World; Catholic Social Tradition; Christianity and Judaism in Antiquity; The Collected Works of Jacques Maritain; Contemporary European Politics and Society; The Conway Lectures in Medieval Studies; Critical Problems in History; Ernest Sandeen Prize in Poetry; Kellogg Institute Series on Democracy and Development; From the Joan B. Kroc Institute for International Peace Studies/Kroc Institute Series on Religion, Conflict, and Peacebuilding; John W. Houck Notre Dame Series in Business Ethics; Latino Perspectives; Liturgical Studies; Michael Psellos in Translation; Notre Dame Conferences in Medieval Studies; Notre Dame Review Book Prize; Notre Dame Studies in Ethics and Culture; Notre Dame Studies in Medical Ethics; Notre Dame Texts in Medieval Culture; Poetics of Orality and Literacy; Reading the Scriptures; ReFormations: Medieval and Early Modern; The Review of Politics Series; Richard Sullivan Prize in Short Fiction; Studies in Judaism and Christianity; Studies in Science and the Humanities from the Reilly Center for Science, Technology, and Values; Studies in Spirituality and Theology; Thresholds in Philosophy and Theology; The Yusko Ward-Phillips Lectures in English Language and Literature; The William and Katherine Devers Series in Dante and Medieval Italian Literature; The Works of Cardinal Newman: Birmingham Oratory Millennium Edition.

Ohio University Press

Alden Library, Suite 101
30 Park Place
Athens, OH 45701-2979

Phone: 740.593.1154
Fax: 740.593.4536
Email: (user I.D.)@ohio.edu

Orders:
Ohio University Press
11030 South Langley Avenue
Chicago, IL 60628
Phone: 800.621.2736
Fax: 800.621.8476

Website and Social Media:
Website: www.ohioswallow.com
Facebook: www.facebook.com/OhioUniversityPress
Twitter: @OhioUnivPress

UK/European Representative:
Combined Academic Publishers

Staff
Director and Editor-in-Chief: Gillian Berchowitz (740.593.1159; email: berchowi)
Acquisitions and Permissions Administrator: Sally Welch (740.593.1154; email: welchs)
Acquisitions Editor: Ricky S. Huard (740.593.1157; email: huard)
Managing Editor: Nancy Basmajian (740.593.1161; email: basmajia)
Production Manager: Beth Pratt (740.593.1162; email: prattb)
Sales Manager: Jeff Kallet (740.593.1158; email: kallet)
Marketing Systems and Design: Sebastian Biot (email: biot)
Promotions and Exhibits Manager: Samara Rafert (740.593.1158; email: rafert)
Publicity Assistant: Maryann Gunderson (email: gundersm)
Business Manager: Omar Aziz (740.593.1156; email: azizo)
Business Office Assistant: Sandra Dixon (740.593.1155; email: dixons3)

Regular Member
Established: 1964
Title output 2016: 42
Titles currently in print: 1,324

Admitted to the Association: 1966
Title output 2017: 47

Editorial Program
Imprints: Swallow Press
Special series, joint imprints, and/or copublishing programs: Africa in World History; Biographies for Young Readers; Cambridge Centre of African Studies Series; The Civil War in the Great Interior; The Collected Letters of George Gissing; The Collected Works of William Howard Taft; The Complete Works of Robert Browning; Eastern African Studies; Hollis Summers Poetry Prize; Indian Ocean Studies Series; Modern African Writing; New African Histories; New Approaches to Midwestern Studies; Ohio Bicentennial Series; Ohio Quilt Series; Ohio Short Histories of Africa; The Papers of Clarence Mitchell, Jr.; Perspectives on the History of Congress 1789 – 1877 and Perspectives on the Art and Architectural History of the United States Capitol (for the US Capitol Historical Society); Perspectives on Global Health; Polish and Polish-American Studies Series; Research in International Studies: Southeast Asia, Africa, Latin America, and Global and Comparative Studies Series; Studies in

Conflict, Justice, and Social Change; Series in Continental Thought; Series in Ecology and History; Series in Appalachian Studies; Series in Victorian Studies; Series on Law, Society, and Politics in the Midwest; War and Society in North America; Western African Studies; White Coat Pocket Guide Series

Ohio State University Press

180 Pressey Hall
1070 Carmack Road
Columbus, OH 43210

Phone: 614.292.6376
Fax: 614.292.2065
Email: info@ouspress.org
Indiv. (user I.D.)@osupress.org

Orders:
Ohio State University Press
Chicago Distribution Center
11030 South Langley Avenue
Phone: 800.621.2736
Fax: 800.621.8476

Website and Social Media:
Website: ohiostatepress.org
Twitter: @ohiostatepress
Facebook: www.facebook.com/ohiostatepress

Staff

Director: Tony Sanfilippo (614.292.7818; email: sanfilippo.16@osu.edu) (regional, trade, medical ethics)
Editor-in-Chief: Kristen Elias Rowley (614.292.8256; email: eliasrowley.1@osu.edu) (American studies, race and ethnic studies, Latino studies, gender & sexuality studies, creative nonfiction, fiction, and poetry)
   Acquisitions Editors: Lindsay Martin (literary studies) (614.292.3668; email: lindsay); Eugene O'Connor (medieval studies, gender and sexuality) (614.292.3667; email: eugene)
Managing Editor: Tara Cyphers (614.292.6198; email: tara)
   Editorial Assistant: Michelle Hoffmann (email: michelle)
Production Manager: Juliet Williams (614.292.3686; email: juliet)
   Production Assistant: Debra Jul (614.292.0999; email: debra)
Marketing Manager: Laurie Avery (614.292.1462; email: laurie.avery)
   Marketing Assistant: Meredith Nini (614.292.6824; email: meredith)
Journals Manager: Emily Taylor (614.292.1407; email: emily)
Business Manager: Kathy Edwards (614.292.3692; email: kathy)

Regular Member

Established: 1957

Title output 2016: 33
Titles currently in print: 642

Admitted to the Association: 2014
(prior membership: 1961-2007)
Title output 2017: 49
Journals published: 6

Ohio State University Press continued

Editorial Program
Scholarly books in the humanities and literary studies, with lists in comic studies, Victorian studies, medieval studies, narrative theory, classics, American and African American studies, gender and sexuality studies, Latino and Chicano Studies, creative works, regional and linguistics.
Journals: *Adoption & Culture; American Periodicals; Inks: The Journal of the Comics Studies Society; Narrative; North American Journal of Celtic Studies; Victorians: A Journal of Culture and Literature*
Special series: 21st Century Essays; Abnormativities: Queer/Gender/Embodiment; Bioethics and Medical Humanities; Black Performance and Cultural Criticism; Classical Memories/Modern Identities; Cognitive Approaches to Culture; Formations: Adoption, Kinship, and Culture; Global Latin/o Americas; Interventions: New Studies in Medieval Culture; Intersectional Rhetorics; The Journal Charles B. Wheeler Poetry Prize; The Journal Non/Fiction Prize; LatinoGraphix: The Ohio State Latin/o Comics Series; Literature, Religion and Postsecular Studies; Machete: The Ohio State Series in Literary Nonfiction; New Directions in Rhetoric and Materiality; New Suns: Race Gender and Sexuality in the Speculative; Studies in Comics and Cartoons; Studies in Victorian Life and Literature; Theory and Interpretation of Narrative; Transoceanic Studies; Victorian Critical Interventions
Imprints: Trillium, Mad Creek

University of Oklahoma Press

2800 Venture Drive
Norman, OK 73069

Phone: 405.325.2000
Faxes: 405.325.4000 (director/rights/acquisitions/marketing);
405.307.9048 (manuscript editing/production/finance)
Email: (user I.D.)@ou.edu

Orders:
Phone: 800.627.7377
Fax: 405.364.5798; 800.735.0476

Website and Social Media:
Website: www.oupress.com
Facebook: www.facebook.com/oupress
Twitter: @OUPress
YouTube: OUPress

UK Representative:
Bay Foreign Language Books

Canadian Representative:
Collin Fuller

Staff
Director: B. Byron Price (405.325.5666; email: b_byron_price)
Editorial: Adam C. Kane, Editor-in-Chief (405.325.7991; email: adam.kane)
  Acquisitions Editors: Kent Calder (Texas regional studies, contemporary American West, Borderlands) (405.325.5820; email: kent.calder); Alessandra Jacobi Tamulevich (native studies: North, Central, and South America, classical studies) (817.538.9802; email: jacobi); Adam C. Kane (military history, American West, environmental his-

tory) (405.325.7991; email: adam.kane); Kathleen Kelly (women's history, California & Southwest, race and culture in the American West, literature) (405.325.1216; email: kathleenkelly); Charles E. (Chuck) Rankin (American West, Mormon studies, Borderlands) (405.209.9833; email: cerankin)
Manuscript Editing: Steven Baker, Managing Editor (405.325.1325; email: steven.b.baker)
Manuscript Editors: Stephanie Evans, Assistant Managing Editor (405.325.4922; email: s.evans); Emily Schuster, Associate Editor (405.325.3786; email: ejerman)
Production: Tony Roberts, Production Manager (405.325.3186; email: tonyroberts)
Production Coordinator: Anna Maria Rodriguez (405.325.3876; email: annamaria)
Electronic Publishing Manager: Brent Greyson (405.325.3202; email: bgreyson)
Marketing and Sales: Dale Bennie, Associate Director, Sales and Marketing Manager (405.325.3207; email: dbennie)
Publicity Manager: Katherine Baker (405.325.3200)
Business: Dale Bennie, Associate Director, Business Manager (405.325.3207; email: dbennie)
Accounting: Amy Liu (405.325.2356; email xliu)
Accounts Receivable and Royalties: Diane Cannon (405.325.2326; email: dcannon)
Customer Service: Kathy Benson (405.325.2287; email: presscs)
Rights and Permissions: Shannon Gering (405.325.3182; email: segering)

Regular Member
Established: 1928
Title output 2016: 128
Titles currently in print: 1,930

Admitted to the Association: 1937
Title output 2017: 101

Editorial Program
Scholarly and general interest books, general nonfiction, and some fiction with special interests in the American West, Art and Photography, Classical Studies, Environmental History, Indigenous Studies (North, Central, and South America), Military History, Natural History, Political Science, Popular Music, and Regional Studies.
Imprints: The Arthur H. Clark Company
Book series: American Exploration and Travel Series; American Indian Law and Policy Series; American Indian Literature and Critical Studies Series; American Popular Music Series; American Trails Series (A.H. CLARK); Animal Natural History Series; Before Gold; Campaigns and Commanders; Charles M. Russell Center Series on Art and Photography of the American West; Chicana and Chicano Visions of the Américas Series; Chinese Literature Today; Civilization of the American Indian Series; Congressional Studies Series; Early California Commentaries (A.H. CLARK); Environment in Modern North America, Frontier Military Series (A.H. CLARK); Hidden Springs of Custeriana (A.H. CLARK); International and Security Affairs Series; Julian J. Rothbaum Distinguished Lecture Series; Kingdom in the West (A.H. CLARK); New Directions in Native American Studies; Oklahoma Series in Classical Culture; Oklahoma Western Biographies; Political Violence in North America, Public Lands History; Race and Culture in the American West; Spain in the West Series (A.H. CLARK); Studies in American Constitutional Heritage; Variorum Chaucer; Ways of War, The Western Frontier Library; Western Frontiersmen Series (A.H. CLARK); Western Lands and Waters (A.H. CLARK); Western Legacies Series; The William F. Cody Series on the History and Culture of the American West

Oregon State University Press

121 The Valley Library
Corvallis, OR 97331-4501

Phone: 541.737.3166
Fax: 541.737.3170
Email: osu.press@oregonstate.edu
Indiv: (user I.D.)@oregonstate.edu

Order Fulfillment & Distribution:
Chicago Distribution Center
11030 S. Langley Ave.
Chicago, IL 60628
Phone: 800.621.2736
Fax: 800.621.8476

Website and Social Media:
Website: osupress.oregonstate.edu
Blog: www.osupress.oregonstate.edu/blog
Facebook: www.facebook.com/OregonStateUniversityPress
Twitter: @osupress
YouTube: OregonStateUPress
Instagram: osupress

European, African, & Middle Eastern Dist.:
Eurospan Group

Canadian Distributor:
University of British Columbia Press

Staff
Director: Faye A. Chadwell (541.737.8528; email: faye.chadwell)
Associate Director: Tom Booth (503.796.0547; email: thomas.booth)
Acquisitions Editor: Mary Elizabeth Braun (541.737.3873; email: mary.braun)
Editorial, Design, and Production Manager: Micki Reaman (541.737.4620; email: micki.reaman)
Marketing Manager: Marty Brown (541.737.3866; email: marty.brown)

Regular Member
Established: 1961
Title output 2016: 18
Titles currently in print: 285

Admitted to the Association: 1991
Title output 2017: 17

Editorial Program
The Oregon State University Press publishes scholarly and general interest books in the environmental humanities; forestry; natural resource management; environmental and natural history; Native American and Indigenous studies; and the history, culture, and arts of the Pacific Northwest.
Special series: First Peoples: New Directions in Indigenous Studies; Horning Visiting Scholars Publication Series; Northwest Reprints; Women and Politics in the Pacific Northwest.

Otago University Press

Street Address:
Level One
398 Cumberland Street
Dunedin, New Zealand 9016

Mailing Address:
Box 56
Dunedin, New Zealand 9016

Phone: 64.3.479.4194
Email: university.press@otago.ac.nz
Indiv: (first name.last name)@otago.ac.nz

Orders (NZ):
Nationwide Book Distributors
Phone: 64.3.312.1603
Email: books@nationwidebooks.co.nz

Website and Social Media:
Website: www.otago.ac.nz/press/index.html
Facebook: www.facebook.com/OtagoUniversityPress
Twitter: @OtagoUniPress

UK Representative:
Gazelle Book Services

US and Canadian Representative:
Independent Publishers Group (IPG)
814 N. Franklin Street
Chicago, IL 60610
Phone 800.888.4741

Staff
Publisher: Rachel Scott (64.3.479.4194)
Editorial/Permissions: Imogen Coxhead (64 3 479 4155)
Design and Production: Fiona Moffat, Production Manager (64.3.479.5851)
Marketing & Publicity: Victor Billot (64.3.479.9094)
Accounts: Glenis Thomas (64.3.479.4194)
Sales reps: Archetype Book Agents (neilb@archetype.co.nz)

Regular Member
Established: 1958
Title output 2016: 20
Titles currently in print: 160

Admitted to the Association 2016
Title output 2017: 21
Journals published: 1

Editorial Program
Non-fiction books on New Zealand and the Pacific, including history and regional history (southern New Zealand); natural history; Māori and Pacific studies; biography and memoir; arts, culture and literary studies; poetry.
Journal: *Landfall: Aotearoa New Zealand Arts & Letters*

University of Ottawa Press | Les Presses de l'Université d'Ottawa

542 King Edward Avenue
Ottawa, ON K1N 6N5 Canada

Phone: 613.562.5246
Fax: 613.562.5247
Email: puo-uop@uottawa.ca

Website and Social Media:
Website: www.press.uottawa.ca
Facebook: www.facebook.com/uOttawaPress
Twitter: @uOttawaPress
Fax: 800.361.8088; 450.434.4135

US Orders (English and French titles):
Ingram Academic Services
Ingram Content Group
Customer Service
210 American Drive
Jackson, TN 38301
Phone: 800.343.4499
Fax: 800.351.5073
Email: academicorders@ingramcontent.com

France (French titles):
Distribution du Nouveau Monde
Website: www.librairieduquebec.fr

Belgium, Netherlands, Luxembourg (French titles):
Patrimoine Diffusion Sprl
Avenue Milcamps 119
1030 Bruxelles
Belgique

Canadian Orders (English titles):
University of Toronto Press
Phone: 800.565.9523; 416.667.7791
Fax: 800.221.9985; 416.667.7832
Email: utpbooks@utpress.utoronto.ca

Canadian Orders (French titles):
Prologue Inc.
1650 Lionel-Bertrand Boulevard
Boisbriand, Quebec J7H 1N7 Canada
Phone: 800.363.2864; 450.434.0306
Email: prologue@prologue.ca

UK and European Orders (English titles):
Marston Book Services

Switzerland (French titles):
Servidis SA
Website: www.servidis.ch

Staff
Director: Lara Mainville (613.562.5663; email: lara.mainville@uottawa.ca)
Acquisitions Editor: Caroline Boudreau (613.562.5800 ext. 3065; email: acquisitions@uottawa.ca)
Production Editor: Elizabeth Schwaiger (613.562.5800 ext. 3064; email: eschwaig@uottawa.ca)
Digital Content Manager: Mireille Piché (613.562.5800 ext. 2854; email: mireille.piche@uottawa.ca)
Marketing, Distribution, and Administration: Sonia Rheault (613.562.5246; email: srheault@uottawa.ca)
General email: puo-uop@uottawa.ca

Regular Member
Established: 1936
Title output 2016: 26
Titles currently in print: 505

Admitted to the Association: 2005
Title output 2017: 30
Journals published: 3

Editorial Program
North America's oldest French-language and only fully bilingual university press developed a publishing program in the social sciences and humanities that promotes critical and ethical thinking, first-class research, intellectual integrity, social responsibility, and innovation. UOP fully supports the open access movement and is committed to the open dissemination of scholarship and research insofar as it is financially viable. Titles are published in print and ebook formats.

UOP's mission is 1) To enrich intellectual and cultural life through the publication and dissemination of scholarly works; 2) To extend the reach and influence of the University of Ottawa and associate its name with excellence in research and knowledge creation. In order to fulfill its mission, UOP looks to its rich academic heritage to publish compelling books that engage with today's issues. UOP series are structured along three axes:

Francophonie & Canadian Studies: Amérique française, Archives des lettres canadiennes; Canadian Literature Collection; Canadian Studies; Mercury Series; Reappraisals: Canadian Writers; Perspectives on Translation; and Literary Translation

Politics, Public Policy and Globalization: International Development and Globalization; Law, Technology and Media; and Politics and Public Policy; and

Contemporary Society: Visual Arts; Education; Contemporary Issues; Criminology; Philosophica; Religion and Society; Health and Society; and Cultural Transfers.

A fourth axis, Praxis, is perpendicular to these and comprises textbooks and other pedagogical materials.

Imprints: Harvest House

Oxford University Press, Inc.

Editorial Offices:
198 Madison Avenue
New York, NY 10016
Phone: 212.726.6000
Fax: 212.726.6440
Email: firstname.lastname@oup.com

Website and Social Media:
Website: www.oup.com/us
Blogs: blog.oup.com blog.oxforddictionaries.com/
Twitter: @OUPAcademic

Customer Service:
Orders/Prices: 800.451.7556
Inquiries: 800.445.9714
ELT: 800.542.2442
Journals: 800.852.7323
Music Retail: 800.292.0639
Fax: 919.677.1303

Distribution Center &
Journals Marketing Office:
2001 Evans Road
Cary, NC 27513
Phone: 919.677.0977
Dist. Fax: 919.677.8877
Journals Fax: 919.677.1714

Oxford University Press (UK):
Great Clarendon Street
Oxford OX2 6DP
United Kingdom
Phone: +44 1865 556767
Fax: +44 1865 556646

American English Language Teaching (ELT):
Phone: 212.726.6300
Fax: 212.726.6388

Staff
President: Niko Pfund
  Assistant to the President: Henry Singleton
  Chief Financial Officer, Global Academic: Deborah Stevenson (interim)
  Vice President, Legal, and General Counsel, Global Academic: Barbara Cohen
  Vice President and Publisher, Higher Education Group: John Challice
  Publisher, Reference and Online: Damon Zucca
  Publisher, Trade, Academic and Journals: Niko Pfund
  President, Dictionaries Division: Casper Grathwohl
  Director, Global Business Development and Rights, Academic & US Divisions: Casper Grathwohl
  Vice President, Global Marketing and Digital Strategy: Colleen Scollans
  Vice President, Human Resources: Rosann Ashe
  Vice President, Operations: Laurea Salvatore

Trade and Academic
Publisher: Niko Pfund
  Editorial: David Pervin (economics and finance); Tim Bent (trade, history and politics); James Cook (sociology, criminology); Susan Ferber (history); Nancy Toff (history); Jeremy Lewis (chemistry, sciences); Peter Ohlin (philosophy and linguistics); Cynthia Read (re-

ligion); Theo Calderara (religion); Suzanne Ryan (music); **Norm Hirschy** (music); Stefan Vranka (classics and ancient history); David McBride (politics, law); Angela Chnapko (politics); Steve Wiggins (Bibles); Hallie Stebbins (linguistics); Sarah Pirovitz (technology studies)

Law
Publisher: John Louth
  Editors: Blake Ratcliff (international law and national security law); Alex Flach (all other areas of law)

Medical
Publishing Director, Clinical Medicine: Sean Pidgeon
  Associate Editorial Director: Craig Panner (neurology, clinical neuroscience)
  Senior Editors: Andrea Knobloch (psychiatry); Chad Zimmerman (public health/epidemiology, infectious disease)
  Editor: Marta Moldvai (palliative care, emergency medicine)
  Digital Development Editor/Medical Editorial: Nicholas Liu

Psychology/Social Work Division
Publishing Director, Psychology/Social Work: Sean Pidgeon
  Editorial Director: Joan Bossert (neuropsychology, cognitive neuroscience, cognitive psychology)
  Senior Editors: Dana Bliss (social work); Abby Gross (social psychology, positive psychology, industrial & organizational psychology); Sarah Harrington (clinical psychology, forensic psychology, school psychology)
  Associate Editor: Courtney McCarroll (developmental psychology, educational psychology)

Reference
Publisher: Damon Zucca
  Reference Editorial: Timothy Allen (social work, education, law); Molly Balikov (social science, economics, business, political science); Ada Brunstein (psychology, neuroscience); Louis Gullino (history); Sarah Kain (earth and physical sciences); Alodie Larson (Oxford/Grove Art); Benjamin Leonard (classics); Robert Repino (African American studies); Anna-Lise Santella (Oxford/Grove Music); Anthony Wahl (sociology, communication, criminology); Katherine Martin (US Dictionaries)

Dictionaries
President: Casper Grathwohl
  Dictionaries Editorial: Katherine Martin (Head of US Dictionaries); Allison Wright (online)

Higher Education
Publisher: John Challice
  Editorial: Patrick Lynch (editorial director); Robert Miller (philosophy & religion); Jodi Lewchuk (English & Linguistics); Richard Carlin (art & music); Jennifer Carpenter (politics); Sherith Pankratz (sociology, anthropology, & archaeology); Steve Helba (criminology & criminal justice); Jane Potter (psychology); Jason Noe (life sciences & chemistry); Dan Kaveney (earth & environmental sciences; engineering & computer science); Ann West (economics & finance); Toni Magyar (communication & journalism); Charles Cavaliere (history and classics); Dave Ward (business and management)
  Director of Marketing: Frank Mortimer
  National Sales Manager: William Marting

Content Operations
Head of Content Operations: Deborah Shor

Oxford University Press continued

   Production Managers: Kate Hind, Lisa Grzan
   Demand Planning Manager: Brenda Manzanedo
Business Development and Rights
Director, Global Business Development and Rights: Casper Grathwohl
   Business Development Manager, Language and Dictionaries: Zachary Haynes
   Business Development Manager: Sabrina Jonkhoff
   Business Development Manager, Global Language Solutions: Zachary Haynes
   Rights Clearance Specialist: Charles Devilbiss
Sales and Marketing
Global Chief Marketing Officer: Colleen Scollans
   Global Marketing Director and North American Key Accounts: Kim Craven
   Global Journals Marketing Director: Sarah Ultsch
   Global Publicity and Trade Marketing Associate Director: Sarah Russo
   Director of Library Sales: Rebecca Seger
   Director of Direct and Content Marketing: Rose Pintaudi-Jones
   Associate Director of Distribution Client Management: Brian Hughes
   Digital Strategy: Jessica Chesnutt
Human Resources
Director, Human Resources, Global Academic: Rosann Ashe
Operations (New York)
Office Services Facility Manager, NY: Lorraine Betancourt
Finance
Chief Financial Officer: Deborah Stevenson (interim)
   Director of Finance: Scott Grande
   Director of Accounting: Dottie Warlick
English Language Teaching—New York
   Head of Adult: Stephanie Karras
   US Sales and Marketing Director:
   Head of Digital, Design, and Content Production: Bridget O'Lavin
Journals
Publishing Director: Alison Denby
   US Director, Corporate Sales: Amy Luchsinger
   Journal's Editorial: Deborah Dixon
   Editorial Director STM: Rhodri Jackson
   Editorial Director Humanities, Social Science and Law: David Crotty
   Editorial Director, Journals Policy: Patricia Thomas (humanities)
   Journals Editorial: Laura Bannon (social science); Fiona Williams (life science); Sara McNamara (life sciences); Chris Reid (medical); Ashley Petrylak (medical); Phyllis Cohen (social science); Rachel Warren (medical); Rachel Safer (medical); Anna Hernandez-French (science); Michael Blong (social science); Byron Boneparth (social sciences); Claire Neumann (medical)
Distribution Center (North Carolina)
Cary Facilities Inventory Control/Freight: James Torrence
   Credit and Collection: Dottie Warlick
   Customer Service: Cheryl Ammons-Longtin

Warehouse Operations: Todd Hayes
Accounting Services: Dottie Warlick
<u>Technology</u>
IT & Technology Director: Mike Monaghan
IT Operations Manager: Martin Bodek

Regular Member

Established: 1895   Admitted to the Association: 1950
Title output 2016: 1,500   Title output 2017: 1,500
Titles currently in print: 26,000   Journals published: (US only): 94

Editorial Program

Scholarly monographs; general nonfiction; Bibles; college textbooks; medical books; music; reference books; journals; children's books; English language teaching. Submissions are not invited in the area of fiction or autobiography.

Journals *published in the US from 2017: Aesthetic Surgery Journal; American Entomologist; American Historical Review; American Journal of Agricultural Economics; American Journal of Comparative Law, American Journal of Epidemiology Research; American Journal of Hypertension; American Journal of Legal History; American Literary History; Annals of the Entomological Society of America; Applied Economic Perspectives & Policy; Archives of Clinical Neuropsychology; Arthropod Management Tests; Biology of Reproduction; BioScience; Cerebral Cortex; Children & Schools; Christian Bioethics; Clinical Infectious Diseases; Diplomatic History; Diseases of the Esophagus; Early Music; Environmental Entomology; Environmental History; Epidemiologic Reviews; The Gerontologist; Gigascience, Health & Social Work; Health Education Research; Health Promotion International; Holocaust and Genocide Studies; ILAR Journal; International Journal of Neuropsychopharmacology; ISA Journals; ISLE: Interdisciplinary Studies in Literature and Environment; JAMIA; JNCI: Journal of the National Cancer Institute; Journal of American History; Journal of Analytical Toxicology; The Journal of Applied Poultry Research Journal of Chromatographic Science; Journal of Deaf Studies and Deaf Education; Journal of Economic Entomology; Journal of Gerontology – Series A: Biological Sciences and Medical Sciences; Journal of Hindu Studies; The Journal of Infectious Diseases; Journal of Insect Science; Journal of Integrated Pest Management; Journal of Islamic Studies; Journal of Mammalogy; Journal of Medical Entomology; Journal of Medicine and Philosophy; Journal of Music Therapy; Journal of Pediatric Psychology; Journal of Public Administration Research and Theory; Journal of Social History; Journal of Survey Statistics and Methodology; Journal of the American Academy of Religion; Journal of the History of Medicine and Allied Sciences; Journal of the Pediatric Infectious Diseases Society; Journal of Theological Studies; Journals of Gerontology – Series B: Psychological Sciences and Social Sciences; Literary Imagination; Mammalian Species; Medical Mycology; Modern Judaism: A Journal of Jewish Ideas and Experience; Monist; Multi-Ethnic Literature of the United States; Music and Letters; Music Theory Spectrum; Music Therapy Perspectives; The Musical Quarterly; Neurosurgery; Nicotine and Tobacco Research; Nutrition Reviews; OAH Magazine of History; Open Forum Infectious Diseases; Opera Quarterly; Operative Neurosurgery; The Oral History Review; Pain Medicine; Physical Therapy; Political Analysis; Poultry Science; Public Opinion Quarterly; Public Policy & Aging Report; Publius; Quarterly Journal of Economics; The Review of Asset Pricing Studies; The Review of Corporate Finance Studies; Review of Environmental Economics & Policy; The Review of Financial Studies; Schizophrenia Bulletin; Sleep, Social Forces; Social Problems; Social Work; Social Work Research; Sociology of Religion: A Quarterly Review; The World Bank Economic Review; The World Bank Research Observer; Toxicological Sciences; Western Historical Review; Work, Aging, and Retirement*

University of Pennsylvania Press

3905 Spruce Street
Philadelphia, PA 19104-4112

Phone: 215.898.6261
Fax: 215.898.0404
Email: (user I.D.)@upenn.edu

Order Department:
PO Box 50370
Baltimore, MD 21211-4370
Phone: 800.537.5487
Fax: 410.516.6998
Email (inquiries only):
custserv@pobox.upenn.edu

Website and Social Media:
Website: www.pennpress.org
Blog: pennpress.typepad.com
Facebook: www.facebook.com/PennPress
Twitter: @PennPress

Warehouse & Returns:
Maple Press Company
Lebanon Distribution Center
704 Legionaire Drive
Fredericksburg, PA 17026

UK/European Distributor:
Combined Academic Publishers

Canadian Representative:
Scholarly Book Services

Staff

Director: Eric Halpern (215.898.1672; email: ehalpern)
Assistant to the Director and Rights Administrator: Zoe Gould (215.898.6263; email: zgould)
  Acquisitions: Peter Agree, Editor-in-Chief (human rights, policy and politics, anthropology) (215.573.3816; email: agree)
  Senior Editors: Jerome E. Singerman (literary criticism and cultural studies; ancient, medieval, and Renaissance studies; landscape architecture; Jewish studies) (215.898.1681; email: singerma); Robert Lockhart (American history, regional books) (215.898.1677; email: rlockhar)
  Consulting Editors: Deborah Blake (ancient studies) (44.7867.540881; email: dcblake.pennpress@virginmedia.com); Damon Linker (current affairs, digital shorts) (610.613.4546; email: linkerpennpress@gmail.com)
  Acquisitions Assistants: Amanda Ruffner (215.898.6262; email: aruff); Hannah Blake (215.898.3252; email: hblake)
Manuscript Editing and Production: Elizabeth Glover, Editing & Production Manager (215.898.1675; email: gloverel)
  Assistant Production Manager: William Boehm (215.573.4059; email: boehmwj)
  Managing Editors: Lily Palladino (215.898.1678; email: lilypall); Erica Ginsburg (215.898.1679; email: eginsbur); Noreen O'Connor (215.898.1709; email: nmoconno)
  Production Coordinator: Susan Staggs (215.898.1676; email: sstaggs)
  Art Director: John Hubbard (215.573.6118; email: wmj)
Marketing: Laura Waldron, Marketing Director (215.898.1673; email: lwaldron)
  Publicity & Public Relations Manager: Gigi Lamm (215.898.1674; email: glamm)Electronic Marketing Coordinator: Peter Valelly (215.898.8678; email: pvalelly)
  Direct Mail & Advertising Manager: Tracy Kellmer (215.898.9184; email: tkellmer)
Journals: Paul Chase, Operations Manager (215.573.1295; email: paulbc)

Editing and Production Coordinator: Emily Stevens (215.898.7588; email: emilyste)
Journals Assistant: Syra Ortiz-Blaines (215.573.4585; email: syra)
Business: Joseph Guttman, Business Manager (215.898.1670; email: josephgg)
Financial Coordinator: Kathy Ranalli (215.898.1682; email: ranalli)
Administrative Assistant: Barbara Nolan (215.898.1671; email: custserv@pobox.upenn.edu)

Regular Member

Established: 1890	Admitted to the Association: 1967
Title output 2016: 134	Title output 2017: 137
Titles currently in print: 3,062	Journals published: 18

Editorial Program
Scholarly and semipopular nonfiction, with special interests in American history and culture; ancient, medieval, and early modern studies; human rights; urban studies, politics and public policy; Jewish studies; anthropology; landscape architecture; and Pennsylvania regional studies.

Journals: *Change Over Time; Dissent; Early American Studies; The Eighteenth-Century: Theory and Interpretation; French Forum; Hispanic Review; Humanity; Huntington Library Quarterly; Jewish Quarterly Review; Journal for Early Modern Cultural Studies; Journal of the Early Republic; Journal of Ecumenical Studies; Journal of the History of Ideas; J19: The Journal of Nineteenth-Century Americanists; Magic, Ritual, and Witchcraft; Manuscript Studies; Pennsylvania Magazine of History and Biography; Revista Hispanica Moderna*

Special series: American Business, Politics, and Society; American Governance; American in the Nineteenth Century; Arts and Intellectual Life in Modern America; Contemporary Ethnography; City in the 21st Century; Democracy, Citizenship, and Constitutionalism; Divinations; Early American Studies; Early Modern Americas; Empire and After; Encounters with Asia; Ethnography of Political Violence; Hagley Perspectivs on Business and Culture; Intellectual History of the Modern Age; Jewish Culture and Contexts; Material Texts; The Middle Ages; Penn Studies in Landscape Architecture; Pennsylvania Studies in Human Rights; Politics and Culture in Modern America

Copublishing programs: Ceramics Handbooks

Imprint: University of Pennsylvania Museum of Archaeology and Anthropology

Pennsylvania State University Press

820 North University Drive
USB-1, Suite C
University Park, PA 16802-1003

Orders:
Phone: 800.326.9180
Fax: 877.778.2665

Phone: 814.865.1327
Fax: 814.863.1408
Email: (user I.D.)@psu.edu

Website and Social Media:
Website: www.psupress.org
Twitter: @PSUPress
Facebook: www.facebook.com/psupress

UK Representative:
The Oxford Publicity Partnership

Canadian Distributor:
University of Toronto Press

Staff
Director: Patrick H. Alexander (814.867.2209; email: pha3)
  Assistant to the Director: Teresa Craig (814.867.5443; email: tac6)
Acquisitions Editorial: Kendra Boileau, Editor-in-Chief (814.867.2220; email: klb60)
  Executive Editor, Art History and Humanities: Eleanor Goodman (814.867.2212; email: ehg11)
  Acquisitions Editor: Kathryn Yahner (814.865.1327; email: kby3)
  Editorial Assistants: Hannah Hebert (814.865.1328; email: hnh1); Alex Vose (814.865.1592; email: hav4)
  Editorial, Design, and Production: Jennifer Norton, Associate Director, EDP Manager (814.863.8061; email: jsn4)
Managing Editor: Laura Reed-Morrisson (814.865.1606; email: lxr168)
  Senior Designer: Regina Starace (814.867.2215; email: ras35)
  Production Coordinator and Data Administrator: Brian Beer (814.867.2210; email: bxb110)
  Production Assistant: Jon Gottshall (814.867.2213; email: jeg31)
Marketing/Sales: Brendan Coyne, Sales and Marketing Director (814.863.5994; email: bcc5228)
  Advertising and Direct Mail Manager: Heather Smith (814.863.0524; email: hms7)
  Publicity Manager: Cate Fricke (814.865.1329; email: crf16)
  Sales and Exhibits Manager: Kathleen Scholz-Jaffe (814.867.2224; email: kxs56)
Rights and Permissions Manager: Sheila S. Reyes (814.867.2831; email: sss2)
Journals Manager: Diana Pesek (814.867.2223; email: dlp28)
  Production Coordinator: Julie Lambert (814.863.5992; email: jas1035)
  Managing Editor: Astrid Meyer (814.863.3830; email: aum38)
  Production Assistant: Jessica Karp (814.867.2211; email: jxk82)
  Production Assistant: Rachel Ginder (814.863.1307; email: rlg5195)
Business Office/Order Fulfillment: Tina Laychur, Business Manager (814.863.5993; email: txs17)
  Assistant Business Manager: Kathy Vaughn (814.863.6771; email: kmv1)

Shipping Clerk: Dave Buchan (814.863.5496; email: dcb11)
Fulfillment Support Associate: Curtiss Smith (814.865.6056; email: ces36)
Information Systems Manager: Ed Spicer (814.865.1327; email: res122)

Regular Member

Established: 1956   Admitted to the Association: 1960
Title output 2016: 40   Title output 2017: 56
Titles currently in print: 1,735   Journals published: 71
(does not include new in paper or distributions)

Editorial Program

Scholarly books in the humanities and social sciences, with current emphasis on animal studies; architecture; art history; American, European, and Latin American history; communication studies and rhetoric; graphic medicine; interdisciplinary literary studies; medieval studies; occultism and esoterism; religion. Submissions are not invited in fiction, poetry, or drama.

Journals: *ab-Original: Journal of Indigenous Studies and First Nations' and First Peoples' Cultures; The Author Miller Journal; Bustan: The Middle East Book Review; The Chaucer Review; Comedia Performance; Comparative Literature Studies; Cormac McCarthy Journal; Critical Philosophy of Race; Dickens Study Annual; The Edgar Allan Poe Review; The Edith Wharton Review; The Eugene O'Neill Review; The F. Scott Fitzgerald Review; George Eliot-George Henry Lewes Studies; Gestalt Review; The Good Society; The Harold Pinter Review; Interdisciplinary Literature Studies; International Journal of Persian Literature; Journal of Africana Religions; Journal of Asia-Pacific Pop Culture; Journal of Assessment and Institutional Effectiveness; Journal of Austrian-American History; The Journal of Ayn Rand Studies; Journal of Development Perspectives; Journal of Eastern Mediterranean Archaeology and Heritage Studies; Journal of General Education; Journal of Information Policy; Journal of Jewish Ethics; Journal of Medieval Religious Cultures; Journal of Modern Periodical Studies; Journal of Moravian History; Journal of Natural Resources Policy Research; Journal of Nietzsche Studies; Journal of the Pennsylvania Academy of Science; Journal of Posthuman Studies; Journal of Speculative Philosophy; Journal of World Christianity; Korean Language in America; Libraries: Culture, History, and Society; Milton Studies; The Mark Twain Annual; Mediterranean Studies; Nathaniel Hawthorne Review; Pacific Coast Philology; Pennsylvania History; Philosophy and Rhetoric; Preternature; Reception: Texts, Readers, Audiences, History; Resources for American Literary Study; SHAW: The Journal of Bernard Shaw Studies; Soundings; Steinbeck Review; Studies in American Humor; Studies in American Jewish Literature; Style; Transformations: The Journal of Inclusive Pedagogy; Transportation Journal; Utopian Studies; Wesley and Methodist Studies; William Carlos Williams Review*

Special series: Africana Religions; Animalibus: Of Animals and Cultures; AnthropoScene: The SLSA Book Series; Buildings, Landscapes, and Societies; Edinburgh Edition of Thomas Reid; Dimyonot: Jews and the Cultural Imagination; The Frick Collection Studies in the History of Art Collecting in America; Graphic Medicine; Iberian Encounter and Exchange, 475–1755; Inventing Christianity; Latin American Originals; Magic in History; Magic in History Sourcebooks; The Max Kade Research Institute Series: Germans beyond Europe; Medieval and Renaissance Literary Studies; Penn State Series in Critical Theory; Penn State Series in the History of the Book; Pietist, Moravian, and Anabaptist Studies; RSA Series in Transdisciplinary Rhetoric; Refiguring Modernism; Religion Around; Rhetoric and Democratic Deliberation; Signifying (on) Scriptures; World Christianity

Special imprints: Keystone Books; Eisenbrauns

University of Pittsburgh Press

7500 Thomas Boulevard
Pittsburgh, PA 15260
info@upress.pitt.edu
Phone: 412.383.2456
Fax: 412.383.2466
Email: (user I.D.)@upress.pitt.edu

Order Fulfillment:
University of Pittsburgh Press
Chicago Distribution Center
11030 South Langley Avenue
Chicago, IL 60628
Phone: 773.568.1550; 800.621.2736
Fax: 773.660.2235

Website and Social Media:
Website: www.upress.pitt.edu
Facebook: www.facebook.com/pages/University-of-Pittsburgh-Press/319974668123448
Facebook (Poetry): www.facebook.com/pittpoetry.series
Twitter: @UPittPress
Twitter(Poetry): @PittPoetry

UK Representative:
Eurospan

Canadian Representative:
Scholarly Book Services

Staff
Director: Peter Kracht (email: pkracht)
  Assistant to the Director: Kelley H. Johovic (email: kjohovic)
Editorial Director: Sandy Crooms (email: scrooms)
  Senior Acquisitions Editor: Joshua Shanholtzer (email: jshanholtzer)
  Acquisitions Editor: Abby Collier (email: acollier)
  Assistant Editor: Amberle Sherman (email: editorial.assistant)
Editorial & Production Manager: Alex Wolfe (email: awolfe)
  Design & Production Editor: Joel Coggins (email: jcoggins)
  Marketing Director: David Baumann (email: dbaumann)
  Web & Social Media Coordinator/Graphic Designer: Greta Polo (email: gpolo)
  Publicist: Maria Sticco (email: msticco)
  Copywriter, Promotional & Social Media Coordinator: Chloe Wertz (email: cwertz)
Subsidiary Rights Manager: Margie Bachman (email: mbachman)
Business Manager: Cindy Wessels (email: cwessels)

Regular Member
Established: 1936
Title output 2016: 48
Titles currently in print: 1,290

Admitted to the Association: 1937
Title output 2017: 69

Editorial Program
History; Russian and East European studies; Central Eurasian studies; Latin American studies; composition and literacy studies; poetry; history and philosophy of science; history of architecture; urban studies; environmental history; Pittsburgh and western Pennsylvania. The Press does not invite submissions in the hard sciences, original fiction (except DHLP), festschriften, memoirs, symposia, or unrevised doctoral dissertations.

  The Press co-publishes and distributes Hebrew Union College Press titles. The Press distributes selected titles with the Carnegie Museum of Art, the Carnegie Museum of Natural History, the Frick Art and Historical Center, the Historical Society of Western Pennsylvania,

the Mattress Factory, and the Westmoreland Museum of American Art.
Special series: Agnes Lynch Starrett Poetry Prize; Ayn Rand Society Philosophical Studies; Central Eurasia In Context; Cuban Studies; Culture, Politics, and the Built Environment; Drue Heinz Literature Prize; History of the Urban Environment; Illuminations: Cultural Formations of the Americas; Pitt Latin American Series; Pitt Poetry Series; Pitt Series in Russian and East European Studies; Pittsburgh Series in Composition, Literacy, and Culture; Pittsburgh/Konstanz Series in Philosophy and History of Science

Princeton University Press

Executive Offices:
41 William Street
Princeton, NJ 08540-5237

Phone: 609.258.4900
Fax: 609.258.6305
Email:
firstname_lastname@press.princeton.edu

Website and Social Media:
Website: press.princeton.edu
Blog: blog.press.princeton.edu
Facebook:@PrincetonUniversityPress
Twitter: @PrincetonUPress
Instagram: @PrincetonUPress
YouTube: www.youtube.com/user/PUPress
Vimeo: www.vimeo.com/princetonuniversity press
Tumblr: pupdesign.tumblr.com
Linkedin: linkedin.com/company/princeton-university-press
Google+: princetonuniversitypress

Order Fulfillment (US and Canada):
Perseus Distribution
210 American Drive
Jackson, TN 38301
Phone: 800.343.4499
Fax: 800.351.5073
Email: orderentry@perseusbooks.com

European Editorial Office:
6 Oxford St.
Woodstock, Oxfordshire OX20 1TW
United Kingdom
Phone: +44 1993 814500
Fax: +44 1993 814504
Email:
firstname_lastname@press.princeton.edu

UK/European Sales Representation:
The University Press Group Ltd.
California | Columbia | MITP | Princeton
1 Oldlands Way, Bognor Regis
West Sussex P022 9SA
United Kingdom
Phone: +44 1243 842165
Fax: +44 1243 842167

China Office: Princeton Asia (Beijing) Consulting
Unit 2602, NUO Centre, 2A Jiangtai Rd., Chao yang Distr.
Beijing, People's Republic of China, 100016
Phone: +86 181 8661 2519
Email: firstname_lastname@press.princeton.edu

Princeton University Press continued

Staff
Director: Christie Henry (609.258.8704)
Assistant to the Director: Martha Camp (609.258.4953)
Associate Director and CFO: Scot Kuehm (609.258.8602)
Associate Publishing Director/Editor-in-Chief: Al Bertrand (609.258.5775)
Assistant Director/Director of Global Development: Brigitta van Rheinberg (609.258.4935)
Acquisitions Editorial: Al Bertrand, Associate Publishing Director/Editor-in-Chief (humanities, history of science) (609.258.5775)
    Humanities: Eric Crahan, Executive Editor (political science, American history) (609.258.4922); Michelle Komie, Executive Editor (art, architecture) (609.258.4569); Anne Savarese, Executive Editor (literature) (609.258.4937); Rob Tempio, Associate Editor-In-Chief/Humanities Publisher (philosophy, ancient world, political theory) (609.258.0843)
    Field Guides and Natural History: Robert Kirk, Executive Editor and Publisher (609.258.4884)
    Mathematics & Natural Sciences: Eric Henney, Editor (physical and computer sciences) (609.258.1739); Alison Kalett, Executive Editor (biology, earth science) (609.258.9232); Vickie Kearn, Executive Editor (mathematics, computer science) (609.258.2321)
    Social Sciences: Fred Appel, Executive Editor (anthropology, religion) (609.258.2484); Peter Dougherty, Editor At Large (economic history, education) (609.258.6778); Joe Jackson, Senior Editor (economics) (609.258.9428); Meagan Levinson, Senior Editor (sociology, psychology) (609.248.4908)
    Editorial Manager: Lyndsey Claro (609.258.0183)
Manuscript Editorial: Neil Litt, Assistant Director/Director of Editing, Design, and Production (609.258.5066)
    Managing Editor: Elizabeth Byrd (609.258.2589)
    Manager of Digital Production: Ken Reed (609.258.2485)
    Assistant Manager of Digital Production: Eileen Reilly (609.258.2719)
    Creative Director: Maria Lindenfeldar (609.258.7557)
Marketing: TBA, Director of Marketing (609.258.4896)
    Associate Director of Marketing: Leslie Nangle (609.258.5881)
    Director of Sales: Tim Wilkins (609.258.4898)
    Associate Director of Sales: Laurie Schlesinger (609.258.4898)
    Director of Publicity: Andrew DeSio (609.258.5165)
    Assistant Director of Publicity: Julia Haav (609.258.2831)
    Advertising and Social Media Design Director: Donna Liese (609.258.4924)
    Social Media Manager: Debra Liese (609.258.4283)
    Director of Digital Sales: Priscilla Treadwell (609.258.9387)
    Director of Exhibits: Melissa Burton (609.258.4915)
    Senior Text Promotion Manager: Julie Haenisch (609.258.6856)
    Director of Web Technology and Services: Ann Ambrose (609.258.7749)
Business: Scot Kuehm, Associate Director and CFO (609.258.8602)
    Associate Controller: Debbie Greco (609.882.0550)
    Director of Human Resources: Kate Danser (609.258.9387)
Information Systems: Dennis Langlois, Chief Information Officer (609.258.7782)

Director of Contracts: Shaquona Crews (609.258.5799)
European Office: Caroline Priday, Head of Office, Europe and European Director of Publicity: (+44 1993 814503)
Editors: Sarah Caro, Publisher, Social Science, Europe (+44.1993 804501); Ingrid Gnerlich, Publisher, Sciences in Europe (+.44.1517.096972); Ben Tate (humanities) (+44 1993 814502)
International Rights Manager: Kimberley Williams (+44 1993 814509)
China Office: Lingxi Li, Chief Representative (86 181 8661 2519)

Regular Member
Established: 1905
Title output 2016: 300
Titles currently in print: 8,221

Admitted to the Association: 1937
Title output 2017: 331

Editorial Program
Humanities: American, European, World, Asian, Slavic, and Jewish history; ancient world; classics; architecture and art history; philosophy; poetry; literature; religion
Reference: humanities; social sciences; and science

University of Puerto Rico Press

Street Address:
Jardín Botánico Norte Carr.
#1 Km. 12.0 Río
Piedras, San Juan PR 00927

Mailing Address:
PO Box 23322
U.P.R. Station
San Juan, PR 00931-3322

Phone: 787.758.8345
Email: info@laeditorialupr.com

Website and Social Media:
Website: www.laeditorialupr.com
Facebook: www.facebook.com/editorialupr/

Staff
Director: Neeltje van Marissing (email: neeltje.vanmarissing@upr.edu)
Editor: Rosa V. Otero
Sales: José Burgos (email: jburgos@upr.edu)
Marketing and Promotion: Ruth Morales (email: ruth.morales2@upr.edu)
Exhibits and Special Projects: José Burgos (email: jburgos@upr.edu), Ruth Morales (email: ruth.morales2@upr.edu)
Shipping, Receiving and Inventory: Carlos Santiago (email: carlos.santiago36@upr.edu)
Warehouse: Ángel Ortiz
Journals Marketing: Ruth Morales

Regular Member
Established:1943
Title output 2016: 5
Titles currently in print: 989

Admitted to the Association: 1971
Title output 2017: NR
Journals published: 1

University of Puerto Rico Press continued

Editorial Program
Scholarly studies on Puerto Rico, the Caribbean and Latin America; philosophy; history; architecture; law; social sciences; health; women's studies; economics; literary theory and criticism; creative poetry and prose; literary anthologies; nature studies; flora; fauna; ecosystems; children's books; reference; other general interest publications.
Journals: *Revista La Torre* (the humanities). In distribution: *Revista de Estudios Hispánicos* (Spanish language studies); and *Historia y Sociedad* (Puerto Rican and Caribbean history); *Diálogos* (philosophy)
Special series: literary anthologies; philosophy; creative literature; scholarly nonfiction; nature
Special imprints: Antología Personal (Selections by renowned hispanic writers); Clásicos no tan clásicos (Faithful re-edition of works written between 1890 and 1930 with annotations by 21st century scholars); Books on Puerto Rican Cooking; Colección Eugenio María de Hostos (complete works); San Pedrito (children's books); Colección Nueve Pececitos (young readers); Cuentos de un mundo perdido (middle school readers)

Purdue University Press

Stewart Center
504 West State Street
West Lafayette, IN 47907-2058

Phone: 765.494.2038
Fax: 765.496.2442
Email: pupress@purdue.edu
Indiv: (user I.D.)@purdue.edu

Orders:
Purdue University Press
PO Box 388
Ashland, OH 44805
Phone: 800.247.6553
Fax: 419.281.6883
Email: order@bookmasters.com

Website and Social Media:
Website: www.press.purdue.edu; www.lib.purdue.edu/publishing
Facebook: www.facebook.com/purduepress
Twitter: @publishpurdue

European Distributor:
Eurospan

Canadian Distributor:
Scholarly Book Services

Staff
Director: Peter Froehlich (765.494.8251; email: pfroehli)
Editorial, Design, and Production Strategic Manager: Katherine Purple (765.494.6259; email: kpurple)
Sales and Marketing Strategic Manager: Bryan Shaffer (765.494.8428; email: bshaffer)
Graphic Designer: Lindsey Organ (765.494.0441; email: lorgan)
Marketing and Outreach Specialist: TBA
   Senior Production Editor: Kelley Kimm (765.494.8024; email: kkimm)
Administrative Assistant: Becki Corbin (765.494.8144; email: rlcorbin)
Editorial Assistants: Alexandra Hoff (765.494.2909; email: hoff1); Liza Hagerman (765.494.4943; email: lhagerma)

Digital Repository Specialist: Marcy Wilhelm-South (765.494.6311; email: wilhelms)
Scholarly Publishing Specialist: Nina Collins (765.494.8511; email: nkcollin)
Journals and Serials Strategic Manager: G. Jake Jaquet (765.494.6430; email: gjaquet)

Regular Member

Established: 1960
Title output 2016: 27
Titles currently in print: 522

Admitted to the Association: 1993
Title output 2017: 22
Journals published: 22

Editorial Program

Dedicated to the dissemination of scholarly and professional information aligned with the strengths of its parent institution, the Press provides quality resources in technology and engineering, library and information science, public policy, aeronautics and astronautics, Indiana history, agriculture, health and human sciences, veterinary studies, European history, Jewish studies, and global languages and literatures.

Journals (Purdue University Press): *CLCWeb: Comparative Literature and Culture; Education and Culture: The Journal of the John Dewey Society; First Opinions—Second Reactions; Global Business Languages; The Interdisciplinary Journal of Problem-Based Learning; Journal of Aviation Technology and Engineering; Journal of Pre-College Engineering Education Research; Journal of Problem Solving; Phillip Roth Studies; Shofar: An Interdisciplinary Journal of Jewish Studies; Studies in Jewish Civilization*

Journals (Scholarly Publishing Services): *Journal of Applied Farm Economics; Artl@s Bulletin; CLARITAS: Journal of Dialogue and Culture; Data Curation Profiles Directory; IMPACT Profile Directory; Journal of Human Performance in Extreme Environments; People and Animals: The International Journal of Research and Practice; Purdue Journal of Service-Learning and International Engagement; Journal of Purdue Undergraduate Research; Journal of Southeast Asian American Education and Advancement*

Special series: Central European Studies; Comparative Cultural Studies; New Directions in the Human-Animal Bond; Purdue Handbooks in Building Construction; Purdue Studies in Aeronautics and Astronautics; Purdue Studies in Romance Literatures; Purdue Information Literacy Handbooks; and Charleston Insights in Library, Archival, and Information Sciences with Against the Grain Press.

RAND Corporation

Street Address:
1776 Main Street
Santa Monica, CA 90407

Mailing Address:
PO Box 2138
Santa Monica, CA 90407-2138

Phone: 310.393.0411
Fax: 310.451.7026

Customer Service:
Phone: 877.584.8642
Fax: 412.802.4981
Email: order@rand.org

Website and Social Media:
Website: www.rand.org/publications
Facebook: www.facebook.com/RANDCorporation
Twitter: @RANDCorporation
YouTube: www.youtube.com/user/TheRANDCorporation
Blog: www.rand.org/blog.html

US Distributor:
National Book Network
Phone: 800.462.6420 or 717.794.3800
Fax: 800.338.4550

UK/European Distributor:
NBN International

Staff
Director: Paul Murphy (ext. 7806; email: murphy@rand.org)
Business Manager, OEA: Laura Shaw (ext. 6722; email: lshaw@rand.org)
Managing Editor: Erin-Elizabeth Johnson (ext. 5450; email: ejohnson@rand.org)
Computing Manager: Edward Finkelstein (ext. 7417; email: edwardf@rand.org)

Regular Member
Established: 1948
Title output 2016: 400
Titles currently in print: 21,900

Admitted to the Association: 2000
Title output 2017: 425
Journals published: 2

Editorial Program
The RAND Corporation is a research organization that develops solutions to public policy challenges to help make communities throughout the world safer and more secure, healthier and more prosperous. RAND is nonprofit, nonpartisan, and committed to the public interest. Publication topics include policy issues such as education; environment and energy; health care; immigration, labor, and population; international affairs; national security; public safety and justice; science and technology; and terrorism and homeland security. Unsolicited manuscripts are not accepted.
Journals: *RAND Health Quarterly; RAND Journal of Economics*

University of Regina Press

Street/Courier Address:
246 – 2 Research Drive
Regina Research Park
Regina, SK S4S 7J7
Canada

Phone: 306.585.4758
Fax: 306.585.4699
Email: uofrpress@uregina.ca
Indiv.: (User I.D.)@uregina.ca

Website and Social Media:
Website: www.uofrpress.ca
Facebook: facebook.com/uofrpress
Twitter: @UofRPress
Instagram: @UofR_Press
YouTube: www.youtube.com/user/CPRCPRESS (U of R Press TV)

Mailing Address:
University of Regina Press
University of Regina
3737 Wascana Parkway
Regina, SK S4S 0A2 Canada

Orders (U.S.)
Ingram Publisher Services
Account No. S210
Phone: 800.565.9523
Fax: 800.838.1149
Email: utpbooks@utpress.utoronto.ca

UK Representative:
Gazelle Academic

Staff
Director: Bruce Walsh (306.585.4795; email: bruce.walsh)
Acquisitions Editorial (scholarly): Karen Clark, Acquisitions Editor (306.585.4664; email: karen.clark)
Acquisitions Editorial (trade): Sean Prpick, Editor (306.585.4789; email: sean.prpick)
Manuscript Editorial: Donna Grant, Senior Editor (306.585.4787; email: donna.grant)
Design and Production: Duncan Campbell, Art Director (306.585.4326; email: duncan.campbell)
Marketing: Morgan Tunzelmann, Sales and Marketing Manager(306.337.3325; email: morgan.tunzelmann)
Publicist: Melissa Shirley (587.389.9510; email: melissa.shirley)
Business: Wendy Whitebear, Office Manager (306.585.4758; email: wendy.whitebear)

Introductory Member
Established: 2014 (predecessor Canadian Plains Research Centre Press)
Admitted to the Association: 2014
Title output 2016: 18   Title output 2017: 19
Titles currently in print: 31 (192 with CPRC Press backlist)

Editorial Program
Scholarly and trade books on Indigenous Studies, the environment, Canadian Studies, American Studies, biography, gender studies, gay and lesbian studies, the arts, public affairs, anthropology, sociology, and more (see the subject area listings for further details).
Special series: First Nations Language Readers; The Regina Collection; Oskana Poetry & Poetics; The Exquisite Corpse; Digestions; The Henry and Mary Bibb Series of Black Canadian Studies

RIT Press

90 Lomb Memorial Drive
Rochester, NY 14623-5604

Phone: 585.475.6766
Fax: 585.475.4090
Email: lmdwml@rit.edu

Orders:
Phone: 585.475.6766

UK and Asian Distributor:
Boydell & Brewer, Ltd.

Website and Social Media:
Website: ritpress.rit.edu
Facebook: www.facebook.com/pages/RIT-Press/172326337130?ref=hl
Twitter: @RITPress
Instagram: @ritpress
Pinterest: ritpress

Staff
Director: Bruce A. Austin (585.475.2879; email: baagll@rit.edu)
Managing Editor: Molly Q. Cort (585.475.4088; email: mqcwml@rit.edu)
Business Manager: Laura DiPonzio Heise (585.475.5819; email: lmdwml@rit.edu)
Design & Marketing Specialist: Marnie Soom (585.475.4089; email: mxswml@rit.edu)

Regular Member
Established: 2001

Admitted to the Association: 2009 (intro. member)
Admitted to the Association: 2014 (full member)

Title output 2016: 8
Titles currently in print: 95

Title output 2017: 5
Journals published: 1

Editorial Program
RIT Press is the scholarly book publishing enterprise at Rochester Institute of Technology. RIT Press is dedicated to the innovative use of new publishing technology while upholding high standards in content quality, publication design, and print/digital production. The Press publishes specialized titles for niche academic audiences, trade editions for mass-market audiences, and occasional limited edition books with unique aesthetic standards. Established in 2001 as RIT Cary Graphic Arts Press, the Press initially focused on publishing titles documenting graphic communication processes, printing history, and bookmaking. As its editorial policies evolved, the Press broadened its reach to include content supporting all academic disciplines offered at RIT.
Special series: Graphic Design Archives Chapbook; Philosophy and the Future; Popular Culture Series (Comics Monograph Series); Printing Industry Series, Sports Studies
Journal: *HAYDN* an online journal of the Haydn Society of North America, peer-reviewed, bi-annual digital-only publication of musicological research.

The University of Rochester Press

668 Mount Hope Avenue
Rochester NY 14620-2731

Phone: 585.275.0419
Fax: 585.271.8778

Orders:
Phone: 585.275.0419
Email: boydell@boydellusa.net

Website and Social Media:
Website: www.urpress.com
Facebook: www.facebook.com/boydellandbrewer
Twitter: @boydellbrewer
Pinterest: boydellbrewer
Instagram: boydellandbrewer

UK Representative:
Boydell & Brewer, Ltd.

Canadian Representative:
Scholarly Book Services

Staff
Editorial Director: Sonia Kane (585.273.5778; email: sonia.kane@rochester.edu)
Managing Editor/Manuscript Editorial: Ryan Peterson (585.273.4429; email: peterson@boydellusa.net)
Associate Editor: Julia Cook (585.273.4356; email: cook@boydellusa.net)
Production Manager: Sue Smith (585.273.2817; email: smith@boydellusa.net)
    Production Editor: Tracey Engel (585.273.2818; email: engel@boydellusa.net)
Sales and Marketing Manager: Sue Miller (585.273.5787; email: miller@boydellusa.net)Associate Marketing Manager: Katie Kumler (585.273.5779; email: kumler@boydellusa.net)
    Marketing Assistant: Rosemary Shojaie (585.275.0391; email: shojaie@boydellusa.net)
Customer Service: Jennifer Shannon (585.273.2959; email: shannon@boydellusa.net)
    Accounts Assistant: Olga Reshota (585.273.5780; email: reshota@boydellusa.net)

Regular Member
Established: 1989

Admitted to the Association: 2008 (intro. member)
Admitted to the Association: 2011 (full member)

Title output 2016: 22
Titles currently in print: 654

Title output 2017: 24

Editorial Program
Central Europe; Rochester Studies in Medical History; Rochester Studies in Medieval Political Thought

The Rockefeller University Press

950 Third Avenue, 2nd Floor
New York, NY 10022-2705

Phone: 212.327.7938
Fax: 212.319.1080
Email: (user I.D.)@rockefeller.edu

Website and Social Media:
Websites: www.rupress.org, jcb.rupress.org, jem.rupress.org, jgp.rupress.org
Facebook: www.facebook.com/RockefellerUniversityPress, www.facebook.com/JCellBiol, www.facebook.com/JExpMed, www.facebook.com/JGenPhysiol
Twitter: @RockUPress, @JCellBiol, @JExpMed, @JGenPhysiol

Staff
Executive Director: Susan L. King (212.327.8881; email: sking01)
Finance Director: Raymond T. Fastiggi (212.327.8567; email: fastigg)
Office Administrator: Sati Motieram (212.327.8583; email: motierd)
Manuscript Editorial: Rebecca Alvania, Executive Editor, *The Journal of Cell Biology*, Director of Editorial Development, Rockefeller University Press (212.327.8011; email: ralvania); Teodoro Pulvirenti, Executive Editor, *The Journal of Experimental Medicine* (212.327.8361; email: tpulvirent); Meighan Schreiber, Managing Editor, *The Journal of General Physiology* (212.327.8651)
Advertising: Lorna Petersen, Sales Director (212.327.8880; email: petersl)
Journals: Robert O'Donnell, Director of Publishing Technologies (212.327.8545; email: odonner)
Business: Raymond T. Fastiggi, Finance Director (212.327.8567; email: fastigg)
  Business Development Director: Gregory Malar (212.327.7948; email: malarg)
Communications and Marketing Director: Rory Williams (212.327.8603; email: rwilliams02)

Regular Member

Established: 1958
Title output 2016: 0
Titles currently in print: 40

Admitted to the Association: 1982
Title output 2017: 0
Journals published: 3

Editorial Program
The Rockefeller University Press publishes three biomedical research journals. *The Journal of Cell Biology* provides a rigorous forum for publication of topics across the complete spectrum of cell biology. *The Journal of Experimental Medicine* publishes papers providing novel conceptual insight into immunology, cancer biology, vascular biology, microbial pathogenesis, neuroscience, and stem cell biology. Articles in *The Journal of General Physiology* elucidate important biological, chemical, or physical mechanisms of broad physiological significance.

Russell Sage Foundation

112 East 64th Street
New York, NY 10065

Phone: 212.750.6000
Fax: 212.371.4761
Email: pubs@rsage.org
Indiv: firstname@rsage.org

Website and Social Media:
Website: www.russellsage.org/about/press-list
Blog: www.russellsage.org/blog
Facebook: www.facebook.com/russellsagefoundation
Twitter: @RussellSageFdn

Orders:
Russell Sage Foundation
Chicago Distribution Center
11030 Langley Avenue
Chicago, IL 60628

Phone: 773.702.7010
Fax: 800.621.8476

UK/European Distributor:
NBN International

Staff
Director of Publications: Suzanne Nichols (212.750.6026)
Publications Assistant: Thalia Bloom (212.750.6038)
Director of Communications: David A. Haproff (212.750.6037)
Assistant Book Marketing Manager and Web Programmer: Bruce Thongsack (212.750.6021)
Web Editor and Staff Writer: Jennifer Pan (212.750.2024)
Production Manager: Marcelo Agudo (212.750.6034)
Exhibits/Permissions: Thalia Bloom (212.750.6038)
Foundation President: Sheldon Danziger

Regular Member
Established: 1907
Title output 2016: 10
Titles currently in print: 600

Admitted to the Association: 1989
Title output 2017: 8
Journals published: 1

Editorial Program
Scholarly books on current research and policy issues in the social sciences. Recent research programs sponsored by the Russell Sage Foundation include the future of work, sustainable employment, current US immigration, the analysis of the US Census, the social psychology of cultural contact, the social dimensions of inequality, carework, and behavioral economics. The foundation no longer enters into copublishing agreements.

Journal: *RSF: The Russell Sage Foundation Journal of the Social Sciences*

Rutgers University Press

106 Somerset Street, 3rd Floor
New Brunswick, NJ 08901

Phone: 848.445.7762
Fax: 732.745.4935
Email: (user I.D.)@press.rutgers.edu

Website and Social Media:
Website: www.rutgersuniversitypress.org
Facebook: www.facebook.com/RutgersUPress/
Twitter: @RutgersUPress
Pinterest: rutgersuniv0180
Instagram: rutgersupress

Warehouse, Fulfillment, & Cust. Service
(until July 1, 2018)
c/o Longleaf Services, Inc.
PO Box 8895
Chapel Hill, NC 27515-8895
Phone: 800.848.6224
Fax: 800.272.6817
Email: longleaf@unc.edu

Warehouse, Fulfillment, & Cust. Service
(after July 1, 2018)
c/o Chicago Distribution Center
11030 S Langley Ave, Chicago, IL 60628
Phone: 773.702.7010
Fax: 800.621.8476

UK/European/Asian Representative:
Eurospan

Canadian Representative:
Scholarly Book Services

Staff
Director: Micah Kleit (848.445.7784; email: micah.kleit)
  Assistant to the Director/Permissions and Subsidiary Rights Manager/E-book Coordinator: Elisabeth Maselli (848.445.7785; email: esm102)
Acquisitions Editorial: Kimberly Guinta, Editor-in-Chief designate (anthropology, Caribbean studies, and women's studies) (848.445.7786; email: kimberly.guinta)
  Senior Editor: Peter Mickulas (regional studies, health, sociology, environment, and criminology) (848.445.7752; email: mickulas)
  Editors: TBA (American studies, humanities, Latino studies, popular culture, film, and media); Lisa Banning (Asian American studies, human rights, new media, higher education) (848.445.7791; email: lmb333)
  Assistant Editor: Elisabeth Maselli (Jewish studies) (848.445.7785; email: esm102)
  Editorial Assistant: Jasper Chang (848.445.7791; email: jasper.chang)
Production: Jennifer Blanc-Tal, Production and Art Director (848.445.7761; email: jfb131)
  Production Editors: Daryl Brower (848.445.7764; email: djb147); Alissa Zarro (848.445.7756; email: ajz45)
Marketing: Jeremy Grainger, Sales and Marketing Director (848.445.7781; email: jeremy.grainger)
Publicity Director: Courtney Brach (848.445.7775; email: clb103)
  Senior Promotion Manager/Webmaster: Brice Hammack (848.445.7765; email: bhammack)
  Marketing Associate: Victoria Verhowsky (848.445.7782; email: victoria.verhowsky)
Business: David Flum, Chief Financial Officer (848.445.7763; email: dflum)
  Business Assistant: Bryan Martinez (email: bmart10)
IT Manager: Penny Burke (848.445.7788; email: pborden)

Regular Member
Established: 1936
Title output 2016: 80
Titles currently in print: 2,788

Admitted to the Association: 1937
Title output 2017: 120

Editorial Program
American Literatures Initiative; American studies; anthropology; Asian American studies; African American studies; Caribbean studies; childhood and family studies; criminology; film and media; food studies; higher education studies; history of science and technology; human rights; Jewish studies; Latino/a studies; popular culture; public policy; regional studies; sociology; women's studies

Special series: The American Campus; Asian American Studies Today; Behind the Silver Screen; Comics Culture; Critical Caribbean Studies; Critical Issues in Crime and Society; Critical Issues in Health and Medicine; Critical Issues In Sport and Society; Families in Focus; Genocide, Political Violence, Human Rights; Global Perspectives on Aging; Jewish Cultures of the World; Junctures: Case Studies in Women's Leadership; Key Words In Jewish Studies; Latinidad: Transnational Cultures in the United States, Nature, Society, and Culture; New Directions in International Studies; The Politics of Marriage and Gender: Global Issues in Shifting Local Contexts;; Quick Takes: Movies and Popular Culture; Rivergate Regionals Collection; Rutgers Series in Childhood Studies; Techniques of the Moving Image; Violence Against Women and Children; War Culture

Joint imprints and co-publishing programs: Co-publishing with Bucknell University Press and caboose

Saint Joseph's University Press

5600 City Avenue
Philadelphia, PA 19131-1395

Phone: 610.660.3402
Fax: 610.660.3412
Email: sjupress@sju.edu
Indiv: (user I.D.)@sju.edu

Orders:
Phone: 610.660.3402
Email: orders@sjupress

Website and Social Media:
Website: www.sjupress.com

Staff
Director: Carmen Robert Croce (610.660.3402; email: ccroce)
Editorial Director: Joseph F. Chorpenning (610.660.1214; email: jchorpen)

Introductory Member
Established: 1997
Title output 2016: 4
Titles currently in print: 78

Admitted to the Association: 2011
Title output 2017: 4

Editorial Program
Jesuit studies (with an emphasis on history and the visual arts), regional studies (Philadelphia and environs)

Special series: Early Modern Catholicism and the Visual Arts (1500-French Revolution)

SBL Press

The Society of Biblical Literature
The Luce Center
825 Houston Mill Road, Suite 350
Atlanta, GA 30329

Phone: 404.727.3100
Fax: 404.727.3101
Email: SBLPressM@sbl-site.org
Indiv: SBLPressP@sbl-site.org

Orders:
Phone: 877.725.3334
Fax: 802.864.7626
Email: sblpressorders@aidcvt.com

Journal Subscriptions and Membership:
Phone: 866.727.9955
Fax: 404.727.2419
Email: sblservices@sbl-site.org

Website and Social Media:
Website: www.sbl-site.org/publications
Twitter: @SBLsite

Staff
Executive Director: John F. Kutsko (404.727.3038; email: john.kutsko@sbl-site.org)
Director, SBL Press: Bob Buller (970.669.9900; email: bob.buller@sbl-site.org)
Production Manager: Nicole Tilford (404.727.2327; email: nicole.tilford@sbl-site.org)
Publishing Marketing Manager: Kathie Klein (404.727.2325;
    email: kathie.klein@sbl-site.org)
Sales Manager: Heather McMurray (404.727.3096; email: heather.mcmurray@sbl-site.org)
Manager of Membership & Subscriptions: Navar Steed (404.727.9494; email: navar.steed@
    sbl-site.org)

Regular Member
Established: 1880
Title output 2016: 40
Titles currently in print: 794

Admitted to the Association: 2003
Title output 2017: 47
Journals published: 2

Editorial Program
The Society of Biblical Literature publishes works in biblical and religious studies through SBL Press. Monographic publications include major reference works; commentaries; text editions and translations; collections of essays; revised doctoral dissertations; tools for teaching and research fields; archaeological, sociological, and historical studies; volumes that use archaeological and historical data to illuminate Israelite religion or the culture of biblical peoples; scholarly works on the history, culture, and literature of early Judaism; scholarly works on various aspects of the Masorah; scholarly congress proceedings; critical texts of the Greek Fathers including evaluations of data; philological tools; studies employing the methods and perspectives of linguistics, folklore studies, literary criticism, structuralism, social anthropology, and postmodern studies; studies of the Septuagint including textual criticism, manuscript witnesses and other versions, as well as its literature, historical milieu, and thought; studies related to the Jewish apocryphal and pseudepigraphical works of the Hellenistic period, and the subsequent development of this literature in Judaism and early Christianity; studies in biblical literature and/or its cultural environment; text-critical works related to the Hebrew Bible/Old Testament and New Testament, including investigations of methodology, studies of individual manuscripts, critical texts of a selected book or passage, or examination of more general textual themes; translations of ancient Near Eastern texts; translations of ancient

texts from the Greco-Roman world; translations of early Jewish and Christian texts from the Islamic world; and studies in the history of interpretation and reception history of biblical traditions. SBL Press also publishes *The SBL Handbook of Style*, now in its second edition.

SBL Press is the exclusive North American distributor for Sheffield Phoenix Press's backlist titles (UK) and the sole producer and distributor of volumes in the Brown Judaic Studies series (Brown University) and the History of Bible Translations series (NIDA). SBL Press also distributes the Manuscripts of the Greek New Testament Series by Reuben Swanson.

Journals: *Journal of Biblical Literature; Review of Biblical Literature*

Special series: Ancient Israel and Its Literature; Ancient Near East Monographs; Archaeology and Biblical Studies; the Bible and Its Interpretation; the Bible and its Reception; the Bible and Women; Biblical Encyclopedia; Biblical Scholarship in North America; Commentary on the Septuagint; Early Christianity and Its Literature; Early Judaism and Its Literature; Emory Studies in Early Christianity; Global Perspectives on Biblical Scholarship; the Hebrew Bible: A Critical Edition; History of Biblical Studies; International Voices in Biblical Studies; The New Testament in the Greek Fathers; Resources for Biblical Study; Rhetoric of Religious Antiquity; Semeia Studies; Septuagint and Cognate Studies; Studia Philonica Annual and Monographs; Text-Critical Studies; Wisdom Literature from the Ancient World; Writings from the Ancient World; Writings from the Ancient World Supplements; Writings from the Greco-Roman World; Writings from the Greco-Roman World Supplements; Writings from the Islamic World

Joint imprints and co-publishing programs: *HarperCollins Study Bible* (NRSV); *HarperCollins Bible Dictionary*, revised edition; *HarperCollins Bible Commentary*, revised edition, and *Harper's Bible Pronunciation Guide* with HarperCollins; *The Greek New Testament: SBL Edition*, with Logos Bible Software; Ancient Near East Monographs/Monografias Sobre el Antiguo Cercano Oriente, co-published with the Centro de Estudios de Historia del Antiguo Oriente (Argentina); *A User's Guide to the Nestle-Aland 28 Greek New Testament*, with the Deutsche Bibelgesellschaft; and *A New Approach to Textual Criticism: An Introduction to the Coherence-Based Genealogical Method* with DBG.

Online books: SBL Press, along with six participating partners, provides PDF files of academic books for free download to individuals and libraries in underresourced areas of the globe. Through software that recognizes the IP address of the web visitor, persons from countries whose GDP is considerably less than the average GDP of the US and the EU are given access to the files. The program, as of late 2012, includes almost 350 titles. In addition, SBL Press also publishes two open-access book series: Ancient Near East Monographs, and International Voices in Biblical Studies.

EBooks: SBL Press has entered the e-book market and partners with Bibliovault to make titles available in multiple formats. We also use Amazon Print Replica to make Kindle-compliant e-books available through Amazon.

The University of South Carolina Press

1600 Hampton Street
5th Floor
Columbia, SC 29208-3400

Phone: 803.777.5245
Fax: 803.777.0160
Email: (user I.D.)@sc.edu

Business Office and Warehouse:
718 Devine Street
Columbia, SC 29208-0001
Phone: 800.768.2500
Fax: 800.868.0740
Email: (user I.D.)@sc.edu

Website and Social Media:
Website: www.sc.edu/uscpress
Facebook: www.facebook.com/USC.Press
Twitter: @USCPress

UK/European Distributor:
Eurospan

Canadian Distributor:
Scholarly Book Services

Staff
Director: Richard Brown (803.777.4423; email: brownri) (rights)
Assistant Director for Operations: Linda Haines Fogle (803.777.4848; email: lfogle)
  Assistant to the Director's Office: Vicki Bates (803.777.5245; email: batesvc)
Acquisitions Editors: Linda Haines Fogle (regional, trade) (803.777.4848; email: lfogle); Jim Denton (literature, religious studies, rhetoric/communication, social work) (803.777.4859; email: denton); TBA (African American studies, history, Southern studies); TBA (literature, religious studies, rhetoric/communication, social work)
Manuscript Editorial: Bill Adams, Managing Editor (803.777.5075; email: adamswb)
  Editorial Assistant: Lynne Parker (803.777.5231; email: parkerll)
Design and Production: Pat Callahan, Design and Production Manager (803.777.2449; email: mpcallah)
  Book Designer: Brock Henderson (803.777.9056; email: hende225)
  Design and Production Assistant: Ashley Mathias (803.777.2238; email: samathi)
Marketing: Suzanne Axland, Director (803.777.2021; email: axland)
  Promotions Manager: Carolyn Martin (803.777.5029; email: clmartin)
Business/Warehouse: Vicki Sewell, Acting Business Manager and Permissions (803.777.7754; email: sewellv)
  Customer Service Representative: Lee Heckle (803.777.1774); (1.800.768.2500)
  Warehouse Assistant: Eddie Hill (803.777.0184; email: jehill)

Regular Member
Established: 1944
Title output 2016: 55
Titles currently in print: 1,250

Admitted to the Association: 1948
Title output 2017: 52

Editorial Program
Scholarly works, mainly in the humanities and social sciences, and general interest titles, particularly those of importance to the state and region. Subjects include African American studies; history, especially American history, military history, maritime history, and South-

ern history; literature and literary studies; religious studies, including comparative religion; Southern studies; rhetoric/communication; and social work.

Special series, joint imprints, and/or copublishing programs: AccessAble Books; The Belle W. Baruch Library in Marine Science; The Carolina Lowcountry and the Atlantic World; Chief Justiceships of the United States Supreme Court; Historians in Conversation; Joseph M. Bruccoli Great War Series; Palmetto Poetry Series; The Papers of John C. Calhoun; The Papers of Henry Laurens; The Papers of Howard Thurman; Social Problems and Social Issues; South Carolina Encyclopedia Guides; South Carolina Poetry Book Prize; Southern Classics; Southern Revivals; Story River Books; Studies in Comparative Religion; Studies in Maritime History; Studies in Rhetoric/Communication; Studies on Personalities of the New Testament; Studies on Personalities of the Old Testament; Understanding Contemporary American Literature; Understanding Contemporary British Literature; Understanding Modern European and Latin American Literature; Women's Diaries and Letters of the South; Young Palmetto Books

South Dakota Historical Society Press

South Dakota Historical Society Press
900 Governors Drive
Pierre, SD 57501

Orders
Phone: 605.773.6009
Email: orders@sdhspress.com

Phone: 605.773.6009
Fax: 605.773.6041
Email: info@sdhspress.com
Indiv.: (firstname.lastname)@state.sd.us

Website and Social Media:
Website and blog: www.sdhspress.com
Pioneer Girl Project website: www.pioneergirlproject.org
Facebook: www.facebook.com/SDHSPress/
Twitter: @sdhspress

International (outside of North America) Representative:
Eurospan

Sales Representative:
Miller Book Trade Marketing
Email: bruce@millertrade.com

Staff
Director/Acquisitions: Nancy Tystad Koupal (605.773.4371; email: nancy.koupal)
Managing Editor of *South Dakota History*: Jeanne Ode (605.773.6008; email: Jeanne.ode)
Marketing Director/Rights and Permissions: Jennifer McIntyre (605.773.8161; email: jennifer.mcintyre)
Associate Editor/Production: Amy Kucera (605.773.8380; email: amy.kucera)
Accounting Assistant/Order Fulfilment: Judy Uecker (605.773.6009; email: judy.uecker)

South Dakota Historical Society Press continued

Affiliate Member
Established: 1997
Title output 2016: 3
Titles currently in print: 65

Admitted to the Association: 2017
Title output 2017: 5
Journals published: 1

Editorial Program
The Press editorial program considers serious nonfiction works that detail the history, culture, people, and day-to-day experiences of those who live in South Dakota and throughout the Northern Great Plains. For the State Historical Society's quarterly journal, *South Dakota History*, all article manuscripts or proposed material must relate to state and region. The Press does consider submissions of fictional children's picture books and early reader chapter books, but these works must directly pertain to the region's vibrant culture and landscape.
Journal: *South Dakota History*
Special series: Historical Preservation Series; South Dakota Biography Series

Southern Illinois University Press

1915 University Press Drive
SIUC Mail Code 6806
Southern Illinois University
Carbondale, IL 62901-6806

Orders:
Southern Illinois University Press
c/o Chicago Distribution Center
11030 South Langley Avenue
Chicago, IL 60628-3830

Phone: 618.453.2281
Fax: 618.453.1221
Email: (user I.D.)@siu.edu

Phone: 800.621.2736
Fax: 800.621.8476
Email: custserv@press.uchicago.edu
EDI; PUBNET at 202-5280

Website and Social Media:
Website: www.siupress.com
Facebook: www.facebook.com/siupress
Twitter: @SIUPress

UK/European Distributor:
Eurospan

Canadian Representative:
Scholarly Book Services

Staff
Interim Co-Directors: Angela Moore-Swafford, Amy Etcheson
Business Manager, Rights and Permissions and Interim Co-Director: Angela Moore-Swafford (618.453.6617; email: angmoore) (rights email: rights)
Executive Editor: Sylvia Frank Rodrigue American History (African-American studies, Chicago, Civil War, Ulysses S. Grant, Abraham Lincoln, Illinois, medical, Midwestern, women's studies, true crime) (508.297.2162; email: sylvia@sylverlining.com)
Acquisitions Editor: Kristine Priddy (composition, criminology, poetry, rhetoric, theater) (618.453.6631; email: mkpriddy)
Acquisitions Assistant: Judy Verdich (618.453.7405; email: jverdich)
Editing, Design, and Production Manager/Book Designer: Linda Buhman (618.453.6612; email: ljbuhman)

Project Editor: Wayne Larsen (618.453.6628; email: wlarsen)
Editorial Assistant: Amy Alsip (618.453.6635; email: ala5391)
Marketing and Sales Manager and Interim Co-Director: Amy Etcheson (618.453.6623; email: aetcheson)
IT Specialist: Jerry Richardson (618.453.6624; email: jerryric)

Regular Member

Established: 1956   Admitted to the Association: 1980
Title output 2016: 50   Title output 2017: 33
Titles currently in print: 1,200

Editorial Program

Scholarly books, primarily in the humanities and social sciences. Particular strengths are theatre and stagecraft; regional and Civil War history; rhetoric and composition; aviation; contemporary poetry. Submissions in fiction and festschriften are not invited.

Special series: Civil War Campaigns in the Heartland; The Collected Works of John Dewey; The Concise Lincoln Library; The Crab Orchard Series in Poetry; The Elmer H. Johnson and Carol Holmes Johnson Series in Criminology; Engaging the Civil War; The Illustrated Flora of Illinois; Landmarks in Rhetoric and Public Address; Looking for Lincoln in Illinois; The Papers of Ulysses S. Grant; Perspectives on Crime and Justice; Rhetoric in the Modern Era; Shawnee Books; Shawnee Classics; Studies in Rhetorics and Feminisms; Theater in the Americas; World of Ulysses S. Grant; Writing Research, Pedagogy, and Policy.

Stanford University Press

500 Broadway
Redwood City, CA 94063

Phone: 650.723.9434
Fax: 650.725.3457
Email: (user I.D.)@stanford.edu

Order Fulfillment (US and Canada):
IPS/Perseus Distribution
One Ingram Blvd
La Vergne, TN 37086
Phone: 866.400.5351
Email: ips@ingramcontent.com

Website and Social Media:
Website: www.sup.org
Blog: stanfordpress.typepad.com
Facebook: www.facebook.com/stanforduniversitypress
Twitter: @stanfordpress

European/Asia Pacific Representative:
Combined Academic Publishers Ltd

Staff

Director: Alan Harvey (650.723.6375; email: aharvey)
Acquisitions: Kate Wahl, Publishing Director and Editor-in-Chief (Middle East studies) (650.498.9420; email: kwahl)
Executive Editor: Emily-Jane Cohen (philosophy, religion, literature) (650.725.7717; email: beatrice)
Senior Editors: Steve Catalano (business, economics) (650.724.7079; email: catalan); Michelle Lipinski (anthropology, law) (650.736.4641; email: mlipinsk)

Stanford University Press continued

Acquisition Editors: Margo Irvin (history, Jewish studies) (650.498.9023; email: mcirvin); Marcela Maxfield (sociology, Asian studies) (650.498.3396; email: mmaxfiel); Friederike Sundaram (digital projects) (650.721.5616; email: fsundaram)
Associate Editor: Faith Wilson Stein (650.497.4991; email: fwstein)
Assistant Editors: Leah Pennywark (650.498.9420; email: lpennyw); Nora Spiegel (650.724.7080; email: nspiegel)
Editorial Assistant: Olivia Bartz (650.736.0597; email: obartz)
Editorial, Design, and Production: Patricia Myers, EDP Director (650.724.5365; email: pmyers)
Senior Production Editor: Emily Smith (650.736.0686; email: emilys)
Production Editors: Gigi Mark (650.724.9990; email: vmark); Anne Fuzellier Jain (650.736.0719; email: anne7); Jessica Ling (650.725.0828; email: jessling)
Digital Production Associate: Jasmine Mulliken (email: jmullike)
Art Director: Rob Ehle (650.723.1132; email: ehle)
Senior Designer: Bruce Lundquist (650.723.6808; email: brucel)
Production Manager: Mike Sagara (650.725.0839; email: msagara)
Production Coordinator: Vicki Vandeventer (650.725.0836; email: vickiv)
Sales and Marketing: Stephanie Adams, Marketing Manager (650.736.1782; email: sadams3)
Sales and Exhibits Manager: Kate Templar (650.725.0820; email: ktemplar)
Publicist: Ryan Furtkamp (650.724.4211; email: furtkamp)
Digital Media Specialist: Kalie Caetano (650.497.3033; email: kcaetano)
Marketing Specialist: Linda Stewart (650.725.0823; email: stewartl)
Marketing Assistants: Kendra Schynert (650.736.1781; email: kschyner); Maxwell Shanley (650.724.9280; email: mshanley)
Business: Jean Kim, Director of Finance and Operations (650.725.0838; email: jean.h.kim)
Royalties/Accounts Receivable: Su-Mei Lee (650.725.0837; email: sumeilee)
Accounts Payable: Aurelia Hernandez (650.724.8697; email: aureliah)
Systems: Chris Cosner, IT Manager (650.724.7276; email: ccosner)
Desktop Support Administrator: Meide Guo (650.723.9598; email: meideguo)

Regular Member
Established: 1892
Title output 2016: 135
Titles currently in print: 3,350

Admitted to the Association: 1937
Title output 2017: 119

Editorial Program
Anthropology, Asian Studies, Business, Economics, History, International Relations, Jewish Studies, Latin American Studies, Law, Literature, Middle East Studies, Philosophy, Politics, Religion, Security Studies, Sociology.
Special series: Anthropology of Policy; Asian America; Asian Security; Cold War International History Project; The Complete Works of Friedrich Nietzsche; Contemporary Issues in Asia and the Pacific; The Cultural Lives of Law; Cultural Memory in the Present; Emerging Frontiers in the Global Economy; Encountering Traditions; Global Competition Law and Economics; High Reliability and Crisis Management; Innovation and Technology in the World Economy; Jurists: Profiles in Legal Theory; Meridian: Crossing Aesthetics; Post*45; RaceReligion; Social Science History; Square One: First Order Questions in the Humani-

ties; Stanford Business Classics; Stanford Nuclear Age Series; Stanford Series in Comparative Race and Ethnicity; Stanford Studies in Human Rights; Stanford Studies in Jewish History and Culture; Stanford Studies in Law and Politics; Stanford Studies in Middle Eastern and Islamic Societies and Cultures; Studies in Asian Security; Studies in Social Inequality; Studies in the Modern Presidency; Studies of the Weatherhead East Asian Institute; Studies of the Walter H. Shorenstein Asia-Pacific Research Center; Thinking Theory Now

Special imprints: Redwood Press; Stanford Briefs; Stanford Business Books; Stanford Economics and Finance; Stanford Law Books, Stanford Security Studies; Stanford Social Sciences

State University of New York Press

Street Address:
10 North Pearl Street
Albany, NY 12207

Phone: 518.944.2800
Fax: 518.320.1592
Email: info@sunypress.edu
Indiv: firstname.lastname@sunypress.edu

Website and Social Media:
Website: www.sunypress.edu
Facebook: www.facebook.com/pages/SUNY-Press/112308762113504
Twitter: @SUNYPress

Canadian Representative:
Lexa Publishers' Representatives

Mailing Address:
353 Broadway
State University Plaza
Albany, NY 12246-0001

Customer Service:
SUNY Press
PO Box 960
Herndon, VA 20172-0960
Phone: 703.661.1575
Toll free: 877.204.6073 (US only)
Fax: 703.996.1010
Toll free: 877.204.6074 (US only)
Email: suny@presswarehouse.com

UK/European Distributor:
NBN International

Staff
Co-Directors: Donna Dixon (518.944.2802); James Peltz (518.944.2815)
   Executive Assistant to the Co-Directors: Janice Vunk (518.944.2821)
   Receptionist: Diana Altobello (518.944.2804)
Acquisitions Editorial:
   Co-Director: James Peltz (518.944.2815) (Excelsior Editions, film studies, transpersonal psychology)
   Senior Acquisitions Editors: Christopher Ahn (Asian studies, religious studies); Michael Rinella (518.944.2811) (African American politics and sociology, environmental studies, political science)
   Acquisitions Editors: Rebecca Colesworthy (518.944.2813) (education, Hispanic studies, queer studies, women's and gender studies); Andrew Kenyon (518.944.2808) (philosophy); Amanda Lanne-Camilli (518.944.2809) (New York State studies, native and indigenous studies, Italian American studies)
   Assistant Acquisitions Editor: Rafael Chaiken (518.944.2828)(Jewish studies)
   Editorial Assistant: Chelsea Miller (518.944.2805)
Production:
   Co-Director: Donna Dixon (518.944.2802) (journals)
   Senior Production Editors: Diane Ganeles (518.944.2825); Ryan Morris (518.944.2814);

SUNY Press continued

Eileen Nizer (518.944.2812)
Production Editor: Jenn Bennett (518.944.2801)
Production and Composition Coordinator: Aimee Harrison (518.944.2816)
Marketing and Publicity:
  Director of Marketing and Publicity: Fran Keneston (518.944.2807)
  Executive Promotions Manager: Anne Valentine (518.944.2820)
  Senior Promotions Manager: Michael Campochiaro (518.944.2827)
  Exhibits and Awards Manager: Michelle Alamillo (518.944.2824)
  Promotions Manager: Kate Seburyamo (518.944.2810)
  Marketing & Publicity Assistant: Katherine Dias (518.944.2817)
Revenue and Business Operations:
  Accounting Manager: Sharla Clute (518.944.2803)
  Sales and Digital Programs Assistant: Renee Jones (518.944.2806)
  Digital Programs Manager: Greg Smith (518.944.2819)

Regular Member
Established: 1966
Title output 2016: 165
Titles currently in print: 5,930

Admitted to the Association: 1970
Title output 2017: 160
Journals published: 5

Editorial Program
Scholarly titles and serious works of general interest in many areas of the humanities and the social sciences, with special interest in African American studies; Asian studies; education; gender studies; Hispanic studies; native and indigenous studies; philosophy; political science; psychology; queer studies; religious studies; transpersonal psychology; and women's and gender studies.

  SUNY Press distributes books from the Albany Institute of History and Art, Codhill Press, Global Academic Publishing, Hudson River Valley National Heritage Area, Mount Ida Press, Muswell Hill Press, New Netherland Institute, Parks & Trails New York, Rockefeller Institute Press, Samuel Dorsky Museum and the Uncrowned Queens Institute.
Journals: *The Journal of Buddhist Philosophy; The Journal of Japanese Philosophy; Mediaevalia; Palimpsest; philoSOPHIA*
Imprints: Excelsior Editions

Syracuse University Press

621 Skytop Road, Suite 110
Syracuse, NY 13244-5290

Phone: 315.443.5534
Fax: 315.443.5545
Email: (user I.D.)@syr.edu

Website and Social Media:
Website: syracuseuniversitypress.syr.edu
Blog: syracusepress.wordpress.com/
Facebook: www.facebook.com/pages/
   Syracuse-University-Press/224301261901
Twitter: @supress
YouTube: www.youtube.com/channel/UCOtUPRTWoHyQ9NL4QQlM32g

Warehouse:
Longleaf Publishers c/o
Ingram Publisher Services
1550 Heil Quaker Blvd
La Vergne, TN 37086

Orders:
Longleaf Services
Phone: 800.848.6224
Fax: 800.272.6817
Email: orders@longleafservices.org

Canadian Distributor:
Scholarly Book Services, Inc.

UK Distributor:
Eurospan

Staff
Director: Alice R. Pfeiffer (315.443.5535; email: arpfeiff)
   Office Coordinator: Mary Doyle (315.443.5541; email: mdoyle)
Acquisitions Editorial: Suzanne E. Guiod, Editor-in-Chief (315.443.5539; email: seguiod)
   Acquisitions Editors: Deborah Manion (315.443.5647; email: dmmanion); Alison Shay (315.443.5543; email: amshay)
   Assistant Editor: Kelly Balenske (315.443.5541; email: klbalens)
Editorial and Production Manager: Kay Steinmetz (315.443.9155; email: kasteinm)
   Senior Designers: Victoria Lane (315.443.5540; email: vmlane); Fred Wellner (315.443.5540; email: fawellne)
   Project Editor: Kaitlin Carruthers-Busser (315.443.5544; email: klcarrut)
Marketing: Lisa Kuerbis, Marketing Coordinator (315.443.5546; email: lkuerbis)
   Marketing Analyst: Mona Hamlin (315.443.5547; email: mhamlin)
   Design Specialist: Lynn Wilcox (315.443.1975; email: lphoppel)
Business: Karen Lockwood, Senior Business Manager (315.443.5536; email: kflockwo)
   Accounting Clerk: Bobbi Claps (315.443.5538; email: baclaps)

Regular Member
Established: 1943
Title output 2016: 46
Titles currently in print: 1,460

Admitted to the Association: 1946
Title output 2017: 51

Editorial Program
Scholarly books and works of general interest in the areas of Middle East, Irish, Jewish, New York State, women's, Native American, ethnic, disability studies; religion; television; popular culture; sports history; journalism; human and urban geography; politics; peace and conflict resolution; Arab American studies; and selected fiction.

   The Press distributes books bearing the imprints of Adirondack Museum; Moshe Dayan Center for Middle Eastern and African Studies (Tel-Aviv University); New Netherlands Proj-

Syracuse University Press continued

ect; Arlen House; Dedalus Press; Blackhall Publishing; Litteraria Pragensia; Ethnic Heritage Studies Center of Utica College; Syracuse University In Florence; Graduate School Press, Syracuse University; Syracuse University; and the Pucker Gallery, Boston.

Special series, joint imprints, and/or copublishing programs: The Adirondack Museum; The Albert Schweitzer Library; America in the Twentieth Century; Arab-American Studies; Contemporary Issues in the Middle East; Critical Perspectives on Disability; Gender, Culture, and Politics in the Middle East; Gender and Globalization; Irish Studies; Iroquois and Their Neighbors; Judaic Traditions in Literature, Music, and Art; Library of Modern Jewish Literature; Middle East Beyond Dominant Paradigms; Middle East Literature in Translation; Modern Intellectual and Political History of the Middle East; Modern Jewish History; New York State Studies; Religion and Politics; Sports and Entertainment; Syracuse Studies in Geography; Syracuse Studies in Peace and Conflict Resolution; Television and Popular Culture; Writing, Culture, and Community Practices

Teachers College Press

1234 Amsterdam Avenue
New York, NY 10027-6696

Phone: 212.678.3929
Fax: 212.678.4149
Email: (user I.D.)@tc.edu
(unless otherwise indicated)

Orders:
Teachers College Press
PO Box 20
Williston, VT 05495-0020
Phone: 800.575.6560
Fax: 802.864.7626

Website and Social Media:
Website: www.tcpress.com
Facebook: www.facebook.com/TCPress
Twitter: @TCPress
Instagram: @tcpress

European Representative:
Eurospan

Canadian Representative:
University of Toronto Press

Staff

Director: Carole Pogrebin Saltz (212.678.3927; email: saltz)
  Rights and Permissions Manager/Special Sales Coordinator: Christina Brianik (212.678.3827; email: brianik)
Acquisitions Editorial: Brian Ellerbeck, Executive Acquisitions Editor (administration, school change, leadership, policy, special and gifted education, multicultural education, teacher research, curriculum studies) (212.678.3908; email: ellerbeck)
  Acquisitions Editor: Emily Spangler (language and literacy, technology and education) (212.678.3909; email: spangler)
  Consulting Senior Acquisitions Editor: Jean Ward (curriculum, professional development, literacy) (847.224.02785; email: ward)
  Assistant Acquisitions Editor: Noelle De-La-Paz (212.678.3905; email: de-la-paz)
Production: Michael Weinstein, Production Manager (212.678.3926; email: weinstein)

Senior Production Editor: Karl Nyberg (212.678.3806; email: nyberg)
Production Editors: Aureliano Vazquez (212.678.3945; email: vasquez); Lori Tate (212.678.3907; email: tate); John Bylander (212.678.3914; email: bylander); Jennifer Baker (212.678.3902; email: baker)
Production Assistants: Debra Jackson-Whyte (212.678.3926; email: jackson-whyte)
Marketing: Leyli Shayegan, Director, Sales and Marketing and Assistant Director (212.678.3475; email: shayegan)
Business Development/Sales Manager: Sarah (Sally) Kling (212.678.7439; email: kling@tc.columbia.edu)
Marketing Manager: Nancy Power (212.678.3915; email: power)
Graphic Arts Manager: David Strauss (212.678.3982; email: strauss)
Publicity Coordinator: Emily Renwick (212.678.3963; email: renwick)
Outreach Coordinator: Michael McGann (212.678.3919; email: mcgann)
Business: TBA, Financial Controller (212.678.3913)
Secretary/Receptionist: Marcia Ruiz (212.678.3929; email: myr3@columbia.edu)

Regular Member
Established: 1904
Admitted to the Association: 1971
Title output 2016: NR
Title output 2017: NR
Titles currently in print: 767

Editorial Program
Scholarly, professional, text, and trade books on education, education-related areas, and parenting. Multimedia instructional materials, tests, and evaluation materials for classroom use at all levels of education.

Specific areas of interest in education are: curriculum; early childhood; school administration and educational policy; counseling; mathematics; philosophy; psychology; language and literacy; multicultural education; science; sociology; special education; social justice; social studies; teacher education; cultural studies; technology and education; women and higher education.

Special series: Advances in Contemporary Educational Thought; Between Teacher & Text; Counseling and Development; Critical Issues in Educational Leadership; Disability, Culture, and Equity; Early Childhood Education; Education and Psychology of the Gifted; International Perspectives on Education Reform; John Dewey Lecture; Language and Literacy; Multicultural Education; Practitioner Inquiry; Professional Ethics in Education; Reflective History; The Series on School Reform; Teaching for Social Justice; Technology, Education—Connections (TEC); Ways of Knowing in Science and Mathematics

Temple University Press

Mailing Address:
TASB
1852 N. 10th Street
Philadelphia, PA 19122

Phone: 215.926.2140
Fax: 215.926.2141
Email: firstname.lastname@temple.edu

Website and Social Media:
Website: www.temple.edu/tempress
Blog: templepress.wordpress.com
Facebook: www.facebook.com/pages/
   Temple-University-Press/21638877349
Twitter: @TempleUnivPress

Street Address:
TASB
2450 West Hunting Park Avenue
Philadelphia, PA 19129

Orders:
Chicago Distribution Center
11030 South Langley Avenue
Chicago, IL 60628
Phone: 800.621.2736
Fax: 800.621.8476

UK Distributor:
Combined Academic Publishers

Staff
Director: Mary Rose Muccie (215.926.2145)
Rights and Permissions: Nikki Miller (215.926. 3181)
Electronic Publishing Manager: Mary Rose Muccie (215.926.2145)
Editor-in-Chief: Aaron Javsicas (215.926.2159)
   Editors: Sara Cohen (215.926.2146); Ryan Mulligan (215.926.2157)
   Editorial Assistant: Nikki Miller (215.926. 3181)
   Senior Production Editors: Joan Vidal (215.926.2148); Dave Wilson (215.926.2147)
Art Manager: Kate Nichols (215.926.2167)
Marketing: Ann-Marie Anderson, Assistant Director and Director of Marketing (215.926.2143)
   Advertising and Promotion Manager: Irene Imperio (215.926.2153)
   Publicity Manager: Gary Kramer (215.926.2154)
Business: Karen Baker, Finance Manager (215.926.2156)

Regular Member
Established: 1969
Title output 2016: 42
Titles currently in print: 1,204

Admitted to the Association: 1972
Title output 2017: 46
Journals published: 2

Editorial Program
African American studies; American studies; anthropology; Asian studies; Asian American studies; cinema and media studies; communication; criminology; disability studies; education; ethnicity and race; LGBTQIA studies; gender studies; geography; immigration; labor studies; Latin American studies; law and society; Philadelphia regional studies; political science and public policy; race and class studies, religion; sexuality studies; sociology; social justice; sports; urban studies; US and European history; women's studies.

Journals: *Commonwealth: A Journal of Pennsylvania Politics and Policy*; *Kalfou: A Journal of Comparative and Relational Ethnic Studie*s
Special series: Animals and Ethics; Asian American History and Culture; Global Youth; History and the Public; Insubordinate Spaces; Pennsylvania History; Politics, History, and Social Change; Religious Engagement in Democratic Politics; Sexuality Studies; Sporting; Studies in Latin American and Caribbean Music; Urban Life, Landscape, and Policy
Co-publishing program: Pennsylvania Historical Association

University of Tennessee Press

Mailing Address:
110 Conference Center
Knoxville, TN 37996-4108

Shipping Address:
600 Henley Street
Suite 110 Conference Center
Knoxville, TN 37902-2911

Phone: 865.974.3321
Fax: 865.974.3724
Email: custserv@utpress.org
Indiv: (user I.D.)@utk.edu

Orders:
Chicago Distribution Center
11030 South Langley Ave.
Chicago, IL 60628
Phone: 800.621.2736
Fax: 773.702.7212

Website and Social Media:
Website: utpress.org
Blog: utpress.org/utpressblog
Facebook page: www.facebook.com/pages/
   University-of-Tennessee-Press/80814711590?ref=ts
Twitter: @utennpress

Staff
Director: Scot Danforth (email: danforth)
Acquisitions Editorial: Thomas Wells (email: twells)
Editorial Assistant: Jon Boggs (email: jboggs6)
Production Coordinator: Stephanie Thompson (email: sthomp20)
Designer: Kelly Gray (email: kgray14)
Exhibits/Publicity Manager: Tom Post (email: tpost)
Marketing Assistant: Linsey Sims (email: lsims9)
Business Manager: Lisa Davis (email: ldavis49)
IT Manager: Jake Sumner (email: jsumner2)

Regular Member
Established: 1940
Title output 2016: 33
Titles currently in print: 913

Admitted to the Association: 1964
Title output 2017: 31

Editorial Program
American studies; Appalachian studies; African American studies; history; religion; folklore; vernacular architecture; historical archaeology; material culture; literature; and literary fiction. Submissions in poetry, textbooks, and translations are not invited.
Special series, joint imprints, and/or copublishing programs: America's Baptists; Appalachian Echoes; Charles K. Wolfe American Music Series; Correspondence of James K. Polk;

University of Tennessee Press continued

Legacies of War, Outdoor Tennessee; The Papers of Andrew Jackson; Sport and Popular Culture; Tennessee Studies in Literature; Vernacular Architecture Studies; Voices of the Civil War; and The Western Theater in the Civil War

University of Texas Press

Street Address:
3001 Lake Austin Blvd
Stop E4800
Austin, TX 78703-4206

Mailing Address:
PO Box 7819
Austin, TX 78713-7819

Phone: 512.471.7233
Fax: 512.232.7178
Email: info@utpress.utexas.edu
Indiv: firstinitiallastname@utpress.utexas.edu

Orders:
Phone: 800.252.3206
Fax: 800.687.6046
Warehouse: 512.471.7656

Website and Social Media:
Website: www.utexaspress.com
Blog: utpressnews.blogspot.com/
Facebook: www.facebook.com/utexaspress
Twitter: @UTexasPress
Instagram: instagram.com/utexaspress
Pinterest: www.pinterest.com/utpress
YouTube: www.youtube.com/c/utexaspress
Tumblr: www.utexaspress.tumblr.com
Soundcloud: www.soundcloud.com/university-of-texas-press

Staff
Director: David Hamrick (512.232.7604)
   Assistant to the Director: Allison Faust (512.232.7603)
International Rights Manager: Ines ter Horst (512.232.7605)
Rights and Permissions Coordinator: Peggy Gough (512.232.7624)
Assistant Director and Editor-in-Chief: Robert Devens (architecture, history, American studies, Texas) (512.232.7615)
   Senior Editors: Jim Burr (classics, Jewish studies, film and media studies, Middle Eastern studies) (512.232.7610); Kerry Webb (Latin American and pre-Columbian studies, Latin American history, Latina/o studies) (512.232.7612)
   Sponsoring Editor: Casey Kittrell (anthropology, archaeology, nature and environment, food studies, music, Texas) (512.232.7616)
   Assistant Editors: Angelika Lopez-Torres (512.232.2589); Sarah McGavick (512.232.7608)
   Acquisitions and Rights Fellow: Stephanie Malak (512.232.7625)
Managing Editor: Robert Kimzey (512.232.7614)
   Senior Manuscript Editor: Lynne Chapman (512.232.7607)
   Manuscript Editor: Bruce Bethell (512.232.7668)
   Assistant Manuscript Editor: Amanda Frost (512.232.7639)

Copyediting and Marketing Fellow: David Juarez (512.232.7643)
Design and Production Manager: Dustin Kilgore (512.232.7640)
  Designers: Derek George (512.232.7642); Lindsay Starr (512.232.7641)
  Production Coordinator: Sarah Mueller (512.232.7627)
  Production Assistant: Cassandra Cisneros (512.232.7638)
Assistant Director and Marketing and Sales Manager: Gianna LaMorte (512.232.7647)
  Assistant Marketing Manager: Nancy Bryan (512.232.7628)
  Publicity and Communications Manager: Kathryn Marguy (512.232.7634)
  Senior Publicist: Cameron Ludwick (512.232.7633)
  Website and Digital Marketing Coordinator: Bailey Morrison (512.471.1728)
  Advertising and Exhibits Manager: TBA (512.232.7630)
  Marketing and Sales Assistant: Demi Marshall (512.232.7637)
  Regional Sales Manager: Bob Barnett (502.345.6477)
Journals Manager: Christopher Farmer (512.232.7620)
  Journals Production Editors: Karen Broyles (512.232.7622); Stacey Salling (512.232.7600)
  Journals Marketing and Advertising Coordinator: Sheila Scoville (512.232.7618)
  Journals Customer Service: Elizabeth Fairman (512.232.7621)
Financial Officer: Allison Lambert (512.232.7646)
  Royalty and HR Manager: Kristin Duvall (512.232.7648)
  Accounts Payable Manager: Linda Ramirez (512.232.7649)
  Accounts Receivable Manager: Jennifer Nuzzo (512.232.7602)
  Customer Service Supervisor: Brenda Jo Hoggatt (512.232.7650)
  Customer Service Assistant: Dawn Bishop (512.232.7652)
  Assistant Director and Information and Business Systems Manager: William Bishel (512.232.7609)
  Digital Publishing Manager: Sharon Casteel (512.232.7631)
Warehouse (512.232.7656)
  Warehouse Supervisor: Paul Guerra (512.232.7657)
  Warehouse Staff: David Guerrero (512.232.7655); Rey Renteria (512.232.7654)

Regular Member
Established: 1950
Title output 2016: 93
Titles currently in print: 2,784
Admitted to the Association: 1954
Title output 2017: 93
Journals published: 13

Editorial Program
American studies, anthropology, archaeology, architecture, art, classics, film and media studies, photography, food studies and cookbooks, history, Jewish studies, Latin American and pre-Columbian studies, Latina/o studies, Middle Eastern studies, music, nature and environment, and Texas and the Southwest.

The Press distributes publications for the Jack S. Blanton Museum of Art; Center for Mexican American Studies; Center for Middle Eastern Studies; Dolph Briscoe Center for American History; Harry Ransom Center; and Teresa Lozano Long Institute of Latin American Studies.

Journals: *Asian Music; Cinema Journal; Diálogo; Information and Culture; The Journal of the History of Sexuality; The Journal of Individual Psychology; Journal of Latin American Geography; Latin American Music Review; Studies in Latin American Popular Culture; Texas Studies in Literature and Language; The Textile Museum Journal; US Latina & Latino Oral History Journal; The Velvet Light Trap*

University of Texas Press continued

Special series, joint imprints, and/or copublishing programs: American Music; Border Hispanisms; Center for Creative Photography; Cities of the Etruscans; CMES (Center for Middle Eastern Studies) Modern Middle East Literatures In Translation; CMES Modern Middle East Series; CMES Emerging Voices from the Middle East; CMES Middle East Monograph Series; CMES Binah Yitzrit Foundation Series in Israel Studies; Exploring Jewish Arts and Culture (with Schusterman Center for Jewish Studies); Focus on American History (with Briscoe Center for American History); Handbook of Latin American Studies (with Library of Congress); Historia USA; Information; The Katrina Bookshelf; Lateral Exchanges: Architecture, Urban Development, and Transnational Practices; The Oratory of Classical Greece; ; Terry and Jan Todd Series on Physical Culture And Sports; Texas Film and Media Studies; Texas Natural History Guides; World Comics and Graphic Nonfiction Series
Endowed book series: Ashley and Peter Larkin Series in Greek and Roman Culture; Bill and Alice Wright Photography Series; Brad and Michele Moore Roots Music Series; Bridwell Texas History Series; Charles N. Prothro Texana Series; Clifton and Shirley Caldwell Texas Heritage Series; The Corrie Herring Hooks Series; Ellen and Edward Randall Series; Jack and Doris Smothers Series in Texas History, Life, and Culture; Jamal and Rania Daniel Series in Contemporary History, Politics, Culture, and Religion of the Levant; Jess and Betty Jo Hay Series; Joe R. and Teresa Lozano Long Series in Latin American and Latino Art and Culture; Linda Schele Series in Maya and Pre-Columbian Studies; Louann Atkins Temple Women and Culture Series; M. Georgia Hegarty Dunkerley Contemporary Art Series; Mildred Wyatt-Wold Series in Ornithology; Peter T. Flawn Series in Natural Resources; Roger Fullington Series in Architecture; William and Bettye Nowlin Series in Art, History, and Culture of the Western Hemisphere

Texas A&M University Press

Street Address:
John H. Lindsey Building, Lewis Street
College Station, TX 77843

Mailing Address:
4354 TAMU
College Station, TX 77843-4354

Phone: 979.845.1436
Fax: 979.847.8752
Email: upress@tamu.edu
Indiv: (user I.D.)@tamu.edu

Orders:
Phone: 800.826.8911
Fax: 888.617.2421
Email: bookorders@tamu.edu

Website and Social Media:
Website: www.tamupress.com
Blog: tamupress.blogspot.com/
Facebook: www.facebook.com/tamupress
Twitter: @TAMUPress
YouTube: www.youtube.com/channel/UCFFpUgvj4qVlaQTf0r5-RxA

European Representative:
Eurospan

Staff
Edward R. Campbell '39 Press Director: Shannon Davies (979.458.3980; email: sdavies)
Acquisitions Editorial: Jay Dew, Editor-in-Chief (Texas, Western, and Southern history; military history; Texas women's history; environmental history; borderland studies; political history) (979.845.0759; email: jaydew)
  Senior Editor: Thom Lemmons (physical anthropology; archaeology; nautical archaeology; sports; Texas art, music, and culture) (979.845.0758; email: thom.lemmons)
  Acquisitions Editor: Stacy Eisenstark (natural history and natural sciences; agriculture; gardening and horticulture; conservation and the environment) (979.458.3976; email: s_eisenstark)
  Editorial Assistant: Emily Seyl (979.845.2521; email: emilyseyl@exhange.tamu.edu)
Manuscript Editorial: Katie Duelm, Managing Editor (979.458.3975; email: katie.duelm)
  Associate Editor: Patricia Clabaugh (979.458.3979; email: pclabaugh)
Design/Production: Mary Ann Jacob, Design & Production Manager (979.845.3694; email: m-jacob)
  Assistant Design and Production Manager: Kevin Grossman (979.458.3995; email: k-grossman)
  Design and Production Assistant: Kristie Lee (979.458.1331; email: K-lee)
Marketing: Gayla Christiansen, Marketing Manager (979.845.0148; email: gayla-c)
  Publicity and Advertising Manager: Christine Brown (979.458.3982; email: christinebrown)
  Promotional Design and Electronic Marketing Manager: Kyle Littlefield (979.458.3983; email: k-littlefield)
  Marketing Communications and Exhibit Manager: Katelyn Knight (979.458.3984; email: k_knight)
  Sales Manager: Kathryn Lloyd (979.458.3988; email: k-krol)
Financial Manager: Dianna Sells (979.845.0146; email: d-sells)
  Business Operations Manager: Wynona McCormick (979.845.0136; email: wynona)
  Order Fulfillment Supervisor: Genny Jennings (979.458.3991; email: genny.howard)Warehouse Manager: Mike Martin (979.458.3986; email: mike.martin)
  Assistant Warehouse Manager: Cliff O'Connell (979.458.3987; email: c-oconnell)

Regular Member
Established: 1974   Admitted to the Association: 1977
Title output 2016: 57   Title output 2017: 60
Titles currently in print: 1,355

Editorial Program
American, Western, and Southern history; Texas and the Southwest; borderlands; Texas women's history; military history; business history; environmental history; natural history; conservation; agriculture; natural resource science; veterinary medicine; consumer health; physical anthropology; archaeology; nautical archaeology; architecture; Texas music, art, and culture; political history. Submissions are not invited in poetry or fiction.
Special series: AgriLife Research and Extension Service Series; Brannen Series in Military Studies; Centennial Series of the Association of Former Students; Connecting the Greater West; Cox Books on Conservation Leadership; Dickson Series in Texas Music; Fay Series in Analytical Psychology; Gulf Coast Books; Harte Research Institute for Gulf of Mexico Studies; Lindsey Series in the Arts and Humanities; Marine, Maritime, and Coastal Books; Merrick Natural Environment; Montague Business and Oil History; Moody Natural His-

Texas A& M University Press continued

tory; Moore Texas Art; Peoples and Cultures of Texas; Peopling of the Americas; Perspectives on South Texas; Presidential Rhetoric and Political Communication; Prothro Texas Photography; Rachal Foundation Series in Nautical Archaeology; Red River Valley Books; River Books; Sam Rayburn Rural Life; Seventh Generation: Survival, Sustainability, Sustenance in a New Nature; Southwestern Studies in the Humanities; Spencer Series in the West and Southwest; Swaim-Paup-For an Spirit of Sports Series; University of Houston Mexican American Studies; Wardlaw Books; Williams-Ford Series in Military History; Williams Texas Life

TCU Press

Mailing Address:
ThCU Box 298300
Fort Worth, TX 76129

Phone: 817.257.7822
Fax: 817.257.5075

Street Address:
3000 Sandage
Fort Worth, TX 76109

Orders:
Phone: 800.826.8911

Website and Social Media:
Website: www.prs.tcu.edu
Facebook: www.facebook.com/pages/
 Fort-Worth-TX/TCU-PRESS/291943790611
Twitter: @TCUPress
Instagram: @tcupress
Tumblr: tcupress.tumblr.com

Staff
Director Dan Williams (email: d.e.williamms@tcu.edu)
Editor: Kathy Walton (email: k.s.walton@tcu.edu)
Production Manager: Melinda Esco (email: m.esco@tcu.edu)
Marketing Coordinator: Rebecca Allen (email: rebecca.a.allen@tcu.edu)
Office Manager: Molly Spain (email: molly.spain@tcu.edu)

Regular Member
Established: 1966
Title output 2016: 16
Titles currently in print: 400

Admitted to to the Association: 1982
Title output 2017: NR

Editorial Program
Humanities and social sciences, with special emphasis on local, Texas, and Southwestern history and literature; American studies, especially Border Studies; fiction; and poetry; also publishes, *descant*, the Fort Worth literary journal.
Special series: Chaparral Books for Young Readers; The Chisholm Trail Series; Literary Cities; The Texas Tradition Series; The Texas Biography Series; TCU Texas Poets Laureate

Texas Review Press

Street Address:
SHSU Department of English
1901 University Ave, Ste. 152
Huntsville, TX 77341 Huntsville,

Mailing Address:
SHSU Department of English
Box 2146
TX 773471-2146

Phone: 936.294.1992
Fax: 936.294.3070
Email: TexasReview@shsu.edu

US Orders
Texas A&M University Press
Orders: 800-826-8911
Email: bookorders@tamu.edu

Website and Social Media:
Website: www.texasreviewpress.org
Blog: texasreviewpress.wordpress.com/
Facebook: www.facebook.com/TexasReviewPress/
Twitter: @TxReviewPress
Instagram: @texasreviewpress

UK, Europe, Africa & the Middle East
Eurospan

Canada
Scholarly Book Services Inc.

Staff
Director: TBA
Assistant to the Director: Kimberly Davis (936.294.1429; email: kpdavis@shsu.edu)
Office Manager: Claude Wooley (936.294.1992; email: cww006@shsu.edu)
Editor, *The Texas Review*: Nick Lantz (936.294.1990; email: nick.lantz@shsu.edu)

Introductory Member
Established: 1979
Title output 2016: 24
Titles currently in print: 290

Admitted to the Association: 2017
Title output 2017: 18
Journals published: 3

Editorial Program
Texas Review Press publishes fiction, nonfiction, memoir, literary criticism, and poetry with a focus on regional works from Texas and the Deep South. We sponsor four annual competitions that invite submissions from around the world. These are the Robert Phillips Poetry Chapbook Competition, The X.J. Kennedy Competition for a full-length poetry collection, the George Garrett Fiction Competition for novel or a collection of short stories, and the Clay Reynolds Novella Competition.
Journals: *The Texas Review, The Gordian Review,* and *The Beacon*
Special series: The Southern Poetry Anthology and Best Creative Nonfiction of the South.

Texas Tech University Press

Street Address:
1120 Main Street
Second Floor
Lubbock, TX 79409-1037

Phone: 806.742.2982
Fax: 806.742.2979
Email: firstname.lastname@ttu.edu

Website and Social Media:
Website: www.ttupress.org
Facebook: www.facebook.com/TTUPress
Twitter: @TTUPress

Mailing Address:
Box 41037
Lubbock, TX 79409-1037

Orders:
Grantham Building
608 North Knoxville Avenue #120
Lubbock, TX 79415
Phone: 800.832.4042;
International: 806.742.2982
Fax: 806.742.2979
International fax: 806.742.2979

UK and European Distributor:
Eurospan

Staff
Director: TBA
Acquisitions: Joanna Conrad, Interim Director and Editor-in-Chief
Managing Editor: TBA
Design and Production Manager: Kasey McBeath
Marketing Coordinator: John Brock
Customer Service: LaTisha Roberts

Regular Member
Established: 1971
Title output 2016: 11
Titles currently in print: 445

Admitted to the Association: 1987
Title output 2017: 10
Journals published: 6

Editorial Program
American legal studies; American Indian studies; history and culture of Texas and the American West, the Great Plains, and modern Southeast Asia during and after the Vietnam War; border studies; natural history and natural science; poetry (by invitation only); nonfiction for young readers; sport in the American West; American roots music; renewable energy studies; and environmental history

Journals: *Conradiana; Helios; Intertexts; Archivation Exploration; Journal of the Vernacular Music Center; Texas Journal of Rural Health*

Special series: American Liberty and Justice; The Americas; Grover E. Murray Studies in the American Southwest; Modern Southeast Asia; Plains Histories; Sport in the American West; Walt McDonald First-Book Series in Poetry; Voice in the American West; Women, Gender, and the West

University of Tokyo Press

4-5-29 Komaba, Meguro-ku
Tokyo 153-0041, Japan

US Representative:
Columbia University Press

Phone: +81.3.6407.1921, +81.3.6407.1904
Fax: +81.3.6407.1582, +81.3.6407.1991
Email: info@utp.or.jp

Staff
President: Junichi Hamada
Chairman of the Board: Shunya Yoshimi
Managing Director: Takuya Kuroda (email: kuroda@utp.or.jp)
Editorial Director: Mika Komatsu
Marketing Director: Hiroki Hashimoto
Production Director: Hiroshi Takagi
Editor-in-Chief & International Liaisons Executive: Kensuke Goto
   (email: gauteau@utp.or.jp)

Regular Member
Established: 1951
Title output 2016: 122
Titles currently in print: 4,600

Admitted to the Association: 1970
Title output 2017: 124

Editorial Program
Titles published in Japanese reflect the research carried out at the university in the humanities, social sciences, and natural sciences. Continuing series are published in biology, earth sciences, sociology, economics, philosophy, and Japanese art and historical studies. Special projects include publication of textbooks and reprinting of historical source materials.

English-language publishing began in 1960; special strengths include Japanese and Asian studies (including art, history, economics, law, and sociology). English-language publications also include translations of historical and important literary works and diaries.

University of Toronto Press

Books Division (Toronto Office):
10 St. Mary Street, Suite 700
Toronto, ON M4Y 2W8 Canada

Phone: 416.978.2239
Fax: 416.978.4738
Email: publishing@utpress.utoronto.ca

Books Division (Guelph Office):
199 Woolwich Street, 2nd Floor
Guelph, ON N1H 3V4 Canada

Phone: 519.837.1403
Fax: 519.767.1643
Email: requests@highereducation.com

P-Shift:
5201 Dufferin Street
Toronto, ON M4H 2T4 Canada
Phone: 416.667.7777

Journals Division:
5201 Dufferin Street
North York, ON M3H 5T8 Canada

Phone: 416.667.7810
Fax: 416.667.7881; 800.221.9985
Email: journals@utpress.utoronto.ca

UTP Distribution:
5201 Dufferin Street
North York, ON M3H 5T8 Canada

Phone: 416.667.7791; 800.565.9523
Fax: 416.667.7832; 800.221.9985
Email: utpbooks@utpress.utoronto.ca

US Warehouse:
2250 Military Road
Tonawanda, NY 14150
Phone: 716.693.2768

Websites and Social Media:
Publishing: www.utorontopress.com
Blog: utorontopress.com/ca/blog
Journals: www.utpjournals.press
P-Shift: www.utpshift.com
Distribution: www.utpdistribution.com
Facebook: www.facebook.com/utpress; www.facebook.com/utpjournals
Twitter: @utpress; @utpjournals

UK Representative:
Oxford Publicity Partnership Ltd.
gary.hall@oppuk.co.uk

UK/Europe Distribution:
NBN International

Staff
Administration
Indiv. email: firstinitiallastname@utpress.utoronto.ca
  President, Publisher and CEO: John Yates (ext. 2222)
  Vice President, HR & Administration: Lindsay Whillans (ext. 2224)
  Vice President, Finance: Shawn O'Grady (416.667.7765)
Book Publishing
Indiv. email: firstinitiallastname@utpress.utoronto.ca
  Vice President, Book Publishing: Lynn Fisher (ext. 2243)
  Publishing Coordinator: Charley LaRose (ext. 2237)
  Permissions & Rights Coordinator: Lisa Jemison (ext. 2226)

Acquisitions Editorial
  Manager Humanities Acquisitions: Suzanne Rancourt (classics, medieval, renaissance studies, Erasmus) (ext. 2239)
  Manager Social Sciences Acquisitions: Jennifer DiDomenico (business & economics) (ext. 2259)
  Acquisitions Editors: Len Husband (Cdn history, native studies, philosophy) (ext. 2238); Mark Thompson (film, literature, cultural studies, book history, communications) (ext. 2231); Stephen Shapiro (history, literature, semiotics) (ext. 2233); Daniel Quinlan (political science & law) (ext. 2254); Jodie Lewchuk (anthropology, geography, sociology, urban studies)(ext. 2251); Meg Patterson (social work, education, medicine & health) (ext. 2230); Textbooks: Anne Brackenbury (anthropology, criminology, geography, indigenous studies, social work, sociology, women's and gender studies) (ext. 4234); Natalie Fingerhut (history, Medieval studies) (ext. 4236); Mat Buntin (politics, international development studies, human rights, security studies, Latin American studies, environmental studies, business) (ext. 4236)

Manuscript Editorial & Production
  Managing Editor: Anne Laughlin (ext. 2236)
  Production Manager: Ani Deyirmenjian (ext. 2227)
  Production Editor: Beate Schwirtlich (ext. 4228)

Electronic Publishing
  Electronic Publishing Coordinator: Barry Meikle (ext. 2232)

Sales & Marketing
  Sales and Marketing Manager: Brian MacDonald (ext. 2253)
  Publicist: Chris Reed (ext. 2248)
  Advertising, Journal Review Coordinator: Deepshikha Dutta (ext. 2247)
  Sales & Electronic Marketing Coordinator: Inae Heo (ext. 2250)
  Catalogue & Copy Coordinator: Luciano Nicassio (ext. 2257)
  Exhibits & Examination Copies Coordinator: Marilyn McCormack (ext. 2260)
  Data & Web Coordinator: Bob Currer (ext. 2249)
  Marketing Manager: Anna Del Col (519.837.1403 ext. 4224)
  Sales Manager: Michelle Lobkowicz (519.837.1403 ext. 4231)
  Sales & Marketing Assistant (also responsible for examination copies): Joanna Kincaide (519.837.1403 ext. 4221)

Journals (5201 Dufferin St.) (416.667.7777)
Indiv. email: firstinitiallastname@utpress.utoronto.ca
  Director, Journals: Antonia Pop (416.667.7838)
  Production Manager, Journals: Katie Yantzi (ext. 7971)
  Circulation & Distribution Manager: Adele D'Ambrosio (ext. 7781)
  Marketing Manager: Vesna Micic (ext. 7849)

P-Shift
Indiv email: firstinitiallastname@utpress.utoronto.ca
  Manager: Nick Hilton (ext. 7830)
  Starting from Word files, P-Shift embeds XML code (semantic markup) within your manuscript. Identifies key information, validates and crosschecks references, and produces active, user-friendly files for editing, InDesign-friendly XML for typesetting, fully featured EPUB, and archival XML.

University of Toronto Press continued

UTP Distribution Centre
Indiv email: firstinitiallastname@utpress.utoronto.ca
  Vice President, Distribution & MIS: Hamish Cameron (416.667.7773)
  Manager, Customer Service: Tom Skudra (416.667.7845)
  Manager, Client Publisher Services: Bessie Luciano (416.667.7946)
  Credit Manager: Clive Williams (416.667.7774)

Regular Member
Established: 1901
Title output 2016: 185
Titles currently in print: 4,000

Admitted to the Association: 1937
Title output 2017: 180
Journals published: 40

Editorial Program
UTP publishes scholarly books, serious non-fiction, course books and books for business professionals with a particular focus on: Business & economics; classical studies; medieval studies; renaissance studies; Slavic studies; environmental studies; Erasmian studies; Victorian studies; English literature; Canadian studies; North American Studies; Canadian literature; cultural studies; literary theory and criticism; modern languages and literatures; philosophy; political science; law and criminology; religion and theology; education; Canadian and international history; history of science and medicine; sociology; anthropology; gender studies; Native studies; social work; geography; urban studies; and women's studies. Submissions are not invited in poetry or fiction. Our textbook publishing program provides an alternative to larger textbook publishers, both for instructors looking for a refreshing change from the standard course book offerings and for potential authors who value creative and editorial license as well as the personal attention provided by our editors. The possibilities for rethinking how texts can be used in the classroom, along with new formats for their delivery, are endless, and we looks to partner with instructors and scholars in this innovative endeavour.

Journals: *Anthropologica; Canadian Bulletin of Medical History; Canadian Historical Review; Canadian Journal of Criminology and Criminal Justice; Canadian Journal of Film Studies; Canadian Journal of History; Canadian Journal of Human Sexuality; Canadian Journal of Information and Library Sciences; Canadian Journal of Mathematics; Canadian Journal of Program Evaluation; Canadian Journal of Women and the Law; Canadian Mathematical Bulletin; Canadian Modern Language Review; Canadian Public Policy; Canadian Review of American Studies; Canadian Theatre Review; Cartographica; Diaspora: A Journal of Transnational Studies; Eighteenth-Century Fiction; Florilegium; Genocide Studies International; International Journal of Canadian Studies; IJFAB: International Journal of Feminist Approached to Bioethics; Journal of the Association of Medical Microbiology and Infectious Disease Canada (JAMMI); Journal of Canadian Studies; Journal of Education for Library and Information Science; Journal of Military, Veteran and Family Health; Journal of Religion and Popular Culture; Journal of Scholarly Publishing; Journal of Veterinary Medical Education; Lexicons of Early Modern English; Modern Drama; Mouseion; National Gallery of Canada Review; Physiotherapy Canada; Publications of the Champlain Society; Seminar; The Tocqueville Review; Toronto Journal of Theology; Ultimate Reality and Meaning; University of Toronto Law Journal; University of Toronto Quarterly; Yearbook of Comparative Literature*
Joint imprints: Rotman-UTP Publishing Imprint.
New series: Provincial and Territorial Health System Profiles.

Ongoing series Anthropological Horizons; Asian Canadian Studies; Benjamin Disraeli Letters; Business & Sustainability Series; Canadian Cinema; Canadian Social History Series; Collected Works of Bernard Lonergan; Collected Works of Erasmus; Collected Works of Northrop Frye; Cultural Spaces; Dictionary of Canadian Biography; Digital Futures; Erasmus Studies; European Union Studies; Frye Studies; Global Suburbanisn; Innovation, Creativity, and Governance in Canadian City-Regions; IPAC Series in Public Management and Governance; Japan and Global Society; Joanne Goodman Lectures; The Kenneth Michael Tanenbaum Series in Jewish Studies; Lonergan Studies; Lorenzo DaPonte Italian Library; Medieval Academy Books; Medieval Academy Reprints for Teaching; New Studies in Phenomenology and Hermeneutics; Osgoode Society for Canadian Legal History; Phoenix Supplementary Volumes; Renaissance Society of America Reprint Texts; Robson Classical Lectures; Selected Correspondence of Bernard Shaw; Studies in Book and Print Culture; Studies in Comparative Political Economy and Public Policy; Studies in Gender and History; The Munk Series on Global Affairs; Themes in Canadian History; Toronto Anglo Saxon Series; Toronto Iberic; Toronto Italian Studies; Toronto Old Norse-Icelandic Series; Toronto Studies in Medieval Law; Toronto Studies in Philosophy; Toronto Studies in Semiotics and Communication; UCLA Clark Memorial Library Series; University of Toronto Romance Series; UTP Insights; The James Scarth Gale Library of Korean Literature. Textbook Series: Teaching Culture: UTP Ethnographies for the Classroom (see www.utpteachingculture.com); Anthropological Insights (short foundation texts); ethnoGRAPHIC (new approaches to pedagogy, ethnography meets graphic novel); Readings in Medieval Civilizations and Cultures; Companions to Medieval History; Rethinking the Middle Ages; CHA/UTP International Themes and Issues; Johnson-Shoyama Series on Public Policy.

Truman State University Press

Street Address:
112 East Patterson St.
Kirksville, MO 63501

Phone: 660.785.7336
Fax: 660.785.4480
Email: tsup@truman.edu

Website and Social Media:
Website: tsup.truman.edu
Blog: tsup.truman.edu/blog-posts/
Facebook: trumanstateunivpress
Twitter: @TSUPress
Pinterest: @TSUPress

Mailing Address:
100 East Normal Ave.
Kirksville, MO 63501

Orders:
Longleaf Services Inc.
Phone: 800.848.6224

Staff
Interim Director/Editor-in-Chief: Barbara Smith-Mandell (660.785.4525; email: bsm@truman.edu)
Production Editor: Lisa Ahrens (660.785.7299; email: lahrens@truman.edu)

Truman State University Press continued

Introductory Member
Established: 1986
Title output 2016: 14
Titles currently in print: 240

Admitted to the Association: 2016
Title output 2017: 11
Journals published: 1

Editorial Program
Truman State University Press was established in 1986 to publish peer-reviewed research and literature for the scholarly community and the reading public, originally focusing on sixteenth-century European history, and later moving into American studies, poetry, and contemporary nonfiction. In 2017, TSUP narrowed its publication program to focus on literary publications.

TSUP's literary publications include poetry in the New Odyssey Series, the Contemporary Nonfiction series, and a literary journal, *Chariton Review*. Since 1997, the Press has sponsored the T. S. Eliot Prize for Poetry, an annual award for the best collection of poetry in English named in honor of native Missourian T. S. Eliot. The Notable Missourians series for young readers was launched in 2014. The Young Voices of Missouri project, begun in 2016 as a special issue of *Chariton Review*, publishes the work of high school students in Missouri.
Journal: *Chariton Review*
Special series: T. S. Eliot Prize for Poetry/New Odyssey; Notable Missourians; Contemporary Nonfiction

United States Institute of Peace Press

2301 Constitution Avenue, NW
Washington, DC 20037

Phone: 202.457.1700
Fax: 202.223.9320
Email: (user I.D)@usip.org

Orders:
PO Box 605
Herndon, VA 20172
Phone: 800.868.8064; 703.661.1590
Fax: 703.661.1501
Email:
usipmail@presswarehouse.com

Website and Social Media:
Website: bookstore.usip.org
Facebook: United States Institute of Peace
Twitter: @USIP

UK/European Distributor:
NBN International

Canadian Representative:
Renouf Books

Asia and the Pacific:
East-West Export Books (EWEB)

Staff
Director of Publishing Operations: Jake Harris (email: jharris)
Sales, Rights, and Marketing Specialist: Cecilia Stoute (email: cstoute)
Publications Coordinator: Delsena Draper (email: ddraper)
Publications Assistant: Erica Holsclaw (email: eholsclaw)

Regular Member

Established: 1991
Title output 2016: 12
Titles currently in print: 209

Admitted to the Association: 1993
Title output 2017: 12

Editorial Program

The Press publishes books that are based on work supported by the Institute. Created by Congress in 1984, the Institute is an independent, nonpartisan institution that works to prevent, mitigate, and resolve violent international conflicts. The Institute's publications range across the spectrum of international relations, including conflict prevention, management, and resolution; diplomacy and negotiation; human rights; mediation and facilitation; foreign policy; gender; ethnopolitics; political science; and religion and ethics.
Special series: Academy Guides; Cross-Cultural Negotiation Series; Peacemaker's Toolkits

W. E. Upjohn Institute for Employment Research

300 South Westnedge Avenue
Kalamazoo, MI 49007-4686

Orders:
Phone: 888.227.8569

Phone: 269.343.4330
Fax: 269.343.7310
Email: publications@upjohn.org
Indiv: lastname@upjohn.org

Website and Social Media:
Website: www.upjohn.org
Facebook: facebook.com/Upjohn.Institute
Twitter: @upjohninstitute

Staff

Director of Publications: TBA (269.343.5541)
   Assistant to the Director: Claire Black (269.343.5541)
Manager of Publications and Marketing: Richard Wyrwa (269.343.5541)
Editor: Ben Jones (269.343.5541)
Editor: Allison Colosky (269.343.5541)
Production Coordinator: Erika Jackson (269.343.5541)

Regular Member

Established: 1945
Title output 2016: 7
Titles currently in print: 2,225

Admitted to the Association: 1997
Title output 2017: 7

Editorial Program

Scholarly works on employment-related issues; labor economics; current issues in the social sciences, with an emphasis on public policy. Books are authored by resident research staff and other scholars in the academic and professional communities. The Institute also publishes working papers, policy papers, and technical reports authored by the resident research staff and grantees; a quarterly journal on the West Michigan economy, *Business Outlook for West Michigan*, and a quarterly newsletter, *Employment Research*.

University of Utah Press

J. Willard Marriott Library, Suite 5400
295 South 1500 East, Suite 5400
Salt Lake City, UT 84112-0860

Fax: 801.581.3365
Indiv: (user I.D.)@utah.edu

Orders:
Chicago Distribution Center
11030 South Langley Ave
Chicago, IL 60628
Phone: 800.621.2736
Fax: 800.621.8476

Website and Social Media:
Website: www.UofUpress.com
Facebook: www.facebook.com/uofupress
Twitter: @UofUPress

UK/European Representative:
Eurospan University Press Group

Staff
Director: Glenda Cotter (801.585.0083; email: glenda.cotter)
Acquisitions: John Alley, Editor-in-Chief (American history; American West, Mormon studies, folklore, Middle East studies, religious studies, environment) (801.585.3203; email: john.alley)
Editor: Reba Rauch (anthropology and archaeology, linguistics, natural history, regional guidebooks) (801.585.0081; email: reba.rauch)
Managing Editor: Patrick Hadley (email: patrick.hadley)
Design & Production Manager: Jessica Booth (email: jessica.booth)
Sales and Marketing Manager: Hannah New (801.585.9786; email: hannah.new)
Business Manager, Rights and Permissions: Janalyn Guo (email: janalyn.guo)

Regular Member
Established: 1949
Title output 2016: 36
Titles currently in print: 523

Admitted to the Association: 1979
Title output 2017: 32

Editorial Program
Anthropology and archaeology, linguistics, Mesoamerica, America Indian studies, creative nonfiction, environmental history, folklore, history of the North American West, Utah and Mormon studies, Middle East studies, natural history, nature writing, regional guidebooks, and general titles of regional interest.

Special series: Agha Shahid Ali Prize in Poetry; Foundations of Archaeological Inquiry; Don D. and Catherine S. Fowler Prize (Anthropology & Archaeology); The Juanita Brooks Prize in Mormon Studies; Perspectives on the Mormon Experience; Tanner Lectures on Human Values; Utah Series in Middle East Studies; University of Utah Anthropological Papers; The Wallace Stegner Prize in Environmental Humanities

Vanderbilt University Press

Street Address:
2014 Broadway
Suite 320
Nashville, TN 37203

Mailing Address:
VU Station B 351813
Nashville, TN 37235

Phone: 615.322.3585
Fax: 615.343.8823
Email: vupress@vanderbilt.edu
Indiv: firstname.lastname@vanderbilt.edu

Customer Service/Order Fulfillment:
OU Press Book Distribution Center
2800 Venture Drive
Norman, OK 73069
Phone: 800.627.7377
Fax: 800.735.0476

Website and Social Media:
Website: www.vanderbiltuniversitypress.com
Facebook: www.facebook.com/pages/Vanderbilt-University-Press/46334873151
Twitter: @VanderbiltUP

Canadian Distributor:
Scholarly Book Services

UK/European Distributor:
Eurospan

Staff
Director: Michael Ames
Acquisitions Editor: Beth Kressel Itkin
Managing Editor: Joell Smith-Borne
Editing, Design, and Production Manager: Dariel Mayer
Marketing Manager: Betsy Phillips
Marketing and New Media Associate: Jenna Phillips
Business Manager: Greta Thomas

Regular Member
Established: 1940
Title output 2016: 20
Titles currently in print: 345

Admitted to the Association: 1993
Title output 2017: 17

Editorial Program
Scholarly books and serious nonfiction in most areas of the humanities, the social sciences, health care, and higher education. Special interests include health care and social issues; caregiving and family policy; studies of race, class, gender, and sexuality; human rights and social justice; public policy; Hispanic and Latin American studies; African American studies; sociology and anthropology; and regional books.
Copublishing program: Country Music Foundation

The University of Virginia Press

Street Address:
Bemiss House
210 Sprigg Lane
Charlottesville, VA 22903-0608

Phone: 434.924.3468
Fax: 434.982.2655
Email: vapress@virginia.edu
Indiv: (user I.D.)@virginia.edu

Mailing Address:
PO Box 400318
Charlottesville, VA 22904-4318

Warehouse Address:
Longleaf Services, Inc
116 S. Boundary Street
Chapel Hill, NC 27514-3808
Telephone: 800-848-6224
Fax: 800-272-6817
orders@longleafservices.org

Website and Social Media:
Website: www.upress.virginia.edu
Facebook: www.facebook.com/uvapress
Twitter: @uvapress

UK/European Representative:
Eurospan

Canadian Representative:
Scholarly Book Services

Staff

Director: Mark H. Saunders (434.924.6064; email: msaunders)
Intellectual Property and Database Manager: Mary MacNeil (434.924.3468; email: mmm5w)
Acquisitions Editorial: Eric Brandt, Assistant Director and Editor-in-Chief (humanities) (434.982.3033; email: ebrandt)
　Editors: Richard K. Holway, Senior Executive Editor (history and social sciences) (434.924.7301; email: rkh2a); Boyd Zenner (architecture, environmental studies, ecocriticism, and regional) (434.924.1373; email: bz2v)
　Associate Editor: Angie Hogan (eighteenth-century studies, history of science) (434.924.3361; email: arhogan)
　Acquisitions Assistant: Nicholas Rich (434.924.4725; email: nr3pf)
　Electronic Imprint: Mark H. Saunders, Rotunda Manager (434.924.6064; email: mhs5u)
　Editorial and Technical Manager: David Sewell, Manager of Digital Initiatives, UVAP (434.924.9973; email: dsewell)
　Rotunda Marketing and Sales Manager: Jason Coleman (434.924.1450; email: jcoleman)
　Editorial and Technical Specialist: Patricia Searl (434.982.2310; email: pls4e)
Editorial: Ellen Satrom, Managing Editor (434.924.6065; email: egs6s)
　Assistant Managing Editor and Senior Editor (BUS/SAH Archipedia): Mark Mones (434.924.6066; email: emm4t)
　Project Editor: Morgan Myers (434.924.6067; email: jm3yg)
　Design and Production: Ellen Satrom, Editorial, Design, and Production Manager (434.924.6065; email: egs6s)
　Production Manager: Anne Hegeman, (434.924.3585; email: aeh7v)
　Senior Designer and Assistant Production Manager: Cecilia Sorochin (434.924.6069; email: scs6ak)

Marketing: Jason Coleman, Marketing & Sales Director (434.924.4150; email: jcoleman
   Publicity and Social Media Director: Emily Grandstaff (434.982.2932; email: egrandstaff)
   Marketing Associate: Emma Donovan (434.924.6070; email: efd4s)
Business Manager: Duncan Pickett (434.924.6068; email: fdp7e)
   Customer Service and Operations Manager: Brenda Fitzgerald (434.924.3469; email: bwf)

Regular Member

Established: 1963   Admitted to the Association: 1964
Title output 2016: 65   Title output 2017: 62
Titles currently in print: 1,510

Editorial Program

Scholarly and general trade publications in humanities and social sciences, with concentrations in American history; African American studies; Southern studies; political science; literary and cultural studies, with particular strengths in African and Caribbean studies; Enlightenment studies; Victorian studies; religious studies; architecture and landscape studies; environmental studies; animal studies; Virginiana.

   The Press also publishes digital publications, primarily critical and documentary editions, and an architectural dictionary, through Rotunda. Documentary editions (ongoing): Selected Papers of John Jay; The Papers of Abraham Lincoln; The Papers of James Madison; The Diaries of Gouverneur Morris; The Eleanor Roosevelt Papers; The Papers of George Washington; The Papers of Andrew Jackson Digital Edition; The Dolly Madison Digital Edition; The Papers of Woodrow Wilson Digital Edition.

Special series: The American South; American Spirituality; Buildings of the United States; CARAF Books (Caribbean and African Literature translated from the French); The Carter G. Woodson Institute Series in Black Studies; Constitutionalism and Democracy; Contemplative Sciences; Cultural Frames, Framing Culture; Early American Histories; Jeffersonian America; Kapnick Lectures; MidCentury: Architecture, Landscape, Urbanism, and Design; Miller Center Studies on the Presidency; A Nation Divided: Studies in the Civil War Era; New World Studies; The Page-Barbour and Richard Lecture Series; Phi Beta Kappa Lecture Series; Race, Ethnicity, and Politics; Reconsiderations in Southern African History; SAH/BUS City Guide; Studies in Early Modern German History; Studies in Pure Sociology; Studies in Religion and Culture; Traditions and Transformations in Tibetan Buddhism; Under the Sign of Nature: Explorations in Ecocriticism; Victorian Literature and Culture; Walker Cowen Memorial Prize in Eighteenth-Century Studies; Writing the Early Americas

University of Washington Press

Street Address:
4333 Brooklyn Avenue NE
Seattle, WA 98105

Phone: 206.543.4050
Fax: 206.543.3932
Email: (user I.D.)@uw.edu

Website and Social Media:
Website: washington.edu/uwpress
Facebook: facebook.com/UniversityofWashingtonPress
Twitter: twitter.com/uwapress/
YouTube: youtube.com/uwashingtonpress/
Pinterest: pinterest.com/uwapress/
Instagram: instagram.com/uwpress/
Tumblr: uwpress.tumblr.com/

Mailing Address:
Campus Box 359570
Seattle, WA 98195

Orders:
Hopkins Fulfillment Services
Phone: 800.537.5487 or 410.516.6956
Fax: 410.516.6998
Email: hfscustserv@press.jhu.edu

EU, Middle East, & Asia-Pacific Reps.
Combined Academic Publishers

Canadian Representative:
University of British Columbia Press

Staff
Administration:
  Director: Nicole Mitchell (206.685.9373; email: nfmm)
  Assistant to the Director: Rebecca Brinbury (206.221.3597; email: rbrinson)
  Grants and Digital Projects: Beth Fuget (206.616.0818; email: bfuget)
  Assistant Director of Advancement: Meredith Wisti (206.543.3056; email: wistim)
Acquisitions:
  Editor-in-Chief: Larin McLaughlin (206.221.4995; email: lmclaugh)
  Executive Editor: Lorri Hagman (206.221.4989; email: lhagman)
  Senior Acquisitions Editor: Catherine Cocks (206.221.4984; email: cathec4)
  Assistant Editor: Niccole Leilanionapae'aina Coggins (206.221.4940; email: ncoggins)
Editorial, Design, and Production:
  EDP Manager: Margaret Sullivan (206.221.4987; email: mksu)
  Senior Project Editor: Julie Van Pelt (206.685.9165; email: jvp)
  Production Manager and Coordinator: Shirley Woo (206.221.4993; email: surely2)
  Art Director: Katrina Noble (206.221.7004; email: krnoble)
Marketing and Sales:
  Publicity Director: Casey LaVela (206.221.4994; email: kclavela)
  Exhibits, Advertising, and Direct Mail Manager: Katherine Tacke (206.221.4996; email: ktacke)
  Catalog and Metadata Manager: Kathleen Pike Jones (206.221.4986; email: kpike)
Finance and Operations:
  CFO: Tom Helleberg (206.221.5892; email: thh200)
  Intellectual Property Manager: Puja Boyd (206.221.4997; email: ptboyd)

Accounts Receivable: Linda Tom (206.543.4722; email: lindatom)
Accounts Payable: Heidi Olson (206.543.2858; email: hoatar)

Regular Member

Established: 1920
Title output 2016: 53
Titles currently in print: 1,198

Admitted to the Association: 1937
Title output 2017: 53

Editorial Program

American studies; anthropology; art history and visual culture; Asian American studies; Asian studies; critical ethnic studies; environmental history; Jewish studies; Native American and Indigenous studies; nature and environment; Scandinavian studies; sustainable design; women's, gender and sexuality studies; and Western and Pacific Northwest history. The press also publishes a broad range of books about the Pacific Northwest for general readers, often in partnership with regional museums, cultural organizations, and local tribes.

Special series and imprints: Center for Korea Studies Publications; Classics of Asian American Literature (no editor); Classics of Chinese Thought; Critical Dialogues in Southeast Asian Studies; Culture, Place, and Nature: Studies in Anthropology and Environment; Decolonizing Feminisms: Antiracist and Transnational Praxis; Feminist Technosciences; Food, People, Planet; Gandharan Buddhist Texts; Gandharan Studies; Global Re-Visions; Global South Asia; Indigenous Confluences; Korean Studies of the Henry M. Jackson School of International Studies; Native Art of the Pacific Northwest: A Bill Holm Center Series; New Directions in Scandinavian Studies; Pacific Northwest Poetry Series; Samuel and Althea Stroum Lectures in Jewish Studies; Scott and Laurie Oki Series in Asian American Studies; Studies on Ethnic Groups in China; Sustainable Design Solutions from the Pacific Northwest; Weyerhaeuser Environmental Books

Publishing partners (world rights unless noted): University of British Columbia Press (US); Anchorage Museum; Art Gallery of New South Wales; British Museum; Frye Art Museum; Hallie Ford Museum; Krannert Art Museum; LM Publishers; Lost Horse Press; Lynx House Press; Museum for African Art; National Gallery of Australia (NA); Paul Holberton Publishing; Power Institute of Fine Arts (NA); Seattle Art Museum; Silkworm Books (world outside Southeast Asia); Tacoma Art Museum; Tate Gallery; UCLA Chicano Studies Research Center; UCLA Fowler Museum

Washington State University Press

Cooper Publications Building
2300 Grimes Way
PO Box 645910
Pullman, WA 99164-5910

Orders:
Phone: 800.354.7360; 509.335.7880

Phone: 509.335.7880
Fax: 509.335.8568
Email: wsupress@wsu.edu
Indiv: (user I.D.)@wsu.edu

Canadian Representatives:
Ingram Book Company
Baker & Taylor Books

Website and Social Media:
Website: wsupress.wsu.edu
Facebook: www.facebook.com/pages/
    Washington-State-University-Press/121327661093
YouTube: www.youtube.com/channel/UCIaaQ895LjckK41nt7MmIzA

Staff
Director: Edward Sala (509.335.3518; email: sala)
Editor-in-Chief: Robert Clark (509.335.3518; email: robert.clark)
Manuscript Editor: Beth DeWeese (509.335.8821; email: beth.deweese)
Marketing Manager: Caryn Lawton (509.335.3518; email: lawton)
Order Fulfillment/Operations: Kerry Darnall (509.335.7880; email: kdarnall)
Permissions: Beth DeWeese (509.335.8821; email: beth.deweese)
Graphic Design/Layout: Pat Brommer, Jeff Hipp, Tracy Randall, Scott Swanger
    (509.335.7880; email: wsupress@wsu.edu)

Regular Member
Established: 1927
Title output 2016: 10
Titles currently in print: 155

Admitted to the Association: 1987
Title output 2017: 9
Journals published: 2

Editorial Program
Pacific Northwest; natural history; history, science, politics, and culture relating to the region; Western American history; ethnic studies; Native American studies; women's studies; and environmental issues.

The Press distributes publications for the Oregon-California Trails Association, Oregon Writers Colony, Wenatchee Valley Museum and Cultural Center, WSU Museum of Art, WSU School of Hospitality Business Management, WSU Thomas S. Foley Institute, Washington State Historical Society, and Anarene Books.

Journals: *Northwest Science*; *We Proceeded On*

Wayne State University Press

The Leonard N. Simons Bldg.
4809 Woodward Avenue
Detroit, MI 48201.1309

Phone: 313.577.6126
Fax: 313.577.6131
Email: (user I.D.)@wayne.edu

Website and Social Media:
Website: wsupress.wayne.edu
Facebook: www.facebook.com/wsupress
Instagram: www.instagram.com/wsupress
Pinterest: www.pinterest.com/wsupress
Youtube: www.youtube.com/user/wsupress1
Tumblr: wsupress.tumblr.com
Twitter: @WSUPress

Canadian Distributor:
Scholarly Book Services

Orders:
Phone: 800.WSU.READ (978.7323)

International Distributor:
East-West Export Books

UK/European Distributor:
Eurospan Group

Staff
Interim Director: Kathryn Wildfong (313.577.6070; email: k.wildfong)
Rights and Permissions: Ceylan Akturk (313.577.6130; email: ceylan.akturk)
Acquisitions Editorial: Annie Martin, Editor-in-Chief (313.577.8335; email: annie.martin)
 Acquisitions Editor: Marie Sweetman (313.577.4220; email: marie.sweetman)
Editorial, Design, and Production: Kristin Harpster, EDP Manager (313.577.4604; email: khlawrence)
 Assistant Editorial Manager and Reprints Manager: Carrie Downes Teefey (313.577.6123; email: carrie.downes)
 Senior Designer: Rachel Ross (313.577.4626; email: rachelsross)
Marketing/Sales: Emily Nowak, Marketing and Sales Manager (313.577.6128; email: enowak)
 Promotion and Direct Mail Manager: Kristina Stonehill (313.577.6127; email: kristina.stonehill)
 Advertising and Exhibits Manager: Jamie Jones (313.577.6054; email: jamie.jones2)
Journals: Tara Reeser, Journals Manager (313.577.4607; email: tara.reeser)
 Journals Marketing and Sales Coordinator: Julie Wahrheit (313.577.4603; email: julie.wahrheit)
Business: Andrew Kaufman, Business Manager (313.577.3671; email: akaufman)
 Fulfillment Manager: Theresa Martinelli (313.577.6126; email: theresa.martinelli)
 Accounts Receivable: DeLisa Fields (313.577.6257; email: delisafields)
 Warehouse Manager: Todd Richards (313.577.4619; email: aa5764)
 Shipping: Aaron Hearn (313.577.4609; email: eu7890)
IT: Bonnie Russell, Technical Project Manager (313.577.1283; email: bonnie.russell)

Wayns State University Press continued

Regular Member
Established: 1941
Title output 2016: 32
Titles currently in print: 1,018

Admitted to the Association: 1956
Title output 2017: 44
Journals published: 11

Editorial Program
Scholarly books and serious nonfiction, with special interests in regional and local history, literature, and culture; African American studies; Jewish studies; film and media studies; fairy tales and folklore; speech and language pathology; citizenship studies; and gender and ethnic studies. Poetry, short fiction, and creative nonfiction by Michigan authors
Journals: *Antipodes; Criticism; Discourse; Fairy Tale Review; Framework; Human Biology; Jewish Film & New Media; Marvels and Tales; Merrill Palmer Quarterly; Narrative Culture; Storytelling, Self, Society*
Special series: Contemporary Approaches to Film and Media; Series in Fairy-Tale Studies; Great Lakes Books; Made in Michigan Writers Series; Painted Turtle Books; Queer Screens; Raphael Patai Series in Jewish Folklore and Anthropology; TV Milestones
Joint imprints, copublishing, and distribution programs: University of Alberta Press; Broadside/Lotus Press; Cranbrook Institute of Science; Detroit Institute of Arts; Ladyslipper Press; Sherwood Forest Association; Watchman Ink, LLC

Wesleyan University Press

Editorial Offices:
215 Long Lane
Middletown, CT 06459

Phone: 860.685.7711
Fax: 860.685.7712
Email: (user I.D.)@wesleyan.edu

Book Distribution Center:
Wesleyan University Press
c/o University Press of New England
1 Court Street, Suite 250
Lebanon, NH 03766-1358
Phone: 800.421.1561
Fax: 603.643.1540

Website and Social Media:
Website: www.wesleyan.edu/wespress/
Facebook: www.facebook.com/pages/Middletown-CT/
   Wesleyan-University-Press/101994439844863
Twitter: @weslpress

UK/European Representative:
Eurospan

Canadian Representative:
University of British Columbia Press

Staff
Director/Editor-in-Chief: Suzanna Tamminen (860.685.7727; email: stamminen)
Marketing Manager: Jaclyn Wilson (860.685.7725; email: jwilson05)
Publicist: Stephanie Elliott (860.685.7723; email: selliott)

Regular Member
Established: 1957

Title output 2016: 29
Titles currently in print: 512

Admitted to the Association: 2001
(Former membership: 1966-1991)
Title output 2017: 28

Editorial Program
The current editorial program focuses on poetry, music, dance, science fiction studies, film/TV/media studies, regional studies, and American studies.
Special series: Early Classics of Science Fiction; Music/Culture; Music/Interview; Wesleyan Poetry; Wesleyan Film; Garnet Books

The University of the West Indies Press

7A Gibraltar Hall Road
Kingston 7
Jamaica, West Indies
Phone: 876.977.2659/702.4082
Fax: 876.977.2660
Email: uwipress@uwimona.edu.jm

US and Caribbean Orders:
Longleaf Services
116 South Boundary St.
Chapel Hill, NC 27514-3808
Phone: 800.848.6224
Fax: 800.272.6817

Website and Social Media:
Website: www.uwipress.com
Facebook: www.facebook.com/uwipress
YouTube: www.youtube.com/user/uwipress
Twitter: @UWIPRESS

UK/European Distributor:
Eurospan Group

Canadian Distributor:
Scholarly Book Services

Staff
Director: Dr. Joseph B. Powell (email: joseph.powell@uwimona.edu.jm)
Rights & Permissions/Finance Manager: Nadine D. Buckland (email: nadine.buckland@uwimona.edu.jm)
Marketing & Sales Manager: Donna Muirhead (email: donna.muirhead@uwimona.edu.jm)
Editorial & Production Project Manager: Shivaun Hearne (email: uwipress.edp@uwimona.edu.jm)

Regular Member
Established: 1992
Title output 2016: 13
Titles currently in print: 401

Admitted to the Association: 2005
Title output 2017: 16
Journals published: 2

Editorial Program
Scholarly books in the humanities and social sciences with an emphasis on Caribbean cultural studies, gender studies, history, literature, economics, education, environmental studies, sociology, political science, linguistics, legal studies, medical studies, psychology, media studies, and general interest.
Special series: Caribbean Biography Series

The University of West Indies Press continued

Journals: *Journal of Caribbean History* (a peer-reviewed journal published by the University of the West Indies Press on behalf of the Departments of History and Archaeology of the University of the West Indies); *Caribbean Journal of Psychology* (a peer-reviewed journal published by the University of the West Indies Press on behalf of the University of the West Indies School for Graduate Studies and Research and the Departments of Sociology, Psychology and Social Work, University of the West Indies, Mona campus)

West Virginia University Press

Street Address:
Bicentennial House
1535 Mileground Road
Morgantown, WV 26506

Phone: 304.293.8400
Fax: 304.293.6585

Website and Social Media:
Website: www.wvupress.com
Facebook: www.facebook.com/westvirginiauniversitypress
Twitter: @wvupress

Mailing Address:
PO Box 6295
Morgantown, WV 26506-6295

Order Fulfillment and Distribution:
Chicago Distribution Center
11030 South Langley Ave.
Chicago, IL 60628
Phone: 800.621.2736
Fax: 800.621.8476

UK Representative:
Eurospan

Staff
Director: Derek Krissoff (304.293.8403; email: derek.krissoff@mail.wvu.edu)
Marketing Manager/Fiction Editor: Abby Freeland (304.293.6188; email: abby.freeland@mail.wvu.edu)
Production Manager/Art Director: Than Saffel (304.293.6185;
  email: than.saffel@mail.wvu.edu)
Managing Editor: Sara Georgi (304.293.6186; email: sara.georgi@mail.wvu.edu)
Editor-at-Large: Andrew Berzanskis (email: aberzanskis@wvupressonline.com)
Office Manager: Floann Downey (304.293.8402; email: floann.downey@mail.wvu.edu)

Regular Member
Established: 1963
Title output 2016: 19
Titles currently in print: 183

Admitted to the Association: 2003
Title output 2017: 19
Journals published: 5

Editorial Program
Serious works of nonfiction in the social sciences, with a particular emphasis on energy, environment, and resources; American history; Appalachian studies; and higher education. Vandalia Press, the creative imprint of WVU Press, publishes fiction and creative nonfiction.
Journals: *Education and Treatment of Children; Essays in Medieval Studies; Tolkien Studies; Vic-*

torian Poetry; West Virginia History
Special series: Histories of Capitalism and the Environment; Energy and Society; Radical Natures; In Place; Gender, Feminism, and Geography; Sounding Appalachia; Regenerations: African American Literature and Culture; Rural Studies; Teaching and Learning in Higher Education; West Virginia and Appalachia Series; Salvaging the Anthropocene

Wilfrid Laurier University Press

75 University Avenue West
Waterloo, ON N2L 3C5 Canada

Phone: 519.884.0710 ext. 6124
Fax: 519.725.1399
Email: press@wlu.ca
Indiv: (user I.D.)@ wlu.ca

Canadian Distributor:
UTP Distribution

US Distributor:
Ingram Publisher Services

UK/European Distributor:
Gazelle Book Services Limited

Website and Social Media:
Website: www.wlupress.wlu.ca
Blog: nestor.wlu.ca/blog/
Facebook: www.facebook.com/wlupress
Twitter: @wlupress

Staff
Director: Lisa Quinn (ext. 2843; email: lquinn)
Senior Editor: Siobhan McMenemy (ext. 3782; email: smcmenemy)
Managing Editor: Rob Kohlmeier (ext. 6119; email: rkohlmeier)
Production Coordinator: Michael Bechthold (ext. 6122; email: mbechthold)
Digital Projects Coordinator: Murray Tong (ext. 3029; email: mtong)
Sales and Marketing Coordinator: Clare Hitchens (ext. 2665; email: chitchens)

Regular Member
Established: 1974
Title output 2016: 31
Titles currently in print: 545

Admitted to the Association: 1986
Title output 2017: 28

Editorial Program
Canadian literature; cultural studies; environmental studies; family studies; film and media studies; history; indigenous studies; life writing; literary criticism; literature in translation; military history; music; poetry; politics; religious studies; social work; sociology; women's studies.
Special series and joint imprints: Canadian Commentaries; Centre for Memory and Testimony Studies; Collected Works of Florence Nightingale; Cultural Studies; Early Canadian Literature); Environmental Humanities; Film and Media Studies; Indigenous Studies; Laurier Centre for Military, Strategic and Disarmament Studies; Laurier Poetry; Laurier Studies in Political Philosophy; Life Writing; SickKids Community and Mental Health; Studies in Childhood and Family in Canada; Toronto International Film Festival; TransCanada, WCGS German Studies

The University of Wisconsin Press

1930 Monroe Street, 3rd Floor
Madison, WI 53711-2059

Phone: 608.263.1110
Fax: 608.263.1120
Email: uwiscpress@uwpress.wisc.edu
Indiv: (user I.D.)@wisc.edu

Orders:
Chicago Distribution Center
11030 South Langley Ave.
Chicago, IL 60628-3892
Phone: 800.621.2736; 773.702.7000
Fax: 800.621.8476; 773.702.7212

Website and Social Media:
Website: uwpress.wisc.edu
Blog: uwpress.wisc.edu/blog
Facebook: University of Wisconsin Press
Twitter: @UWiscPress
GoodReads: UW Press

UK Distributor:
Eurospan

Staff
Director: Dennis Lloyd (608.263.1101; email: dlloyd2)
Subsidiary Rights and Permissions Manager: Anne McKenna (608.263.1131; email: rights@uwpress.wisc.edu)
  Executive Editors: Gwen Walker (608.263.1123; email: gcwalker) (American history and politics, environmental studies, Irish history, human rights, Latin American studies, Russian/East European studies, Southeast Asian studies, regional Wisconsin history and natural history); Raphael Kadushin (608.263.1062; email: kadushin) (biography, Classics, fiction, creative nonfiction, performing arts, folklore, LGBT, 20th-C European history, Jewish interest, foodways, travel)
  Acquisitions Assistants: Amber Rose (608.263.1134; email: ajrose2); Anna Muenchrath (608.263.1134; email: muenchrath)
Managing Editor: Adam Mehring (608.263.0856; email: amehring)
  Senior Editor: Sheila McMahon (608.263.1133; email: samcmahon)
  Production Manager: Terry Emmrich (608.263.0731; email: temmrich)
  Assistant Production Manager: Jennifer Conn (608.263.0732; email: jeconn)
  Senior Compositor: Scott Lenz (608.263.0794; email: sjlenz)
Marketing and Sales Manager: Andrea Christofferson (608.263.0814; email: aschrist)
  Communications Director: Sheila Leary (608.263.0734; email: smleary)
  Exhibits and Data Coordinator: Lindsey Meier (608.263.1136; email: lindsey.meier)
  Metadata and Database Manager: Lisa Mensink (608.263.0573; email: lisa.mensink)
Journals Manager: Toni Gunnison (608.263.0667; email: toni.gunnison)
  Journals Production Manager: John Ferguson (608.263.0669; email: john.ferguson)
  Editorial Assistant: Chloe Lauer (608.263.0534; email: chloe.lauer)
  Journals Marketing Assistant: TBA
Business and Operations Manager: Ryan Pingel (608.263.1137; email: rpingel)

Accountant: Pahnia Lee (608.890.4615; email: plee76)
Bookkeeper and Customer Service: Rebecca Forbes (608.263.0654; email: rlforbes)
Office Manager: Jim Hahn (608.263.1128; email: jhahn3)

Regular Member

Established: 1936
Title output 2016: 44
Titles currently in print: 1,438
Admitted to the Association: 1945
Title output 2017: 57
Journals published: 11

Editorial Program
Scholarly and general-interest works in African and African American studies; agriculture; American history and politics; Classics; environmental studies; fiction; performing arts (primarily film and dance); folklore; foreign language learning; human rights; Jewish studies; LGBT; Latin American studies; memoir and autobiography; modern European and Irish history; poetry; Russian and East European studies; Southeast Asian studies; and Wisconsin and the Upper Midwest

Journals: *African Economic History; Arctic Anthropology; Contemporary Literature; Ecological Restoration; Ghana Studies; Journal of Human Resources; Land Economics; Landscape Journal; Luso-Brazilian Review; Monatshefte; Native Plants Journal*

Special series: Africa and the Diaspora: History, Politics, Culture; Critical Human Rights; Folklore Studies in a Multicultural World; George L. Mosse Series in Modern European Cultural and Intellectual History; Harvey Goldberg Series for Understanding and Teaching History; History of Ireland and the Irish Diaspora; The History of Print and Digital Culture; Languages and Folklore of the Upper Midwest; Living Out: Gay and Lesbian Autobiographies; New Perspectives in Southeast Asian Studies; Publications of the Wisconsin Center for Pushkin Studies; Studies in Dance History; Wisconsin Film Studies; Wisconsin Land and Life; Wisconsin Poetry Series; Wisconsin Studies in Autobiography; Wisconsin Studies in Classics; Women in Africa and the Diaspora

Imprints: Terrace Books, Popular Press

Wits University Press

Street Address:
Fifth Floor, University Corner
University of the Witwatersrand,
Jorissen Street, Braamfontein, Johannesburg.

Mailing Address:
Private Bag 3, Wits, 2050
Johannesburg
South Africa

Phone: +27 11 717 8700 / 1

Orders in Africa
Blue Weaver
Tel: + 27 21 701 4477
orders@blueweaver.co.za

Website and Social Media:
Website: www.witspress.co.za
Facebook: www.facebook.com/Wits-University-Press
Twitter: @WitsPress

Orders in UK, Europe, Middle East:
The Eurospan Group

Orders in North and South America:
Independent Publishers' Group (IPG)
Phone: 800.888.4741
orders@ipgbook.com

Wits University Press continued

Staff
Publisher: Veronica Klipp (+27 11 717 8704l; email: Veronica.klipp@wits.ac.za)
Administrator: Matselane Monggae (+ 27 11 717 8700; email: matselane.monggae@wits.ac.za)
Commissioning Editor: Roshan Cader (+27 11 717 8707; email: roshan.cader@wits.ac.za
Digital Publisher: Andrew Joseph (+27 11 717 8703; email: andrew.joseph@wits.ac.za)
Marketing Coordinator: Corina van der Spoel (+27 11 717 8705; email: corina.vanderspoel@wits.ac.za)

Regular Member
Established: 1922
Title output 2016: 24
Titles currently in print: 450

Admitted to the Association: 2016
Title output 2017: 27

Editorial Program
Wits University Press is strategically placed at the crossroads of African and global knowledge production and dissemination. We are committed to publishing well-researched, innovative books for both academic and general readers. Our areas of focus include art and heritage, popular science, history and politics, biography, literary studies, women's writing and select textbooks.

The Woodrow Wilson Center Press

Woodrow Wilson International Center for Scholars
One Woodrow Wilson Plaza
1300 Pennsylvania Avenue, N.W.
Washington, DC 20004-3027

Phone: 202.691.4042
Fax: 202.691.4001

Website and Social Media:
Website: www.wilsoncenter.org/press

Regular Member
Established: 1987
Title output 2016: 12
Titles currently in print: 174

Admitted to the Association: 1992
Title output 2017: NR

Editorial Program
Woodrow Wilson Center Press shares in the mission of the Wilson Center by publishing outstanding scholarly and public policy books for a worldwide readership. Written by the Center's worldwide network of scholars and its expert staff, our books concentrate on subjects of the Center's greatest strength, especially energy, security, environmental and social resilience, urban studies, U.S. foreign policy, cold war history, and area studies.

All the Press's books are copublished. Partners include Columbia University Press, Stanford University Press, Cornell University Press, Cambridge University Press, University of California Press, Johns Hopkins University Press, Indiana University Press, and University of Pennsylvania Press. The Cold War International History Project Series is copublished with Stanford.

Yale University Press

Street Address:
302 Temple Street
New Haven, CT 06511

Main: 203.432.0960
203.432.6129 (Receptionist)
203.432.0900 (Acquisitions Editorial)
203.432.4060 (Design/Production)
203.432.0961 (Marketing)
203.432.0163 (Publicity)
Email: (firstname.lastname)@yale.edu

Yale Press Fax Numbers:
203.432.6862 (Accounting)
203.432.0948 (Administration)
203.436.1064 (Acquisitions 1st Floor)
203.432.2394 (Acquisitions 2nd Floor)
203.432.8485 (Marketing 3rd Floor)
203.432.5455 (Promotion)
203.432.4061 (Design/Production)
401.658.4193 (Warehouse)

Mailing Address:
PO Box 209040
New Haven, CT 06520-9040

Distribution/Customer Service:
Triliteral LLC
Customer Service Toll Free: 1.800.405.1619
Customer Service Fax 800.406.9145

London Office:
47 Bedford Square
London WC1B 3DP
United Kingdom
Phone: +44-20 7079 4900
Fax: + 44-20 7079 4901
Email: firstname.lastname@yale.co.uk

Website and Social Media:
Website: www.yale.edu/yup/
Blog: yalepress.typepad.com/yalepresslog/
Facebook: www.facebook.com/yalepress
Twitter: @yalepress

Staff

Director: John E. Donatich (203.432.0933)
Sr. Executive Assistant to the Director: Danielle Di Bianco Caracas (203.432.4301)
Chief Operating Officer: Katherine Brown (203.432.8496)
Director of Legal Affairs: Pam Chambers (203.432.0936)
Contracts Associate: Kristy Leonard (203.432.0934)
Permissions and Ancillary Rights Manager: Donna Anstey (203.432.0932)
Acquisitions Editorial: Seth Ditchik, Editorial Director (economics) (203.432.0935); Jean E. Thomson Black, Senior Executive Editor (life sciences, physical sciences, environmental sciences, medicine) (203.432.7534); William Frucht, Executive Editor (law, political science international relations, and economics) (203.432.7571); Patricia Fidler, Art Publisher (art and architectural) (203.432.0927); Jennifer Banks, Executive Editor (religion, literature, classics, philosophy) (203.432.6807); Joseph Calamia, Sr. Editor (science & technology) (203.432.0904); Jaya Chatterjee, Associate Editor (world history, geopolitics, and international relations); Heather Gold, Assistant Editor (religion) (203.432.8541); Katherine Boller, Senior Acquisitions Editor (art and architecture) (203.432.7217); Sarah Miller, Editor (language and literature) (203.432.0901); Adina Popescu Berk (American history) (203.432.9698)

Yale University Press continued

Director of Editorial Design & Production: Jenya Weinreb (203.432.0914)
Manuscript Editorial: Assistant Managing Editor: Mary Pasti (203.432.0911)
   Editors: Dan Heaton (203.432.1017); Ann-Marie Imbornoni (203.432.0903); Phillip King (203.432.1015); Susan Laity (203.432.0922); Margaret Otzel (203.432.0918); Jeffrey Schier (203.432.4001); Heidi Downey (203.432.2390)
   Art Workshop: Kate Zanzucchi, Managing Editor (203.432.0916)
   Assistant Managing Editor: Heidi Downey (203.432.2390)
Production: Maureen Noonan, Associate Production Manager (203.432.4064)
   Reprint Controller: Orna Johnston (203.432.4060)
   Design and Production Manager Art Books: Mary Mayer (203.432.0925)
   Production Controller: Katherine Golden (203.436.8022)
   Senior Production Controller: Aldo Cupo (203.432.7484)
Design: Nancy Ovedovitz, Art Director (203.432.4067)
   Designers: Sonia Scanlon (203.432.4066); Mary Valencia (203.432.8092)
Sales: Jay Cosgrove, Sales Director (203.432.0968)
   General Sales Queries: (203.432.0966)
   Assistant Director, Sales: Stephen Cebik (203.432.2539)
   Marketing and Promotions Director: Heather D'Auria (203.432.8193)
   Publicity Director: Brenda King (203.432.0917)
   Publicists: Robert Pranzatelli (203.432.0972); Alden Ferro (203.432.0909); Elizabeth Pelton (410.467.0989); Jennifer Doerr (203.432.0969); Roland Coffey (203.432.0964)
   General Publicity Inquiries: Publicity Assistant (203.432.0163)
   Online Marketing Manager: Michael Hoak (203.432.0961)
   Educational Marketing Manager: Debra Bozzi (203.432.0959)
   Academic Discipline Marketer: Karen Stickler (203.436.8467)
   Direct Mail Assistant: Lisa Scecina (203.432.0957)
   Exhibits/Advertising Manager: Ellen Freiler (203.432.0958)
   New Business and Product Manager: Sara Sapire (203.432.0965)
   Digital Product and Production Editor: John Carlson (203.436.9298)
Business:
Deputy Director of Finance: Timothy Haire (203.436.1924)
   Accounting Manager: Wendy DeNardis (203.432.0951)
   Accounting Assistant: Stephanie Pierre (203.432.0949)
   Royalty Accountant: Kim Jones (203.432.0946)
   Database Analyst: Marc Benigni (203.432.8446)
   Inventory & Building Operations Manager: Jim Stritch (203.432.0939)
London Office:
Managing Director, London and Editorial Director (Humanities): Heather McCallum
Head of Marketing: Noel Murphy
Foreign Rights Manager: Karen McTigue

Regular Member

Established: 1908   Admitted to the Association: 1937
Title output 2016: 430   Title output 2017: 432
Titles currently in print: 6,453

Editorial Program
Humanities, social sciences, natural sciences, physical sciences, medicine. Poetry is not accepted except for submissions to the Yale Series of Younger Poets contest, held annually. Festschriften and collections of previously published articles are not invited and very rarely accepted.

Special series, joint imprints and/or co-publishing programs: Agrarian Studies; Anchor Bible and Commentaries; Annals of Communism; The Annotated Shakespeare; Babylonian Collection; Bard Graduate Center; Carnegie Endowment for International Peace; The Castle Lectures in Ethics, Politics, and Economics; A Century Foundation Book; Complete Prose Works of John Milton; Complete Works of St. Thomas More; Council on Foreign Relations; Cowles Foundation; Culture and Civilization of China; Darden Innovation and Entrepreneurship; David Brion Davis Lectures; Democracy in America; The Diary of Joseph Farington; Dodge Lectures; Dura-Europos; Economic Census Studies; Economic Growth Center; Economic History; Elizabethan Club; English Monarchs; Faith and Globalization; George Elliot Letters; The Henry McBride Series in Modernism and Modernity; Henry Roe Cloud Series for American Indigenous Peoples and Modernity; History of the Soviet Gulag System; Horace Walpole Correspondence; Institute for Social and Policy Studies; Institute of Far Eastern Languages; Institution of Human Relations; Intellectual History of the West; Italian Literature and Culture; James Boswell; Jewish Lives; Lamar Series In Western History; Library of Medieval Philosophy; Neighborhoods of New York City; Margellos World Republic of Letters; New Directions In Narrative History; The New Republic; Oak Spring Garden Library; Okun; Open University; Page Lectures; The Papers of Benjamin Franklin; The Papers of Benjamin Latrobe; Papers of Frederick Douglass; Papers on Soviet & East European, Economic & Political Science; Paul Mellon Centre for Studies in British Art; Pelikan History of Art; Percy Letters; Petroleum Monographs; Pevsner Series: Buildings of England, Scotland, and Ireland; Phillips Andover Archaeology; Philosophy and Theory and Art; Poems of Alexander Pope; Posen Library of Jewish Culture and Civilization; Psychoanalytic Study of the Child; The Relations of Canada and the United States; Rethinking the Western Tradition; Russian Classics; Science in Progress; The Selected Papers of Charles Willson Peale and His Family; Silliman Lectures; Society and the Sexes; Stalin Archives; Storrs Lectures; Studies in Comparative Economics; Studies in Hermeneutics; Studies in Modern European Literature and Thought; Terry Lectures; Theoretical Perspectives in Archaeological History; Walpole Series in Eighteenth Century Studies; Why X Matters; The Works of Jonathan Edwards; The Works of Samuel Johnson; Yale Classical Monographs; Yale Classical Studies; Yale Contemporary Law Series; Yale Drama Series; Yale Edition of the Unpublished Works of Gloria Stein; Yale French Studies; Yale Guide to English Literature; Yale Health and Wellness; Yale Historical Publications; Yale Judaica; Yale Law Library Publications; Yale Law School Studies; Yale Library of Military History; Yale Liebniz; Yale Linguistics; Yale New Classics; Yale Publications in Religion; Yale Romantic Studies; Yale Series of Younger Poets; Yale Studies in Economics; Yale Studies in English; Yale Studies in History & Theory of Religious Education; Yale Studies in Political Science

ASSOCIATION PARTNERS

The Association's Partner Program was launched in 2008. For more details about the Partner Program, visit the Association's website The following companies enrolled as Partners in 2017.

Baker & Taylor

New Jersey Office:
1120 US Highway 22 East
Bridgewater, NJ 08807

Website and Social Media:
Website: www.baker-taylor.com
Facebook: www.facebook.com/pages/Baker-Taylor/140688295944178
Twitter: @BakerandTaylor
YouTube: www.youtube.com/user/BakerandTaylorTV?feature=mhw5

Staff Contacts
VP, Academic Library and Higher Education Merchandising: Sally Neher (908.541.7460; email: sally.neher@baker-taylor.com)
Director, Ad Sales, Co-op and Editorial: Lynn Bond (908.541.7374; email: lynn.bond@baker-taylor.com)
Merchandise Manager, Academic: Lorraine Ferry (908.541.7435; email: lorraine.ferry@baker-taylor.com)

Year enrolled as an Association Partner: 2009

Company Description
Baker & Taylor, a Follett company, is the premier worldwide distributor of digital and print books and entertainment products. We love books and leverage our unsurpassed distribution network to deliver rich content in multiple formats, anytime and anywhere, to readers worldwide. Baker & Taylor offers cutting-edge digital media services, a full range of publisher services, and innovative technology platforms to thousands of publishers, libraries and retailers globally.

BAKER & TAYLOR PUBLISHER SERVICES

30 Amberwood Parkway
Ashland, OH 44805

Phone: 888.814.0208
Toll-free: 567.215.0030

<u>Website and Social Media:</u>
Website: www.btpubservices.com

Staff Contacts
SVP, Sales/Client Svcs: Mark Suchomel (email: mark.suchomel@baker-taylor.com)
SVP, Operations: Ken Fultz (email: kfultz@btpubservices.com)
VP, Client Svcs: Jeff Tegge (email: jeffrey.tegge@baker-taylor.com)
Director, Publisher Relations: Larisa Elt (email: lelt@btpubservices.com)
Director, Mktg/Publisher Relations: Kristen Steele (email: ksteele@btpubservices.com)

Year enrolled as an Association Partner: 2009

<u>**Company Description**</u>
Baker & Taylor Publisher Services is the publishing industry's most effective client service organization, driven by the combined forces of the industry's leading suppliers to public and school libraries, higher education, the general book trade, the Christian book trade, and specialty retailers: Follett and Baker & Taylor.

BTPS offers higher education and academic publishers, as well as children's, trade, and K-12 publishers economical solutions for warehousing and order fulfillment; sales and marketing support; inventory management and virtual inventory programs; book manufacturing including offset, digital short run, and print-on-demand (POD); and editorial services.

Books International

BOOKS INTERNATIONAL
Fulfillment / Print / Digital

22883 Quicksilver Dr.
Dulles, VA 20166

Phone: 703.661.1500
Fax: 703.661.1501
Website: www.booksintl.com

Staff Contacts
Vice President: Vartan Ajamian (703.661.1519; email: vartan@booksintl.com)
Vice President, Print Sales: Bill Clockel (703.996.1025; email: bclockel@booksintl.com)
Director Business Development: Ellen Loerke (703.661.1512;
    email: eloerke@booksintl.com)
Chief Information Officer: Charles Thies (703.661.1514; email: charles@booksintl.com)

Year enrolled as an Association Partner: 2009

Company Description
Third party print, fulfillment and digital services. Complete fulfillment services including EDI, standing orders, collections, and royalties provided on publisher-branded databases. Internet access to data and reports. We provide on-site digital printing (color, b&w) for stock replenishment or print to order, as well as ONIX feeds, electronic title and digital asset management, and ebook sales and distribution.

Brian Murphy Group

101 Vickery St.
Roswell, GA 30075

Website and Social Media:
www.bmurphygroup.com

Staff Contacts:
President: Brian Murphy (774.641.1537); email: brian@bmurphygroup.com
Vice President of Sales and Operations: Nick Murphy (617.901.5618); email: nick@bmurphygroup.com
Senior Marketing Director: Allison Doherty (email: Allison@bmurphygroup.com)

Year enrolled as an Association Partner: 2016

Company Description
BMG, LLC provides outsourced text book adoption services specifically for University Presses. Our proprietary-software driven marketing campaigns leverages 30 years of text book sales experience and engages more professors at a fraction of the cost of traditional, publishing industry sales methods. Our team of marketing experts and sales professionals focuses on raising the profile and prestige of every title, significantly increasing adoptions in all educational markets. Our no-risk pricing requires no fixed monthly fee, no additional budget and is based entirely on our success in driving adoptions. In short, our only service charge comes directly from revenue that we create.

Firebrand Technologies

44 Merrimac Street
Newburyport, MA 01950

Phone: 978.465.7755

<u>Website and Social Media:</u>
Website: www.firebrandtech.com
Facebook: www.facebook.com/FirebrandTechnologies
Twitter: @firebrandtech
Instagram: firebrandtech

Staff Contacts
Director of Sales and Marketing: Steve Rutberg (845.893.8402; email: steve.rutberg@firebrandtech.com)
CEO: Fran Toolan (email: fran@firebrandtech.com)
President: Doug Lessing (email: doug@firebrandtech.com)
Chief Community Officer: Robert Stevens (email: robert@firebrandtech.com)

Year enrolled as an Association Partner: 2013

Company Description
Firebrand Technologies, a dedicated industry partner, provides leading software and services to help publishers achieve success, and presents seamless information flow throughout the publishing process.
 • **Title Management Enterprise** provides you with the ability to manage every part of the publishing process from the very beginnings of your title acquisition through editorial, production, marketing, and publicity.
 • **Eloquence on Demand** metadata services are the most accurate and cost-effective way to manage, store, and distribute final print and eBook metadata and digital assets for discovery and sales.
 • **Eloquence on Alert** augments Title Management and Eloquence on Demand, applying data analysis to provide Actionable Market Intelligence about your books, metadata, and retail merchandising efforts in key retail channels. By analyzing the marketplace carefully, Eloquence on Alert will highlight metadata issues, helping your product sales to surge.
 • **NetGalley** provides secure, digital galleys to a vibrant and growing community of professional readers. Small and large publishers; PR/marketing firms; and hundreds of indie authors in the US, Canada, UK, and Australia are using NetGalley to generate early buzz about their titles.
 • **Preview-a-Book** is the largest aggregator and distributor of in print book excerpts. A database of more than 400,000 excerpts of current titles is used by booksellers, distributors, libraries, and global bibliographic information sources for their online catalogs.

ITHAKA

ITHAKA
ARTSTOR / ITHAKA S+R / JSTOR / PORTICO

2 Rector Street, 18th Floor
New York, NY 10006

Website and Social Media:
Website: ithaka.org
Twitter: @ITHAKA_org

Staff Contacts:
President – ITHAKA: Kevin Guthrie
Director – JSTOR Journals: Barbara Chin
Director – Books at JSTOR Frank Smith
Associate Director, Marketing & Communications, Ithaka S+R: Kimberly Lutz
Director – Portico Publisher Relations: Stephanie Orphan
VP, Communications: Heidi McGregor (212.358.6400; email: heidi.mcgregor@ithaka.org)

Year enrolled as Association Partner: 2012

Company Description
ITHAKA is a not-for-profit organization that works with the global higher educational community to advance and preserve knowledge and to improve teaching and learning through the use of digital technologies. ITHAKA has launched some of the most transformative and widely used services in higher education: Ithaka S+R, JSTOR, and Portico. Recently ITHAKA has enhanced its mission through a strategic alliance with Artstor, facilitating access to its services for researchers, teachers, and students worldwide.

ProQuest

161 E. Evelyn Ave
Mountainview, CA 94041

Phone: 650.475.8700
Fax: 650.475.8881

Website and Social Media:
Website: www.proquest.com
Twitter: @ProQuestEbooks

Staff Contacts
Director Content Strategy: Anna Bullard (650.475.8758; email:
   anna.bullard@proquest.com)
Publisher Relations Manager: Matthew Kull (650.475.8794;
   email: matthew.kull@proquest.com)

Year enrolled as an Association Partner: 2009

Company Description
ProQuest connects people with vetted, reliable informtaion. Key to serious research, the company's products are a gateway to the world's knowledge including dissertations, governmental and cultural archives, news, historical collections and books—both print and digital. ProQuest's technologies serve users across the critical points in research, helping them discover, accesss, share, create and manage information.

Publishr.cloud

publishr.cloud
an outcome labs business

1533 Cecilia Ave
Coral Gables, FL 33146

Phone: 305.608.0074

<u>Website and Social Media:</u>
Website: publishr.cloud
Facebook: @Publishr

Staff Contacts:
Founder and CEO: John Fleming (email; john@publishr.cloud)

Year enrolled as an Association Partner: 2017

<u>**Company Description**</u>
Publishr.cloud provides customizable sales and marketing platforms for authors and publishers that are fully optimized for search. social and mobile.

Thomson-Shore

THOMSON-SHORE
Helping you put your best book forward®

7300 West Joy Road
Dexter, MI 48130

Phone: 734.426.3939
Fax: 800.706.4545
Email: info@thomsonshore.com

Website and Social Media:
Website: www.thomsonshore.com
Facebook: www.facebook.com/ThomsonShore
Twitter: @ThomsonShore
Instagram: instagram/thomsonshore
LinkedIn: www.linkedin.com/company/thomson-shore-Inc-

Staff Contacts
Kevin Spall - President (734-426-3939; email: kevins@thomsonshore.com)
Kelley Jones - University Press Market Sales Coordinator (734.426.6237; email: kelleyj@thomsonshore.com)
Customer Service Representatives:
Kelley Jones (734.426.6237; email: kelleyj@thomsonshore.com)
Carrie Gamblin (734.426.6229; email: carrieg@thomsonshore.com)
Julie McLean (734.426.6203; email: juliem@thomsonshore.com)
Dawn Rice (734.426.6299; email: dawnr@thomsonshore.com)

Year enrolled as an Association Partner: 2008

Company Description
Thomson-Shore is an employee-owned book manufacturer with capabilities of printing soft and case bound books in 1-color or 4-color text both digitally and offset (1-50,000 books at a time). We offer short-run digital printing, 1-off print-on-demand, retail distribution and fulfillment along with eBook conversion. Our Specialty Bindery department is well known for book repair and unique bindings and tray cases.

Ubiquity Press

]u[ubiquity press

part of the]u[partner network

155 Grand Avenue, Suite 400
Oakland, CA 94612-3758

Phone: 510.473.2717

Website and Social Media:
Website www.ubiquitypress.com
Twitter: @ubiquitypress

Staff Contacts
CEO: Brian Hole (email: brian.hole@ubiquitypress.com
Community Manager: Chealsye Bowley (email: chealsye.bowley@ubiquitypress.com)

Year enrolled as an Association Partner: 2017

Company Description
Ubiquity Press provides a comprehensive platform and suite of services to support university press open access publishing, including books, journals, conferences and research data. We also run the Ubiquity Partner Network, enabling the presses on our platform to collaborate and work more efficiently.

Virtusales Publishing Solutions

virtusales
PUBLISHING SOLUTIONS

Third Floor, Sheridan House
112-116 Western Road
Brighton & Hove
BN3 1DD   UK

Phone: 212.461.3686
Fax: +44 8454584021
Email: info@virtusales.com

Website and Social Media:
Website: www.virtusales.com

Staff Contacts
Vice President and Commercial Operations: Rodney Elder (212.461.3686; email: rodney.elder@virtusales.com)

Year enrolled as an Association Partner: 2013

Company Description
Virtusales develops Biblio3, BiblioLIVE, BiblioRoyalties and BiblioDAM which are used by many University Press publishers including Harvard University Press, Wayne State University Press, Syracuse University Press, Penn State University Press and University of Georgia Press. The software suite is an advanced publishing management system available in the cloud, allowing publishers to track their data from pre-acquisition to publication. It covers functional areas including ONIX & eBook feeds, production management, contracts, rights, royalties and digital asset management.

Westchester Publishing Services

4 Old Newtown Road
Danbury, CT 06810

Phone: 203.791.0080

Website and Social Media:
Website: westchesterpublishingservices.com
Twitter: @WestchesterPub
LinkedIn: www.linkedin.com/company/10627500

Staff Contacts
Chief Revenue Officer: Tyler M. Carey (203.658.5681; email: tyler.carey@westchester-pubsvcs.com)
Key Accounts Manager: Bill Foley (203.791.0080 ext. 104; email: bill.foley@westchester-pubsvcs.com)
Business Development Manager: Tim Cross (203.717.4187; email: tim.cross@westchester-pubsvcs.com)
Director, Editorial Services: Susan Baker (email: susan.baker@westchesterpubsvcs.com)
Director of Technology: Michael Jensen (email: michael.jensen@westchesterpubsvcs.com)

Year enrolled as Association Partner: 2015

Company Description
Westchester Publishing Services is a U.S. employee-owned company that provides U.S.-based and offshore editorial, composition, and digital conversion services to the publishing industry, with specialties in supporting university presses and journal publishers.

International Sales Agents and Distributors

Asia Publishers Services Ltd.
Units B&D, 17th Flr Gee Chang
Hong Centre
65 Wong Chuk Hang Rd
Aberdeen, Hong Kong
Phone: 852.2553.9289
Fax: 852.2554.2912

Baker & Taylor International
1120 Route 22 East
Bridgewater, NJ 08807 USA
Phone: 800.775.1500; 908.541.7000
Email: btinfo@baker-taylor.com
Website: www.baker-taylor.com
 international.cfm

Bay Foreign Language Books Ltd.
Unit 4, Kingsmead
Park Farm
Folkestone, Kent CT19 5EU United Kingdom
Fax: + 44 (0) 1233 721 272
Email: sales@baylanguagebooks.co.uk
Website: www.baylanguagebooks.co.uk

Boydell & Brewer, Ltd.
Bridge Farm Business Park
Top Street
Martlesham, Suffolk IP12 4RB United Kingdom
Phone: +44 (0) 1394 610600
Fax: +44 (0) 1394 610316
Website: www.boydellandbrewer.com

Brunswick Books
20 Maud St. Suite 303
Toronto, Ontario, M5V 2M5
Phone: 416.703.3598
Fax: 416.703.6561
Email: info@brunswickbooks.ca
Website: brunswickbooks.ca/

Casemate Academic (formerly the David Brown Book Company)
1950 Lawrence Road
Havertown, PA 19083 USA
Phone: 610.853.9131
Email: info@casemateacademic.com
Website: www.oxbowbooks.com/dbbc

Codasat Canada Ltd.
Phone: 604.228.9952
Email: info@codasat.com
Website: www.codasat.com

Combined Academic Publishers, Ltd.
Windsor House
Cornwall Road
Harrogate, North Yorkshire HG1 2PW
United Kingdom
Phone: +44 (0) 1423 526350
Email: enquiries@combinedacademic.co.uk
Website: www.combinedacademic.co.uk

Distribution du Nouveau Monde
30, rue Gay Lussac
F-75005 Paris, France
Phone: +33 1 43 54 50 24
Fax: +33 1 43 54 39 15
Website: www.librairieduquebec.fr/distribution.html

Artbook LLC & D.A.P. | Distributed Art Publishers, Inc.
75 Broad Street, Suite 630
New York, NY 10004 USA
Phone: 212.627.1999
Fax: 212.627.9484
Website: www.artbook.com

East West Export Books
University of Hawaii Press
2840 Kolowalu Street
Honolulu, Hawaii 96822 USA
Phone: 888 UHPRESS (847.7377)
Fax: 800.650.7811
Email: eweb@hawaii.edu
Website: uhpress.wordpress.com/eweb/

Eurospan Group
3 Henrietta Street
Covent Garden
London WC2E 8LU United Kingdom
Email: info@eurospangroup.com
Website: www.eurospangroup.com

Exportlivre
505, rue Bélanger, bureau 223
Montreal, QC H2S 1G5 Canada
Phone: 450.671.3888 ext. 111
Fax: 450.671.2121
Email: commande@exportlivre.com
Website: www.exportlivre.com

Footprint Books
4/8 Jubilee Avenue
Warriewood NSW 2102 Australia
Phone: +61 (0) 2 9997 3973
Fax: +61 (0) 2 9997 3185
Website: www.footprint.com.au

Gazelle Book Services, Ltd.
White Cross Mills
Hightown
Lancaster, Lancashire LA1 4XS United Kingdom
Phone: +44 (0) 1524 528500
Fax: +44 (0) 1524 528510
Email: sales@gazellebookservices.co.uk
Website: www.gazellebookservices.co.uk

Georgetown Terminal Warehouses
34 Armstrong Avenue
Georgetown, ON L7G 4R9 Canada
Phone: 905.873.2750
Fax: 905.873.6170
Email: info@gtwcanada.com
Website: www.gtwcanada.com

Libro Co. Italia srl.
Via Borromeo, 48
50026 San Casciano V.P.
Firenze, Italy
Phone: +39 055 822.84.61
Fax: +39 055 822.84.62
Email: libroco@libroco.it
Website: www.libroco.it

Login Brothers Canada
300 Saulteaux Crescent
Winnipeg, MB R3J 3T2 Canada
Phone: 800.665.1148 or 204.837.2987
Website: www.lb.ca

Marston Book Services, Ltd.
160 Eastern Avenue
Milton Park
Oxfordshire OX14 4SB United Kingdom
Phone: +44 (0) 1235 465500
Fax: +44 (0) 1235 465509
Website: www.marston.co.uk

NBN International
10 Thornbury Road
Plymouth PL6 7PP United Kingdom
Phone: +44 (0) 1752 202301
Email: cservs@nbninternational.com
Website: distribution.nbni.co.uk

Orca Book Services
160 Eastern Ave
Milton Park
Abingdon OX14 4SB United Kingdom
Phone: +44 (0) 1235 465500
Email: tradeordcrs@orcabookservices.co.uk
Website: www.orcabookservices.co.uk

Oxbow Books
The Old Music Hall
106-108 Cowley Road
Oxford OX4 1JE United Kingdom
Phone: +44 (0) 1865 241249
Fax: +44 (0) 1865 794449
Website: www.oxbowbooks.com/oxbow

Oxford Publicity Partnership Ltd.
2 Lucas Bridge Business Park
Old Greens Norton Road
Towcester NN12 8AX United Kingdom
Phone: +44 (0) 1327 357770
Email: info@oppuk.co.uk
Website: www.oppuk.co.uk

Publishers Group UK
63-66 Hatton Garden
London EC1N 8LE United Kingdom
Phone: +44 (0) 207 405 1105
Fax: +44 (0) 207 242 3725
Email: info@pguk.co.uk
Website: www.pguk.co.uk

Renouf Publishing Co. Ltd.
22-1010 Polytek Street
Ottawa, ON K1J 9J1 Canada
Phone: 866.767.6766
Fax: 613.745.7660
Email: orders@renoufbooks.com
Website: www.renoufbooks.com

Roundhouse Group
Unit B
18 Marine Gardens
Brighton BN2 1AH United Kingdom
Phone: +44 (0) 1273 603 717
Fax: +44 (0) 1273 697 494
Email: sandy@roundhousegroup.co.uk
Website: www.roundhousegroup.co.uk

Scholarly Book Services Inc.
289 Bridgeland Avenue, Unit 105
Toronto, ON M6A 1Z6 Canada
Phone: 800.847.9736
Fax: 800.220.9895
Email: lstevens@sbookscan.com
Website: www.sbookscan.com

Servidis SA
Chemin des Chalets, 7
1279 Chavannes-de-Bogis, Switzerland
Phone: +41 22 960 95 25
Fax: +41 22 776 63 64
Website: www.servidis.ch

University of Toronto Press Distribution
5201 Dufferin St.
Toronto, ON M3H 5T8 Canada
Phone: 416.667.7791
Fax: 416.667.7832
Email: utpbooks@utpress.utoronto.ca
Website: www.utpress.utoronto.ca/UTP_Distribution/

Yale Representation Ltd
47 Bedford Square
London WC1B 3DP United Kingdom
Phone: +44 020 7079 4900
Email: yalerep@yaleup.co.uk
Website: www.yalerep.co.uk

THE ASSOCIATION

The Association of University Presses was established by a small group of university presses in 1937. In the subsequent years, the association has grown steadily. Today the Association consists of 143 member presses, ranging in size from those publishing a handful of titles each year to those publishing more than a thousand.

The Association is a nonprofit organization. Its sources of financing are limited to membership dues and to revenues derived from such activities as organizing national conferences and seminars, producing publishing-related books and catalogs, and operating cooperative marketing programs.

The Association's member presses provide much of the personnel that guide the association and carry out its work. A Board of Directors sets policy for the organization. Many individuals serve on committees and task forces. Their activities reflect the diverse concerns of the membership, including keeping up with emerging technologies, production and analysis of industry statistics, maintaining copyright protections, professional development, marketing, and journals publishing.

The Association has office space in both New York City and Washington, DC. The executive director and a small professional staff manage member programs and coordinate the work of the board and committees.

Association members currently fall into three categories—regular, affiliate, and introductory. For a complete description of membership requirements, consult the "Guidelines on Admission to Membership and Maintenance of Membership," on page 256.

Association of University Presses Central Office

Association of University Presses
1412 Broadway, Suite 2135
New York, NY 10018

Phone: 212.989.1010
Email: info@aupresses.org

DC Office:
1775 Massachusetts Avenue, NW
Washington, DC 20036

Website and Social Media:
Website: www.aupresses.org
Facebook: www.facebook.com/universitypresses
Twitter: @aupresses

Staff
Executive Director: Peter Berkery (917.288.5594; email: pberkery@aupresses.org)
Marketing and Communications Director: Brenna McLaughlin (917.244.2051; email: bmclaughlin@aupresses.org)
Membership Manager: Susan Patton (917.244.1915; email: spatton@aupresses.org)
Business Manager Kim Miller (917.244.1264; email: kmiller@aupresses.org)

2017-2018 Association Board of Directors

Nicole Mitchell, University of Washington Press, President (2017-2018)
Jennifer Crewe, Columbia University Press, President-Elect (2017-2018)
Darrin Pratt, University Press of Colorado, Past President (2017-2018)
Nadine Buckland, University of West Indies Press, Treasurer (2017-2018)
Robbie Dircks, University of North Carolina Press, Treasurer-Elect (2017-2018)
Patrick Alexander, Penn State University Press (2015-2018)
Lisa Bayer, University of Georgia Press (2015-2018)
Greg Britton, Johns Hopkins University Press (2017–2020)
Becky Clark, Library of Congress Publications (2015-2018)
John Donatich, Yale University Press (2016-2019)
Dennis Lloyd, University of Wisconsin Press (2017–2020)
Gita Manaktala, MIT Press (2017–2020)
Donna Shear, University of Nebraska Press (2017-2018)
Peter Berkery, Executive Director, AUPresses, *ex officio*

2017-2018 Association Committees and Task Forces

The work of Committees and Task Forces, staffed by volunteer members, is essential to the Association. To learn more about the charges and projects of each, visit the Associaiton's Website.

Committees of the Board

Admissions and Standards
Mark Simpson-Vos, North Carolina, Chair
Patrick Alexander, Penn State
Walter Biggins, Georgia
Jennifer Crewe, Columbia
Dennis Lloyd, Wisconsin
Melissa Pitts, British Columbia

Audit
Mike Bieker, Arkansas, Chair
Nadine Buckland, West Indies
Robbie Dircks, North Carolina
Darrin Pratt, Colorado

Nominating
Meredith Babb, Florida, Chair
Doug Armato, Minnesota
Lisa Bayer, Georgia
Gillian Berchowitz, Ohio
Greg Britton, Johns Hopkins
Ellen Chodosh, NYU
John Donatich, Yale
Alan Harvey, Stanford
Stephanie Williams, Kentucky

Committees of the Association

Acquisitions
Mary Elizabeth Braun, Oregon State, Chair
Matt Bokovoy, Nebraska
Beth Bouloukos, Amherst
Allyson Carter, Arizona
Catherine Cocks, Washington
Brian Halley, Massachusetts
Kim Hogeland, Kansas
Michael McGandy, Cornell
Clark Whitehorn, New Mexico

Annual Meeting 2018
Erich van Rijn, California, Chair
Kathy Bail, New South Wales
Kim Bryant, North Carolina
Chris Cosner, Stanford
Jocelyn Dawson, Duke
Susan Donnelly, Harvard
Bridget Flannery-McCoy, Columbia
Mary Francis, Michigan
Dan Williams, TCU

Annual Meeting 2019
Mary Francis, Michigan, Chair

Book, Jacket, and Journal Show
Marianne Jankowski, Northwestern, Chair
Karen Copp, Iowa
Rachel Ross, Wayne State
Alan Brownoff, Alberta
Joel W. Coggins, Pittsburgh

Business Systems
Brent Oberlin, MIT, Chair
Duane Anderson, Abilene Christian
Lynn Benedetto, Cornell
Davida Breier, Johns Hopkins
Alice Ennis, Illinois
Ryan Pingel, Wisconsin
Ioan Suciu, Georgetown

Digital Publishing
TBA, Chair
Nicky Agate, Modern Language Association
Michael Boudreau, Chicago
Terry Ehling, MIT
Lynn Fisher, Toronto
Kevin Hawkins, North Texas
Beth Kressel Itkin, Vanderbilt
Jeremy Morse, Michigan

Editorial, Design, and Production
Michele Quinn, Alabama, Co-Chair
Janet Rossi, MIT, Co-Chair
Angela Anderson, Marine Corps
Melissa Bugbee Buchanan, Georgia
Kathryn Owens, Georgetown
Jillian Downey, Michigan
Dariel Mayer, Vanderbilt
Lisa Tremaine, New Mexico

Faculty Development
Patrick Alexander, Penn State, Chair
Ann Baker, Nebraska
Seth Denbo, American Historical Association
Angela Gibson, Modern Language Association
Ilene Kalish, NYU
Gita Manaktala, MIT
Larin McLaughlin, Washington
Trevor Perri, Northwestern

IP and Copyright
Cathy Rimer-Surles, Duke, Chair
Puja Boyd, Washington
Margie Guerra, NYU
Jenny Hunt, Baylor
Lisa Jemison, Toronto
Charles Myers, Chicago
Kelly Rogers, Johns Hopkins
Jordan Stepp, Georgia
Stephen Williams, Indiana

Investment
Susan Doerr, Minnesota, Chair
Mike Bieker, Arkansas
Nadine Buckland, West Indies
Robbie Dircks, North Carolina
Donna Shear, Nebraska
Erik Smist, Johns Hopkins

Journals
Ann Snoeyenbos, Johns Hopkins, Chair
Clare Hooper, Liverpool
Julie Lambert, Penn State
Katie Luu, MIT
Levi Rubeck, MIT
Brian Shea, Johns Hopkins
Katie Smart, Duke
Emily Taylor, Ohio State

Library Relations
Kathryn Conrad, Arizona, Co-Chair
Beth Fuget, Washington, Co-Chair
Karen DeVinney, North Texas
Jeremy Grainger, Rutgers
Liz Hamilton, Northwestern
Geoffrey Little, Concordia
Katherine Purple, Purdue

Marketing
Mark Heineke, Nebraska, Chair
Michelle Alamillo, SUNY
Jennie Collinson, Liverpool
Amy Harris, Kentucky
Abby Mogollón, Arizona
Bailey Morrison, Texas
Kathryn Pitts, Notre Dame
Erin Rolfs, LSU

Professional Development
Dawn Durante, Illinois, Chair
James Ayers, New Mexico
Ciara O'Connor, NYU
Michael Regoli, Indiana
Brian Roach, Catholic
Allison Shay, Syracuse
Jill Shimabukuro, Chicago
Christine Thorsteinsson, Harvard

Task Forces

Book, Jacket, and Journal Show
Linda Secondari, Studiolo Secondari, Co-Chair
Jill Shimabukuro, Chicago, Co-Chair
Greg Britton, Johns Hopkins
Jeffrey Cohen, Getty
Colleen Devine Ellis, Texas
Than Saffel, West Virginia

Diversity and Inclusion
Gita Manaktala, MIT, Co-Chair
Larin McLaughlin, Washington, Co-Chair
Ellen C. Bush, North Carolina
Susan Doerr, Minnesota
Gisela Concepción Fosado, Duke
Brian Halley, Massachusetts
Alexandria Leonard, Princeton
Jill Petty, Northwestern

Research
Elizabeth Windsor, Project MUSE/John
    Hopkins, Chair
Anthony Cond, Liverpool
Toni Gunnison, Wisconsin
Mary Frances Gydus, MIT
Kimberly Lutz, ITHAKA S+R
Cason Lynley, Duke
Alphonse MacDonald, National Academies
Brigitte Shull, Cambridge
Rebecca Welzenbach, Michigan
Stephanie Williams, Kentuckyi

Small Press
Jim McCoy, Iowa, Chair
Mike Bieker, Arkansas
Jane Bunker, Northwestern
Trevor Lipscombe, Catholic
Lara Mainville, Ottawa
Alice Pfeiffer, Syracuse
Justin Race, Nevada
Dan Williams, TCU

University Press Week
Fred Nachbaur, Fordham, Chair
Rosemary Brandt, Arizona
Chris Hart, Manchester
Sara Henning-Stout, Princeton
Catherine Hobbs, Columbia
Ilene Kalish, NYU
Colleen Lanick, MIT
Cameron Ludwick, Texas
Jess Massabrook, Princeton
Mark Saunders, Virginia
Laura Sell, Duke

By-Laws (As revised August 29, 2017)

ARTICLE I Preamble
ARTICLE II Purposes
ARTICLE III Membership
Section 1. Regular Membership
Section 2. Definition of a Press Eligible for Regular Membership
Section 3. Eligibility Criteria for Regular Membership
Section 4. Associate Membership
Section 5. Affiliate Membership
Section 6. Introductory Membership
Section 7. Voting and Other Privileges
Section 8. Cancellation of Membership and Resignation
Section 9. Determination of Membership Category
ARTICLE IV Membership Meetings
Section 1. The Annual Meeting
Section 2. Special Meetings
Section 3. Notice of Meetings
Section 4. Representation by Proxy
Section 5. Quorum
Section 6. Voting
ARTICLE V Directors and Officers
Section 1. The Board of Directors
Section 2. Election Procedure and Term of Office
Section 3. Officers
Section 4. Duties of Officers
Section 5. Removal from Office and Replacement
Section 6. Board Meetings
Section 7. Board Quorum
Section 8. Board Voting

ARTICLE VI	Executive Committee
ARTICLE VII	Committees of the Board
ARTICLE VIII	Other Committees and Task Forces
ARTICLE IX	The Executive Director
ARTICLE X	Dues
ARTICLE XI	Books and Records
ARTICLE XII	Changes in By-Laws

ARTICLE I: PREAMBLE

This Corporation, existing under the Not-for-Profit Corporation Law of the State of New York, shall be known as the Association of University Presses, Inc. (hereinafter referred to as the "Association"). The Association expects members to recruit, employ, train, compensate, and promote their employees without regard to race, ethnic background, national origin, status as a veteran or handicapped individual, age, religion, gender, gender orientation, marital status, or sexual orientation.

ARTICLE II: PURPOSES

The purposes of the Association shall be:

a) To encourage dissemination of the fruits of research and to support university presses in their endeavor to make widely available the best of scholarly knowledge and the most important results of scholarly research;

b) To provide an organization through which the exchange of ideas and information relating to university presses and other non-profit publishers within the scholarly communications ecosystems may be facilitated;

c) To afford technical advice and assistance to learned bodies, scholarly associations, and institutions of higher learning; and

d) To do all things incidental to and in furtherance of the fore¬going purposes without extending the same.

ARTICLE III: MEMBERSHIP

The Association admits members in three categories: (1) regular membership, (2) affiliate membership, and (3) introductory membership.

Section 1: Regular Membership.

The regular membership of the Association shall consist of those members who were in good standing at the time of the incorporation of the Association in 1964, except those who have since resigned or whose membership has been otherwise terminated, and all other members who have since been admitted in accordance with the procedures set forth in Section 3 of this Article. Presses with associate member or international member status as of June 2016 (both of which have now been eliminated as membership categories) will be instated as regular members.

Section 2: Definition of a Press Eligible for Regular Membership.

A press eligible for regular membership is hereby defined as: (i) the nonprofit scholarly publishing arm of a university or college, or of a group of such institutions within a defined geographic region, or (ii) the scholarly publishing arm of a non-profit organization (as constituted under local law) that functions in a manner substantially similar to an entity described in clause (i) herein. A non-profit scholarly publisher eligible for membership as here defined must be an integral part of one or more such non-profit institutions, and should be so recognized in the manual of organization, catalog, website, or other official publication of at least one such parent institution. The organization and functions of the non-profit scholarly publisher described herein must lie within the prescription of its parent institution or institutions.

Section 3: Eligibility Criteria for Regular Membership.
Any non-profit scholarly publisher described in Section 2 of these Bylaws and satisfying the requirements set forth in the "Guidelines on Admission to Membership and Maintenance of Membership" (hereinafter, the "Guidelines") that are in force at the time of application shall be eligible for election to regular membership in the Association. A non-profit scholarly publisher shall be elected to membership by a majority vote of the membership on the recommendation of the Board of Directors at the Annual or a Special Meeting of the membership. Such action shall be taken by the Board only on the prior recommendation of the Committee on Admissions and Standards, which shall be responsible for determining that the applying non–profit scholarly publisher satisfies the minimum requirements for membership. Annual dues for regular members shall be set from time to time by the Board of Directors.

Section 4: Associate Membership.
This category of membership shall be closed to new applicants as of June 2016.

Section 5: Affiliate Membership.
The affiliate membership of the Association shall consist of those affiliate members who have been admitted since the time of the incorporation of the Association in 1964, in accordance with the procedures in force at the time of application.

Affiliate membership may be applied for by a non-profit scholarly publisher that meets some but not all of the criteria for regular membership. To qualify for affiliate membership in the Association, a non-profit scholarly publisher must submit the same application as applicants for regular member status, but only will need to meet a subset of the editorial, staffing and organizational requirements applicable to regular members, as that subset may be set forth from time to time in the Guidelines. Admission to affiliate membership shall be by a majority vote of the membership at an Annual or Special Meeting, a quorum being present, on the prior recommendation of the Committee on Admissions and Standards and the Board of Directors.

Affiliate members shall enjoy such rights and privileges as determined by the Board of Directors, but in no event shall their rights extend to: (i) service on the Board of Directors; (ii) vote in any business being con¬ducted by the Association, the Board of Directors, or the membership; (iii) receive without charge any compilation of member or other statistics undertaken by the Association from time to time; (iv) serve in any capacity on the Committees of the Board; or serve as chair of the Annual Meeting Program Committee. Any reference elsewhere in these By-Laws to a voting right, therefore, shall be read so as to exclude affiliate members. Annual dues for affiliate members shall be set from time to time by the Board.

As a condition of membership, an Association affiliate member shall include the term "affiliate" in any reference to its Association membership.

As a condition of membership, an Association affiliate member shall refrain from referring to itself as a "university press" unless it is recognized as such in the manual of organization, catalog, website, or other official publication of its parent institution.

Section 6: Introductory Membership.
Eligible for introductory membership are nonprofit scholarly publishers that intend to apply for Association membership in one of the other categories either during their introductory term or at the end of that term. Introductory members may not stay in that category for more than five years.

Candidates for introductory membership will be expected to provide evidence concerning the scholarly character of their publishing programs and information about present staffing, reporting relationships, editorial review processes, and also any changes or developments proposed in these areas, but they will not be expected to meet the requirements of regular or affiliate membership. Admission to introductory membership shall be made at the discretion of the Executive Director of the Association after favorable review by the Committee on Admissions & Standards upon receipt of an application that includes the requested information.

At any time during the introductory period introductory members may apply for regular or affiliate membership. After five years, introductory membership is automatically terminated.

Introductory members shall enjoy such rights and privileges as determined by the Board of Directors, but in no event shall their rights extend to: (i) service on the Board of Directors; (ii) vote in any business being conducted by the Association, the Board of Directors, or the membership; (iii) receive without charge any compilation of member or other statistics undertaken by the Association from time to time; (iv) chair any Association committee (v) serve in any capacity on the Committees of the Board of the Association. Any reference elsewhere in the By-Laws to a voting right, therefore, shall be so read as to exclude introductory members. Annual dues for introductory members shall be set from time to time by the Board.

Section 7: Voting and Other Privileges.
Each regular member of the Association shall be entitled to one vote in such business as may come before the Association. Only regular members in good standing shall be entitled to vote, and only members in good standing shall be entitled to enjoy the other privileges of membership in the Association.

Section 8: Cancellation of Membership and Resignation.
An Association member, by its very nature, must be devoted to scholarly and educational ends; the failure of a member to pursue such ends as its fundamental business shall constitute grounds for canceling its membership in the Association. Any accusation of such a failure will be brought to the Committee on Admissions and Standards for a recommendation to the Board.

A membership may also be canceled for continued nonpayment of dues or for continued failure, after admission to membership, to meet the minimum requirements set forth in the Guidelines.

Cancellation of membership shall be effected, on recommendation of the Board of Directors, by a two-thirds vote of the members present and voting at the Annual Meeting or a Special Meeting, a quorum being present.

Any member may resign at any time if its current annual dues are paid, provided its resignation is confirmed in a written communication to the Executive Director and President of the Association from a responsible officer or group of officers of the parent institution or institutions.

Should a member in any class of membership resign after the due date of the annual dues payment and before the next annual dues payment date, the member is responsible for the payment of such dues at the time of resignation.

Section 9: Determination of Membership Category.
All Association members are expected to maintain their membership in the Association at the highest level of membership for which they qualify. Association members are expected to notify the Association promptly of any material change in circumstance which might impact the category in which they are eligible to maintain their membership.

ARTICLE IV: MEMBERSHIP MEETINGS

Section 1: The Annual Meeting.
The Annual Meeting of members shall be held at such time and place within or without the State of New York as may be designated by the Board of Directors after giving due weight to preferences ex¬pressed by members. Such meetings shall be held for the purpose of electing the Board of Directors, approving the annual budget, and transacting such other business as may be properly brought before the meeting. At each Annual Meeting of members, the Board of Directors shall cause to be presented to the membership a report verified by the President and the Treasurer, or by a majority of the Board, in accordance with the requirements of Section 519 of the New York Not-for-Profit Corporation Law.

Section 2: Special Meetings.
Special Meetings of the members shall be held at such time and place within or without the State of New York as may be designated by the Board of Directors. Such meetings may be called by (a) the Board of Directors; or (b) the Executive Committee; or (c) the President, the President-elect, or the Executive Director, acting on a request received in writing that states the purpose or purposes of the meeting and signed by 30 percent or more of the members of the Association.

Section 3: Notice of Meetings.
Notice of the purpose or purposes and of the time and place of every meeting of members of the Association shall be in writing and signed by the President, President-elect, or the Executive Director, and a copy thereof shall be delivered personally, by first class mail, by facsimile or by electronic mail not less than ten or more than fifty days before the meeting, to each member entitled to vote at such meeting. In the case of a special meeting, such notice shall also set forth the purpose or purposes of the meeting.

Section 4: Representation by Proxy.
A member may authorize a person or persons to act by proxy on all matters in which a member is entitled to participate by providing such authorization in writing, including by facsimile or electronic mail, to the person who will be the holder of the proxy, provided that any such authorization by electronic mail shall set forth information from which it can be reasonably determined that the authorization by electronic mail was authorized by the member. If it is determined that such authorization by electronic mail is valid, the inspectors or, if there are no inspectors, such other persons making that determination shall specify the nature of the information upon which they relied. No proxy shall be valid after the expiration of eleven months from the date thereof unless otherwise provided in the proxy. Every proxy shall be revocable at the pleasure of the member executing it.

Section 5: Quorum.
Except for a special election of Directors pursuant to Section 604 of the New York Not-for-Profit Corporation Law, the presence at a meeting in person or by proxy of a majority of the members entitled to vote thereat shall constitute a quorum for the transaction of any business, except that the members present may adjourn the meeting even if there is no quorum.

Section 6: Voting.
In the election of members of the Board of Directors and the election of Officers, a plurality of the votes cast at an Annual Meeting shall elect. Any other action requires a majority of votes cast except as otherwise specifically provided in these By-Laws. Any action required or permitted to be taken at a meeting of members may be taken without a meeting, without

prior notice, if all of the members consent to the adoption of a resolution authorizing the action. Such consent may be written or electronic. If written, the consent must be executed by each member by signing such consent or causing his or her signature to be affixed to such consent by any reasonable means including, but not limited to, facsimile signature. If electronic, the transmission of the consent must be sent by electronic mail and must set forth, or be submitted with, information from which it can reasonably be determined that the transmission was authorized by the member. The resolution and consents thereto shall be filed with the minutes of the proceedings of the members.

ARTICLE V: DIRECTORS AND OFFICERS

Section 1: The Board of Directors.
The Association shall be managed by its Board of Directors, and, in this connection, the Board of Directors shall establish the policies of the Association while considering the wishes of the membership and the constituency of the Association (which constituency consists of the employees of the member presses), and shall evaluate the performance of the Executive Director. The Board of Directors shall meet at least three times each year, once in the fall and once in the winter, and in conjunction with the Annual Meeting of the membership of the Association. The Board of Directors shall consist of not fewer than nine or more than thirteen Directors, all of whom shall be at least nineteen years of age, at least two-thirds of whom shall be citizens of the United States, four of whom shall be the elected Officers of the Association as described in Section 3 (hereinafter, "Officers"). Directors other than Officers (hereinafter, "Directors-at-Large"), like Officers, must be on the staff of a member press, except that the Executive Director shall serve ex officio as a nonvoting member of the Board of Directors and the Executive Committee.

Section 2: Election Procedure and Term of Office.
Directors shall be elected by a plurality vote of the members present at the Annual Meeting. Candidates may be nominated by the Nominating Committee appointed by the President or from the floor. Officers shall be elected for a one-year term, except that the President shall remain on the Board of Directors for an additional year as Past-President. Directors-at-Large shall be elected for a three-year term. Directors shall not succeed themselves except that (a) Directors who are elected Officers shall continue as Directors as long as they remain Officers, and (b) the Treasurer shall remain on the Board for an additional year as a Director-at-Large. Each newly elected Director and Officer shall assume office at the close of the Annual Meeting at which the election is held. Any Director or Officer may resign by notifying the President, the President-elect, or the Executive Director. The resignation shall take effect at the time therein specified. Except as provided for in Article IX ("The Executive Director"), Directors shall not receive any compensation for serving as Directors. However, nothing herein shall be construed to prevent a Director from serving the Association in another capacity for which compensation may be received.

Section 3: Officers.
The elected Officers of the Association, each of whom must be on the staff of a member press, shall be a President, a President-elect, a Treasurer, and a Treasurer-elect, each to be elected for a one-year term by a plurality vote of the members present at the Annual Meeting. No employee of the Association may serve as President. Between Annual Meetings of members, a Special Meeting of members may elect, by a plurality vote of the members present, an Officer to complete the term of an Officer who has resigned or otherwise ceased to act as an Officer.

Section 4: Duties of Officers.
The President shall serve as presiding officer at all meetings of the membership and all meetings of the Board of Directors and the Executive Committee. The President, with the Executive Director, serves as spokesperson for the Association. At the Annual Meeting of members, the President and the President-elect shall provide a forum for the Association membership and constituency to discuss and assess the Association's program. The President-elect shall discharge the duties of the President in the President's absence, and shall succeed to the office of President in the event of a vacancy in that office, filling out the unexpired term as well as the term to which he or she subsequently may be elected President.

The Treasurer shall be custodian of the Association's funds, shall be responsible for the preparation of its financial records as the basis for an annual audit, and shall report at the Annual Meeting of members on the Association's financial condition. The Treasurer-elect shall discharge the duties of the Treasurer in the Treasurer's absence, and shall succeed to the office of Treasurer in the event of a vacancy in that office, filling out the unexpired term as well as the term to which he or she may be elected Treasurer.

Section 5: Removal from Office and Replacement.
Any Director or elected Officer may be removed from office at any time, for cause or without cause, by a majority vote of the membership or may be removed for cause by a majority vote of the Board, in either case acting at a meeting duly assembled, a quorum of not less than a majority being present. If one or more Director-at-Large vacancies should occur on the Board for any reason, the remaining members of the Board, although less than a quorum, may by majority vote elect a successor or successors to hold office until the next Annual Meeting of members at which the election of directors is in the regular order of business and until the election and qualification of a successor or successors.

Section 6: Board Meetings.
Meetings of the Board of Directors shall be held at such place within or without the State of New York as may from time to time be fixed by resolution of the Board, or as may be specified in the notice of the meeting. Notice of any meeting of the Board need not be given to any Director who submits a signed waiver of such notice. Special Meetings of the Board may be held at any time upon the call of the Executive Committee, the Executive Director, the President, or the President-elect.

Section 7: Board Quorum.
A majority of the members of the Board of Directors then acting, but in no event less than one-half of the entire board of Directors, acting at a meeting duly assembled, shall constitute a quorum for the transaction of business. If at any meeting of the Board there shall be less than a quorum present, a majority of those present may adjourn the meeting without further notice from time to time until a quorum shall have been obtained. The "entire Board of Directors" shall mean the total number of Directors entitled to vote that the Association would have if there were no vacancies.

Section 8: Board Voting.
Except as otherwise specified in these By-Laws, all decisions of the Board shall be by majority vote of the Directors in attendance, a quorum being present. Any Board action may be taken without a meeting if all members of the Board or committee thereof consent to the adoption of a resolution authorizing the action. Such consent may be written or electronic. If written, the consent must be executed by the director by signing such consent or causing

his or her signature to be affixed to such consent by any reasonable means including, but not limited to, facsimile signature. If electronic, the transmission of the consent must be sent by electronic mail and must set forth, or be submitted with, information from which it can reasonably be determined that the transmission was authorized by the director. The resolution and consents thereto shall be filed with the minutes of the proceedings of the board or committee as applicable. The resolution and consents thereto shall be filed with the minutes of the proceedings of the Board. Any member of the Board or of any committee thereof may participate in a meeting of such Board or committee thereof by means of a conference telephone or similar communications equipment or by electronic video screen communication al¬lowing all persons participating in the meeting to hear each other at the same time. Participation by such means shall constitute presence in person at a meeting.

ARTICLE VI: EXECUTIVE COMMITTEE
The Executive Committee of the Board of Directors shall consist of the President, Past-President, President-elect, Treasurer, Treasurer-elect, and the Executive Director (ex officio, nonvoting). The Executive Committee shall advise and confer with the Executive Director, call Special Meetings of the Board of Directors as necessary, appoint committee members not otherwise appointed pursuant to these By-Laws, and unless otherwise delegated serve as the investment committee for the Association. The Executive Committee shall, if necessary, act for the full Board of Directors between meetings of the Board, but only in those matters not establishing policy or not requiring a vote of more than a majority of Directors in attendance. Neither the Executive Committee nor any other committee shall have the power to (a) submit to the members any action requiring the approval of the members, (b) amend, repeal or adopt By-Laws, (c) fill vacancies in the Board of Directors or in any committee of the Board, (d) fix the compensation of Directors for serving on the Board or on any Committee of the Board, or (e) amend or repeal any resolution of the Board which by its terms shall not be so amendable or repealable.

ARTICLE VII: COMMITTEES OF THE BOARD
The Board, by resolution adopted by a majority of the entire Board, may designate from among its members other Committees of the Board, each including three or more Directors. Such Committees of the Board, to the extent provided in a resolution, shall have the authority of the Board, except as limited by the Board of Directors or by law. The Committees of the Board (in addition to the Executive Committee) shall be the Committee on Admissions and Standards, the Committee on the Audit, and the Nominating Committee. The Committee on Admissions and Standards shall be constituted as provided in the Guidelines. Appointments to the Committee on the Annual Meeting Program and the Nominating Committee shall be made in accordance with Article VIII of these By-Laws.

ARTICLE VIII: OTHER COMMITTEES AND TASK FORCES
Other committees and task forces may be established by agreement of the Executive Director and the Board, to include a Committee on the Annual Meeting Program.
Such committees shall be advisory in nature and shall not have the authority to bind the Board of Directors or the Association. The President-elect shall appoint chairs of said committees (and the Committees of the Board) and such of their members as the Executive Committee may care to designate. The President-elect shall charge the said committees with such duties, including reporting duties, as he or she may deem appropriate. Task forces shall be established for a limited time to accomplish a specific goal. The President shall appoint chairs of task forces and provide their charges. Reports of Committees of the Board and

all other committees and task forces shall be made to the Board of Directors, in writing or orally, as requested by the Executive Director.

ARTICLE IX: THE EXECUTIVE DIRECTOR

The Board of Directors may appoint at such times, and for such terms as it may prescribe, an Executive Director of the Association who shall report to the Board of Directors and who is responsible for implementing policy through fiscally sound programs; monitoring the work of committees and task forces; and managing the Central Office (such Central Office consisting of salaried employees hired by the Executive Director in order to carry out the business of the Association). The Executive Director shall prepare an operating plan and budget and shall participate in meetings of the Board of Directors and Executive Committee in an ex officio nonvoting capacity as appropriate. Under the authority of the Board of Directors, the Executive Director shall have responsibility for the execution of Association policy, for the furtherance of the Association's interests, and for the day-to-day operation of the Association's business and programs. The Executive Director or his or her designee shall act as secretary at all Board meetings, Executive Committee meetings, and Annual and Special Meetings of the Association, and shall prepare and distribute minutes of the same. The Executive Director shall serve as Corporate Secretary. The Executive Director's salary shall be fixed annually by the Board, or by the Executive Committee if the Board so decides.

ARTICLE X: DUES

The amount of the annual dues payment by members shall be voted each year at the Annual Meeting on recommendation of the Board of Directors. The fiscal year of the Association shall be April 1 to March 31. Dues shall be payable by September 30, at which time any member which has not paid its dues shall be subject to suspension at the Board's discretion. When a member is suspended for nonpayment of dues, the President of the Association shall so notify the director of the said member and the responsible officer or officers of its parent institution or group of institutions, and shall further advise them that if such member has not paid its dues by the end of the Association's fiscal year its membership shall be subject to cancellation.

ARTICLE XI: BOOKS AND RECORDS

The Association shall keep at its office within the State of New York correct and complete books and records of account; minutes of meetings of the members, of the Board of Directors, and of the Executive Committee; and an up-to-date list of the names and addresses of all members. These books and records may be in written form or in any other form capable of being converted to written form within a reasonable time.

ARTICLE XII: CHANGES IN BY-LAWS

Members may propose changes to these By-Laws by submitting the proposed change and its rationale to the Executive Director. S/He will arrange for the Board's review of any such proposal at the next appropriate Board Meeting. If the Board recommends Association approval of the proposed change, the change will be presented with at least thirty days advance notice to the membership at the next Annual Meeting or Special Meeting called for that purpose at which a quorum is present. A change to the By-Laws requires a two-thirds majority of all Members eligible to vote (in person or by proxy). Whenever there is a conflict between these By-Laws and the Guidelines, any Statement of Governance, or a resolution of the membership, Board of Directors, or Executive Committee, or any other document published by the

Association, these By-Laws shall prevail.

In the event the Board recommends against approval of a proposed change, the member proposing the change may call a vote on the measure at the Annual Meeting or at a Special Meeting for that purpose, provided thirty days' notice is given and thirty percent of the Association's voting members sign a request that said proposal be voted upon. Requirements for adoption of the measure in such circumstance are as stated elsewhere in this Article.

Guidelines on Admission to Membership and Maintenance of Membership

As revised August 29, 2017
(Hereinafter, "Guidelines")

A. Preamble
The mission of the Association is to advance the essential role of a global community of publishers whose mission is to ensure academic excellence and cultivate knowledge.

The purposes of the Association are to encourage dissemination of the fruits of research and to support university presses and other non-profit scholarly publishers in their endeavor to make widely available scholarly knowledge and the most important results of scholarly research; to provide an organization through which the exchange of ideas relating to the functions of university presses and other non-profit scholarly publishers may be facilitated; to afford technical advice and assistance to learned bodies, scholarly associations, and institutions of higher learning; and to do all things incidental to and in furtherance of the foregoing purposes without extending the same.

B. Types of Membership
The Association admits members in three categories: (1) regular membership, (2) affiliate membership, and (3) introductory membership.

1. Regular Membership
Eligible for regular membership are: (i) the non-profit scholarly publishing arm of a university or college, or of a group of such institutions within a defined geographic region, or (ii) the scholarly publishing arm of a non-profit organization (as constituted under local law) that functions in a manner substantially similar to as an entity described in clause (i) herein, which satisfies the following criteria:

(a) Eligible university presses and other non-profit scholarly publishers must be an integral part of one or more such parent institutions, and should be so recognized in the manual of organization, catalogue, website, or other official publication of at least one such parent institution. The organization and functions of the university press or other non-profit scholarly publisher must lie within the prescription of its parent institution or institutions.

(b) Both of the following editorial criteria: (i) a committee or board of the scholars (or other officials of directly comparable rank and authority) of the parent institution or institutions shall be charged with certifying the scholarly quality of the publications that bear the institutional imprint; and, (ii) the peer review of their scholarly publications in a manner consistent with commonly understood notions of peer review among university presses, including such notions as they may be expressed in any written guidelines for best practice which the Association may from time to time issue or update.

(c) Publication of ten or more scholarly titles in a given twenty-four month period. Scholarly books, journals, and digital projects that include original scholarly content will all be counted to satisfy this requirement. The word "scholarly" is used here in the sense of original research of a character usually associated with the scholarly interests of a college, university or comparable research institution college. (Publications for which the press serves solely as a printer and/or distributor for other departments or divisions of the parent institution are not to be included in the aforementioned minimum scholarly publishing requirement.)

(d) An acceptable scholarly publishing program shall have the benefit of the service of not fewer than three full-time equivalent staff, of whom one shall have the functions of director. This official shall report, organizationally, to the president of the university or college, or to an officer at the vice-presidential or decanal level (i.e., an officer reporting either to the president or to the chief academic officer) having both academic and fiscal authority, or to the designated representative of a group of such institutions who shall have both kinds of authority, or to an individual of directly comparable rank and authority to one of the three proceeding classes of individuals.

Any university press or other non-profit scholarly publisher satisfying these requirements shall be eligible in principle for election to regular membership in the Association.

2. Affiliate Membership

Eligible for affiliate membership shall be university presses and other non-profit scholarly publishers who meet some but not all of the criteria for regular membership, and more specifically which satisfy at least the following criteria:

(a) The non-profit institutional affiliation required for regular membership.
(b) Either of the following editorial criteria: (i) the committee or review board criteria required for regular membership; or, (ii) the peer review of their scholarly publications in a manner consistent with commonly understood notions of peer review among university presses, including such notions as they may be expressed in any written guidelines for best practice which the Association may from time to time issue or update.
(c) Either of the following indicia of sustained commitment: (i) publication of five or more scholarly titles in a given twenty-four month period; or, (ii) the benefit of the service of at least one full-time equivalent staff.

3. Introductory Membership

Eligible for introductory membership are non-profit scholarly publishers that intend to apply for Association of University Presses membership in one of the other categories either during their introductory term or at the end of that term.

Candidates for introductory membership will be expected to provide evidence concerning the scholarly character of their publishing programs and information about present staffing, reporting relationships, review processes, and also any changes or developments proposed in these areas, but they will not be expected to meet the publication rate, staffing, or organizational requirements of full membership. Presses may not stay in the introductory category for more than five years.

At any time during the introductory period introductory members may apply for membership in the regular or affiliate category. If a press does not wish to continue as an introductory member for five years, it may resign from the Association after payment of its current annual dues. At the end of five years, the introductory membership is automatically terminated.

C. Application, Admission, and Cancellation

1. Application

All inquiries from prospective applicants for membership in the Association are to be directed to the Association's Executive Director, or such staff member as he or she may designate. The Executive Director, or his or her designee, shall advise the candidate of the substance of these Guidelines on Admission to Membership and Maintenance of Membership, and shall require as evidence of satisfactory compliance with the following materials for submission to the

Committee on Admissions and Standards:
(a) One copy of each of 10 or more different scholarly titles published by the applicant and certified by its faculty editorial board or committee in the twenty-four months preceding the date on which the application for membership is filed, and full runs of the issues of any journals for the year or years in which a journal serves as one of the titles. If original digital publications are submitted, the applicant will provide access to committee members.
(b) A list of the peer reviewers (names and affiliations) for each of the books or original digital publications submitted as part of the application. Published reviews of the titles and information about scholarly awards received may be submitted as part of the application.
(c) Copies of the applicant press's catalogs for the past two years for each member of the Committee on Admissions and Standards.
(d) A complete list, by name and title, of the staff of the applicant press, to be prepared in that form in which such information is given for active members in the most recent edition of the Directory of the Association of American University Presses. For part-time staff the list should indicate the percentage of time each person devotes to the press.
(e) A statement from a senior administrative officer of the parent institution, or the designated representative of a group of institutions, outlining the immediate and long-term intentions and financial expectations of the institution or group of institutions for its press, and reflecting a realistic appreciation of the cost of supporting a serious program of scholarly publication.
(f) Copies of its financial operating statements for the two most recently completed fiscal years.
(g) Documentation demonstrating the non-profit status of the applicant and/or its parent institution.

With respect to the scholarship of published works, the Association will in general accept the certification of the press's own faculty board or committee and will not pass judgment on the scholarship of any individual work. However, the Committee on Admissions and Standards will take into account the observance by the press of commonly accepted standards of editorial review, ordinarily including at least one positive evaluation by a qualified scholar not affiliated with the author's own institution.

Applicants for regular membership shall be expected to adhere strictly to all submission requirements.

Applicants for affiliate membership shall be expected to adhere strictly to those submission requirements relevant to the eligibility criteria upon which they are basing their application for membership.

Applicants for introductory membership shall be expected to make a good faith effort to adhere to as many submission requirements as practicable.

2. Admission

Following the filing of a formal application for regular, affiliate, or introductory membership and notification by the Association's Executive Director to the applicant of its acceptance for consideration, the candidate press shall be regarded as having entered a period of probation, which will last for a period of time no longer than one year.
A press shall be elected to regular or affiliate membership by an affirmative vote of a ma-

jority of the Association's regular members at the Annual Meeting or a Special Meeting, a quorum being present, on the recommendation of the Board of Directors. Such action shall be taken by the Board only on the prior recommendation of the Committee on Admissions and Standards, which shall be responsible for determining that the applying press satisfies the minimum requirements for membership. Admission of a new member to the Association shall take effect immediately following approval by the members as described herein.

Admission to introductory membership shall be made at the discretion of the Executive Director after favorable review by the Committee on Admissions & Standards.

To maintain its active membership status, each member shall be required to submit each year to the Central Office of the Association, for publication in the annual Directory of members, both a roster of its current staff and an indication of the number of books, journals, and original digital publications that it has published in each of the two calendar years preceding and that have been certified as to scholarship by its editorial board or committee.

3. Cancellation
An Association of University Presses member, by its very nature, must be devoted to scholarly and educational ends; the failure of a press to pursue such ends as its fundamental business shall constitute grounds for canceling its membership in the Association. Any accusation of such a failure will be brought to the Committee on Admissions and Standards for a recommendation to the Board. Cancellation of membership shall be effected, on recommendation of the Board of Directors, by a two-thirds majority vote of the members present and voting at the Annual Meeting or a Special Meeting, a quorum being present.

It shall be the responsibility of the Executive Director, or his or her designee, to review each listing of an active member in each annual edition of the membership Directory, and to undertake action as follows when any member seems to have fallen below the qualifying criteria for membership: (a) to make an inquiry and, if current standards are not being met, offer the assistance and cooperation of the Association in bringing about satisfactory corrections to the member's deficiencies; (b) to advise the Committee on Admissions and Standards, and the Board when notification of an apparent delinquency has been sent and an offer of assistance made; (c) to inform the Committee on Admissions and Standards, and the Board of any response received from the member press following the offer of assistance.

Should the delinquent press fail to resolve its deficiencies within one year of the Executive Director's notice, the Committee on Admissions and Standards shall submit to the Board of Directors a full report of the situation, and recommend, for endorsement by the Board and transmission to the membership for ratification, that the membership of the delinquent press be terminated. Two years from the date of its expulsion, a press shall be entitled to apply for readmission through initiation of the application procedures herein prescribed.

D. The Committee on Admissions and Standards
The official agency for the administration of these Guidelines shall be the Committee on Admissions and Standards, which shall operate under authority delegated by the Board of Directors, and which shall consist of between four and six members, at least three of whom shall be members of the Board of Directors and at least two of whom shall be the director of a member press. The incoming President will appoint the chair of the committee from among members of the current committee with at least one year of service. The chairs shall

each serve a term of one year as part of their three-year term on the committee and may not succeed themselves in office. Consistent with the requirements of the Association's Policies & procedures, and in consultation with the President and the Executive Director, the chair shall appoint the remaining committee members. Terms of the committee members normally will be three years. Committee members will not be eligible to serve more than two successive terms.

E. Amendments

Members may propose changes to these Guidelines by submitting the proposed change and its rationale to the Executive Director. S/He will arrange for the Board's review of any such proposal at the next appropriate Board Meeting. If the Board recommends Association approval of the proposed change, the change will be presented with at least thirty days advance notice to the membership at the next Annual Meeting or Special Meeting called for that purpose at which a quorum is present. A change to the Guidelines requires a majority of all Members eligible to vote (in person or by proxy). Whenever there is a conflict between the By-Laws and these Guidelines, any Statement of Governance, or a resolution of the membership, Board of Directors, or Executive Committee, or any other document published by the Association, the By-Laws shall prevail.

In the event the Board recommends against approval of a proposed change, the member proposing the change may call a vote on the measure at the Annual Meeting or at a Special Meeting for that purpose, provided thirty days' notice is given and thirty percent of the Association's voting members sign a request that said proposal be voted upon. Requirements for adoption of the measure in such circumstance are as stated elsewhere in this Article.

PERSONNEL INDEX

Abe, Carol	84	Arab, Ranjit	93
Abel, Susan A.	136	Arain, Maryam	141
Abley, Mark	113	Arakaki, Ku'ulei	84
Abrams, Robert	62	Arkin, Emily	82
Acerra, Stephen	50	Arlow, Noah	63
Adams, Bill	182	Armato, Douglas	122, 243
Adams, Sandy	128	Arndt, Henriette	34
Adams, Stephanie	186	Arrington, Lisa	51
Adams, Tiffany	57	Arroyo, Paul	87
Ade, John	51	Ashe, Rosann	158, 160
Adkins, Jad	143	Ashenfelter, Paul	149
Agarwal, Kritika	29	Aten, Alison	121
Agate, Nicky	127, 243	Atwan, Helene	41
Agree, Peter	162	Audet, Janice	82
Agudo, Marcelo	177	Ault, Elizabeth	70
Ahn, Christopher	187	Austin, Bruce A.	174
Ahrens, Lisa	205	Auten, Lindsey	133
Ajamian, Vartan	228	Avery, Laurie	151
Akturk, Ceylan	215	Avouris, Ann	50, 51
Alamillo, Michelle	188	Axland, Suzanne	182
Alamillo, Michelle	244	Aycock, David	40
Albers, Greg	81	Ayers, James	138, 244
Albury, Susan	70	Aziz, Omar	150
Alexander, Patrick	164, 242, 243, 244	Babb, Meredith	243
Alexander, Sandy	125	Bachman, Margie	166
All, Emma	95	Baggaley, Richard	113
Allen, Latrice	57	Baida, Laura	44
Allen, Patrick	79	Bail, Kathy	140, 243
Allen, Rebecca	198	Baines, Jennika	90
Allen, Timothy	159	Bajorat, Valerie	57
Alley, John	208	Bakely, Emily	131
Alsip, Amy	185	Baker-Young, Melissa	118
Alston, Edith	142	Baker, Ann	133, 244
Altobello, Diana	187	Baker, Donna Cox	25
Altreuter, Judith	127	Baker, Jennifer	191
Alvania, Rebecca	176	Baker, Karen	192
Alvaro, Gabe	49	Baker, Katherine	153
Amador, Marisol	73	Baker, Steven	153
Ambrose, Ann	168	Baker, Susan	237
Amega, Madje G.	89	Balenske, Kelly	189
Ames, Michael	209	Balestracci, Julia	36
Ammons-Longtin, Cheryl	160	Balikov, Molly	159
Amoroso, Connie	52	Balskus, Ben	56
Anderson, Angela	107, 244	Banducci, JoAnne	135
Anderson, Ann-Marie	192	Bandy, Emily	124
Anderson, Duane	23	Banfi, Aniko	51
Anderson, Duane	243	Banks, Jennifer	223
Anderson, Erik	122	Banning, Lisa	178
Anderson, Odessa	133	Bannon, Laura	160
Andree, Courtney	109	Banward, Darrell	138
Andreou, George	82	Barbasa, Santos	84
Andrew, Emily	66	Barbee, Jennifer	87
Angress, Miriam	70	Barla-Szabo, Agnes	54
Anstey, Donna	223	Barnes, Jacqline	131
Aono, Lucille	84	Barnes, Marcy	41
Appel, Fred	168	Barnett, Andre M.	94
Appleyard, David	105	Barnett, Bob	195

Barrett, Sheila	83		Bielstein, Susan	56
Barry, Bridget	132		Biggins, Walter	79, 243
Barton, Kate	103		Billot, Victor	155
Bartz, Olivia	186		Biot, Sebastian	150
Basmajian, Nancy	150		Birchmeier, Bryan	118
Bassford, Alison K. Syring	86		Bisberg, Laura	142
Bastion, Cynthia	57		Bishel, William	195
Bates, Tristan	56		Bishop, Dawn	195
Bates, Vicki	182		Bixler, Gina	149
Bathgate, Linda	72		Blachere, Natalie	113
Battista, Dino	144		Black, Claire	207
Bauer, Nate	27		Black, George	71
Bauerle, Ellen	117		Blake, Deborah	162
Baumann, David	166		Blake, Hannah	162
Bayer, Lisa	79, 242, 243		Blakeslee, Kristine	119
Beard, Elliott	44		Blanc-Tal, Jennifer	178
Beardow, Jim	89		Bliss, Dana	159
Beaver, Adrienne	46		Blobaum, Dean	57
Bechthold, Michael	219		Blon, Matthew	141
Beck, Elizabeth	105		Blong, Michael	160
Becker, Matt	109		Bloom, Thalia	177
Beeny, Martyn	67		Bodek, Martin	161
Beer, Brian	164		Boehm, William	162
Beerman, Brian	57		Boehmer, Susan Wallace	82
Beermann, Tera	132		Boggs, Jon	193
Beilhart, Jacqueline	78		Bohannan, Adam	142
Belan, Allison	69		Bohlen, Ivis	144
Bell, Kewon	58		Boileau, Kendra	164
Bellows, David R.	137		Bokovoy, Matthew	132, 243
Benedetto, Lynn	67, 243		Boldan, Terry	133
Benigni, Marc	224		Boller, Katherine	223
Bennett, Jason	80		Bond, Lynn	226
Bennett, Jenn	188		Boneparth, Byron	160
Bennett, Matthew	50		Booth, Jessica	208
Bennie, Dale	153		Booth, Tom	154
Bennion, Greta	147		Bors, Deborah L.	94
Benson, Barbara A.	137		Bortz, Eli	149
Benson, Frances	66		Bossert, Joan	159
Benson, Kathy	153		Bossier, Erica	103
Bent, Tim	158		Boudreau, Caroline	156
Benton, Emily	84		Boudreau, Michael	57, 243
Berchowitz, Gillian	150, 243		Bouloukos, Beth	33, 243
Beres, Gabriela	118		Bourgogne, Beatrice	56
Bergen, Glenn	106		Bower, Kim	91
Berger, Courtney	69		Bowley, Chealsye	235
Berger, John	50		Bowman, David	131
Berger, Susan	149		Boyd, Puja	212, 244
Bergeron, Catherine	95		Bozzi, Debra	224
Bergstrom, Krista	43		Brach, Courtney	178
Berkery, Peter	242		Brackenbury, Anne	203
Bernal, Jennifer	149		Bradley, Jessica	51
Berrada, Houda	89		Bradley, Venus	70
Berry, Jon	25		Brand, Amy	110
Berk, Adina Popescu	223		Brand, Megan	43
Bertrand, Al	168		Brandon, Robert	100
Berzanskis, Andrew	218		Brandt, Eric	210
Besen, Rachel	111		Brandt, Rosemary	245
Betancourt, Lorraine	160		Brandt, Rosemary	36
Bethell, Bruce	194		Brannon, Mandy	71
Bieker, Mike	37, 243, 244, 245		Braun, Mary Elizabeth	154, 243

Breichner, William	95	Bylander, John	191
Breier, Davida G.	95, 243	Byrd, Elizabeth	168
Brennan, Emma	105	Byron, Robert	105
Brennan, Katie	130	Cader, Roshan	222
Brenneman, John	89	Caetano, Kalie	186
Brereton, Patrick	102	Cahen, Ben	44
Brewer, Tony	90	Cahill, Kerry	95
Brianik, Christina	190	Calamia, Joseph Sr.	223
Briggs, Barbara L.	136	Calder, Kent	152
Brinbury, Rebecca	212	Calderara, Theo	159
Britton, Greg	94, 242, 243, 244	Caldwell, Amy	41
Broaddus, Kaelin	79	Callahan, Pat	182
Brock, John	200	Callaway, MaryKatherine	103
Brock, Taylor	70	Cameron, Hamish	204
Brommer, Pat	214	Cameron, Linda	121
Brook, Matt	95	Camp, Martha	168
Brook, Susan Todd	130	Campbell, Duncan	173
Brooks, Christine A.	98	Campochiaro, Michael	188
Brooks, Eric M.	136	Candreva-Szwet, Gail	58
Broughan, Connor	63	Cannon, Diane	153
Brouwer, Anouk	34	Caputo, Kara L.	136
Brower, Charles	70	Carey, Amber	70
Brower, Daryl	178	Carey, Edward	51
Brown, Christine	197	Carey, Tyler M.	237
Brown, Katherine	223	Carlin, Richard	159
Brown, Marty	154	Carlson, John	222
Brown, Rebekah	103	Caro, Sarah	169
Brown, Richard	182	Carpenter, Jennifer	159
Browne, Matthew	110	Carr, David	106
Brownoff, Alan	28, 243	Carr, Rosalyn	25
Broyles, Karen	195	Carrick, Brendan	57
Brunstein, Ada	159	Carroll, Brian	56
Bryan, Nancy	195	Carroll, Meredith	105
Bryant, Kim	143, 243	Carrollo, Sandra	89
Bryant, Virginia	78	Carruthers-Busser, Kaitlin	189
Bryfogle, Tam	129	Carruthers, Meredith	64
Buchan, Dave	165	Carter, Allyson	36, 243
Buchanan, Amy	70	Cascio, Al	51
Buchanan, Melissa Bugbee	79, 244	Cash, Susan L.	98
Buchanan, Rob	133	Casteel, Sharon	195
Buchholz, Roger	133	Castillo, Amy	38
Buckland, Nadine D.	217, 242, 243, 244	Castro-Rappl, Jessica	71
Buckles, Kristen	36	Castro, Grey	133
Buckley, Susan	110	Catalano, Steve	186
Buhman, Linda	185	Catanese, Chris	70
Bullard, Anna	232	Catlos, Alicia C.	95
Buller, Bob	180	Cavaliere, Charles	159
Bunker, Jane	147, 245	Caviness, Mary	143
Buntin, Mat	203	Cebik, Stephen	224
Burgess, Kathy	124	Cedillos, Felicia	138
Burgos, José	169	Cerbone, Will	74
Burke, Brendan	51	Cercone, Philip J.	113
Burke, Penny	178	Chadwell, Faye A.	154
Burr, Jim	194	Chaffin, Jennifer	91
Burris, Glen	95	Chaiken, Rafael	188
Burton, Angela	87	Challice, John	158
Burton, Melissa	168	Chambers, Pam	223
Burton, Michael P.	136	Chan, Derick	43
Bush, Ellen	144, 244	Chan, Tina	59
Butchart-Bailey, Chris	117	Chaney, Margo	87

Chang, Jasper	178
Chapman, Lynne	194
Chase, Paul	162
Chatterjee, Jaya	223
Chen, Angela	49
Chesnutt, Jessica	160
Chin, Barbara	231
Ching, Emma	84
Chnapko, Angela	159
Chodosh, Ellen	141, 243
Chorpenning, Joseph F.	179
Chrisman, Ronald	145
Christensen, Alicia	132
Christiansen, Gayla	197
Christofferson, Andrea	220
Christofides, Marika	86
Chun, Stephanie	84
Church, Lucas	143
Ciaccio, Michele	81
Cisneros, Cassandra	195
Clabaugh, Patricia	197
Claps, Bobbi	189
Clark, Becky	242
Clark, Jennifer	86
Clark, Karen	173
Clark, Rakia	41
Clark, Robert	214
Clarke, Paul	105
Claro, Lyndsey	168
Clay, Jami	144
Cleland, Jaime	127
Clevenger, Beth	110
Clingham, Greg	45
Clockel, Bill	228
Cloutier, Suzanne	156
Clute, Sharla	188
Coates, Laraine	43
Coatney, Susan	138
Cobb, Caelyn	63
Cobb, David	99
Cobra, Alison	47
Cockerham, Jamison	143
Cocks, Catherine	212, 243
Coffey, Roland	224
Coggins, Joel	166, 243
Coggins, Niccole Leilanionapae'aina	212
Cohen, Barbara	158
Cohen, Emily-Jane	186
Cohen, Jeffrey	244
Cohen, Phyllis	160
Cohen, Sara	192
Cohn, Stephen A.	69
Coleff, Patrick	71
Colella, Alexa	87
Coleman, Jason	210, 211
Coleman, Robin	94
Colesworthy, Rebecca	187
Collier, Abby	166
Collins, Don P.	58
Collins, Mike	65
Collins, Nina	171
Collins, Teresa W.	100
Collinson, Jennie	102
Collinson, Jennie	244
Colman, Jason	118
Colosky, Allison	207
Comeau, Jennifer	86
Comer, Heather	117
Cond, Anthony	102, 245
Congdon, David	97
Conley, Mary	126
Conn, Jennifer	220
Connell, Carol	25
Connelly, Rich	57
Conner, Bonnie	69
Connery, Lisa	86
Connors, Logan J.	45
Conover, Roger	110
Conrad, Joanna	200
Conrad, Kathryn	36, 244
Contrucci, Jason	118
Cook, James	158
Cook, Julia	175
Cook, Rick	25
Cook, Tonya	66
Cooper, Kevin	142
Cooper, Pam	51
Cope, Kevin L.	45
Copp, Karen	93, 243
Corbin, Becki	170
Corrado, Susan	131
Cort, Molly Q.	174
Corwin, Erica	133
Cosgrove, Jay	224
Cosner, Chris	186, 243
Cosseboom, Joel	84
Costanzo, Gerald	52
Cotter, Christina	80
Cotter, Glenda	208
Coty, Danielle	118
Coulson, Krista	56
Couture, Christie	30
Cowles, Lauren	50
Coxhead, Imogen	155
Coxon, Khadija	113
Coyne, Brendan	164
Crago, Jonathan	113
Crahan, Eric	168
Craig, Teresa	164
Craven, Kim	160
Cresswell, Marilyn	105
Crevier, Yvonne	109
Crewe, Jennifer	62, 242, 243
Crews, Shaquona	169
Croce, Carmen Robert	179
Cronin, John	95
Cronin, Susan	118
Crooks, Cathie	28
Crooms, Sandy	166
Crosby, Darryl M.	98

Name	Page
Cross, Tim	237
Crotty, David	160
Crowe, Sean	60
Cuddy, Erin	133
Cuesta, Ethel	47
Cullen, Darcy	43
Cunningham, David Scott	37
Cunningham, Kevin	87
Cupo, Aldo	224
Currer, Bob	203
Cusano, Melina	47
Cutler, Thomas J.	130
Cyphers, Tara	151
Czarnowsky, Lora	94
D'Ambrosio, Adele	203
d'Arbonne, Jessica	61
D'Auria, Heather	224
D'Onofrio, Joseph	57
Dailey, Heidi	118
Dailey, Pamela	45
Dalton, Emily	148
Dalzell, Sam	144
Danforth, Scot	193
Danser, Kate	168
Danziger, Sheldon	177
Dark, Tom	105
Darling, Karen	56
Darnall, Kerry	214
Davey, Kate	58
Davidson, Andrew	126
Davies, Jon	79
Davies, Shannon	197
Davis, Deanna	126
Davis, Jacqueline	114
Davis, Julie	91
Davis, Kimberly	199
Davis, Lisa	193
Davulis, Laura	131
Dawson, Jocelyn	71, 243
de Bueger, Vanessa	34
de Choisy, Gemma	93
de Garmo, Jennifer	138
De Laet, Veerle	101
De-La-Paz, Noelle	190
Dean Dotson, Anne	99
Dean-Grossmann, Kristen	87
Dean, Jeff	82
DeHerrera, Scott	36
Del Col, Anna	203
Delodder, Blake	57
DeLucia, Leslie	87
Demers, Elizabeth	118
DeNardis, Wendy	224
DeNaro, Rio	129
Denbo, Seth	29, 244
Denby, Alison	160
Dennison, Kirsten	86
Denton, Jim	182
Dermody, Meagan	66
Des Jardines, David	80
DeShano, Rachael	109
DeSio, Andrew	168
DeTratto, Eric	56
Deumens, Eleanor	73
Devens, Robert	194
Devilbiss, Charles	160
Devine, Thomas	69
DeVinney, Karen	145, 244
Dew, Jay	197
DeWeese, Beth	214
Deyirmenjian, Ani	203
Dhamee, Saleem	57
Di Bianco Caracas, Danielle	223
di Costanzo, Patricia	101
Dias, Katherine	188
Diaz, Gemma	89
Dickey, Sonia	138
DiDomenico, Jennifer	203
Diehl, Debra	97
Dilworth, Rob	70
Ding, Kristine	86
Dircks, Robbie	144, 242, 243, 244
Ditchik, Seth	223
Dixon, Deborah	160
Dixon, Donna	187
Dixon, Sandra	150
Doboszenski, Amanda	144
Doerr, Jennifer	224
Doerr, Susan	123, 244
Doherty, Allison	229
Dolbow, Jim	130
Doll, Rachel	73
Donatich, John E.	223, 242, 243
Donnelly, Susan	83, 243
Donovan, Emma	211
Dorr, Yuni	146
Doskow, Sara	50
Dotson, Rand	103
Dotto, Gabriel	119
Dougan, Jill	42
Dougherty, Mary	109
Dougherty, Peter	168
Dougherty, Sarah	118
Dowd, Matthew	149
Downey, Floann	218
Downey, Heidi	224
Downey, Jillian	118, 244
Doyle, Mary	189
Draper, Delsena	206
Dreesen, Robert	50
Dreyer, Christopher	118
Duckworth, Michael	60
Duelm, Katie	197
Duff, Kate	57
Dufy, Daniel	73
Duggan, Cait	53
Dunbar, Christine	62
Duncan, Michael	51
Dunham, Chantel	79
Dunham, Gary	90

Dupuis, Amanda A.	136
Durante, Dawn	86, 244
Durham, Cynthia	69
Dutta, Deepshikha	203
Duvall, Kristin	195
Dwyer, Michaela	144
Dyson, Elizabeth Branch	56
Dyson, Sandra	73
Eager, Leslie	70, 71
Eckhart, Carol	95
Edington, Mark	33
Edwards, Kathy	151
Ehle, Rob	186
Ehling, Terry	110, 243
Eidenier, Natalie	120
Eidson, Ryan	126
Eisenstark, Stacy	197
El Manialawi, Basma	32
El-Elaimy, Tarek	32
El-Hadi, Nadine	32
Elam, Tim	100
Elder, Rodney	236
Ellerbeck, Brian	190
Elliott, Stephanie	216
Elliott, Steve	50
Ellis, Colleen Devine	244
Elt, Larisa	227
Emmrich, Terry	220
Engel, Carrie	44
Engel, Tracey	175
Engelhardt, James	86
Ennis, Alice	87, 243
Erickson, Lesley	43
Esco, Melinda	198
Etcheson, Amy	184, 185
Eubanks, April	145
Eubanks, Debra	30
Evans-Reitz, Nora	36
Evans, Claire Lewis	25
Evans, Justine	62
Evans, Rebecca	143
Evans, Sally	76
Evans, Stephanie	153
Ezernack, Kristi	124
Fagan, Teresa	57
Fahmy, Miriam	32
Fairman, Elizabeth	195
Faison, Anna	144
Falocco, Filomena	114
Famiano, David	48
Farmer, Christopher	195
Farr, Clay	144
Farranto, Amy	146
Fasciani, Susan	36
Fastiggi, Raymond T.	176
Faust, Allison	194
Faust, Jana	133
Faust, Jessica	104
Fehrenbacher, Micah	57
Feinsod, Denise	48, 49
Felland, Kirstie	148
Ferber, Susan	158
Ferguson, John	220
Ferguson, Sara	67
Fernandez, Maya	41
Ferrence, Susan	92
Ferro, Alden	224
Ferry, Lorraine	226
Fidler, Patricia	223
Fields, DeLisa	215
Fields, LeAnn	117
Figueira, Sarah George	31
Fikes, Jason	23
Finan, William	44
Fingerhut, Natalie	203
Finkelstein, Edward	172
Fisher, Jennie	87
Fisher, Lynn	202, 243
Fitzgerald, Brenda	211
Fitzgerald, Patrick	62
Fiyak-Burkley, Michele	73
Flach, Alex	159
Flannery-McCoy, Bridget	62, 243
Fleming, John	233
Fletcher-Jones, Nigel	32
Flum, David	178
Fobben, Tish	133
Fogle, Linda Haines	182
Foley, Bill	237
Fontaine, Cerise	127
Fontana, Virginia	135
Forbes, Rebecca	221
Forde, Simon	34, 115
Fortner, Shannon	95
Fosado, Gisela Concepción	70, 244
Foss, David	82
Foster, Cynthia	124
Fowler, Marjorie	144
Francis, Mark	133
Francis, Mary	117, 243
Franklin, Tom	144
Fraser, Kathleen	114
Freeland, Abby	218
Freels, Amy	24
Freiler, Ellen	224
Fricke, Cate	164
Friedman, Paloma	113
Frisch, Janice	90
Froehlich, Peter	170
Frost, Amanda	194
Frost, Matthew	105
Frucht, William	223
Fry, Jenni	56
Fuget, Beth	212, 244
Fugini, Richard	138
Fuller, Molly	122
Fuller, Timothy D.	94
Fultz, Ken	227
Furney, Laura	61
Furtkamp, Ryan	186

Gabriele, Louis	63
Galante, Edward	51
Gallagher, Heather	102
Gallaway, Matt	50
Galle, Suzanne	97
Gamblin, Carrie	234
Gammon, Julie	24
GAN, Qi	59
Ganeles, Diane	188
Garcia, Sydney	142
Garrett, Susan	144
Garrison, Patrick	67
Gasbarrini, Tiffany	94
Gasso, Ale	73
Gawronski, William	63
Gemignani, Nathan	67
Gendler, Anne	147
George, Derek	195
Georgi, Sara	218
Gering, Shannon	153
Gernenz, Heather	87
Gershenowitz, Deborah	50
Gettman, Joyce	133
Gibson, Angela	126, 244
Gibson, Katie Cross	100
Gieling, Saskia	34
Gill, Craig W.	124
Gillespie, Carmen	45
Gillooly, Diana	50
Ginder, Rachel	164
Ginsburg, Erica	162
Gleason, Laura	103
Glover, Elizabeth	162
Gnerlich, Ingrid	169
Godlewski, Cynthia	81
Gold, Heather	223
Goldberg, David	111
Golden, Katherine	224
Goldstead, Catherine	94
Gonzales, Pat	100
Gonzalez, Anibal	45
Goodman, Eleanor	164
Goodman, Robert White	95
Goranescu, Elena	114
Gordon, Ariel	106
Gosnell, Jason	107
Goto, Kensuke	201
Gottshall, Jon	164
Gough, Peggy	194
Gould, Zoe	162
Goussy, Patrick	118
Grabill, Catherine A.	136
Grainger, Jeremy	178, 244
Grande, Scott	160
Grandstaff, Emily	211
Grant, Donna	173
Grathwohl, Casper	158
Gray, Kelly	193
Greco, Debbie	168
Green, Joanna	41
Greenhalgh, Adam	130
Greig, Justine	102
Grench, Charles	143
Greyson, Brent	153
Gribbin, Laura	143
Griffin, Don	69
Griffith, Glenn	131
Griffiths, Drew	126
Grodsky, Larry	51
Gross, Abby	159
Grosse, Diane	69
Grossman, James R.	29
Grossman, Kevin	197
Grossman, Maggie	147
Grossman, Sarah E. M.	66
Grotophorst, Wally	76
Grzan, Lisa	160
Guagnini, Valeria	51
Guerra, Margie	141, 142, 244
Guerra, Paul	195
Guerrero, David	195
Guinta, Kimberly	178
Guiod, Suzanne E.	189
Gullino, Louis	159
Gunderson, Maryann	150
Gunnison, Toni	220, 245
Guo, Janalyn	208
Guo, Meide	186
Gurganus, Cynthia	70
Gusinde-Duffy, Mick	79
Guthrie, Kevin	231
Gutierrez, Romi	73
Guttman, Joseph	163
Guttormsen, Kate	38
Gydus, Mary Frances	245
Haav, Julia	168
Habib, Sylvia	32
Hadley, Patrick	208
Haenisch, Julie	168
Hagerman, Liza	170
Hagman, Lorri	212
Hahn, Jim	221
Haire, Timothy	224
Hajnoczky, Helen	47
Hall, Charles	73
Hall, Emily	127
Hall, Jonathan	67
Hall, Marie	74
Hall, Megan	39
Hall, Sue	70
Halley, Brian	109, 243, 244
Halliday, Dorothea	142
Halliday, Mark	140
Hallock, Tom	41
Halpern, Eric	162
Halter, Theresa	91
Halverson, Pete	124
Ham, Scott	118
Hamada, Junichi	201
Hamblem, Carol	95

Hames, Charles	142		Henry, Christie	168
Hamilton, Emily	123		Henry, Marcia E.	127
Hamilton, Liz	148, 244		Henry, Tricia	113
Hamilton, Susan	142		Hensley, Heather	70
Hamlin, Mona	189		Hensley, Kate	111
Hamm, Lisa	63		Henson, Kristi	25
Hammack, Brice	178		Heo, Inae	203
Hammer, Jennifer	141		Hernandez-French, Anna	160
Hammer, Melissa	99		Hernandez, Aurelia	186
Hamrick, David	194		Hernandez, Terika	119
Hannan, Jack	114		Herrera-Diaz, Maritza	63
Hansard, Patrick	30		Hildebrand, Douglas	28
Hansen, Kathleen	127		Hill, Amanda	50
Haproff, David A.	177		Hill, Eddie	182
Harper, Allie	25		Hill, Mindy B.	136
Harpster, Kristin	215		Hilton, Nick	203
Harrington, Marjorie	115		Hind, Kate	160
Harrington, Sarah	159		Hindley, Victoria	110
Harris, Amy	111, 244		Hipp, Jeff	214
Harris, Jake	206		Hirashima, Steven	84
Harrison, Aimee	188		Hirschberg, Adam	51
Harrison, Joyce	97		Hirschy, Norm	159
Harrison, Kristen	44		Hirst, Bethan	105
Hart, Chris	105, 245		Hiscox, Abbie	111
Hart, Gary	57		Hitchens, Claire	219
Harvey, Alan	185, 243		Hivnor, Margaret	56
Hashimoto, Hiroki	201		Hoagland, Nancy	70
Hashman, Mary	118		Hoak, Michael	224
Haskell, Michael	63		Hobbs, Catherine	63, 245
Hatch, James C.	127		Hodorowicz, Cate	143
Hatfield, Ed	80		Hoff, Alexandra	170
Hawkins, Kevin	243		Hoffman, Robert	57
Hayden, Jeffrey	88		Hoffman, Susan	138
Haydon, Brett	140		Hoffmann, Michelle	151
Haydon, Roger	66		Hogan, Angie	210
Hayes, Stacey	80		Hogeland, Kim	97, 243
Hayes, Todd	160		Hoggatt, Brenda Jo	195
Haynes, Zachary	160		Hohman, Laura	90
Headrick, Jeri	80		Hole, Brian	235
Headrick, Marianne	51		Holland, Claudia	76
Hearn, Aaron	215		Holmes, Jack	95
Hearne, Shivaun	217		Holmes, Nathan	146
Heath, Mary	124		Holsclaw, Erica	206
Heaton, Dan	224		Holway, Pamela	39
Hebel, Brad	62		Holway, Richard K.	210
Hebert, Hannah	164		Hooper, Clare	102, 244
Heckle, Lee	182		Hooper, Niels	48
Hegeman, Anne	210		Hoover, MaryhNell	57
Heineke, Mark	133, 244		Hop, Kristen	25
Heise DiPonzio, Laura	174		Hope, Katie	111
Heiser, Christopher	56		Houck, Anna	52
Helba, Steve	159		Houlihan, Connor	39
Helke, Katie	110		Howard, Jesse	120
Helleberg, Tom	212		Howard, Meredith	63
Helms, Derek	97		Howells, Richard	83
Henderson, Brock	182		Huard, Ricky S.	150
Henderson, John	123		Hubbard, John	162
Hendricksen, Sara	135		Hubbart, Dustin	87
Henney, Eric	168		Hudson, Christopher	127
Henning-Stout, Sara	245		Hudson, Liz	43

Hughes, Brian	160
Hull, Stephen P.	136
Hulsey, Dave	90
Hunt, Jenny	40, 244
Hunt, Val	83
Hunter, Sian	72
Hunter, Stephanye	73
Husband, Len	203
Hutchinson, Emma	140
Hwa, Karen T.	67
Hyzy, Karen	57
Iaffa, Elena	63
Igali, Monika	28
Iguchi, Yasuyo	111
Ikeda, Masako	84
Imbornoni, Ann-Marie	224
Imperio, Irene	192
Inkei, Peter	54
Ireland, Brad	129
Irvin, Margo	186
Isaacs, Olivia	73
Itkin, Beth Kressel	209, 243
Morse, Jeremy	243
Jackson-Wyte, Debra	191
Jackson, Erika	207
Jackson, Joe	168
Jackson, Rhodri	160
Jackson, Zoe	29
Jacob, Mary Ann	197
Jacobs, Donald	78
Jacobs, Joanna	25
Jacobson, Tanjam	53
Jacobson, Tony	95
Jacqmin, Hilary S.	95
Jacques, Kelly Chrisman	97
Jain, Anne Fuzellier	186
Jajuga, Elise	120
Jankowski, Marianne	147, 243
Janssen, Karl	97
Jaquet, G. Jake	171
Jarrad, Mary Beth	142
Javsicas, Aaron	192
Jemison, Lisa	202, 244
Jennings, Genny	197
Jensen, Michael	237
Jerome, Jennifer	63
Jestis, Cheryl	87
Jimenez, Anja	73
Johnson, Aaron	50
Johnson, Chris	49
Johnson, Claudette	105
Johnson, Erin-Elizabeth	172
Johnson, Harmony	43
Johnson, Kimberly F.	94
Johnson, Thomas M.	136
Johnston, Orna	224
Johovic, Kelley H.	166
Jolley, Marc A.	116
Jones, Ben	207
Jones, Briony	138
Jones, Christopher	58
Jones, Elizabeth	70
Jones, Jamie	215
Jones, Kathleen Pike	212
Jones, Kelley	234
Jones, Kim	224
Jones, Parneshia	147
Jones, Renee	188
Jones, Tim	82
Jones, Valerie	124
Jones, Zina	128
Jongkind, Marina	36
Jonkhoff, Sabrina	160
Joseph, Andrew	222
Joseph, Kennia	42
Juarez, David	195
Jul, Debra	151
Juskewitch, Adam	44
Kachergis, Anne	53
Kadair, Catherine	103
Kadis, Linda	39
Kadushin, Raphael	220
Kaelin, Stephanie	51
Kaemmer, Beverly	122
Kain, Sarah	159
Kalett, Alison	168
Kalish, Ilene	141, 244, 245
Kallet, Jeff	150
Kalna, Josef	144
Kane, Adam C.	152
Kane, Sonia	175
Kaneshiro, Norman	84
Kanter, Greg	42
Karby, Amanda	118
Karkiewicz, Robyn	149
Karp, Jessica	164
Karras, Stephanie	160
Kasper, Carol	56, 57
Kasprzak, Danielle	122
Kass, Gary	126
Kaufman-Fox, Keller	70
Kaufman, Andrew	215
Kaur, Manjit	133
Kaveney, Dan	159
Kean, Linda Griffin	88
Keane, Robert	103
Kearn, Vickie	168
Keegan, Jennifer	103
Keene, Katie	124
Kehoe, Michael	97
Keller, Holly	43
Kelley, Pamela	84
Kellmer, Tracy	162
Kelly, Jennifer Savran	67
Kelly, Kathleen	153
Kemball, Kate	87
Kembrey, Jane	140
Kendzejeski, Nicole	94
Keneston, Fran	188
Kennedy, Melinda	56

Name	Page
Kenney, Mary Lou	95
Kenyon, Andrew	187
Kerr, Karen	67
Kessler, John	57
Kharbanda, Sanj	42
Kiely, Garrett P.	56
Kilgore, Dustin	195
Killian, Sam	118
Killoh, Kathy	39
Kilmartin, Kerry	43
Kim, Elizabeth L.	67
Kim, Hannah	128
Kim, Jean	186
Kim, Sulah	78
Kimberling, Clint	25
Kimm, Kelley	170
Kimzey, Robert	194
Kincaide, Joanna Moore	203
Kindell, Alexandra	107
Kindler, Rachel	90
King, Brenda	224
King, Frederick	44
King, Melissa	37
King, Phillip	224
King, Susan L.	176
Kingra, Mahinder S.	66
Kingsley, Stephanie	29
Kinney, Andrew	82
Kirk New, Erin	79
Kirk, Kara	81
Kirk, Robert	168
Kirkpatrick, Kristin	125
Kittrell, Casey	194
Kleczewski, Alison	84
Klein, Kathie	180
Kleit, Micah	178
Kling, Sarah (Sally)	191
Klipp, Veronica	222
Klopfenstein, Amy	141
Klopping, John	133
Klose, Lisa	95
Knight, Katelyn	197
Knobloch, Andrea	159
Knox, Helena	71
Knutsen, Trond	84
Ko, Christina	51
Kocher, Rob	107
Kohlmeier, Rob	219
Kolander, Mikala	133
Kolman, Amanda	70
Komatsu, Mika	201
Komie, Michelle	168
Kondrick, Maureen	108
Konecy, Mark	60
Kornbluh, Gregory	83
Kos, Krisztina	54
Kosowski, Mary Beth	116
Kosturko, Bob	41
Koupal, Nancy Tystad	183
Kowal, Basia	28
Kozakov, Sergiy	39
Kracht, Peter	166
Kramer, Gary	192
Kraus, Dennis	58
Krause, Amanda	36
Krebs, Paula M.	126
Kretzer, Kyle Howard	95
Kriesel, Leslie	63
Krissoff, Derek	218
Krol, Thomas P.	115
Krouse, Young-hee	107
Krum, Jeff	51
Kucera, Amy	183
Kuehm, Scot	168
Kuerbis, Lisa	189
Kull, Matthew	232
Kumler, Katie	175
Kunos, Linda	54
Kuny, Greg	30
Kuroda, Takuya	201
Kurtz, Kevin	63
Kushnirsky, Julia	63
Kutsko, John F.	180
La Mantia, Katherine	79
LaBrenz, Marcia	118
Lacy, Rosemary	118
Lage, Amy	133
Laity, Susan	224
Lamb, Cynthia	52
Lambert, Allison	195
Lambert, Julie	164, 244
Lambert, Ray	70
Lamm, Gigi	162
LaMorte, Gianna	195
Lance, James	66
Lane, Victoria	189
Langlois, Dennis	168
Lanick, Colleen	111, 245
Lanne-Camilli, Amanda	187
Lantz, Nick	199
Lape, Todd	124
Lara, Greg	62
Larkin, Sheniqua	62
LaRose, Charley	202
Larsen, David	106
Larsen, Wayne	185
Larson, Alodie	159
Laska, Elizabeth	27
Latture, Richard	131
Lauer, Chloe	220
Laughlin, Anne	203
Laughlin, Philip	110
Laun, Karen	67
Laur, Mary	56
Laurent, Amy	51
Laut, Julie R.	86
LaVela, Casey	212
Lawrence-Hurt, Jessica	111
Lawrence, Emily	71
Laws, Andrea	97

Name	Page
Lawton, Caryn	214
Lay, Thomas	74
Laychur, Tina	164
Lazarus, Todd	63
Leach, Kaitlyn	50
Leary, Dan	121
Leary, Sheila	220
Leas, Mary E.	57
LeBien, Thomas	82
Ledendecker, Thea	24
Lee, Chang Jae	63
Lee, Kristie	197
Lee, Marie	110
Lee, Milenda	63
Lee, Pahnia	220
Lee, Su-Mei	186
LeGro, Hope	77
Leichum, Laura	56
Lemmons, Thom	197
Lenz, Scott	220
Leonard, Alexandria	244
Leonard, Benjamin	159
Leonard, Kristy	22
Leone, Sara	70
Leppig, Angela	7
Leshan, Larry	73
Lessing, Doug	230
Lester, Liz	37
Levay, Rachel	61
Leventhal, Josh	121
Leventhal, Philip	62
Levine, Karen	81
Levine, Scott	67
Levinson, Meagan	168
Levy, Rachel	128
Lewchuk, Jodi	159
Lewchuk, Jodie	203
Lewek, Tom	127
Lewis, Dorothy	128
Lewis, Jeremy	158
Li, Danny	85
Li, Lingxi	169
Lichtenstein, Alex	29
Liese, Debra	168
Liese, Donna	168
Lightfoot, Nancy	90
Lilly, James	56
Lilly, Nick	56
LIN, Ying	59
Lindenfeldar, Maria	168
Lindsay, Nick	111
Ling, Jessica	186
Linker, Damon	162
Lipinski, Michelle	186
Lipp, Michelle	47
Lipscombe, Trevor	53, 245
Litkey, Jozsef	54
Litt, Neil	168
Little, Geoffrey	64, 244
Little, Nadine	48
Little, Stephen	149
Littlefield, Kyle	197
Liu, Amy	153
Liu, Katherine H.	66
Liu, Nicholas	159
Lloyd, Alice	56
Lloyd, Dennis	220, 242, 243
Lloyd, Kathryn	197
Lloyd, Matt	50
Lobkowicz, Michelle	203
Lochner, Wendy	62
Lockhart, Robert	162
Lockwood, Karen	189
Loe, Cheryl	84
Loehr, Julie L.	119
Loerke, Ellen	228
Long, James	103
Long, John	129
Long, Linda	89
Lonie, Tonia	125
Loo, Patricia	89
Lopez-Torres, Angelika	194
Lord, Tayler	133
Losh, Lacey	133
Louth, John	159
Love, Alexa	43
Lovecraft, Margaret	103
Lowenthal, Marc	110
Luber, Joel	70
Luchsinger, Amy	160
Luciano, Bessie	204
Ludwick, Cameron	195, 195
Lumenello, Susan	41
Lundquist, Bruce	186
Luttrell, Marsha	116
Lutz, Brian	73
Lutz, Kimberly	231, 245
Luu, Katie	244
Ly, David	43
Lynch, Patrick	159
Lynley, Cason	70, 245
Ma, Kingsley	59
MacBrien, Nathan	147
MacColl, Pamela	42
MacDonald, Alphonse	128, 245
MacDonald, Brian	203
Macdonald, Jane	56
Mackie, Rob	114
Macklem, Ann	43
MacNeil, Mary	210
MacNevin, James	43
Madden, Kyla	113
Magoulias, Michael	57
Magyar, Toni	159
Mahalek, Gina	144
Mainville, Lara	156, 245
Maisner, Elaine	143
Malak, Stephanie	194
Malar, Gregory	176
Malashewsky, Megan	43

Malcolm-Clarke, Darja	90
Malcolm, Ian	82
Malcolm, Reed	49
Maloney, Karen	50
Manaktala, Gita	110, 242, 244
Manion, Deborah	189
Manko, Cliff	42
Manning, Linda	25
Manning, Shaun	118
Manzanedo, Brenda	160
Marchenkova, Maria	128
Marcus, Rachel	128
Marguy, Kathryn	195
Mark, Gigi	186
Markell, Amanda	111
Markova, Lyudmila	138
Marks, Rachel	41
Marney, Tim	30
Marshall, Demi	195
Marshall, Kate	49
Marshall, Stewart	138
Marsland, Joanna Ruth	143
Marson, Rosie	140
Martin, Annie	215
Martin, Carolyn	182
Martin, Dawn	120
Martin, Katherine	159
Martin, Larisa	97
Martin, Lindsay	151
Martin, Mike	197
Martin, Miranda	56
Martin, Pieter	122
Martinelli, Theresa	215
Martinez, Bryan	178
Marting, William	159
Martino, John	53
Maselli, Elisabeth	178
Mason, Jacqueline	113
Mason, Tony	105
Massabrook, Jess	245
Matheson, Laurie	86
Mathias, Ashley	182
Mattern, Margaret	133
Matthews, Jermey	111
Maxfield, Marcela	186
Mayer, Dariel	209, 244
Mayer, Mary	224
Mazzarra, Chris	70
Mazzocchi, Jay	143
McAdam, Matthew	94
McAnespie, Elena	49
McArdle, Jeff	87
McBeath, Kasey	200
McBeth, Barbara F.	137
McBride, David	159
McCallum, Heather	224
McCarroll, Courtney	159
McCarthy, Juliana M.	94
McConkey, Jill	106
McCormack, Marilyn	203
McCormick, Mack	100
McCormick, Wynona	197
McCoy, Jim	93, 245
McCreary, Courtney	125
McCullough, Michael	71
McDermott, Kathleen	82
McDonald, Leigh	36
McDuffie, John J.	30
McEntire, Ila	100
McFee, Mollie	56
McGandy, Michael	66, 243
McGann, Michael	191
McGaughey, Tyler	56
McGavick, Sarah	194
McGlone, Jonathan	118
McGraw, Tom	57
McGregor, Heidi	231
McGuinness, Phillipa	140
McHugh, Elise	138
McIntosh, Susan	114
McIntyre, Jennifer	183
McKenna, Anne	220
McLaughlin, Brenna	242
McLaughlin, Larin	212, 244
McLean, Julie	234
McLeod, John	143
McMahon, Sheila	220
McMenemy, Siobhan	219
McMillen, Wendy	149
McMurray, Heather	180
McMurtray, Lisa	124
McNamara, Sara	160
McTigue, Karen	224
Means, Allison Thomas	93
Meekers, M'Bilia	103
Meerdink, Jon	91
Mehring, Adam	220
Meier, Lindsey	220
Meijer, Margreet	101
Meikle, Barry	203
Melina, Valerie	73
Melton, Mardee	84
Melvin, Terrence J.	95
Mendez, Jose Antonio	51
Mendonça, Megan R. M.	31
Mennel, Timothy	56
Mensink, Lisa	220
Menzies, Elspeth	140
Merzlak, Paul	130
Mesker, Louis W.	87
Meszaros, Abel	54
Meyer, Astrid	164
Meyer, Caitlin	42
Micic, Vesna	203
Mickulas, Peter	178
Midgley, Peter	28
Milberger, Kurt	119
Miles, Terry	144
Miller, Allison	29
Miller, Chelsea	188

Name	Page
Miller, David	90
Miller, Jon	24
Miller, Kim	242
Miller, Nikki	192
Miller, Robert	159
Miller, Robyn L.	69
Miller, Sarah	223
Miller, Stephani	107
Miller, Sue	175
Miller, William M., III	131
Milliken, Leif	132
Mills, Eric	131
Miniard, Kathi	60
Mitchell, David	67
Mitchell, Douglas	56
Mitchell, Nicole	212, 242
Mixon, Jennifer	124
Miyasato, Terri	84
Modi, Akshay	89
Moeller, Rachel	122
Moen, Jeff	122
Moffat, Fiona	155
Mogollón, Abby	36, 244
Moir, Robin	121
Moldvai, Marta	159
Monaghan, Mike	161
Mones, Mark	210
Monggae, Matselane	222
Montagna, Marlena	131
Montano, Dawn	27
Moode, Michelle	93
Moody, David	140
Moore-Swafford, Angela	184
Moore, Hal	51
Moore, Nathan	70
Moos, Katja	71
Morales, Ruth	169
Moravetz, Jeff	107
Morgan, Dan	48
Morris Babb, Meredith	72
Morris, Michael	67
Morris, Ryan	188
Morrison, Bailey	195, 244
Morrison, Richard W.	74
Morrone, Cathy	111
Morrow, Lettie	23
Morse, Jeremy	118
Mortensen, Dee	90
Mortimer, Frank	159
Mortimer, Rebecca	105
Mosser, Gianna	147
Motherwell, Elizabeth	25
Motieram, Sati	176
Muccie, Mary Rose1	92
Mueller, Sarah	195
Muenchrath, Anna	220
Muirhead, Donna	217
Mullervy, Deirdre	75
Mulligan, Ryan	192
Mulliken, Jasmine	186
Mumford, Abigail	83
Munson, Heather	87
Munson, Stephanie	67
Muranaka, Royden	84
Murphy, Barbara	128
Murphy, Brian	229
Murphy, Ellen F.	66
Murphy, Nick	229
Murphy, Noel	224
Murphy, Paul	172
Murray-Harrison, Marissa	51
Myers, Charles	56, 244
Myers, Morgan	210
Myers, Patricia	186
Myers, Will	41
Myree, Deborah	60
Nachbaur, Fredric W.	74, 245
Nadkarni, Alicia	141
Nair, Valerie	43
Nakata, Kyle	85
Nangle, Leslie	168
Naqib, Nadia	32
Nasr, Laili	130
Nasset, Daniel	86
Nasson, Melissa	41
Naylor, Trevor	32
Neher, Sally	226
Nelson, Priya	56
Nemens, Emily	104
Nettles, Jordan	125
Neumann, Claire	160
New, Hannah	208
Newalu, Clifford	85
Newcomb, Paula	118
Newkumet, Libby	53
Newman, Carey	40
Newman, Eric	74
Newman, Jessica	143
Newton, Susan Hill	93
Nicassio, Luciano	203
Nichols, Kate	192
Nichols, Sally	109
Nichols, Suzanne	177
Nichols, Wendalyn	51
Nicolaes, Chantal	34
Nini, Meredith	151
Nishimoto, Kiera	84
Nixon, Deborah	140
Nizer, Eileen	188
Noble, Claire	131
Noble, Katrina	212
Noe, Jason	159
Nolan, Barbara	163
Noonan, Margaret M.	74
Noonan, Maureen	224
Noonan, Robin	131
Norell, Randy	29
Normansell, John	105
Norton, Jennifer	164
Norton, Rebecca	79

Norton, Scott	49		Patterson, Meg	203
Noth, Michael	91		Pattishall, Roy	70
Nowak, Emily	215		Patton, Susan	242
Nuzzo, Jennifer	195		Paul, Tammy	58
Nyberg, Karl	191		Paulson, Jennifer	95
O'Connor, Ciara	244		Pazik, Steven	57
O'Beirne, Paul	140		Pearson, Janie	91
O'Brien-Nicholson, Kate	74		Pedersen, Nadine	43
O'Connell, Cliff	197		Peeler, Denise	87
O'Connell, Robert	176		Pelton, Elizabeth	224
O'Connor, Eugene	151		Peltz, James	187
O'Connor, Noreen	162		Peluse, Michael	50
O'Donovan, Maria	65		Pennefeather, Shannon	121
O'Dowd, Patrick	99		Pennywark, Leah	186
O'Grady, Shawn	202		Pensak, Susan	63
O'Handley, Robert	111		Perez, Peter	4509
O'Lavin, Bridget	160		Perkel, Bonnie	69
O'Neal, Natalie	131		Perri, Trevor	147
O'Neill, Kathy	86		Perri, Trevor	244
O'Rourke, Kellie	51		Pervin, David	158
O'Shea, Patti	56		Pesek, Diana	164
Oakes, Ian	143		Petersen, Lorna	176
Oaks, Kelly	131		Peterson, Bob	57
Oates, William L.	67		Peterson, Joseph	57
Oberlin, Brent	110, 243		Peterson, Ryan	175
Ochsner, Courtney	132		Petilos, Randolph	56
Ochsner, Daniel	122		Petrik, Katrina	43
Ode, Jeanne	183		Petrylak, Ashley	160
Oestreich, Julia	68		Petty, Jill	147, 244
Ohlin, Peter	158		Pfeiffer, Alice R.	189, 245
Olson, Heidi	213		Pfund, Niko	158
Olson, Sarah	100		Phillips, Betsy	209
Ombadykow, Dolma	142		Phillips, Jenna	209
Oreshkov, Chaz	57		Phillips, Lauren	73
Organ, Lindsey	170		Phillips, Peter	50
Orphan, Stephanie	231		Piché, Mireille	156
Ortiz-Blaines, Syra	163		Pickett, Duncan	211
Ortiz, Ángel	169		Pidgeon, Sean	159
Osterman, Anne	56		Pierre, Stephanie	224
Otero, Rosa V.	169		Pimm, Matthew	128
Otzel, Margaret	224		Pinchefsky, Andrew	114
Ovedovitz, Nancy	224		Pingel, Ryan	220, 243
Owen, Susan	48		Pinnone, Daniela	34
Owens, Kathryn	78, 244		Pintaudi-Jones, Rose	160
Pagan, Cristina	89		Pirovitz, Sarah	159
Pakiela, James	62		Pisano, Joanne	114
Palladino, Lily	162		Pitts, Kathryn	149, 244
Pan, Jennifer	177		Pitts, Melissa	43, 243
Panetta, Jackie	73		Plant, Alisa	132
Pankratz, Sherith	159		Platter, Clara	141
Panner, Craig	159		Plummer, Herbert	63
Park, Josh Hyoun Woo	89		Podraza, Morgan	138
Parker, Andrea	57		Poe, Marshall	33
Parker, Erika	30		Poggione, Mary	121
Parker, Lynne	182		Polivka, Raina	48
Pasha, Cherylann	78		Pollack, Jane	73
Pastel, Sara	127		Polo, Greta	166
Pasti, Mary	224		Poor, Weston	133
Patnaik, Gayatri	41		Pop, Antonia	203
Patrick, Richanna	67		Pope, Barbara Kline	94

Name	Page
Poss, Marielle	62
Post, Tom	193
Potter, Jane	159
Powell, Joseph B.	217
Power, Danielle	51
Power, Nancy	191
Powers, Emily	42
Pranzatelli, Robert	224
Pratt, Beth	150
Pratt, Dan	61
Pratt, Darrin	61, 242, 243
Price, B. Byron	152
Price, Destini	31
Priday, Caroline	169
Priddy, Kristine	184
Prior, Robert	111
Procopio, Joseph	89
Proefrock, Jim	86
Proia, Brandon	143
Propheter, Lori	146
Prpick, Sean	173
Puchalla, Joel	133
Pullano, Michelle	111
Pult, Richard	136
Pulvirenti, Teodoro	176
Purcell, Finn	114
Purple, Katherine	170, 244
Putens, Nathan	133
Pyle, Dan	90
Queen, Wendy J.	94
Quick, Pamela	111
Quinlan, Daniel	203
Quinn, Lisa	219
Quinn, Michele	25, 244
Quinn, Yelba	44
Race, Justin	135, 245
Racette, Ann-Christine	74
Raddatz, Kristen	56
Rafert, Samara	150
Rainbow, Fred	131
Ramirez, Linda	195
Ramsey, Tasha	99
Ranalli, Kathy	163
Rancourt, Suzanne	203
Randall, Tracy	214
Rankin, Charles E. (Chuck)	153
Rasmussen, Paige	90
Ratcliff, Blake	159
Ratzlaff, Richard	113
Rauch, Reba	208
Rawls, Tiffany	138
Read, Cynthia	158
Reaman, Micki	154
Reaume, Julie	120
Rector, Molly	37
Reed-Morrisson, Laura	164
Reed, Chris	203
Reed, Ken	168
Reedy, Nora	94
Reeser, Tara	215
Regan, Ann	121
Regoli, Michael	90, 244
Rehl, Beatrice	50
Reid, Chris	160
Reilly, Eileen	168
Reitmeier, Ami	87
Rennells, Kevin	118
Rennison, Robin	95
Renteria, Rey	195
Renwick, Devon	95
Renwick, Emily	191
Repeta, Kasia	71
Repetto, David	50
Repino, Robert	159
Repta, Bob	87
Reshota, Olga	175
Reyes, Sheila S.	164
Rheault, Sonia	156
Rhyne, Edward	57
Rice, Dawn	234
Rich, Nicholas	210
Richards, Alun	105
Richards, Melanie	105
Richards, Todd	215
Richardson, Jerry	185
Rickard, John S.	45
Ridge, Sam	37
Rimer-Surles, Cathy	69, 244
Rinella, Michael	187
Ringblom, Jenny	57
Ringo, Tad	86
Rittenhouse, Rose	57
Roach, Brian	53, 244
Roane, Kari	57
Roberts, Conrad	97
Roberts, Jennifer	114
Roberts, LaTisha	200
Roberts, Laura	30
Roberts, Lisa	83
Roberts, Rebecca	128
Roberts, Tony	153
Robinson, Brett	120
Robinson, Chris	51
Robinson, Christopher	71
Robinson, Kim	48
Robinson, Morris (Dino)	147
Roche, Thomas	79
Rodrigue, Sylvia Frank	184
Rodriguez, Anna Maria	153
Roessner, Maura	49
Rogers, Kelly	94, 244
Rold, Alison	133
Rolfs, Erin	103, 244
Rollins, Leslie	81
Roman, Steven	44
Romeo-Hall, Ange	67
Roper, Sarah	105
Rose, Amber	220
Rosenbaum, David	126
Rosolina, Rachel	90

Name	Page
Ross, Briana	83
Ross, Marsha	57
Ross, Rachel	215, 243
Ross, Simon	105
Rossetti, Chip	141
Rossi, Janet	111, 244
Rotella, Giuseppe	51
Routh, Andrew	144
Routon, Anne	32
Rouw, Ebisse	34
Roux, Michael	87
Rowley, Kristen Elias	151
Rowley, Linda	118
Roy, Mary Lou	28
Roy, Michael	30
Royal, Chad	71
Rubeck, Levi	244
Ruccia, Dan	71
Rude, Pam	90
Rudy, Gordon	57
Ruffner, Amanda	162
Ruiz, Marcia	191
Runyon, Ashley	90
Rusko, Joe	94
Russell, Bonnie	215
Russell, Richard A.	130, 131
Russo, Sarah	160
Rutberg, Steve	230
Ryan, Jessica	70
Ryan, Ray	50
Ryan, Suzanne	159
Rye, Olivia	105
Sacher, Jennifer	31
Safer, Rachel	160
Saffel, Than	218, 244
Sagara, Mike	186
Sain, Elizabeth	149
Sala, Edward	214
Salas, Lauren	57
Salisbury, Leila W.	99
Saller, Carol	57
Salling, Stacey	195
Saltz, Carole Pogrebin	190
Saltzman, Glenn	78
Salvatore, Laurea	158
Sampson, Nancy	70
Samuel, Adedoyin	128
Sanders-Buell, Sara	129
Sanfilippo, Tony	151
Santella, Anna-Lise	159
Santiago, Carlos	169
Sapir, Marc	128
Sapire, Sara	224
Sarratt, Blanche	25
Satrom, Ellen	210
Sattler, Maggie	123
Saunders, Mark H.	210, 245
Savage, Lisa	70
Savarese, Anne	168
Scallan, Amanda	103
Scanlon, Sonia	224
Scarpelli, Elizabeth	60
Scecina, Lisa	224
Schaffner, Melanie B.	94
Schaper, Jennifer	71
Schier, Jeffrey	224
Schleicher, Wendy	129
Schlesinger, Laurie	168
Schmidt, Eric	49
Schmidt, Karen	81
Schmidt, Randy	43
Schnaufer, Wendi	25
Schneider, Naomi	49
Scholz-Jaffe, Kathleen	164
Schramm, Kate	90
Schreiber, Meighan	176
Schuetz, Richard	138
Schuster, Emily	153
Schutjer, Karin	45
Schwartz, Barry L.	132
Schwartz, Eric I.	62
Schwartz, J. Alex	119
Schwarz, Jessica	63
Schwinck, Claire	133
Schwirtlich, Beate	203
Schynert, Kendra	186
Scollans, Colleen	158
Scott, Rachel	155
Scott, Rebecka	23
Scoville, Sheila	195
Scrivener, Brian	47
Scruggs, Sally	144
Seagram, Andrew	57
Searl, Patricia	210
Seburyamo, Kate	188
Secondari, Linda	244
Seger, Rebecca	160
Sekora, Rosemary	133
Sell, Laura	71, 245
Sells, Dianna	197
Seltzer, Joyce	82
Semple, Timothy E.	137
Sen, Sharmila	82
Sery, Doug	111
Sewall, Martha	95
Sewell, David	210
Sewell, Vicki	182
Seyl, Emily	197
Shaffer, Bryan	170
Shah, Vijay	124
Shahan, Andrea	133
Shanahan, Mary	56
Shanholtzer, Joshua	166
Shanklin, Serenity	121
Shanley, Maxwell	186
Shannon, Jennifer	175
Shapiro, Stephen	203
Shaw, Laura	172
Shay, Alison	189, 244
Shay, Mariah	129

Shayegan, Leyli	191
Shea, Brian	95, 244
Shear, Donna A.	132, 242, 244
Shepherd, Danielle	105
Sher, Richard B.	45
Sherer, John	143
Sherman, Amberle	166
Sherman, Gayle	110
Shidlauski, Tamara	86
Shields, Charlie	37
Shimabukuro, Jill	56, 244
Shirley, Melissa	173
Shojaie, Rosemary	175
Shor, Deborah	159
Shull, Brigitte	50, 245
Siewers, Alfred	46
Silva, Diana	67
Simmons, Derek	56
Simmons, Valencia	76
Simpson-Vos, Mark	143, 243
Sims, Linsey	193
Sims, Michael	111
Singerman, Jerome E.	162
Singleton, Henry	158
Sioles, Lee	103
Sipovic, Jaclyn	118
Sippell, Kelly	118
Skidmore, Colleen	28
Skinner, Heather	123
Skord, Taylor	131
Skudra, Tom	204
Slajus, Jen	144
Slavin, Lianne	105
Smart, Katie	71, 244
Smiley, Matt	123
Smist, Erik	94, 244
Smith-Borne, Joell	209
Smith-Mandell, Barbara	205
Smith, Alexa	89
Smith, Bill	110
Smith, BJ	144
Smith, Curtiss	165
Smith, Dean J.	66
Smith, Deborah	105
Smith, Diane E.	40
Smith, Emily	186
Smith, Frank	231
Smith, Greg	188
Smith, Heather	164
Smith, Kelsea	70
Smith, Liz	70
Smith, Marena	80
Smith, Sue	175
Smyre, Terence	123
Snead, Beth	79
Snoeyenbos, Ann	94, 244
Soeterboek, Nella	140
Solic, Peggy	90
Sondervan, Jeroen	34
Soom, Marnie	174
Sorochin, Cecilia	210
Soule, Susan	51
South, James	108
Spain, Molly	198
Spall, Kevin	234
Spangler, Emily	190
Sparenberg, Roberta	87
Specter, Susan	67
Spicer, Ed	165
Spiegel, Nora	186
Springsteen, Sara	133
Stabel, Meredith	93
Stachew, Lauren	118
Staggs, Susan	162
Stahl, Levi	56
Staib, Erich	70
Stallings, Lisa	144
Stanforth, Christi	70
Starace, Regina	164
Starr, Brent	91
Starr, Lindsay	195
Stauffer, Heather	132
Stauss, Bryan	128
Stebbins, Hallie	159
Steed, Navar	180
Steele, Kristen	227
Stein, Carol A.	31
Stein, Faith Wilson	186
Steinle, Kim	71
Steinmetz, Kay	189
Stepp, Jordan	79, 244
Sterns, Stephen	63
Steve, Betsy	142
Stevens, Emily	163
Stevens, Robert	230
Stevenson, Deborah	158
Stewart, Linda	186
Stewart, Mark	57
Stewart, Shane Gong	124
Sticco, Maria	166
Stickler, Karen	224
Stoffel, Michael	122
Stoica, Alex	113
Stone, Jenn	58
Stonehill, Kristina	215
Storm, Douglas	94
Stoute, Cecilia	206
Strand, John	129
Strauss, David	191
Strickland, Deborah	144
Strickland, Sherri L.	136
Stritch, Jim	224
Stroupe, Dylan	144
Suchomel, Mark	227
Suciu, Ioan	78, 243
Suffern, Erika	127
Sullivan, Margaret	212
Sullivan, Nicholas	69
Sullivan, Sandy	87
Sumner, Jake	193

Sundaram, Friederike	186
Sundook, Ali	73
Svinarich, Beth	61
Swanger, Scott	214
Swanson, Tom	132
Sweeney, Kathleen A.	74
Sweetman, Marie	215
Swope, Pamela K.	108
Sybert, Michelle	90
Sylvia, Susan	136
Szabo, Noemi	54
Szczybor, Catherine	53
Szekley, Meagan	131
Taber, Emily	111
Tacke, Katherine	212
Taft, Gene	95
Takagi, Hiroshi	201
Tambeau, Renee	118
Tamberino, Claire McCabe	95
Tamminen, Suzanna	216
Tamulevich, Alessandra Jacobi	152
Tang, Debra	84
Tanner, Annette	120
Tarbell, Kate L.	136
Tate, Ben	169
Tate, Lori	191
Tauch, Matt	70
Taylor, Emily	151, 244
Taylor, Ihsan	144
Taylor, Rob	132
Taylor, Robyn	73
Teefy, Carrie Downes	215
Tegge, Jeff	
Tempio, Rob	168
Templar, Kate	186
ter Horst, Ines	194
Thaxton, Sara	36
Thedford, Sherondra	90
Thies, Charles	228
Thomas, Alan	56
Thomas, Donna	75, 76
Thomas, Glenis	155
Thomas, Greta	209
Thomas, Joanne	144
Thomas, Patricia	160
Thomas, Suela	62
Thompson, Gary	131
Thompson, Mark	203
Thompson, Myles	62
Thompson, Stephanie	193
Thomson Black, Jean E.	223
Thomson, Julie	71
Thongsack, Bruce	177
Thorsteinsson, Christine	82, 244
Tifft, Douglas C.	136
Tilford, Nicole	180
Tjandra, Lia	49
Toews, Regan	113
Toff, Nancy	158
Tolentino, Blaine	84
Tom, Linda	213
Tonegutti, Marta	56
Tong, Murray	219
Tong, Tong	46
Toolan, Fran	230
Toole, Regenia (Jenny)	116
Torrence, James	160
Totten, Clara	77
Towne, Ashley	57
Townsend, Barbara	133
Traganas, Alexia	142
Treadwell, Priscilla	168
Tremaine, Lisa	138, 244
Tripp, Colin	97
Trippe, Bill	110
Tritschler, Tracy	126
Truwant, Mirjam	101
Tucker Woods, Erica	70
Tunzelmann, Morgan	173
Turner, Duncan	28
Turner, Shelly	105
Twardowski, Kristen	71
Uecker, Judy	184
Uhl, Lyn	49
Ultsch, Sarah	160
Underwood, Will	98
Upano, Alicia	84
Usui, Emiko K.	129
Vacca, Carmie	113
Valelly, Peter	162
Valencia, Mary	xyz
Valentine, Anne	188
van der Bijl, Inge	34
van der Drift, Michiel	34
Van Der Dussen, Rhonda	91
van der Spoel, Corina	222
Van Eeghem, Beatrice	101
Van Huijstee, Ryan	114
van Jaarsveld, Judith	34
van Marissing, Neeltje	169
Van Pelt, Julie	212
van Rheinberg, Brigitta	168
van Rijn, Erich	48, 243
Van Woerden, Peter	73
Vanderwill, James	118
Vandeventer, Vicki	186
Vandezande, Annemie	101
Vaughn, Kathy	164
Vazquez, Aureliano	191
Velissariou, Michelle	51
Verdich, Judy	185
Verhowsky, Victoria	178
Vidal, Joan	192
Vinarub, Vanessa	83
Visser, Louise	34
Vogel, Chris	129
Vogelenzang, Atie	34
Voros, Nora	54
Vose, Alex	164
Vranka, Stefan	159

Name	Page
Vunk, Janice	187
Vyce, Stephanie	82
Wackrow, Dan	82
Wadman, Rob	34
Wadsworth-Booth, Susan	98
Wagenaar, Jaap	34
Wagner, Kyle	56
Wahl, Anthony	159
Wahl, Kate	185
Wahrheit, Julie	215
Wainwright, Lisa	129
Waldron, Laura	162
Walker, Gwen	220
Walker, Janet	44
Walker, Laura	27
Walker, Theresa	53
Wallace, Ivey Pittle	75
Wallen, Chip	131
Wallen, Michelle	144
Walsh, Bailey	57
Walsh, Bruce	173
Walsh, Christopher	95
Walter, Amy	70
Walters, Marthe	73
Walton, Kathy	198
Wantland, Clydette	87
Ward, Dave	159
Ward, Jean	190
Ward, Roy	114
Ware, Cynthia	129
Warlick, Dottie	160, 161
Warne, Kate	49
Warnement, Julie	129
Warner, Chris	73
Warren, John W.	76
Warren, Rachel	160
Washburn, Amanda	128
Wasik, Bethany	66
Wassmann, Ingrid	32
Wasti, Shubhash	39
Watanabe, Kyle	84
Waterman, Dan	25
Waters, Lindsay	82
Waters, Suzi	144
Watkinson, Charles	117
Weaver, Caroline	129
Webb, Kerry	194
Weber, Laura	121
Weber, Patty	95
Wehling, William O'Dell	67
Weidemann, Jason	122
Weinberg, Joy	132
Weinreb, Jenya	224
Weinstein, Michael	191
Weir, Anna	133
Welch, Sally	150
Wellner, Fred	189
Wells, Phyllis	80
Wells, Thomas	193
Welsby, Alison	102
Welzenbach, Rebecca	117, 245
Wen, Grace	84
Wendell, Emily	132
Wenzel, Stephanie	143
Wertz, Chloe	166
Wesley, Stephen	63
Wessels, Cindy	166
West, Ann	159
West, Krista	27
Westlund, Laura	122
Whillans, Lindsay	202
Whitaker, Theresa M.	115
Whitby, Elizabeth	145
White, Katherine	138
White, Rebekah	83
Whitebear, Wendy	173
Whitehorn, Clark	138, 243
Whiting, Colin	31
Wieters, Madeline	40
Wiggins, Steve	159
Wilcox, Lynn	189
Wildfong, Kathryn	215
Wilhelm-South, Marcy	171
Wilkins, Tim	168
Williams, Clive	204
Williams, Dan	198, 243, 245
Williams, Fiona	160
Williams, Juliet	151
Williams, Kimberley	169
Williams, Rory	176
Williams, Stephanie	100, 243, 245
Williams, Stephen	91, 244
Willoughby-Harris, H. Lee	71
Willshire, Thomas	51
Willson, Katy	97
Wilson, Andrew	30
Wilson, Dave	192
Wilson, Jackie	100
Wilson, Jaclyn	216
Wilson, JD	147
Wilson, Pamela	84
Windsor, Elizabeth R.	94, 245
Winter, Maureen	81
Winters, Andrew	143
Wisniewski, Cassandra	58
Wisselink, Karyn	39
Wissink, Jan-Peter	34
Wissoker, Ken	69
Wisti, Meredith	212
Witzke, Jennifer	90
Wolfe, Alex	166
Wong, Angelina	59
Wong, Collin	85
Woo, Shirley	212
Wood, Shannon	114
Woods, Mike	51
Wooley, Claude	199
Wraight, Anastasia	120
Wren, Jeanne	118
Wright, Allison	159

Wright, Donald P.	38
Wrinn, Steve	149
Wrzesinski, Julie	120
Wyrwa, Richard	207
Yahner, Kathryn	164
Yantzi, Katie	203
Yates, John	202
Yates, Steve	124
Ybarra, Laurel	133
YE, Minlei	59
Yee, Amanda	141
Yen, Cindy	85
Yenerich, Pat	146
Yoshimi, Shunya	201
Young, Kathleen	95
Young, Mary D.	98
Young, Steve	43
Youngman, Donna	136
Zaboski, Samantha	73
Zadrozny, Mark	51
Zaleski, Elizabeth	133
Zalewski, Ellen M.	56
Zanzucchi, Kate	224
Zarro, Alissa	178
Zenelis, John	76
Zenner, Boyd	210
Zimmerman, Chad	159
Zinner, Eric	141
Zucca, Damon	158
Zucco, Joeth	133